Sustainable Landscaping For Dummies®

Cheat Sheet

Identifying Ways to Make Your Landscape Sustainable

Sustainable landscapes don't happen by themselves. But by answering a few questions, you can begin to get a handle on what you can do to improve the sustainability of your property. Go outside, have a seat in a comfy chair, and consider these questions:

- **How big is your lawn?** The lawn has the most negative impacts of any landscape feature. So, if you can, make it smaller, or replace it with a low-care meadow that requires little water. Or at least tune up your sprinkler system and consider using a push mower. See Chapters 19 and 22.

- **What materials are available on your site?** Do you have stones, salvageable concrete, used lumber, trees, or bamboo that could be made into a structure? Even the soil beneath your feet can be used to make beautiful earthen landscape elements. See Chapter 2.

- **Where does the water go?** Follow the path of rainwater as it moves across your land. See if you could harvest rainwater from the roof of your house or elsewhere using dry streambeds and other site features to let it soak in to the soil. Or perhaps you can even store rainwater in a cistern. See Part III.

- **How could you cut down on maintenance?** If you're spending a lot of time and resources on laborious but unnecessary garden tasks, learn how to redesign your landscape to eliminate troublesome gardening work. See Chapters 20 and 21.

- **How's the climate in and around your house?** Trees and shrubs can shade the house, intercept and lift wind over your property, and cut down on heating and air conditioning bills (see Chapter 17). Shade structures can create cool zones (see Chapter 12).

Following Simple Strategies to Set Up a Water-Thrifty Landscape

Water conservation is a key component of a sustainable landscape. The following list presents the appropriate practices in a nutshell. Check out Part III for more details.

- **Pay attention to design.** Group plants into *hydrozones* (areas containing plants with similar water needs) to ensure that you aren't wasting water.

- **Choose drought-tolerant plants.** Select species that are climate-appropriate and that will thrive on rainfall alone or with very little supplemental irrigation.

- **Downsize your lawn.** The lawn is the big water-sucker in your landscape. Try reducing the size of your lawn to just what you actually use.

- **Harvest rainwater.** The best water for your garden falls out of the sky, so why not gather it? Even something as simple as digging a swale to channel your rainwater or connecting a rain barrel to your downspout can help save water.

- **Irrigate efficiently.** *Drip irrigation* (a type of watering system that applies water directly and slowly to the soil) or judicious hand watering are the best ways to irrigate.

- **Use mulch.** *Mulch* is a layer of organic matter, usually wood chips or bark, that's placed on top of the soil surface. It conserves water by reducing evaporative loss from the soil surface, keeping the roots of the plants cool, and reducing weeds that compete with desirable plants for water.

- **Manage your landscape with conservation in mind.** Run your garden the smart way. Keep weeds down. Top off mulch as needed to maintain a 3- to 4-inch thick layer. Check your irrigation system monthly for proper operation, and then make any necessary repairs as soon as you can. Reprogram your irrigation controller as needed to adjust for seasonal differences in water use.

For Dummies: Bestselling Book Series for Beginners

Sustainable Landscaping For Dummies®

Cheat Sheet

Selecting Plants Suited for Your Yard

Plants are the heart and soul of the sustainable landscape. Here are a few key sustainability-oriented questions to ask when considering a particular plant, shrub, or tree. Find the answers to these questions in plant encyclopedias, at the nursery, on the Internet, or by hiring a professional to help you develop your plant palette.

- **Is it adapted to your climate?** Make sure your plants will tolerate the temperatures, winds, humidity, and seasonal rhythms that occur where you live.

- **Is it the right size?** Plants that grow too big for the space they're in need constant pruning to keep them in bounds. Give your plants (and yourself!) a break by allowing them room to grow.

- **Is it resistant to pests and diseases?** Why create trouble by choosing wimpy plants? Opt for sturdy varieties that never need to see the doctor.

- **Is it long-lived?** This question is especially important with trees and shrubs. Replacing "permanent" plants all the time is definitely not sustainable.

- **Is it safe?** Avoid poisonous or highly flammable plants, thorny plants, and trees that tip over or break apart in windstorms.

- **What does it do?** It's best if your plants are more than just pretty faces on your landscape. Try to use plants that provide food for you or the neighborhood critters, make habitats for wildlife, improve the microclimate around your house, or create privacy.

Choosing Sustainable Alternatives

The following tables show some alternatives to conventional landscaping practices. These alternatives will save you effort and money, and will be a lot friendlier to the environment.

Alternatives to Power Equipment

Power Tool	Sustainable Alternatives
Gas lawn mower	Push mower, electric mower, sheep, alternative lawn such as a meadow
String weed and grass trimmer	Hand shears, scythe, hoe, goat, mulching, knee-high plants to suppress weeds
Gas hedge trimmer	Hand or electric hedge shears, natural unclipped hedges
Chain saw	Hand pruning saw, lopping shears
Rototiller	None (tilling isn't recommended; use a spading fork only when starting new beds)
Gas blower	Rake, broom, allowing leaves to remain in place as mulch
Lawn tractor	Hand cart, wheelbarrow

Alternatives to Harsh Chemicals

Harsh Chemical	Sustainable Alternatives
Fertilizers	Installing low-demand plants, composting, applying green manures, planting cover crops, allowing leaf litter to remain in place, practicing chop and drop pruning, applying organic fertilizers
Pesticides	Selecting pest-resistant plants, improving growing conditions to make plants less susceptible, washing the pests off with a jet of water, releasing beneficial insects that feed on harmful insects, using the least-toxic pesticides such as insecticidal soaps and oil sprays
Herbicides	Blocking out weeds with tall dense plantings, sheet mulching, applying organic herbicides such as corn gluten meal or vinegar, using a drip system to reduce wetting of soil, pulling weeds before they set seed

For Dummies: Bestselling Book Series for Beginners

Sustainable Landscaping

FOR

DUMMIES®

by Owen E. Dell

WILEY

Wiley Publishing, Inc.

Sustainable Landscaping For Dummies®

Published by
Wiley Publishing, Inc.
111 River St.
Hoboken, NJ 07030-5774
www.wiley.com

WILEY

About the Author

Owen Dell got his first serious exposure to landscaping in San Francisco's Golden Gate Park, where he spent his childhood afternoons gamboling about instead of doing his homework. After a brief career in electronics, which taught him where his affections really lay, he turned to horticulture. Two charismatic college botany professors opened his eyes to the wonders of nature. Class field trips made it clear that the gap between the way nature handled landscaping and the way people did was huge — and that it was the people who needed help.

In 1971, Owen went on to start his own landscaping business, which was devoted to developing native-plant gardens for California homeowners. After a brief period of hauling rubbish and landscaping mobile homes, he found a niche for himself. As his career developed, his vision expanded, aided by a series of natural disasters that illuminated the need to make landscaping smarter, safer, and more environmentally friendly. Wildfires led Owen to become an expert in firescaping (a term he coined). Droughts taught him the value of water conservation. The impacts of fossil-fuel use led him to found the Fossil-Free Landscaping Group. Each catastrophe led to a wider vision of what landscaping could and should be.

Today, Owen is an internationally recognized and widely admired expert in sustainable landscaping. He has written numerous articles for *Sunset Magazine, National Gardening Magazine, Southern California Gardener, Pacific Horticulture,* and many others. He's an international speaker who has presented hundreds of truly rousing lectures, classes, and workshops to homeowners and professionals. Owen is also the co-writer and co-host of the popular Santa Barbara, California, television series *Garden Wise Guys* (www. citytv18.com), a sustainable-landscaping sitcom. His other book, *How to Start a Home-Based Landscaping Business* (Globe Pequot), has helped thousands of budding professionals get a healthy start on their careers.

Owen's work has been featured on HGTV, Peak Moment Television, and NBC and in *The Wall Street Journal, Fortune* magazine, *Landscape Architecture Magazine,* the *Los Angeles Times,* and many other publications. He has won numerous awards for his work.

In his spare time, Owen putters in his own garden, hangs out with his cats, spends quality time in wild places, cooks a mean meal from homegrown produce, and dabbles in political and social activism.

Visit Owen's Web site at www.owendell.com.

Dedication

I dedicate this book to those who strive to make the world a better place by starting in their own backyards. What you do matters very much.

Acknowledgments

Let me tell you about my neighbor. I don't want to assume he's eager to see his name in a book, so I'll call him Jack. He's lived in his house for nearly 40 years. He has the same furniture as when he moved in. The same Harvest Gold appliances. The same dial phone. The same 1967 car. And yes, the same landscaping. Far as I can tell, Jack buys food and occasionally some clothing. He's not poor; he just likes to live simply. When I think about how much stuff I've gone through in that time, I'm truly humbled. True, his stuff is not environmentally cool. His car pollutes more than my Prius, and his appliances don't have Energy Star labels. But when you look at the overall impact of our lives, I bet his footprint is way smaller than mine. Jack is the most sustainable person I know, but he doesn't see himself that way. He's my hero, but he doesn't know it. He's just a guy living his life, but he has inspired me to do better, and that inspiration led, in part, to this book. Thanks, Jack, for keeping me honest. You're the best neighbor a person could have.

Many people have helped me become (I hope) worthy of the task of spreading the word about sustainable landscaping. Lacking the space to name them all, I tip my hat to those who have devoted their careers to this worthy work and who have inspired me and taught me so much. My esteemed colleagues — Ken Foster, Misty Gonzales, Billy Goodnick, Alison Jordan, Mark Wisniewski, and many others — provided feedback, information, resources, and encouragement while this book came into being. My staff was consistently supportive as I neglected them to find time to write. Kudos to Bonnie Barabas for keeping the office in one piece and to Octavio Toscano for keeping things together out in the field. Your good work ensured that I have a business to go back to now that the writing is done.

Thanks to my friends for tolerating my reclusive behavior. Special thanks to my sweetie, Jan, for her encouragement, patience, and loving kindness as I subjected her to regular episodes of distraction, inattention, and anxiety.

The staff of the *For Dummies* series was a delight to work with. More than that, they consistently encouraged me not to hold anything back, to create a first-class book filled with substance and solid information. Thanks, Alissa Schwipps and Mike Baker of Wiley. You guys ain't half bad. And I'm grateful to the illustrators, Kathryn Born and Stacey Isaac, for their lovely contributions to the book. What a team!

Publisher's Acknowledgments

We're proud of this book; please send us your comments through our Dummies online registration form located at http://dummies.custhelp.com. For other comments, please contact our Customer Care Department within the U.S. at 877-762-2974, outside the U.S. at 317-572-3993, or fax 317-572-4002.

Some of the people who helped bring this book to market include the following:

Acquisitions, Editorial, and Media Development

Senior Project Editor: Alissa Schwipps

Acquisitions Editor: Mike Baker

Copy Editors: Jessica Smith, Kathy Simpson

Assistant Editor: Erin Calligan Mooney

Editorial Program Coordinator: Joe Niesen

Technical Editor: Ben Falk

Senior Editorial Manager: Jennifer Ehrlich

Editorial Assistants: David Lutton, Jennette ElNaggar

Art Coordinator: Alicia B. South

Cover Photos: © Owen E. Dell

Cartoons: Rich Tennant (www.the5thwave.com)

Composition Services

Senior Project Coordinator: Kristie Rees

Layout and Graphics: Reuben W. Davis, Melissa K. Jester, Christine Williams

Special Art: Kathryn Born, Stacey Isaac

Proofreader: Broccoli Information Management

Indexer: Sherry Massey

Special Help: Elizabeth Rea, Danielle Voirol

Publishing and Editorial for Consumer Dummies

 Diane Graves Steele, Vice President and Publisher, Consumer Dummies

 Kristin Ferguson-Wagstaffe, Product Development Director, Consumer Dummies

 Ensley Eikenburg, Associate Publisher, Travel

 Kelly Regan, Editorial Director, Travel

Publishing for Technology Dummies

 Andy Cummings, Vice President and Publisher, Dummies Technology/General User

Composition Services

 Gerry Fahey, Vice President of Production Services

 Debbie Stailey, Director of Composition Services

Contents at a Glance

Table of Contents

Introduction

· ·

*1*t's a lovely fall day. I'm looking out the French doors that separate my office from the food forest outside. I see lemons, oranges, and tangerines ripening on (what an amazing coincidence!) my lemon, orange, and tangerine trees. A tall stalk of amaranth, a welcome volunteer, is topped by an outrageous pompom of red flowers swaying in the gentle afternoon breeze. Leeks, onions, fava beans, several kinds of basil, sage, bell peppers, hot chilies, blueberries, and a couple dozen other edibles are within my view. There's even a water chestnut plant growing happily in a tiny water garden.

All in all I have more than 130 kinds of edible plants in my very compact yard, along with four water features; what must be hundreds of kinds of ornamental plants; lots of beneficial insects, butterflies, and hummingbirds; and a couple of cats snoozing in the shade on my little meadow of native sedges. I have half a dozen inviting outdoor rooms for entertaining and quiet contemplation, plus a welcoming entry area, a street-side native garden, and plenty of intimate views and surprises. I feel so fortunate to be able to enjoy this place every day.

I guess you could say I'm in love with my garden. I'd do just about anything for it, but the truth is that I hardly work on it at all. A couple of hours of work a week is sufficient to keep it in beautiful condition. It requires very little water, almost no fertilizer, and never, ever any pesticides. It generates almost no waste or bad karma. It feeds me, shelters me, entertains me and the others who experience it, delights all my senses, and provides habitat for many wild things — and it does all this with very little negative impact on the environment. It's an efficient living system that really works.

This amazing spot didn't happen by chance, of course. I spent 28 years creating a sustainable, beautiful garden. And landscaping is my profession, so I do have a leg up on the ordinary Joe. But having spent my adult life creating similar gardens for thousands of clients, I know such a place is within your reach — and you don't have to wait a quarter century to have it.

This book shows you how to develop your property for maximum enjoyment, at minimal cost, and with a net positive impact on your surroundings. That outcome may sound like magic, but then, gardens are full of magic. You just have to know the tricks of the trade, and that's what *Sustainable Landscaping For Dummies* is all about.

About This Book

You may have already struggled and felt overwhelmed with the complexities of creating a landscape, especially if you yearn for something that's good for the environment as well as for you. Admittedly, landscaping is complex — a lot more complex than most people realize. Yet when taken step by step, creating a sustainable landscape isn't difficult. This book does a thorough job of filling you in on the principles of sustainable landscaping and on the all-important details that make the difference between a garden that's just okay and one that will blow everybody away with its beauty and usefulness.

Now, I happen to believe that anything worth doing is worth having fun with. Gardens should be fun, and so should reading about them. You can expect to find some silliness here, the occasional bad pun, and a light touch. But the fun doesn't come at the expense of substance. You'll find all you need to know here — perhaps more than has ever been compiled in one place on this subject. This book isn't fluffy. But I like to believe it isn't tedious, either.

Like all *For Dummies* books, you can dip into the book anywhere to get what you need. You don't need to start at the beginning unless you want to. Go for what attracts you, and move around as you want. You'll always get what you need, quickly and easily (the table of contents and index can help). When I just don't have the space to cover everything, I refer you to handy Web sites or to some of the other gardening and landscaping books in the *For Dummies* series. I don't want to leave you hanging.

Conventions Used in This Book

The following conventions are used throughout the text to make things consistent and easy to understand:

- New terms appear in *italics* and are closely followed by an easy-to-understand definition.
- **Bold** highlights the key words in bulleted lists and the action parts of numbered steps.
- All Web addresses appear in `monofont`.

One thing you should know is that I use the terms *landscape* and *garden* interchangeably. It's easy to argue about semantics, but for most people, the space around their home is their garden or their landscaping. To some degree, the term you prefer to use depends on how you manage things, with *garden* having a more active flavor than *landscape*. But hey, there's really little or no difference, and frankly, I figure that reading the words *landscape* and *landscaping* over and over would be a little irritating after a while.

What You're Not to Read

Every now and then, a special situation comes up in this book: I tell you something that's interesting but not necessarily important to everyone. For instance, the fine details of how to make a handsome retaining wall out of chewed-up dog toys are quite fascinating. But surprisingly, most people probably don't care much about this matter, despite the fact that our very way of life is dependent on it. Unfortunately, I think the dog-toy info ended up on the cutting room floor. But those are the type of fun but unnecessary facts that are placed in *sidebars,* which are boxes with gray backgrounds to separate them from the regular text. I don't take points off for skipping these, and hey, don't mind my feelings. I'll be okay. Really.

Foolish Assumptions

I've been thinking about you. I think I may have your number when it comes to your gardening interests. See whether I'm right:

- ✔ You own a single-family home or hope to. It has some land around it, a little or a lot, and you're wondering what the heck to do with it. You're intrigued by the idea of messing around with land but don't have a lot of background in gardening or landscaping.

- ✔ You care a lot about the environment, and you realize that this is your chance to do something really good — or to really mess things up. You realize that your yard is part of the real world and that what you do there isn't just about your needs and your family's needs. You take your responsibilities seriously.

- ✔ You like tackling do-it-yourself projects, not just to save money but because they're fun. You're no all-star landscaper, but you can dig a hole without ending up in traction, and you like physical work.

- ✔ You may have some gardening experience, but you're facing a project that's bigger than anything you've tackled before. You're maybe just a teeny bit intimidated. You need a friend in the business.

- ✔ Then again, you may be a pro — a landscape contractor, gardener, or builder who's looking for cutting-edge information on sustainable landscaping. You've come to the right place! Pull up a wheelbarrow and have a seat.

How This Book Is Organized

Each part of this book covers a particular major chunk of information. Take a minute to look them over before you dive into the wonderful world of sustainable landscaping.

Part I: Sustainable Landscaping: The Basics

That word *sustainable* is everywhere these days. It has a warm-'n'-fuzzy feeling, but you may not really understand what it means when applied to landscaping. Part I is the place to find out. It helps you understand what makes a landscape sustainable, what a sustainable landscape looks like, why it matters, and what it's going to cost you. It also introduces you to the sustainable materials, practices, and principles that go into a landscape system. Finally, Part I helps you decide what you can do yourself and when to call a pro.

Part II: Good Design: The Key to Sustainable Landscaping

Part II gives you in-depth details on designing a landscape. You discover *site analysis* (a fancy term for looking at stuff with your brain in gear); screening for sustainable features; and basic principles of landscape design, including some of the tricks the pros use to create those killer gardens in the fancy magazines. This part provides information on how to handle special situations and how to stay safe and out of trouble. It also provides you with plenty of information on creating a great landscape plan.

Part III: Water, Water, Everywhere: Water-Conserving Irrigation and Drainage

Most landscapes require some kind of watering system, if only to get new plantings established. Even native plantings need a little water at times. A watering system can be as simple as a hose or as complex as a fully automated irrigation system with a smart controller that gets its programming from outer space (no kidding). Here's where you find out how it all works. In Part III, you see how to manage watering for maximum conservation and how to maintain your irrigation system. You also get up to speed on the all-important, ultra-sustainable topic of water harvesting. Finally, I provide a bit of info about drainage systems. Wear your swim fins while reading this part.

Part IV: Hardscaping Made Easy: Creating Awesome Features without Wrecking the Environment

Even though sustainable landscapes rely primarily on plants and other elements of the biological world, you inevitably need some of the hard stuff: concrete patios, stone retaining walls, fences, arbors, steps, and lighting systems. Here, you find out how to assemble sustainable hardscape elements into outdoor rooms to serve your family's needs as well as how to construct and maintain them. Just to show you that I'm not all business, this part also addresses fun stuff, such as art, water features, outdoor kitchens, and facilities for animals — all done with minimal nasty impacts.

Part V: Great Greenery for a Green Garden

When most people hear the word *landscaping* or *garden,* they think of plants. Plants are the heart of the garden, and with the underpinnings out of the way, the fun of populating your property with trees, shrubs, perennials, and other plants begins in this part. Here you see how to design gorgeous plantings that also really work, demanding little care and few resources. You get the dirt on soil, composting, and mulching. You find out how to buy, install, and care for plants. And of course, you read all about lawns — but not just any old lawns; you find out about alternatives to conventional lawns and lawn care.

Part VI: The Part of Tens

Mere mortals with nongreen thumbs will love the list of ten easy, quick, and inexpensive (or free) projects that can almost instantly hurtle your existing landscaping into the world of sustainability. And everyone should have a look at the ten big mistakes to avoid.

Don't stop there! If you have special interests or needs — such as making your home safer in a wildfire, developing an edible landscape, or making the most of rainfall — check out the appendix, which includes detailed drawings of realistic projects you can create. You also find sections on attracting wildlife to your property, developing a drought-tolerant landscape, and creating a landscape that saves energy by keeping your house cooler in summer and warmer in winter.

Icons Used in This Book

To make this book easier to read and simpler to use, I include some icons that can help you find and fathom key ideas and information.

I know a few landscaping pointers, and I'm not holding any of them back. Paragraphs with this icon next to them are places to get the inside scoop on doing things right.

Some stuff is more important than other stuff. This icon signals you to listen up, because if you blow this topic, you'll regret it. So don't skip any paragraphs marked with this icon.

Sustainable landscaping isn't for sissies. You can get smacked down in lots of ways. Heed the warnings, and nobody gets hurt.

Where to Go from Here

Many sustainable processes don't just make things less bad; they make them a lot better than how they started out. If you really take this advice far enough, your landscaping will go beyond sustainability to become a net producer of great stuff — food, fresh air, cooler homes, more wildlife, happier people, and more.

And now you're on your way. Maybe you feel like you're stepping off the plane in an exotic foreign land: a bit excited and a bit disoriented. If you're the linear type, like me, just keep reading. I think it's important to at least absorb the basic principles in Chapters 1 and 2. But you may have a particularly urgent need, such as getting an existing irrigation system back on its feet (Chapter 10), building a sustainable water feature (Chapter 13), or growing more food on your land (Chapter 18 and the appendix). Go for it.

To make navigation as easy as possible, the table of contents comes in two flavors: Contents at a Glance, which covers the major headings, and a full Table of Contents that spreads everything out. Don't forget the yellow Cheat Sheet in the front of the book and the appendix in the back, which provide some neat special projects. Something for everybody — that's my philosophy.

All kidding aside, I consider it an honor to share my lifetime of experience in — and passion for — sustainable landscaping with you. I wish you the most fun ever in making your dreams come true. Best of luck!

Part I
Sustainable Landscaping: The Basics

In this part . . .

What the heck is a sustainable landscape, anyway? What does it look like, and what makes it tick? You may wonder how to get one (and how much it will cost). If you're unfamiliar with this kind of landscape, you may also wonder whether it really makes any difference to the environment or to you. Finally, you may not know whether you can create a sustainable landscape yourself or have to hire a professional.

Start with this part to make sense of all these concerns and more. It's a great jumping-off point for the rest of the book, because it gives you the core ideas behind sustainable landscaping. It's kind of like a road map for what's to come. You'll feel a lot better after you read these chapters.

Chapter 1

Landscaping the Sustainable Way

In This Chapter

▶ Going through a sustainability overview

▶ Creating a sustainable landscape

▶ Good design: The key to success

▶ Working out your plan

▶ Making maintenance easy and safe

*L*ook at nature. Nobody gardens nature. Nature quietly thrives, while down in town, everyone takes up arms every Saturday morning — hacking, decapitating, shearing, poisoning, ripping, and tearing their yards, not to mention sweating and swearing. Lucky for you, this book is all about how to develop your landscaping along natural models so you can enjoy lovely, environmentally friendly surroundings and get a break from the battle.

This chapter gives you an overview of what sustainable landscaping is, why it matters, how it works, and how you can transform your property into a beautiful, functional sustainable landscape. If you start with this chapter, you'll have a good grasp of the basics, and then you can move on to whatever sections of the book apply to your current situation or whatever you're curious about.

Getting Up to Speed on Sustainability

At one time, all gardens were simple. They were made up of plants, soil, and natural building materials. They didn't cost much to create or care for. Their effect on the environment was positive, because they didn't cause strip mining, release poisons into the atmosphere, or consume huge quantities of fossil fuel. They were sustainable before the word was popular because they could go on essentially forever.

That's what sustainability is all about. Gardens can be that way again. All over the world, people are getting wise to the fact that they have an alternative to the dysfunctional industrial/commercial landscaping model that's been jammed down our throats by advertising and ignorance.

Sustainability is a better way. It's not perfect, but by doing things right, you'll make a huge and important difference. Your land is your opportunity to help create a better future.

What the heck is sustainable landscaping, anyway?

Sustainable landscaping isn't about a look. A Japanese garden can be sustainable. So can an English garden or a desert garden or a woodland garden. A sustainable landscape can be formal or informal, geometric or naturalistic, simple or complex. Other than planting vast swards of mowed lawn in a dry climate, you're pretty much free to choose whatever look you want as long as you follow the principles of sustainability, setting up a smoothly functioning ecosystem that makes minimal demands and creates minimal problems.

The key ideas that make sustainable landscaping work are simple and easy to put into practice:

- **Living system:** Nature is a system of interrelated subsystems that work together to form a smoothly operating whole — a living, functioning ecosystem. There are many examples of living systems, such as your body (made up of various organs), a forest (filled with many kinds of plants and animals), and the ocean (teeming with millions of interdependent life forms). If you make your landscape a highly functioning system patterned after the ways of nature, it will operate like nature — without the need for much control or intervention and without harming any other living system.

- **Homeostasis:** *Homeostasis* is a fancy word for *stability*. It's the balance of forces in a living system, with no force getting out of control to cause harm. Consider your body, which more or less functions automatically. You don't need to will your heart to beat or your eyes to see; those things just happen. With a little care from you, all is groovy. The landscape system can work this way, too, if you set it up right.

- **Deep design:** Homeostasis doesn't happen by accident; it's a product of good design. I'm not talking about the too-common superficial design that creates pretty but dysfunctional gardens. Instead, I mean design that looks beneath appearances to develop a beautiful landscape that also really works. Deep design takes special skills — skills that you discover in this book.

✔ **Cyclical design:** Nature recycles everything. As the Buddhist master Thich Nhat Hanh once said, "When I look at a rose I see compost; when I look at compost I see a rose." Conventional manmade systems are linear. Consider the process:

1. Get a virgin material from nature (usually with disastrous effects at the source).

2. Use toxic and energy-intensive processes to alter it so much that it can never go back to nature.

3. Use it one time.

4. When the material's too-short useful life comes to an end, dispose of it in a landfill, where it plugs up the works of yet another formerly living system.

Nature has been very patient with us, but this linear game is just about up. Mother Nature hates it, and besides, she's running out of merchandise. Going back to the infinite and ancient cyclical way of life makes your garden one with nature, less troublesome, and more enduring.

✔ **Harmony with the local environment:** There are no nonlocal conditions. Your property is unique, with a particular soil type, microclimate, exposure, vegetation, and other factors. By choosing plants and other elements that are well suited to these particulars, you set up a robust ecosystem that will be happy with its lot in life. (Conventional gardens rely on ill-adapted plants and other elements and then depend on continual input of resources to keep from failing.)

✔ **Careful management of inputs and outputs:** The sustainable landscape thrives on what nature offers. It makes efficient use of resources such as building materials, water, and fertilizer. What goes in and out of the landscape is minimized, so as many effects as possible are beneficial.

✔ **Consideration of on-site effects:** What happens on-site is carefully considered at the design stage. Natural features such as soil, native plants, and animal habitat are preserved. All improvements must meet the test of being good players. Each element of the newly formed ecosystem must play a beneficial role: making oxygen, sequestering carbon, providing food, improving the climate inside dwellings, preventing erosion, or protecting against wildfire, to name a few. To minimize negative effects, toxic materials aren't used; neither are energy-intensive processes, noise-generating machinery, or thirsty plantings.

✔ **Consideration of off-site effects:** What happens off-site is important too. By that, I mean that there should be no damage at the source of materials. Your landscape won't be truly sustainable unless it leaves forests intact, mountains unmined, oil unburned, and workers safe and happy.

✔ **Benefits beyond sustainability:** Finally, a sustainable landscape should seek to go beyond mere sustainability. As visionary architect William McDonough observed, we shouldn't just be less bad; we should be good. Landscapes offer so many benefits to users and to nature that it's easy to use the power of the sun, the rain, and the soil to create a paradise for all living beings. You can do that — and you have no reason not to.

Why sustainable landscaping matters to the environment

Where do I start? The traditional landscape is an environmental train wreck:

✔ It fragments and destroys native habitat.

✔ It consumes natural resources.

✔ It causes strip mining, clear cutting of forests, and other negative effects at the source of materials.

✔ It introduces nonnative plants that invade and devastate wild ecosystems.

✔ It wrecks waterways and groundwater through the leaching of pesticides, herbicides and fertilizers. (Of the nitrogen applied to lawns, 40 percent to 60 percent ends up in the water.)

✔ It increases runoff, which results in urban flooding and further damage to waterways.

✔ It fills canyons and landfills with waste.

✔ It increases global warming through the use of fossil fuels.

✔ It wastes precious water to keep useless ornamental plants and lawns alive.

✔ Outdoor power equipment creates noise in every neighborhood.

✔ Pesticides kill 60 million to 70 million birds each year, not to mention their negative effects on beneficial insects and other wildlife.

✔ Pesticide use in the United States is ten times greater for landscaping than for agriculture.

Cowabunga! What a mess! Added to these effects are those on human well-being:

✔ The health of one in every seven people is affected by pesticides.

✔ Air pollution caused by pesticides and fossil-fuel use damages everyone's health.

✔ Each year, 60,000 to 70,000 severe accidents and fatalities are caused just from lawn mowing.

This has got to stop. Sustainable landscaping addresses all these issues by cleaning up the system, making these effects unnecessary, and respecting the environment. Simply put, sustainable landscaping is good for the environment because it does things the right way.

What's in it for you

Suppose that you don't even care about the environment. Fine. You still should have a sustainable landscape because it's cheaper, easier to care for, more satisfying to live with, and much more interesting.

You'll save money because all your inputs are significantly reduced. You'll spend less on materials, water, fertilizer, gasoline, labor, dump fees — the works. Sustainable landscaping is a penny-pincher's delight.

Because sustainable landscaping makes so few demands on you, you spend less time keeping it from falling apart and more time enjoying it (or enjoying something else you love). If you've busted your chops on a conventional landscape for a while, you know how much work it can be. Imagine that work not happening. That's what converting to a sustainable landscape can do for you.

Finally, when you see how beautifully everything works, you'll come to admire the elegance of a finely tuned system. It's soothing to know that things are working smoothly without much help from you.

Doing Your Part: What It Takes to Make a Sustainable Landscape

I assume that you'll be fairly involved with your project, even if you hire someone to do some of the work. That's why you bought this book, right? Well, here's an overview of what it takes to make your landscape sustainable, including tips on how to make the most of your relationship to the job.

Taking the time to do things right

Slow down. Whether your project is small or massive, the practice of deep design (refer to "What the heck is sustainable landscaping, anyway?" earlier in this chapter) demands careful observation and attention to detail. I've been told that in ancient times, Japanese garden designers sat on the site every day, all day, for a year, carefully noticing the way the sun moved; how the trees responded to wind; what animals visited; and many more subtleties that can be grasped only through quiet, intense scrutiny. As the seasons changed, the designers learned in summer what they could never learn in spring, and so on through the full annual cycle. Only after that apprenticeship did they dare to begin the design process. Whether you opt to follow the ancient ways or not, do give yourself time to understand what you're working with. Attention to detail pays off in many ways.

Using your skills to lower your bills

If you're planning to do the work of building a whole new landscape, you can look forward to a lot of physical effort. Even a smaller project can be hard work. Landscaping isn't crocheting doilies. On the other hand, it can be a wonderful opportunity to get outside and get some exercise, and it can be a lot of fun too.

Busting some sustainability myths

As with anything new, concerns come up. You'll be making a big, expensive, long-term commitment to your landscaping, and you need to know that this isn't some goofy New Age idea that doesn't really deliver the goods. Here are some facts to set your mind at ease:

✔ **Myth:** Sustainable landscapes are ugly.

Truth: Plants in a sustainable landscape are healthy and vigorous, and have room to grow into their beautiful natural forms. Structures are made from natural materials, with their inherent beauty showing through. Sustainable landscapes are green, flowery, fresh, and lovely — not parched gravel beds with thorny, nasty-looking plants (unless that's what you want, of course).

✔ **Myth:** Sustainable landscapes are expensive.

✔ **Truth:** All landscaping is expensive, but sustainable landscaping is less expensive for a couple of reasons:

✔ Because the sustainable approach emphasizes plants over hardscape, you save money on the installation. Plants are cheaper than concrete.

✔ Even more important, the ongoing care of the landscape will be much less because it is undemanding of resources and labor.

✔ **Myth:** Sustainable landscapes don't work.

Truth: The whole point of developing a landscape sustainably is to create an ecosystem that functions smoothly without much effort on your part. When you look at what's needed to keep a conventional landscape in one piece — the mowing, watering, pest control, pruning, and all the rest — you see that *conventional* landscaping is what doesn't work.

First, take stock of your ability to dig ditches, lift heavy stuff, and generally grunt out (weekend after weekend for a really big project). Balance that effort against the cost of paying someone else to do some or all of the work. If you do want to tackle it, be sure you know how to work safely, and check with your doctor if you have any qualms about your fitness level. Stay safe, okay?

Doing the work yourself can save up to half the total cost of the project. But before you leap in, it's helpful to assess your abilities. You may know how to run a tractor or sweat copper pipe or program an irrigation controller. But you can also get into things you don't know how to handle. This book, and its companion volume *Landscaping For Dummies* (by Phillip Giroux, Bob Beckstrom, Lance Walheim, and The Editors of the National Gardening Association), will help you to develop skills you may not have. If there's some part of the project that you can't or don't want to tackle, hire an expert. Paying someone else to do the work is cheaper than having to do it over. See Chapter 3 for some guidelines on when to do it yourself and when to hire a professional.

Getting a grip on costs

You have lots of variables to consider, and costs vary wildly depending on the kinds of improvements you'll be making. A flagstone patio can cost 20 or 30 times what a ground cover would for the same area, for example, and generally speaking, landscaping an entire yard front and rear can set you back the price of a new car or two. But many smaller projects and improvements won't break the bank.

No matter the size of your project, you can save tons of money by doing the work yourself and by tapping the waste stream for materials whenever you can. See Chapter 2 for some inspiring waste stream resources.

Developing a good tight budget is difficult when you aren't sure what you'll be doing, so develop your design first. Then do your homework. Talk to contractors, shop for materials, and also consider the value of your own time. Don't get too detailed at this stage. When you know exactly what you'll be doing, you can crunch the numbers to determine the total expense and adjust your plan as needed.

If you'll be doing an entire property, this number will be big. If the number is too big, consider how you could lower costs without compromising quality (smaller plants, less hardscape, and a manual irrigation system, for example).

Or break the project into phases spread out over a few months or even years. For instance, you may tackle just the front yard during the first phase, and then follow up later with paths, patios, lighting, and other features. You have lots of options that help keep the money end of things on track.

Keep track of expenses with a spreadsheet. Log all the elements of the project and what they cost: the tractor used for demolition, tree trimming, topsoil, irrigation equipment, contracted labor (which may be the whole job), incidental expenses like a portable toilet for the workers, and so on. The handy thing about having costs set up this way is that you can keep updating your costs as your design goes through its inevitable changes. You can also use it to track actual costs as the project progresses. Check out Chapter 3 for more help keeping cost in mind.

Scheduling your project

Consider the scope of the work and how much time it will take you to do it or have it done. It's amazing what you can accomplish in a weekend or two, if you've planned things out thoroughly in advance. Not every sustainable landscaping project has to take months out of your life. Looking at the sidebar on the sequence of landscaping operations, you'll see a lot of tasks. Evaluate how many of those tasks are part of your project. A smaller job may involve only a little demolition, some planting, and a layer of mulch. A full-yard remodel could require work in every category and therefore call for some serious advance choreography.

Whatever the scope of your project, keep in mind that many landscaping tasks are dependent on the time of year. If you'll be getting professional help with some or all of the job, talk to your contractor about the timing from his or her perspective. Think about your cash flow, too, if that's a consideration.

For a large project, develop a project calendar, using the sequencing information in the sidebar. Schedules can get off track, of course, but at least you'll have an action plan to work from.

Planning and Design: The Keys to a Sustainable Landscape

When it comes to making your landscaping work properly, good design is everything; it determines once and for all how the system will work. Design is especially important when you have big plans in mind. It's detailed, but it's a lot of fun too.

Sequence of landscaping operations, start to finish

Here's an overview of this whole big monster of a process of turning your nasty ol' yard into a sustainable landscape. Every project has its own particular aspects, quirks, and special needs, but some universals apply to all projects. Landscaping isn't an exact science, and many things can alter the passage from ugly to lovely. You may already have guessed that some of these steps are done concurrently with others. You may still be designing certain aspects of the project while you're building others, for example. (In fact, you probably will be.) Whatever the particulars of your project, the following table will help give you an idea of how things usually go.

Certain sequences are pretty hard to argue with. You have to do your demolition before you build anything new, and it's a whole lot easier to do the grading before the plants are planted and the irrigation is in. Other sequences are more flexible. You may install a patio in one corner of the yard before you even touch another corner. As for design, it can be a continuing process of thinking, learning, and reconsidering throughout the course of the entire project. Overall, though, if you follow this chain of events, you'll be fine.

Category	*Tasks*
Planning and design	Site analysis, landscape plans, budgeting
Permits and approvals	Building permits, zoning approval, and so on
Weed control	Grubbing weeds, sheet mulching
Utilities location	Call the free One-Call coordinating service at 811 (or visit www.call811.com) for line location
Demolition	Remove plants, structures, and so on
Tree trimming	Prune existing trees
Earthwork	Grading, excavating, importing soil
Drainage	Underground drains, dry streambeds, and water-harvesting features
Erosion control	Netting, silt fencing, hydromulching
Water mains	Piping, backflow prevention device(s), valves, hose bibs
Electrical	Irrigation control wires, lighting wires, buried conduits
Sprinklers	Lawn and other sprinklers
Heavy construction	Boulders, retaining walls, fences, and so on
Flatwork	Driveway, patios, walkways
Plantings	Trees, shrubs, ground covers
Drip system	Drip tubing and emitters
Mulching	Cover ground with mulch
Lighting	Install fixtures, transformers
Site furnishings	Benches, tables, artwork, potted plants

Getting to know the site — and your needs

Responding appropriately to conditions is essential to developing the kind of finely tuned landscape that's easy to live with. The first step is making friends with the site so you understand what you're dealing with. Start by spending some quality time with your yard. (It's been a while, hasn't it?) Go outside when you have the time to just hang out and quietly observe the many characteristics of your property: the path of the sun, the condition of the soil, the health of existing plants, and good and bad views, to name a few aspects. Take photos, make notes, and move around to see things from as many perspectives as possible. Get professional advice if you have special concerns, such as an unstable hillside or soil problems. See Chapter 4 for an in-depth discussion of site analysis.

But understanding the site isn't enough; you also have to learn what you want and need. Rushing into the design phase without going through this process leaves you without the information you need to make good decisions. Think about your needs and desires. What do you want from the finished landscape? Make a simple list. Do this outdoors so you can imagine the possibilities better. If you stand in your backyard and dream about what you need, for example, you might list privacy, a shady place with a hammock or a patio, a play space for the kids, a vegetable garden, a few fruit trees, secure fencing, and a water feature. Take the time to get everything down on paper. Include your family in the process, and make sure that everybody gets heard.

Scoping out sustainable avenues of research

I'll be the first to admit that this book is almost all you need to create and maintain a sustainable landscape. Nonetheless, there are some other great resources out there that you should know about. Local government agencies, such as the public works department, often have community-specific resources and tips on water conservation, waste reduction, and other aspects of sustainable landscaping. Visit the gardening section of your local bookstore. Talk to local nurseries and landscape supply stores.

And of course there's the Internet, which is rich with timely information on all aspects of sustainable landscaping (but also rife with unreliable and inaccurate information). I refer you to reliable Web sites throughout this book. But you can also search on a particular topic, such as integrated pest management or water harvesting, and turn up more information than you could ever even read. To cull out the junk and find the best information, focus on university

Web sites (those with the suffix ".edu"), nonprofit sites (with the suffix ".org"), and some government agency sites, such as the Environmental Protection Agency (these sites use the suffix ".gov"). Commercial sites can be great too, but watch out for sales pitches disguised as information.

Developing a design

Design deserves your best thinking because it determines the outcome of the project and how it will function over time. The design phase is a time to slow down and pay attention. Design goes from the general ("I think I want a vegetable garden") to the specific ("I want four 4 x 10 raised stone beds in the northeast corner of the back yard with six kohlrabi plants, a dozen rutabagas, and five Bad Boy tomatoes").

Designing a sustainable landscape is rigorous, but anyone can do it. I discuss design in detail in Part II of this book. For now, here's an overview of the process:

- ✔ **Creating the conceptual design:** When you understand the site and your own needs, you're ready to take a first stab at putting everything together. This draft is called the *conceptual design*. You create it in steps, starting with a bubble diagram and moving through field measuring, a base sheet, and ending with a concept plan.

- ✔ **Refining your design:** When you have a good understanding of how the elements fit together, you can begin to work on all the little details. What will that patio be made of, and precisely what will its shape and location be? Which tree will go on the east side of the house, and what size will it be at planting time? What species of perennials will go in the front border, how many of each kind, and what container size? You can even develop a series of individual plans that detail the construction, planting, irrigation, and other phases of the work. These plans will help you refine your ideas and guide you through the long process of constructing the landscape, and they'll help you share your vision with a contractor if you decide to hire a pro.

Putting Your Plan into Play

It's time to get hot and dirty! Are you really ready for this? Okay. You can do it. Put on those work boots and a good hat, grab your gear, and get out in the hot sun (don't forget sunscreen!). The work won't be easy, but it won't kill you either. Keep the dream of a beautiful new garden alive while you work. And if you poop out, you can always hire eager professionals to pick up where you left off.

Gathering the tools and materials you need

A landscaping project really is many projects rolled into one. Depending on the scope of your project, you may be doing demolition, moving and grading soil, installing irrigation and drainage systems, building all sorts of structures, planting plants, mulching, and doing a lot more. Some tools, such as shovels and rakes, are common to many of these tasks, and you'll get to know them quite well indeed. Other jobs — particularly hardscape construction (see Chapter 14) — require special and sometimes costly tools. You probably already have the basic tools; others can be rented or borrowed. (Buying tools that you only use once or twice isn't very sustainable, is it?)

The right tools make the job easier and safer, and the outcome will be more like what a pro would do. As for materials, you'll be getting these from a variety of sources: lumberyards, concrete plants, nurseries, landscape supply stores, stone and masonry dealers, irrigation supply stores, and others. Scout local resources, looking for places that have a commitment to supplying sustainable materials whenever possible. Try to buy locally, but if a more sustainable material is available elsewhere, it may be a better choice environmentally. Don't forget to tap the waste stream for as many materials as you can (see Chapter 2). Sustainable means buying as little as possible.

Ensuring success along the way

If you're tackling a small project, a day or two may be enough to get the job done. Some projects require more time to get ready than it takes to do the actual work. Plan ahead, gathering up all the materials and tools you need in advance of the big day. Keep in mind that some materials, especially plants, may not be available exactly when you need them, so call around at least a week in advance to be sure you'll have what you need.

If you're taking on an entire landscape remodel, pace yourself. It isn't a one-weekend project. Many people burn out partway through. But *you* have to be sustainable too. If you aren't accustomed to physical work, build up to it slowly, and give yourself lots of breaks.

The best outcome is the result of ongoing design decisions made as the project unfolds. Just because you turn your body on to do the physical work doesn't mean that you turn your mind off.

As you go, don't be afraid to rethink the details as new aspects of the work unfold. Details matter, and they aren't all evident in the design stage. Stay open to new ideas.

Maintaining the Land Nature's Way

You don't have to be a great gardener to have a great garden. Caring for a sustainable landscape should be much easier than caring for a conventional one. It's been designed with low maintenance in mind, remember?

The first year will be somewhat demanding as you nurture your new baby along to maturity, but maintenance will get much easier after that. By contrast, a conventional garden — with its many oversize plants, susceptibility to pests and diseases, and generally entropic nature — can get harder and harder to live with over time.

Even sustainable landscapes require some maintenance, but it's along the lines of removing dead flowers, picking fruit, tidying up a bit, and gently nudging things in the right direction now and then. The work is nonviolent, quiet, and fun. For more information on maintaining your sustainable landscape, flip to Chapter 20.

Minimizing the effects of maintenance, on- and off-site

Conventional maintenance does huge damage to the environment. Every year in the United States alone, we use 800 million gallons of gasoline just to mow lawns — and lots more to power other equipment, such as trimmers, blowers, and chain saws. Power equipment also generates significant air and noise pollution.

The 67 million pounds of pesticides used annually on American lawns destroy native and beneficial insects, cause air pollution, and sicken people and pets. Herbicides and fertilizers also harm the environment.

The result is a mess, but things don't need to be this way. By building a landscape that needs little care, adopting organic methods that don't use harsh chemicals, and using hand tools instead of power equipment, the sustainable landscape becomes a place of peace, purity, and productivity, not a war zone. You find tips for how to do this in Chapters 20, 21, and 22.

Cutting out the chemicals

The reason that conventional gardens depend on chemicals is that they aren't set up to be durable and naturally resistant to pests and diseases. Gardeners often use chemicals because they don't know about natural alternatives or don't believe that natural solutions could possibly work as well. Actually, the opposite is true. Follow the tips on natural weed control and integrated pest management in Chapter 21, and stick with organic fertilizers (see Chapter 22). You'll be safer; so will your family and the environment.

Keeping costs down

Because so much less care is involved, costs drop dramatically in sustainable landscapes. It's easy to prove that around 80 percent of the total cost of a conventional garden is for maintenance over a 20-year life span. That adds up to a huge number — one that most homeowners are shocked to see, realizing that their property is eating up their life savings month by month. In a sustainable system, the cost of everything is less because you have less to do and fewer inputs to provide. Even small savings can add up to make a huge difference in the overall cost of the project.

Chapter 2

Making Good Decisions about What to Include in Your Landscape

....

In This Chapter

▶ Trimming down your resource use

▶ Optimizing what goes into your landscaping and what comes out

▶ Finding the sources of sustainable materials

▶ Buying into biological solutions

▶ Ensuring that each element of the garden has a purpose

....

*O*ne of the coolest things about landscaping your property sustainably is that you, personally, benefit from it. Heck, even if you don't give a hoot about the environment, you're going to save big bucks and avoid having to do a whole lot of hard work that you didn't really want to do anyway. Sustainable landscaping is good for your selfish side *and* for the planet.

In this chapter, I tell you how to make good decisions about what to include in your landscape. I help you select materials and features that make sense for you and the environment, and I show you how to create a dream landscape that's beautiful and easy to live with.

The whole idea of sustainable landscaping is creating a practical, well-thought-out landscape system that works for everybody — including the environment. The total impact of your landscape, both on- and off-site, should be positive. In other words, sustainable landscaping is about considering the life cycle of everything that you bring into your landscape. When you take the life cycle into account, you're well on your way to creating a landscape that's truly sustainable.

Using Materials and Resources Wisely

Putting resources to good (and efficient) use not only reduces the impact of your landscaping project, but it also saves you money. After all, you're buying cheaper materials and using less of them. Creating a conventional landscape requires lots of materials, and over time it requires more and more resources to keep it going. Why? Because most landscapes aren't designed along the lines of nature and its life cycles and systems.

Nature is really good at fostering ecosystems that are self-regulating and able to live on locally available resources. Think about it: Nobody waters, fertilizes, or sprays wild areas with pesticides, and yet they continue growing for millions of years. By making your landscape more in keeping with the rules of nature, you'll enjoy the same benefits found in a natural system.

So an important principle to apply when you're designing your landscape is simply to use fewer materials and resources. For instance, a landscape that's dominated by *hardscape* (constructed features, like a concrete patio or a wrought iron fence) creates enormous impacts off-site where the materials are obtained and processed.

The production of concrete, for instance, requires strip mining of rock, sand, and the other minerals that go into making cement. Manufacturing cement also generates a lot of carbon dioxide — over a billion metric tons per year worldwide. Concrete is just one example of how much damage is done by our addiction to high-tech landscaping materials. And you know what? Concrete is expensive, too!

After a conventional landscape made with lots of materials is completed, its appetite for water, fertilizer, and other resources — not to mention the labor and money that all this requires — will vary depending on how skillfully the landscape was initially designed. On the other hand, a landscape that's an internally stable, highly-functioning ecosystem won't need much help from you or require many materials to keep it going. The remaining sections in this chapter provide you with tons of specific ways to reduce your use of materials and resources.

Getting the Most Out of What You Put Into Your Landscape

If you want to create a highly tuned, efficient landscaping system that rewards you with decades of pleasure and beauty, you need to create a landscape that minimizes the need for *inputs* (the things you bring in) and uses the most efficient and earth-friendly materials when you *do* need them. It should also generate few (or no) *outputs* (things that leave the system; erroneously called "waste").

In this section, I focus on the inputs. Check out the later section "Generating Few (or No) Outputs" for more on minimizing outputs. Landscaping inputs fall into two categories:

- Building materials that are used to initially create the landscape
- Maintenance materials that are required to keep your landscape going

You have to build your landscape out of *something*, but there are huge differences among the materials, and many really great sustainable options are available. The more efficient your landscape is, the fewer maintenance materials you'll need.

Building materials: Turning one person's trash into your landscaping treasure

Your first step when trying to minimize your building material inputs is to consider how much hardscape you really need. It isn't necessary to pour a patio big enough to accommodate a wedding reception when you really just need someplace for the family to have dinner. Get into the habit of self-restraint. After deciding how much hardscape you need, determine what you already have that you can use to build it. The first place you should look for materials is in your own backyard. What you have there is free, doesn't need to be transported from elsewhere (burning up fossil fuels in the process), and isn't doing much other than just sitting around.

At first you may think that you don't have anything useful, but I'm willing to bet you do. As you look around your property, make a list of anything that you could possibly transform into a landscape feature. For instance, here are some ideas:

- Use native stones to build walls, paths, and dry streambeds
- Harvest undesirable trees for lumber
- Break up an old patio and turn the pieces into stepping stones

If nothing else, there's always soil, which you can turn into handsome earthen walls, benches, and even toolsheds. Visit Chapter 13 for details.

Don't overlook the neighbors' yards. Their so-called trash may be just what you need for your hardscape (and won't they be happy if you clean up their yards for them!). Also, consider reusing things that come from the community's waste stream, such as broken concrete (now called *urbanite*, a brand-new mineral!), which you can easily turn into a lovely patio or a handsome dry-stacked low retaining wall. Similarly, old timbers on their way to the land-fill can be used to build a raised bed or handsome footbridge. There are many ways to hunt down usable waste materials. Develop an eye for what might be salvaged from neighborhood remodels, cleanups, and construction projects. Tap local businesses for surplus materials. Scour craigslist, local classifieds, and bulletin boards. Dumpster dive.

Everything old is new again: Salvaged and reclaimed materials

Salvaged and reclaimed materials are resources that could have been wasted but are instead carefully saved and sold to willing buyers. In certain places, for example, you can buy wood that has been taken out of old barns (with the barn owner's permission, of course). You can also purchase logs dredged up from underwater where they sank a century ago. This lumber isn't cheap, but it's sold at a fraction of what you'd pay for similarly gorgeous old-growth wood (if you could even find it).

If you can't get your hands on used wood, note that modern portable lumber mills are circulating around some communities making usable lumber out of urban trees that have to be cut down for one reason or another. This lumber is sold at retail outlets and is usually advertised locally. Similarly, used bricks can be found in nearly any community; you'll find them advertised in the classified section of the newspaper or online.

A search of the Web can often turn up amazingly cool things for sale that you can use to create a one-of-a-kind refuse-chic landscape feature. There are even stores around the country that sell used building materials of all kinds. Most of these are small mom-and-pop operations, but you can also check out the chain of ReStores, which is operated by the nonprofit group Habitat for Humanity. Purchases made at a ReStore benefit good works around the world. Visit www.habitat.org/env/restores.aspx to find a ReStore near you.

Reincarnation: Recycled content materials

The difference between waste-stream or reclaimed materials and recycled ones is the degree of processing involved. You can use a waste-stream mate-rial, such as urbanite, as is, with no special work to make it into something else. It's still just concrete when you're done with it. But a recycled material, such as plastic lumber, goes into a factory as a big load of sticky pop bottles and comes out looking like a 2 x 6. You'd have a hard time guessing what it was made from.

Some people refer to recycling as *downcycling* or *remanufacturing* because the end product is so different from the ingredients that went into it. These folks also use this terminology because in most cases you can never take it in the other direction. For example, you couldn't make soda bottles out of old plas-tic lumber. A few materials, such as aluminum and steel, are truly recyclable.

By using recycled materials, you're having a positive impact on the environment. You're making use of what had once been considered trash, and that reduces the need to cut down trees, strip mine raw materials, and do other environmentally irresponsible things.

Some recycled-content materials, such as plastic lumber, may cost somewhat more than conventional products. Others, like wood chips, are free or available at a very low cost. Refer to Table 2-1 for a list of recycled materials commonly available in most communities.

Table 2-1	Commonly Available Recycled Materials	
Item	*Use*	*Source*
Fly ash	Added to concrete for paving, footings, and so on	Residue from coal-fired power plants
Landscape ties	Walls, steps, and planters	Plastic reclaimed from old cars
Plastic lumber	Decks, planters, railings, fencing, and furniture	Grocery bags, milk and soda containers, and wood shavings and scraps
Recycled plastic	Composters, pots, other materials, and gadgets	Waste plastic of various kinds
Road base	Sub-base under paving	Ground asphalt and concrete
Wood chips	Mulching around plants	Tree trimming operations and municipal green waste

Some recycled materials are controversial. For example, there's concern about crumb rubber that's made of ground up tires and used as mulch, as a base under artificial turf, and in playground mats. Zinc and other chemicals leaching from the rubber can kill plants and permanently toxify soil. The rubber also may be a fire hazard. And of course it stinks to high heaven on a hot day. Similarly, *biosolids* (treated sewage in common parlance) that are used as fertilizer come from uncontrolled sources that may contain contaminants or toxins. Even wood chips can contain weed seeds and contaminants. Some years ago many areas had a problem with persistent herbicides in municipal compost. The moral of this story? Investigate all claims made for recycled materials.

Taking it easy with low-impact materials

Low-impact materials are those that have been produced using practices that create a minimum of harmful effects on the environment. For instance, you can look for lumber that's been certified by an independent organization as having been sustainably grown and harvested. Such organizations include the Forest Stewardship Council in the United States (www.fscus.com) or the Programme for the Endorsement of Forest Certification (www.pefc.org).

Here are a few other low-impact considerations:

- ✔ Use straw bale or earthen construction instead of lumber.
- ✔ Grow your own wood or bamboo for a low-impact, ultra-local resource.
- ✔ Substitute high-density polyethylene (HDPE) or galvanized piping for PVC (polyvinyl chloride). Also avoid copper, because it's strip mined.
- ✔ If you must use paints and finishes, choose those that are low in *volatile organic compounds* (VOCs). Low-VOC paints don't emit as many pollutants into the atmosphere.

Protecting the future with renewable materials

Simply put, a *renewable resource* is one that you can continually get more of. Trees are a renewable resource — you can simply plant more trees. Oil, on the other hand, is not a renewable resource. The amount of oil on the planet today is as much as there will ever be.

By choosing renewable materials, you can ensure that future generations will be able to enjoy them too. Renewable materials are those that come from living sources, because they're the only things that can replicate themselves. Examples include lumber and other wood products, bamboo, straw, animal manures, and organic fertilizers, such as bone meal, fish emulsion, and kelp.

Creating things that last: Heritage materials

A special category of materials includes what I call *heritage materials*. These materials are produced so they can be reused over and over again as circumstances change. An example is the interlocking concrete paver block systems that are beginning to pop up in driveways all over.

For a long time, I truly hated these systems, mainly because of their lack of aesthetic merits. Then one day I realized that the most important thing about these pavers was the fact that they could be taken up and reused. Your driveway, 40 years from now, could become a neighbor's driveway, and then in a few more decades it could end up in the next block as a patio in the backyard of somebody who hasn't even been born yet.

When you create things that last and make them modular so they can be used again or repurposed, you're doing something very sustainable indeed, because the initial environmental impact can be spread over many decades of use.

The totally cool art of junkscaping

Living off the fat of the land is easy in our world, and it's so satisfying to know that you helped clean up a waste problem, got a material for nothing (or next to nothing), and reduced your demands for new materials — all in one fell swoop. That kind of synergy can really make you grin. The idea of junkscaping is simple: Find something that's headed to the landfill, and then take it home and make it a really cool part of your yard.

The possibilities for junkscaping your yard are endless. In fact, you have so much waste going by your door every day that you simply have no excuse for not building something out of it. Heck, I've seen planter beds edged with bowling balls bought for a dollar or two at the thrift store, a planter made out of old car headlights, lovely bonsai pots made from old truck brake drums, furniture crafted from fallen trees, old patios beautified with artfully inlaid scraps of tile and waste wood, and gorgeous wrought iron work made from old oilfield piping. Used materials often have that funky glow that only old things can provide. Think of them as outdoor antiques.

Where do you find this stuff? On craigslist, free-stuff listservs, and Web sites; in classified ads; sitting by the side of the road; at junkyards and used materials stores; in the backs of shopping centers; in dumpsters; and in your neighbor's backyard. Junk is everywhere!

Any durable and movable item — bricks, stones, paving blocks, and segmental retaining walls, for example — could fall into the category of heritage material. The key is understanding the long-term potential of these materials and setting them onto a bed of compacted sand rather than cementing them into place so they can't be reused.

Maintenance materials: Planning ahead to reduce upkeep later

After you've completed your landscaping, it will still require maintenance. After all, there's no such thing as no-maintenance landscaping. But by designing for sustainability and building things so they last, you'll be reducing the materials, effort, and money that go into keeping the place in shape.

In the following sections, I cover the materials commonly needed to maintain a landscape, and I also tell you which chapters help you minimize your need for these materials.

Water

Most folks think of water as being abundant, but out of the 326 million cubic miles of water on the planet, only about three-tenths of a percent of it is fresh, relatively unpolluted potable (drinkable) water that's usable by humans. Overall, that's not much.

Water is a renewable resource, of course. (Refer to the earlier section "Protecting the future with renewable materials" for more on renewable resources.) In fact, the water that falls from the sky in the form of rain and snow is about as renewable as you can get. Plus it's free. Rain even picks up nitrogen on its way down, delivering nice organic fertilizer right to your plants, and then watering it in — all at no charge. You gotta love that.

Water is in short supply in most places now, and it just isn't right to use potable water to irrigate lawns and decorative plants when people in other parts of the world are going thirsty. Fortunately you can greatly reduce your landscape water use without compromising the appearance and function of your garden. Check out the Cheat Sheet as well as the chapters in Part III for everything you need to know about the big subject of water conservation.

Fertilizer

Have you ever wondered why we need to fertilize? Nobody fertilizes the mountains or the forests, yet they grow perfectly well century after century. If you suspect something strange about the constant need to feed garden plants, you're right.

If a plant is well-adapted to local conditions because it's native to your area or comes from a similar environment somewhere else in the world, it'll be satisfied with the nutrients that are naturally available in the soil. And if you can manage to resist raking up all those tree leaves in the fall (they call them leaves because you're supposed to leave them there), you'll be allowing valuable nutrients to remain in place. That means you don't have to replace them with expensive, imported fertilizer. If you just can't stand to see the leaves lying on the ground, compost them and return them to the soil.

Of course there are times to fertilize. Many food-bearing crops need regular fertilizing, and any plant will need a little snack now and then. How do you know? Get a soil test, and watch the plants for signs of nutrient deficiencies (yellowing leaves and slowing growth, for example).

When you do fertilize, be sure to use organic fertilizers, which come from natural, renewable, non-petroleum sources. These types are less likely to burn plants, and they're a lot kinder to the soil. See Chapters 16 and 20 for more on fertilizers.

Pesticides

Pesticides kill — you guessed it — pests, such as bugs. As with fertilizers, it's tempting to ask why we even need this stuff. Plants in nature get pests and diseases just the same as the ones in your garden. In nature, however, there's a better balance of pests and predators, and because the system is in a state of equilibrium things are less likely to go wildly out of control.

You can control most pests pretty easily without resorting to wicked chemicals and war-like ways. First, choose plants that are naturally pest-resistant, and then give them proper growing conditions so they thrive (healthy plants are much less susceptible to pests and diseases). Then wait out any infestations, because beneficial insects often move in to kill pests. If that doesn't work, use the least-toxic control method that you can, such as releasing beneficial insects that you buy at the nursery, washing pests off of plants, or using an insecticidal soap that's not toxic (unless, of course, you're a pest). Refer to Chapter 21 for complete details on pest management.

Herbicides

Herbicides kill weeds (plants that are both undesired and inclined to self-replicate to a troublesome degree). Most weeds are nonnative. Despite decades of herbicide use, you may have noticed that we still have tons of weeds. If these herbicides work so well, how come the planet has more weeds than ever? It's time to take a different track.

Weeds occur most densely in disturbed areas, where bare ground creates a favorable habitat for them. The bare ground in a flowerbed is a perfect example. And though you'll never entirely get rid of weeds, you have some simple, sustainable strategies available to you that work at least as well as the harmful chemicals. For example, you can plant densely. If you don't have much free space in your landscape, the weeds won't have any room to grow, and the plants you *do* want will keep weeds from cropping up. Flip to Chapter 20 for more highly effective — and environmentally safe — weed management techniques.

Fossil fuels

Petroleum products (oil, gasoline, natural gas) are used everywhere in the garden. They're made from crude oil, which is basically made from rotten old dinosaurs and primitive plants that have been festering underground for millions of years — hence the term *fossil fuels*. Gas-powered lawn mowers and other power garden equipment are major consumers of gas and oil. In fact, according to the Environmental Protection Agency (EPA), Americans use over 800 million gallons of gas a year just mowing their lawns!

But there's a whole lot more oil in those gardens. Check out the nearby sidebar for the grim details.

By using hand tools (check out the list on the Cheat Sheet), organic fertilizers, natural materials, and other low-impact inputs, you can significantly reduce your garden's dependence on fossil fuels. And if you use some of your property to grow food, you'll reduce your own dependence on fossil fuels for food production and shipment.

Fossil fuelishness

Have a look at some of the sneaky ways that oil consumption creeps into your gardening and landscaping:

- **Transportation of imported materials:** Every time you buy materials that have to be delivered to your home (either by your own car or by a delivery truck), you're using oil.

- **Manufacturing of nearly everything used in the landscape:** Many landscape materials and products are made from oil, and fossil fuel energy is used in the manufacturing process.

- **Pumping water:** Unless gravity does the job, water is pumped out of wells or over mountains to get to you. Energy to run the pumps comes primarily from fossil fuels.

- **Chemically-based fertilizers and pesticides:** The main ingredient in chemically-based nitrogen fertilizer is natural gas, which is a fossil fuel. Some pesticides are made from oil.

- **Plastics of all kinds, including irrigation pipe and materials, garden structures,** **furniture, and plant containers:** With a few exceptions, plastics are made directly from oil.

- **Construction processes that require power tools and heavy equipment:** Tractors, trenchers, tillers, and similar pieces of equipment all operate on fossil fuels. Even electrically-powered equipment depends on fossil fuels. How? They're burned to generate electricity.

- **Maintenance, including the use of power equipment:** Obviously, mowers, blowers, and the like run on gas, but so do the trucks that bring the workers.

- **Disposal, including trash hauling, green waste processing, and landfill management:** Hauling, grinding green waste, and filling and capping landfills all depend on fuel.

- **Equipment to melt snow and ice:** Increased use of heating equipment to keep walkways, driveways, and pools free of snow and ice uses energy.

Time

Sustainable landscaping is stable landscaping, which means it doesn't turn into a jungle of weeds and overgrown or dying plants when you leave it alone for a couple of weeks. With its own elegant system of checks and balances, sustainable landscaping doesn't really need much from you. A little benevolent nudging now and then is sufficient for the routine care of the landscape. That means you probably need a long day in the garden only once or twice a year. So, you have time to enjoy the garden instead of working in it every weekend! Sustainable gardens save you time.

Money

When you design, construct, and maintain your landscape sustainably, you spend far less money on it over time. The landscaping may or may not cost you less to put in, but for sure it will cost less to care for because it makes fewer ongoing demands. The maintenance cost of a conventionally cared-for landscape can run three times that of a sustainably-maintained one, and there's a huge difference in the environmental impacts too.

Generating Few (or No) Outputs

Outputs, the so-called waste products of landscaping, occur because of inefficiencies in the design of the system. When a landscape is designed as a *linear system* (where materials are taken from nature, used once, and then thrown away), it's inevitable that a lot of waste will occur. On the other hand, nature itself is a *cyclical system.* Each element in a cyclical system stays within that system, eliminating the need for both inputs and waste. The goal of sustainable landscaping is to develop a minimum-waste, minimum-output system.

You can eliminate (or at least minimize) negative outputs by optimizing your inputs. This kind of efficiency is the synergy of a finely-tuned system at work. (Check out the earlier section, "Getting the Most Out of What You Put Into Your Landscape" for more details on optimizing your inputs.)

The following sections focus on less-desirable outputs, but keep in mind that some outputs are good — the oxygen given off by living plants, for instance, or the food you grow in your garden.

Green waste

Green waste is a fancy term for the plant parts we cut off and send to that magical place called "away." Sometimes green waste ends up in landfills, and sometimes it comes back to us as mulch. But the truth is that, in most cases, green waste doesn't need to exist in the first place. It's caused by poor design that puts plants in spaces that are too small for their eventual size, requiring the gardener to trim or prune the plant to fit the size the gardener wants it it be (instead of the size the plant has evolved to be). Plants all have genetic destinies to develop in certain time-honored ways. They grow to fulfill their destinies, often to the detriment of the garden and the gardener. Want proof? I once saw a hedge made of young redwood trees (you know, the ones that grow 30-foot trunks?). Fifty-four of these trees were placed a foot apart in a tiny planter space only 8 inches wide. What do you suppose the people who created this landscaping nightmare were thinking?

Placing the wrong plant in the wrong place is just one example of the commonest of garden afflictions. Other examples include planting invasive vines, choosing spreading junipers for 5-foot-wide parkways, using trees as hedges, picking tall shrubs as ground covers, and planting any plant that has an *indeterminate growth habit* (no reasonable limits to its ultimate size).

The existence of green waste is caused by other factors as well. Consider, for example, over-watering and over-fertilizing. Both make plants grow faster and bigger. Sometimes that's a good thing, but excess growth that just needs to be cut off and thrown away creates problems (without any benefits).

When you design your garden, carefully check the ultimate size of the plants you select, and then locate them so they have enough room to grow. If the plant will grow too large for the space you're considering, choose another plant — one that *will* fit — instead. This is one of the truly essential ideas of the sustainable landscape. Imagine how much time you'll save by maintaining a garden that requires little or no pruning to control size.

Polluted runoff

Polluted runoff is caused by rainfall or irrigation water moving pesticides, herbicides, fertilizers, dog feces, and other nasty stuff into streets, storm drains, and eventually into bodies of water. Polluted runoff is a major problem all over the world. You can become part of the solution simply by not using pesticides, herbicides, and fertilizers in the first place — and by cleaning up after your dog. Nothing in, nothing out.

The other problem is that when water from your property hits the street, it washes curbside pollution into those same bodies of water. Use water harvesting strategies such as underground percolation chambers and careful watering to keep rainwater on site (see Part III). By inviting water into your soil, it remains on site. And beneficial microorganisms in the soil will break pollutants down so they can't cause environmental problems.

Air pollution

When Ronald Reagan was governor of California, he said, "Trees cause more pollution than automobiles do." I was never Reagan's biggest fan, but it turns out that his statement has *some* basis in fact. Here's the fact: Some tree species produce what scientists call *biogenic emissions* (volatile organic compounds that can worsen pollution problems). Because of the emissions, these trees shouldn't be planted in large quantities in urban areas. The worst offenders include some species of Eucalyptus, Ficus, sweet gum, spruce, sycamore, cottonwood, oak, and willow, to name a few. Visit `selectree. calpoly.edu` for information on the emissions of particular tree species. And remember that most trees reduce air pollution and are a significant net benefit to the environment.

Despite what the Gipper said, far more significant than the pollution caused by trees are the emissions produced by humans engaged in destructive gardening activities, such as operating power lawn and garden equipment, spraying pesticides and herbicides, and driving back and forth to the gardening center for another load of feed-and-weed. In fact, the small engines used in powered outdoor gear emit enough hydrocarbons, carbon monoxide, and nitrogen oxides to qualify as the largest single contributor to non-vehicle hydrocarbon emissions.

The solution is simple; it starts with reducing lawn areas and oversized plants so that you don't have to trim and mow as much, using hand tools whenever you can, and avoiding pesticides and herbicides. Check out Chapter 20 for more tips on eliminating power equipment and Chapter 21 for info on cutting out the chemicals.

Noise pollution

Isn't a garden supposed to be a peaceful sanctuary — a place to escape from the racket and hubbub of the outside world? Of course. But gas-powered garden equipment destroys that lovely calm.

In most neighborhoods you hear the incessant din of blowers, mowers, edgers, weed whackers, and all the other gas-powered weapons of horticulture that we need because our properties are filled with lawns and overfed, oversized plants.

The bottom line: By making the garden a more stable system, and by eliminating the power tools for the little work there is, you not only eliminate fossil fuel use and pollution, you also help to make the neighborhood quieter. On top of that, performing gardening tasks manually is better exercise for you. See Chapter 20 for alternatives to power garden equipment.

Paying Attention to What's in the Materials You Buy

One of the best ways to mess up your sustainable game plan is to mindlessly drive over to your local garden-supply store and get a bunch of the same old stuff without asking yourself or the clerks where it came from and what the impacts of the purchase will be, both in your landscape and at the source of the materials. You need to ensure that you're keeping your impact on the environment to a minimum.

Additionally, some of the building materials common to landscaping projects present toxicity problems such as offgassing of chemicals into the atmosphere, leaching them into the soils, and in some cases presenting significant risks to people and animals through direct contact. And don't forget toxicity to the workers who make and use the materials. Table 2-2 shows some toxic and harmful landscape materials and their nontoxic alternatives.

Table 2-2	Toxic Materials and Alternatives
Toxic (or Suspected Toxic) Material	*Safer Alternative*
Arsenic-treated wood	ACQ-treated wood, black locust, white oak, cedar, redwood, steel
Glues	Alternative glues, mechanical fasteners like nails, screws, and bolts
Paints, finishes, and solvents	Low VOC finishes, or best of all, materials that don't need finishing
PVC	High-density polyethylene or other plastics, non-plastic alternatives
Railroad ties	Recycled plastic landscape ties, salvaged timbers

Toxic materials are rarely, if ever, necessary. Folks created beautiful gardens long before the invention of PVC, solvents, and other harmful materials. By choosing natural materials, you end the problem before it begins. Environmentally friendlier materials are showing up everywhere these days. You'll often find them at good prices in major chains as well as at local suppliers. You also can find more and more specialty stores that carry only materials that have been carefully screened for sustainability. And, of course, you can always shop online. Visit www.healthybuilding.net and www.pollutioninpeople.org for even more information. I talk more about hardscaping materials in Chapter 12.

Opting for Biological Solutions before Technical Ones

As the permaculturists always say: Use biological approaches to landscaping before technological ones. (Not sure what a permaculturist is? Check out the nearby sidebar, "What's permaculture?") In other words, use plants to do the job that hardscaping might. For instance, a $50 tree will shade your house more effectively than a $5,000 aluminum patio cover. Besides, it also uses no energy, absorbs pollution, creates oxygen, provides a home for birds, and creates a couple dozen other benefits.

What's permaculture?

Choosing biological solutions before technological ones and stacking functions (making each element serve multiple purposes) are ideas that come from the rich and fascinating world of *permaculture*. Developed in the 1970s in Australia, permaculture is a design system much like sustainable landscaping. The term is difficult to define, but many practitioners have taken a shot. For example, here's one definition by Graham Bell in the book *The Permaculture Way* (Permanent Publications, 2005):

> "Permaculture is the conscious design and maintenance of agriculturally productive systems which have the diversity, stability,

and resilience of natural ecosystems. It is the harmonious integration of the landscape with people providing their food, energy, shelter, and other material and non-material needs in a sustainable way."

It sounds a lot like sustainable landscaping, doesn't it? Well, it is — with an added emphasis on using our gardens to provide food and fulfill other needs. After all, is there any good reason not to use your property to grow food and offer up other tangible benefits? (For resources on permaculture, see the appendix.)

Plants are naturally solar-powered. The sun, the soil, the atmosphere, and the rain provide everything the living landscape needs. In other words, long-lived plants don't need painting, resurfacing, repairs, or replacement. And hey, if you plant a hedge instead of installing a wall or fence, the neighborhood taggers won't be able to paint on it.

I don't mean you have to develop a zero-hardscape garden. That's pretty difficult to pull off. But by choosing as many living (biological) elements as you can, you optimize the system and save yourself trouble.

What Does It Do? Bringing Purpose to Each Element of the Garden

Every element in your landscape should fulfill some purpose. Nothing should be there just because some clever advertising made you buy it or because you're trying to impress the neighbors. For example, a ground cover planting may help control erosion on a slope, a patio can offer a place for you and your family to hang out, and landscape lighting makes your property safer at night.

Many landscape elements serve more than one purpose. That ground cover isn't only holding the slope. It's also providing nectar for the bees, producing oxygen, and perhaps adding fragrance to be enjoyed by people. In the permaculture world (see the nearby sidebar "What's permaculture?"), getting multiple benefits out of one action or element is called *stacking functions*.

When your entire landscape is composed of things that serve one or more purposes, and when all the elements are skillfully combined into a single, highly-functioning whole, you'll have a landscape system that offers maximum benefit to you and to the environment. So when you're making choices of what to put in your new landscape, run things through the "What does it do?" filter. You'll be glad you did.

Sometimes the answer to the "What does it do?" question can be, "It makes me really happy" or "It's beautiful." Don't feel bad about that. Your happiness is important.

Chapter 3

Deciding Whether to Do It Yourself or Call in the Pros

....

In This Chapter

▶ Examining the skills you bring to landscape table

▶ Contemplating how much time and money you want to spend in the garden

▶ Preparing a sustainable landscaping toolkit

▶ Getting professional help when you need it

....

A landscaping project calls up numerous resources. This is less true of the sustainable landscape, of course, but you still have major demands on your time, money, and abilities. If you're considering doing all or part of the work as a do-it-yourself project, you need to get an idea of how much time and energy you have. You also need to examine your ability to do the work. And if you plan to work with professionals in the design and construction of the project, it really helps to know who the players are and how to work with them. In this chapter, I fill you in on all this and more.

Assessing Your Skill Set: Are You Ready for This?

You may come to your landscaping project as a seasoned landscaper or maybe even as a professional. On the other hand, you may not know what a rake is used for. Whatever your skill level, you need to inventory what you bring to the project and then decide how much to do yourself and how much to hire out. In this section, you do a little self-evaluation.

You may find some aspects of your latest project pleasant (or even fun), but you may dread others. Tackle the ones you're enthusiastic about and hire out the rest.

What are your design skills?

Sustainable landscape design differs from ordinary landscape design in that you have to carefully plan for functionality, and you have to have a deep sensitivity to the site to make that functionality happen. In other words, you have to be more aware and think differently to achieve sustainability. You don't have to be a genius, though; you just have to consider a lot of things that you may never have thought of. I get to that in Part II. For now, think in terms of doing what I like to call *deep design* — applying your best thinking to planning your new landscape on many levels.

You won't just be decorating your yard; you'll be developing a complex ecosystem that's finely tuned to operate smoothly with minimal effort or resources, an ecosystem that's productive as well as beautiful and is also good for the larger environment. Deep design is trickier than simply figuring out which plants look pretty together and whether to buy the blue or the mauve cushions for the patio furniture. This concept may seem overwhelming at first, but you can get the hang of it quickly.

In the following list, I introduce some of the talents and resources you may bring to the design phase of your landscaping project. You need these design chops if you're going to figure out the whole project on your own, but they're handy even if you plan to hire a professional landscape architect or designer. It never hurts to be well informed. You can read all about these skills in Part II of the book.

- ✔ **An eye for detail:** The small things seem to make the difference between an average job and a great one. Details are also what make a project sustainable. Choosing a shrub that's the right size, for instance, eliminates the need to prune constantly.

- ✔ **The willingness to spend time really understanding your property:** To achieve sustainability in your landscape, you need to know what you're working with. Moving around your land, observing with a high level of awareness, and researching the environmental conditions present on your property all inform your design work and help you create a landscape that's tuned to your actual circumstances.

- ✔ **A feeling for the laws of natural systems:** By understanding how a natural ecosystem works — the interactions among soil, climate, plants, microorganisms, insects, and animals — you're better prepared to create your own ecosystem.

- ✔ **A basic knowledge of the universal principles of design:** Certain rules are fundamental to all kinds of design, not just landscaping. Following these rules helps you create a landscape that looks as if it were professionally done.

- ✔ **Good taste:** Taste is subjective, of course. And I suppose most people think they have good taste (even the ones with the paisley golf slacks or the plastic flowers tied to their shrubbery). But an artist's eye helps you take the design principles to a higher level.

- ✔ **A love of plants and living things:** Passion may not be a design skill, strictly speaking, but without it your work suffers from mediocrity. It's safe to say you bought this book because you love gardens, so use your enthusiasm to push your design to its highest and best level.

- ✔ **Some basic drafting skills (optional):** You don't need to be an artist — you're going to be making a beautiful garden, not pictures of a beautiful garden — but it helps to be able to draw a plot plan of your project and lay out your ideas on paper before committing to them in the real world.

What are your construction skills?

If you're planning to do some or all of a project's construction work yourself, it certainly helps to know how. Many basic tasks of landscaping may seem like menial work to you — shoveling, digging holes and trenches, and grading soil, for example — but even they must be done properly to achieve success. Other landscape elements, such as constructing arbors, patios, and walls or installing irrigation and lighting, require different skills: carpentry, electrical, plumbing, and others.

I give you tips along the way, but no book can provide hands-on experience. Be realistic about your ability level, and don't let your ego get in the way of calling in professional help when you're really not up to a task. Or consider trading skills with a friend who really knows how to do the work you need. Working side-by-side with an experienced person is much more fun than struggling through it alone.

Without a professional level of construction skill and talent, you're better off limiting yourself to things that don't take years to learn, such as planting, doing some kinds of irrigation work, mulching, and the like. You still save a heap of money, and you make a meaningful contribution to the job without compromising its quality.

How hard can you work?

I'm not going to be coy about this: Landscaping is hard work. Working smart can save you a lot of energy and body aches. Be sure to work safely, and take a look at some ways to make the work easier and to save money on chiropractor bills:

✔ **Lift with your legs, not your back.** In other words, squat down to lift heavy things; don't bend over at the waist.

✔ **Don't overestimate your strength.** This advice especially rings true for you guys. Men — myself included — tend to think that they're all weightlifting champions. Dude, you're not *that* buff, okay? Get help if you need it. Some things are just too heavy to lift alone.

✔ **Use the right tool for the job.** Shovels are made for digging, not for prying out tree stumps. Why bust a perfectly good tool or a perfectly good back when you could have picked up the digging bar and let its weight and strength do the work for you?

If for some reason you aren't able to do heavy labor, you're better off hiring someone.

Determining the Time and Money You Can Devote to a Project

Quality landscaping can be a substantial investment. If you landscape your entire property, assuming you live on a typical suburban lot, you'll spend between $10,000 and $30,000 on materials and that much again in labor if you hire the work out to licensed professionals. However, you can spend much less on materials if you use what's on site and tap the waste stream for materials such as broken concrete and salvaged timbers. The trick is to have a satisfying, durable end result that justifies what you've put into it — in terms of both time and money. In the following sections, I help you get an idea of how much time and money you can expect to devote to a sustainable landscaping project.

Considering the amount of time you have

If you hire a landscaping company to do a major landscaping project, that company will send a crew of maybe four or five people who, depending on the scope of the work, will put in perhaps 1,200 hours of time. Divide that by the 10 hours you'll realistically have on the weekends, and you're in for a rude awakening. That comes out to 120 weekends, which is about 3 to 5 years of work time, depending on how much rain or snow you get where you live. Is that what you had in mind?

How much of this project are you *really* going to do? You may want to put in some plants, spread some mulch, and maybe do a brick walkway yourself. But unless you're qualified, hire a landscaping company to take care of the complicated or labor-intensive tasks — heavy grading, woodwork, and masonry structures to name a few.

Keeping cost in mind

The amount of money you need to spend depends on a number of factors. Check out Chapter 1 for some more budgeting advice, and keep these elements in mind as you tabulate costs:

- ✔ **Location:** Prices are generally higher in big cities and where property values are high. Regional prices vary considerably.
- ✔ **Size:** Naturally, the larger your property, the more you'll spend.
- ✔ **Who does the work:** Doing the job yourself can save you 30 to 80 percent.
- ✔ **The company you hire:** Bids from landscape professionals can vary by 100 percent or more, depending on the company's experience, size, overhead, distance from the job, and yes, your attitude.
- ✔ **The amount of hardscape you want:** *Hardscape* (the stuff made with concrete and rebar and lumber) is way more expensive per square foot of landscaped area than plants are.

As a rule of thumb, count on spending anywhere from $20,000 to $70,000 on the average complete landscaping job for a typical property. Landscaping is a major investment.

Sustainable landscaping can cost less — sometimes much less — than conventional landscaping, especially if you stick with a primarily plant-based project. But the best news of all is that by landscaping sustainably, you save a huge amount in maintenance costs for the life of the project, which is where the real expenses are.

Looking into Your Toolbox: Stuff You Need

Landscaping tools are fairly basic, and chances are that you already have a lot of what you need in your garage just waiting to be put to work. In this section, I go through some main landscaping tools. If you don't know what some of this stuff is, take the list to your local hardware store, and the workers there can help you out.

You don't need to go out and buy all the tools you don't have — many of them can be rented. Renting makes more sense, especially when tools are used for one project and then left to sit in the garage for years. Such a waste of resources! (However, do invest in a few good maintenance tools, which you'll be using over and over again.)

Whenever you're working outdoors, be sure to include the most important tools of all: plenty of sunscreen and a hat. Sunburns aren't limited to the beach — and they make landscape work even tougher.

Creating a plan with some design tools

Landscape architects have cool drafting equipment, including computer-based drafting software, but you don't need that much to develop a good landscape design. In fact, good design is about *thinking,* not about drawing pretty pictures. And all you need to think is your brain.

But if you're willing and able, drawing plans does help for a variety of reasons that I get into in Chapter 6. You can draw a reasonably effective plan on a piece of paper taped to the kitchen table, using a yardstick and an old chewed-up number 2 pencil. But frankly, planning is a lot easier if you're equipped with a few decent drafting tools. Here's what you need:

- An architect's scale (one that's divided into quarters and halves, not the engineer's scale that's divided into tenths)
- A circle template that goes up to about 2 inches in diameter
- A compass
- Drafting paper (vellum with a grid of eight light blue lines per inch)
- A drawing board (at least 24 x 36 inches, but bigger is better)
- A medium-hard pencil (number 2 is fine) and an eraser
- Two tape measures (a 20-foot-long one and a 100-foot-long one)
- A roll of inexpensive tissue paper, which we dignified professionals call *bumwad,* for sketching over your base sheet
- A T-square
- Two drafting triangles (a 45-degree triangle and a 30-60-90-degree triangle)

The truly sustainable thing to do is borrow the stuff you need from this list. You may know someone who has a drafting set or at least some of the items you need. Buy him a six-pack and take his tools home for a while. If that doesn't work, you can find all these items at a drafting or artist supply store.

To arms! Grading, earthmoving, and planting tools

When you need to move large amounts of soil or other earthen matter, do not — I repeat — do *not* go buy a tractor. If you really need one, you can rent a tractor. But think long and hard about even doing that. Tractors burn nasty fossil fuels and belch pollution, and they keep you from having the deeply meaningful experience of shoveling soil into a wheelbarrow day after day. Sustainable landscaping means minimal dependence on powered equipment. You don't have to become a fossil-free zealot, but use human power when you can. Sure, shoveling isn't as much fun as driving a tractor, but just think how fit you'll be!

The following list shows some basic muscle-powered tools that can get you through the majority of your earth-related tasks:

- Round-point shovel for planting and general digging
- Square-point shovel for scooping things up
- Small hand trowel with an ergonomically curved handle
- Digging bar (a long, heavy steel bar with a wide blade on one end and a tamper on the other) to make breaking up hard soil a lot easier
- Mattock or pulaski (these are different versions of a combination axe and wide digging blade) for chopping, trenching, and loosening
- Iron rake to move and smooth soil
- Wide landscaping rake to *really* smooth soil
- Wheelbarrow (the heavy-duty contractor kind) or, for some uses, a two-wheeled garden cart
- Four-tine pitchfork for moving mulch
- Push broom
- Gloves and a pair of good, sturdy boots

Old, ugly tools work just as well as new ones, so getting them at a garage sale — or borrowing them from a friend — is fine.

Long-handled tools are much easier on the back than short-handled ones. If you have to buy tools, be sure you buy ones that are of high quality — they do a better job and last longer (which is *very* sustainable).

Handling hardscape: Construction gear

If you're building a hardscape, you need some construction equipment. What you need depends on the type of work you're doing. I break it down for you in Table 3-1.

Table 3-1	Construction Tools You May Need for Hardscaping		
Basic Construction Tools	*Carpentry Tools*	*Concrete Tools*	*Brick and Masonry Tools*
Hacksaw, mason's twine, pliers, screw-drivers, small and large sledgeham-mers, stakes, stepladder, tape measure, wheelbarrow	Circular saw, chalk line, chisel, claw hammer, hand-saw, level, nail set, pair of sawhorses, plane, post-hole digger, power drill and drill bits, pry bar, sander, square	Cement mixer (or get ready-mix concrete or mix by hand), con-crete trowel, corner tools, darby (a type of concrete finishing tool), edger, finishing broom, floats, form boards and stakes, groover, hose and nozzle, knee pads, level, long 2 x 4 (for leveling out wet concrete after it's placed), rubber boots, shovel, tamper to compact and settle concrete, transit or sighting level, wheelbarrow	Brick trowel, 5-gallon bucket, jointing tool, mason's hammer and chisel, mortar-board, pointing trowel, thin-set applicator, tile saw

Consider having skill- and tool-intensive projects like concrete pouring and finishing done by a qualified professional. A professional job may not cost any more when you consider the investment in tools that's required to do it your-self. Plus, the pros will likely do a better job, and they guarantee their work.

Water workhorses: Getting the irrigation tools you need

The truly sustainable landscape doesn't need an irrigation system, and depending on your climate, this ideal may be easily attainable for you. In drier climates, though, it's difficult to have a nice garden without some supple-mental watering, which is best accomplished with a well-designed, water-conserving irrigation system. The following tools can get you through a typical irrigation system installation:

- ✓ **Pipe shears:** These special cutters do a bang-up job on plastic pipe.

- ✓ **Pressure gauge:** You use this tool only once, so borrow one from your supplier if possible.

✔ **Small screwdriver or proprietary tool:** Use these for adjusting sprinkler heads.

✔ **Trenching shovel:** A special narrow shovel for digging trenches.

✔ **Two pairs of tongue-and-groove pliers:** These are handy for tightening threaded connections. (You need two pairs because you have to twist the two pieces you're fitting together in opposite directions.)

For more on irrigation, see Part III.

Gathering tools for sustainable maintenance

When I look at garden catalogs, I have to marvel at how little of the stuff they sell is really necessary to manage a well-designed garden. After all, by developing a stable, sustainable landscape, you eliminate most of the maintenance and most of the tools that go with it.

For routine maintenance, you really need just a few key tools:

✔ **Hoses:** Black ones disappear into the shadows of your garden better than green ones. Rubber ones last longer and are somewhat less harmful to the environment than vinyl ones. You can pick up a good hose for around $25.

✔ **Hose nozzle:** Get a high-quality one with multiple settings, which allow you to wash off insects, water plants, fill your pond, mist your ferns, wash the pooch, and squirt the kids all with one tool. A nice nozzle sets you back $10.

✔ **Pair of high-quality loppers or a folding pruning saw:** These tools come in handy for occasionally cutting a branch bigger than your pruners can handle. You can get a quality lopper for $30 and a folding pruning saw for about $20.

✔ **Pair of quality pruning shears:** A good pair costs you around $50.

✔ **Push broom and a leaf rake:** You need these only if you're the tidy sort, and at most they cost $30 or so.

✔ **Push mower:** If you do have a lawn, consider a push mower instead of a gas- or electric-powered one. An old-fashioned scythe works, too (after you get the hang of it). Or get a goat, for that matter.

✔ **Weeding tool of some kind:** I like to use an asparagus knife, which costs $7 or less.

That's it. Take the money you would have spent on power gadgets and go have a nice vacation somewhere.

You don't need anything else if you've successfully created a sustainable landscape that's easy to care for. You won't be pruning to control size (your plants are the right size already), you won't be trimming hedges (you don't have trimmed hedges), you won't be mowing the lawn (you have a meadow instead), you won't be spraying for pests (your plants are pest-resistant), and you won't be doing much weed control (the mulch and tall plants smother the weeds). If your trees need pruning, stay safely on the ground and let a professional care for them. The bottom line? You've set up a system that's easy to live with, so now's the time to start enjoying it!

Turning to Landscape Professionals

If you're a die-hard do-it-yourselfer, don't be afraid to tackle your whole landscaping project by yourself. This book won't make a seasoned landscape architect or contractor out of you, but it gives you the information you need to be successful. It also warns you about doing anything that's really dangerous.

There's a time and place to turn to professionals for help with the design or construction of your landscape. Noticing your weak spots and getting help is key. A good landscape architect or garden designer can turn out a better landscape design than you probably can, and the fees can be a good investment in creating a project that costs much less to maintain over time. Similarly, a qualified landscape contractor can get the job done better, faster, and sometimes cheaper.

Be sure to hire professionals who have expertise in truly sustainable landscaping; everyone claims to be "green," but actual skill levels vary tremendously. Ask for references and look at completed projects to be sure your candidates do things the sustainable way.

In the following sections, I fill you in on who the various landscape professionals are and how you can find the ones you need.

Identifying the players

When you've decided that you want to hire professionals to help with all or some part of your landscaping project, you have plenty of choices. There are lots of players on a landscaping team. Here's a quick primer (in the order you may hire them, from design through construction and maintenance):

- **Landscape architect:** A landscape architect is trained to understand and practice design on a sophisticated level. That said, not all landscape architects are familiar with — or care about — sustainability issues; be sure to find one who is. Remember that the landscape architect can design your project, but she can't build it.

✔ **Landscape contractor:** Most landscape contractors are capable of carrying out a wide range of construction tasks, from grading and planting to irrigation, hardscape, lighting, and more. Some contractors have good design ideas; others are mainly hired to install what the landscape architects design.

✔ **Gardener:** Even sustainable landscapes require some maintenance. After your landscaping project is done, you may want to hire a gardener to maintain it. Most gardeners aren't capable of doing much landscaping work beyond putting in some plants. Finding qualified gardeners is difficult — most have no formal training and are more outdoor housekeepers than horticulturists. And few of them pay attention to sustainable-landscape maintenance.

You may be able to find a reputable gardener by asking your green-leaning friends about who takes care of their gardens. Some communities offer sustainability training for gardeners and can provide a list of certified graduates; these folks are a better bet than simply picking somebody out of the phone book.

Because your new landscape is much easier to care for than a nonsustainable one, you may be able to do most of the maintenance yourself. You may need only occasional help for heavy work.

✔ **Arborist:** Specially trained to care for trees, the arborist is a certified professional; look for certification by the International Society of Arboriculture (ISA).

✔ **Tree trimmer:** Tree trimmers may or may not be certified. Quality of care varies widely. A good interview question is whether the tree trimmer does tree topping. If the answer is yes, look elsewhere. Topping trees is a discredited practice, and no qualified professional does it.

The best approach is to hire a company that sends at least one ISA-certified person on each job. This way you know you're getting a real pro.

✔ **Others you may need:** In some states, irrigation work must be done by a licensed plumber or irrigation contractor. And if you suspect that your property has unstable soil or other geological problems, call a consulting geologist. A civil engineer may help you design retaining walls and other structures. Pest control problems are best handled by a licensed pest control advisor or operator. Be aware that licensure and the exact details of these professions vary from place to place.

You may also want to turn to your local nursery for help. Aside from selling plants and supplies, nurseries can offer advice on planting design. Another possible resource is landscape supply stores, which sell tools, equipment, and landscape materials such as gravel, tile, stone, brick, irrigation materials, and so on. They can often recommend landscape professionals, too.

Finding green professionals

Don't sabotage yourself by hiring someone who doesn't share (and work by) your sustainable commitment. Instead, find a green (as in *environmentally friendly*) professional.

By far the best way to find the right professional is to ask around. Generally speaking, the good ones don't advertise; and the heavy advertisers do so because they can't get referrals. So check with your friends, knock on the door of a house with beautiful landscaping, or inquire at your favorite nursery.

When you're considering working with a landscaper, pay attention to the following:

- ✔ **Check for commitment to sustainability.** Not all professionals understand this stuff. Some will tell you they do things sustainably, but get specifics and compare them to the information in this book.

- ✔ **Look at their work.** Get a list of recent jobs that you can drive by and look at. View them in terms of overall quality as well as sustainability.

- ✔ **Get references.** Ask a couple of current or former clients about promptness, professionalism, prices, quality of workmanship, and reliability.

- ✔ **Get detailed estimates.** A proper estimate should have a line item for each aspect of the work, and it should differentiate between firm bid prices and estimates (sometimes called *allowances*).

- ✔ **Get, and carefully read, specifications for the work.** Specifications detail precisely what will be done, what materials will be used, and the outcome of the work. Get drawings where necessary.

- ✔ **Check licenses.** Most professionals are required to be licensed. Be sure licenses are current and in effect.

- ✔ **Get a detailed written contract.** Make sure everything is spelled out. That way you're somewhat protected if the professional reneges on his or her end of the bargain.

- ✔ **Set firm starting and ending dates.** But do keep in mind that these dates may change for legitimate reasons as the work progresses.

Part II
Good Design: The Key to Sustainable Landscaping

The 5th Wave   By Rich Tennant

©RICHTENNANT

"Designing the lawn was easy –just fit the pieces together. As far as sustainability goes, each piece is made of high-impact polystyrene plastic."

In this part . . .

Sustainable landscaping begins with careful design. A sustainable landscape is a highly tuned system, and it doesn't just happen overnight. It's the product of really getting to know your property and applying some basic principles to all the elements of your new landscape. Your best thinking during the design portion of the project means years of smooth sailing later on because good design results in a smoothly functioning landscape that demands less of you and the environment than a poorly-thought-out one would.

In this part, you find out how to analyze your property so you understand what it needs. I coach you through the design process, showing you how professional landscape architects go about turning a nasty-looking yard into a sustainable masterpiece. I walk you through the whole process step by step, and warn you about pitfalls and problems that you may not foresee on your own.

Chapter 4

Getting Better Acquainted with Your Property

*W*hat if I told you I know a technique that can help you design a garden that's more sustainable, more beautiful, and more fun than any you've ever had? You'd be pretty excited, wouldn't you? Well, you're in luck! I've got the goods: The wonder-cure that can help you create sustainable, beautiful, fun gardens is what I call *deep design,* and it's simply the practice of combining the art of making your landscaping look good with the science of making it work properly; it's design that considers more than just appearance.

Most of what passes for landscape design is about exterior decorating: the art of putting pretty plants around in color-appropriate combinations and accenting them with attractive lawn furniture and accessories, much as one decorates a living room. Skillfully done, exterior decorating can make for some lovely effects.

There's nothing wrong with beauty; sustainable landscaping isn't about creating ugly gardens. But there's much more to a sustainable landscape than how it looks. How it works is equally important because if the landscape functions well, it requires fewer resources and less work, and it has a positive effect on the environment instead of harming it as conventional landscapes do.

To build a truly sustainable landscape, you need to have a solid understanding of where you are and what you have to work with — the focus of this chapter. Then you can design a landscape system that responds to the many conditions of the site and to the laws that govern natural systems.

Meeting Your Yard: Site Analysis

Site analysis is the first stage of deep design; it's nothing more than looking critically at your property from many different viewpoints in order to develop a list of conditions, problems, needs, and possible design responses that govern what you eventually build. Site analysis is more than just rushing around making lists, though. You also want to experience subtler aspects of the site, such as how you feel in different areas.

Imagine yourself on vacation sitting under some palm trees on a tropical beach with your favorite beverage in hand. You're totally relaxed, and you feel a sense of connection with the place. You're experiencing it with all your senses. Doing site analysis is a lot like sitting on that beach. First, you have to understand the place itself, which means perceiving it on a deep level. You have to slow down enough to see the details, such as how the sun moves across the land, how neighboring houses impact your site, and which areas feel good to hang out in. You give yourself time to ask and answer important questions about your site that will later inform your design decisions. I refer to this process as "making friends with the site," and I consider it one of the most important steps on the path to a beautiful, sustainable landscape.

Using a lawn chair, the world's best design tool

If you really want to get to know your site, get yourself a comfortable, lightweight lawn chair. (No hammocks, please — I want you to be awake for this.) Put the chair anywhere in the yard. Then sit down in it and be quiet. Notice things. The whole point of this exercise is to stop doing and start perceiving. You see, this stage isn't about design or coming up with answers. For now, you want to just absorb as much as possible.

As you sit and observe your site, don't take any paper, drawing boards, cameras, cellphones, laptops, or other technology with you. The goal is to bond with your yard, so it should be just you and the yard without distractions.

After a few minutes of quiet contemplation, perceptions of all kinds start to pour in. For instance, you may suddenly see the distant tree that could be a lovely part of what landscape architects call a *borrowed view* (a view of something distant, off your property, that's good enough to incorporate into what you see from key points in your own landscape). Or you may notice the way the neighbor's trees cast a shadow on your lawn at this time of day.

As perceptions come to you, don't write down anything, and don't try too hard. Just enjoy the process of hanging out, and trust that your perceptions will still be in your memory when you're making design decisions later. After you've spent some time in your initial spot, move the chair someplace else. Move it to somewhere you never thought you'd sit, such as one of the corners of your yard. Plop down and notice what you perceive from there. Keep moving your chair around the yard, staying in each spot for at least 10 minutes or until impressions start pouring in.

Pay attention to how you feel as you sit in different locations throughout your yard. The goal is to find *power spots* (places where you feel really good and want to stay for a while). Finding these spots can help you make design decisions about the major-use areas in your yard. This exercise also helps you notice factors that you'll have to deal with if you want to enjoy that part of your property (such as noise from the neighbor's garage).

Repeat the entire process a few times: at different times of the day, when you're in different moods, and during different kinds of weather. If you really want to do this right, take several months or even a whole year for this stage of the design process. I suggest spending at least three or four weeks on this part of the process, with a minimum of three or four sessions.

Making a record of your impressions

After you've had a chance to take it all in from your favorite lawn chair (see the preceding section), it's time to start putting your impressions in some physical form, whether you're making notes, sketching, or taking pictures. Put all this information in a folder or binder, which will become Design Central for your project. Keep it close at hand because you'll find yourself referring to it and making additions on a regular basis.

The exact content of the binder varies from person to person and from site to site, but it should include some or all of the following elements:

- **A bubble diagram showing the basic functions of each area:** This diagram helps you through the early design process. For an example and a complete explanation of what a bubble diagram is, check out Chapter 6.

- **A list of your favorite plants:** Even though choosing plants is one of the last steps in designing a landscape, it's good to begin thinking about it now. What plants do you like most? Even if some of them won't work in your yard, thinking about them develops your awareness of the qualities of plants and of your own taste. Also note which plants are already in your yard and think about whether you want to keep them.

- **Any problems you've identified:** For example, maybe your neighbors' garage is really close to one of your property lines and their teenager's band practice is annoying. You may not be able to convert the kid to your style of music, but you can put up a wall to block the sound a bit.

✔ **A list of things you like and dislike about your yard:** For instance, has it always bothered you that there's no privacy in your backyard or that the kids don't have a place to play? Bring those issues to the surface. Talk to the family about them. Also inventory the good things: that cozy place under the elm tree, the handsome Camellia outside the front door, your funky-but-productive veggie patch.

✔ **Articles and pictures that appeal to you in garden books and magazines:** Seeing how others handle garden design always helps. Gather up as many images as you can, especially of situations similar to yours. Read the articles so you understand the considerations that went into the designs.

✔ **A list of possible elements to be used in your design (paving materials, patio furniture, and so on):** Later in the process, you'll choose specific elements. At this stage, shop for prospective materials, keeping sustainability in mind, to develop a palette of possible choices.

✔ **Photos of your property to look at when you're developing your ideas:** Take pictures from the house looking out, from the corners of the property looking toward the house, from the street, and from every other possible angle. You can even get on the roof. Later you'll study these and sketch over them with tracing paper to see how your ideas play out in three dimensions.

✔ **Photos of gardens in the neighborhood that you like:** Walk around the 'hood to see what your neighbors have been up to. Photos of their yards (discreetly taken) can help you think about what you want.

Taking a Closer Look at Your Land

In the following sections, I walk you through some of the many details you begin to examine as you take a closer look at your yard. I show you how to deal with these details in order to create an effective sustainable design. As you gather information, add it to the binder I discuss in the preceding section.

Don't call it dirt: Soils and geological features

As a gardener, you're concerned with two key aspects of soil: how well the soil grows plants and whether the soil is going anywhere anytime soon. You may think of these two aspects as *fertility* and *stability,* respectively.

A large part of sustainability is developing a thriving, low-care plant community, and the basis of this is understanding your soil. For now, just know that the qualities of your soil — whether it's clay or sand, acid or alkaline — in part determine your ultimate plant palette. Because you match plants to soil and not the other way around, the appearance of your plantings depends on this element. In Chapter 16, you find out how to make sustainable plant choices.

Soil is also a base for whatever hardscape you construct. Its ability to support heavy structures is a factor in the design of those structures. You also need to know whether the soil is prone to erosion and other structural problems. Chapter 14 covers this in detail.

Despite soil's complexity, you need to focus on only a few simple techniques to examine your soil:

- ✔ **Look at how plants are growing on the site and in the neighborhood.** Doing so tells you a lot about the potential of your property. If you notice leaves that are stunted or discolored, or if you see plants that are smaller than normal or that display unusual growth habits, your soil may be poorly drained, its chemistry may be unbalanced, or the living organisms in the soil may be compromised. If the existing plants look happy, however, new plants will probably be happy, too. See Chapter 16 for details.

- ✔ **Do a soil test.** A *soil test* is like a blood test; you send a sample to a lab for analysis. Conducting this test is especially important if you suspect problems or see that plants perform poorly in certain areas. For info on the benefits and limitations of soil testing, turn to Chapter 16.

- ✔ **Check your internal soil drainage.** If you've ever had a plant drown because water built up in the soil, you already know about internal soil drainage (or the lack of it). Most plants like to grow in soil that drains away excess water. After the soil pores are filled, the plant really has no need for any more water. In normal soils, water simply leaks down into the lower soil horizons due to the force of gravity. But some soils have an impervious layer of clay or rock present below the surface. This layer creates a *perched water table*, a zone of floating water. Check out Chapter 16 for a simple way to test your internal soil drainage as well as sustainable (and easy) approaches to handling poor drainage.

- ✔ **Check the stability of your soil.** Are the trees and telephone poles in your area leaning over at crazy angles? Are there parallel cracks in the soil? Is there a history of earth movement in the neighborhood? If so, call your local consulting geologist for an evaluation of the stability of your property. A consultation can cost you $200 to $400, but it just may save you the price of an uninsured mudslide.

Adding plants and water to an unstable site can cause a catastrophic landslide, which won't be covered by your insurance policy. Causing a landslide isn't very sustainable, is it?

✔ **Pay attention to surface erosion.** If runoff water is concentrated so that it runs across your land, there's a good chance that the soil will begin to wash away. This process, called *surface erosion,* can be difficult to stop after it starts. You can use various strategies to prevent surface erosion. I explain these in Chapter 14. For now, just know that you need to look for signs of erosion — soil washing away and gullies of any size — and make repairing them a high priority.

Over the river and through the woods: Terrain and landform

Is your property level or sloping? Hilly or smooth? Rocky? Steep? Are the human-made landforms appealing and functional, or do they need to be changed? Where does the water go? When you're planning your landscape, you need to consider all these questions.

Making conscious changes to landform can give you a major environmental payoff: being able to use your land to harvest rainwater, which I cover in Chapter 8. Bad decisions about landform can result in flooding of your house or neighboring properties, poor plant performance, or even landslides. If you're planning to make major changes in your terrain, work with a landscape architect, landscape contractor, or grading contractor so you get it right.

If your land is hilly, pay particular attention to the following:

✔ **The *aspect* of the slope (that is, the direction it faces):** In the Northern Hemisphere, an east-facing slope gets only morning sun, so you'll have a cool place for plants and people. A west-facing slope, however, will be quite hot on summer afternoons. South-facing slopes get all-day sun, and north-facing ones are shady and cool.

✔ **The location of your low and high spots:** Cold air drains to low spots, which can make for especially chilly areas in winter.

Steep properties may need special help, such as erosion protection and particular kinds of irrigation. You really need to contact a landscape architect, landscape contractor, or a civil engineer to find out how to proceed.

Considering the path of the sun

Landscapers in the Northern Hemisphere always want to know where north is because it tells them a lot about the path of the sun during the day and at different seasons of the year. The path of the sun affects nearly everything about the landscape and is therefore important to consider when you're designing your landscape.

As you know, the sun rises in the east and sets in the west. It travels across the sky at a lower arc in winter and a higher arc in summer. The days are longer in summer and shorter in winter. This basic information is critical because the sun's path affects not only the growth of plants but also where you should place your patios and other areas. For instance, you should position your sitting area on the east side of the house if you want to hang out there and be warmed by the morning sun. Put it on the north side if you love to sit in the shade on hot afternoons.

Keeping the sun's movement in mind, visualize when and where you'll enjoy your home and landscape throughout the day (see Figure 4-1). Go out in your yard at different times of the day and make note of where the sun is. Imagine where trees, buildings, and so on will cast shade at different times. If you can, do this throughout the year so you can get a sense of how the path of the sun changes with the seasons.

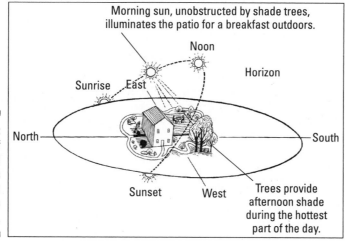

Figure 4-1: The path of the sun and the effects on tree and patio placement.

Assessing your water situation

Water comes in many forms: natural water, applied water, harvested water, problem water, and lack of water. Water is obviously important to your landscaping. It supplies plants with one of their basic needs, and it can also cause damage if you don't deal with drainage issues. By harvesting rainwater, you solve both problems at once. You're moving water safely away from trouble spots like your living room and into parts of your property where it can grow plants and reduce your dependence on city water.

Here are some questions to ask about the water on your property:

- ✔ **What's the annual rainfall in your area, and during what season(s) does it rain?** This information helps you select plants that are adapted to your conditions. It also plays a role in creating outdoor rooms that work with your weather patterns.

- ✔ **How much snow and ice accumulate in winter, and do the snow and ice protect plants or damage them?** Snow can insulate plants and protect them from damaging winter winds. But too much snow and ice can damage your plants, so choose plants that can tolerate whatever your winter throws at them.

- ✔ **What's the source of your irrigation water — a municipal water supply or a private well? And what's the quality of that water?** Get a water report from your water purveyor; it can tip you off to some bad water chemistry that may affect plants or damage your irrigation system.

- ✔ **Where on the property are the existing plumbing features, such as water mains, backflow prevention devices, control valves, and hose bibs?** When you plan your irrigation system, you need to know what's existing, whether it's in the right place, and what condition it's in.

  If your water mains are old, your best bet is to replace them before you put in your landscaping. Otherwise, you may have to tear the landscaping up a year from now when the old galvanized water main finally bursts.

- ✔ **During a rain, how does the water move on the site, and how could you redirect it to more useful and less damaging locations?** Managing rainwater helps the environment by reducing flooding and pollution. Take a look at Chapter 8 to discover how to make rainwater an asset by reducing your need for municipal water.

- ✔ **Are there natural water features such as creeks, streams, ponds, and springs on the property?** If so, lucky you! But do be aware that they can also be sources of flooding.

- ✔ **Where are the site drains, catch basins, and drainage swales (long, shallow ditches)?** These carry rainwater safely away from vulnerable areas. Make sure they're working right. Visit Chapter 8 for details of drainage systems and a more thorough explanation of these terms.

- ✔ **Is runoff from your property causing problems for your neighbors, or vice versa?** Avoid channeling rainwater onto neighboring properties. Determine whether water will be coming onto your land from off-site and whether it'll be an asset or a liability.

- ✔ **Is there standing water anywhere you don't want it on your property?** If so, consider how you can capture that water where it'll be of service to the system instead of creating problems.

Everything on your property is a potential resource. Think of your property as one big water catchment device, and then plan out what you can do with all that lovely, free water. Putting it to use is more sustainable than treating it as a waste product.

Greenery and flowers: Examining existing plants

Plants that currently live on your property are important. They're either an asset (they provide shade, protect a slope against erosion, attract butterflies, or have any of a hundred good qualities, including that you just like them) or a liability (they're in poor condition, poisonous, unstable, or just ugly). You need to make some decisions about what gets to stay and what gets the axe.

Start by considering the location, size, and condition of trees and whether they're native to the area or have been planted by someone. Be sure you know the mature size of any young trees on your site and find out whether they pose any potential problems, such as instability, greedy or lifting roots, brittle limbs, or messy foliage or fruits. Also consider the cost of tree care, which can be expensive.

Call a certified arborist to give you a report on the condition of your trees and to do any major pruning or removals before you put in the rest of the land-scaping. (See Chapter 17 for more information on trees.)

Look beyond the boundaries of your property and identify potential problem trees in neighboring yards. Your neighbors' tree roots may be poised to visit your garden. If they do, the tree may suck away the water and nutrients that your plants need, and they may even crack that nice, new patio you're planning to build.

If a tree is in a bad location, decide whether to take it out or make adjustments to your design. It's easy to believe that keeping a tree is always better for the environment than removing it, but that's not necessarily the case. It depends on whether the whole system is better off with it in place. For instance, if a tree will cause problems for the entire property by sucking all the water out of the soil so that nothing else can grow there, you may be better off taking it out. (Unless it's a native tree; those are generally sacred.)

After examining the trees on your lot, look at the existing shrubs and other plants in the same way, assessing each for condition, suitability, and proper placement. Then make decisions about their fates. I recommend keeping desirable plants, especially natives, that have a clean bill of health, are in the right place, and pass the adorableness test. Consider removing invasive and problematic plants, plants in poor health, and poisonous plants (use gardening books and online resources to identify common poisonous plants and eliminate this hazard). Part V provides more advice for selecting and maintaining plants.

You may find a whole section of your yard where nothing seems to grow. It may be a sort of Bermuda Triangle for plants. Find out whether the performance problems are due to soil issues, pathogens, heavy competition from neighboring trees, or other factors. Correct the problems or find plant varieties that are tough enough to survive the trying conditions.

Room with a view: Making the most of your surroundings

Take a look outside from in your house, especially from those rooms you use the most. What are the pleasant and unpleasant views, and what's the potential for creating focal points that are attractive from inside?

Most people spend 80 percent of their lives indoors, so the views of your garden from inside are at least as important as how it looks when you're out in it. Look at your surroundings from outside too. Choose vantage points that may end up being use areas. If you have an unpleasant view, you can screen it with structures or plants. You can "borrow" attractive views by preserving or creating openings that frame a distant mountain, lake, or stately tree.

Eyeing existing structures and development

Unless you're starting with an empty lot, you need to consider how your house and other existing structures fit into the big design picture, and then you have to decide whether to keep, modify, or eliminate them. Each structure affects the project, even if only because its mass creates small areas that provide welcome shelter for plants or make an otherwise usable area dank and unpleasant. Additionally, new landscape plantings and structures can affect the climate and light levels inside your house.

Here are some things to observe about your house and other buildings on the property, utilities, and other human-made features. Make a list of answers to these questions:

- ✔ **Where are the house and other buildings located?** Evaluate how your house will affect the landscaping and vice versa. Determine whether buildings will provide opportunities, such as leaving a sunny area for a patio, or create problems, such as becoming a fire hazard because of placement at the top of a slope.

- ✔ **What's the orientation of the house with respect to the compass?** The sun moves in a specific and predictable way each day, and each room of your house is exposed to the sunlight in a unique way. Your landscape can work to make the house more comfortable. You may want to shade the east and west sides to protect against hot morning and evening sun, for instance.

- ✔ **How tall are the buildings and other structures, and how will they shade the property at various seasons and times of day?** The sun's path is low in the sky in winter, expanding the shadow that the house casts on the north side of the landscape. And the pool of shade moves throughout the day. Remember that a two-story house casts more shade than a single-story one. Place use areas where they'll get sun in cool seasons and shade in summer, and site other features for optimum performance.

- ✔ **What do each of the house's rooms look out on?** What you do in the landscape has to relate to how the house works. Putting a patio outside the garage is silly, but it makes sense to have a patio outside the living room. High-use areas should be away from bedrooms.

- ✔ **What's the condition of the structures on your property?** If they need work, get it done before you put in the new landscaping.

- ✔ **What's the architectural style of your house?** Match the style of your landscaping to that of your house. A Japanese garden plopped down in front of a Southern colonial mansion looks quite silly.

- ✔ **Where are the doors, and how will people move from inside to outside?** Place landings, patios, and paths in good relationship to the traffic patterns inside the house.

- ✔ **How wide are overhangs, and will they leave some planters dry when it rains?** This means you'll have to water those areas even during the rainy season.

- ✔ **Are there gutters, or does rain fall directly on the beds?** Gutters carry water away from the house (good) but usually deposit it where it goes to waste (bad). Rain sluicing off the roof and crashing onto planter beds can damage plants and soil, and it can damage the house by saturating the soil around it.

✔ **Where are the gas, water, and power sources?** Locate gas mains, drilled wells or town water mains, overhead or underground electric lines, telephone lines, and power outlets. You obviously want to avoid hitting these during construction, and you also want to avoid planting trees directly over them. If you have overhead electric, telephone, and cable wires, you may want to put them underground before you landscape.

✔ **Where are existing site improvements — such as patios, decks, and paths — and are they desirable?** If you have a poorly situated patio or a path that nobody walks on, consider making changes. You can often reuse the salvaged material.

✔ **Where are landscape lights, and do they illuminate effectively?** Are there *hot spots* where light fixtures blind you rather than illuminate the property? Is the safety and security lighting adequate and in good working condition? Where are there dark zones that need to be lit?

✔ **Where do vehicles park?** Cars may be unsustainable, but they're everywhere, and you need to accommodate them. Make sure parking areas are safe, out-of-sight (if possible), and reasonably close to the house. Connect the parking areas to the house via smooth, well-lit paths with as few stairs as possible.

✔ **Which existing features can be repaired or repurposed?** It's definitely more sustainable to save anything that's useful. Figure out how you can transform a shabby but basically sound element into something really cool.

✔ **What's on your site that you could use to make new improvements?** Every site at least has soil to work with, which you can use to make cob or adobe walls, seats, and other structures. You may also have beautiful stones or boulders, you can turn into dry streambeds or garden walls. If you're planning to remove a tree, it may be possible to mill it into lumber that you can use for garden structures. Reusing, repurposing, and recycling are at the very heart of sustainability. (See Chapter 2 for more details on scouring your yard for reusable materials.)

Designing around nice and not-so-nice neighbors

Recognize that your yard is part of the neighborhood. Identify its place in local traffic patterns, in neighborhood land use patterns, and in the overall context of your community. For example, are you in a historical neighborhood that requires special landscape treatment? Do adjacent buildings create problems such as shading or heavy vehicle traffic? Are there trouble spots nearby that may hamper your enjoyment of your own property? Even though these factors don't relate to sustainability, you need to take them into account.

Don't forget about the people who live around you. I have a theory about neighbors. Consider this: The typical suburban lot has five immediate neighbors — one on each side, one directly behind, and two in the back corners. Now I figure that about 20 percent of the people in this world are — how can I say this? — jerks. So the odds are that you're going to have one troublesome neighbor who has family spats out on the deck, keeps wildebeests in the backyard, or rebuilds antique construction cranes in the driveway. Or you may have one who's contentious, contrary, litigious, nosy, noisy, messy, constantly drunk, or otherwise offensive in some way. And because jerks don't realize that they're jerks, they hardly ever change.

Be careful where you place that patio. You may regret your decision (and ripping up concrete and throwing it in the dumpster isn't very sustainable). Consider a solid block wall where needed to hide the distractions, and practice sustainable patience and loving kindness as best you can.

Paying attention to privacy

Some properties naturally lend themselves to taking in their surroundings — it's hard to turn your back on a splendid view. Other sites may lack views or be surrounded by undesirable elements; these sites can be developed inward to create a private world.

Regionally, attitudes about the privacy of people's yards vary a lot. In many places, it's considered uncool to put a fence around your property. In others, it's just the opposite. Neighborhoods that are denser and more urban tend toward privacy, whereas rural areas are more open. If your house and your neighbor's house are too close for comfort, you may want to plant trees between the buildings in an attempt to develop a buffer.

How's the weather? Closing in on climate

Climate affects nearly every aspect of the sustainable landscape. Choose strategies that are best adapted to your climate so that not only is the end result more useful, but it also makes fewer demands on resources. Tuning your design in to the local climate can even make your house more comfortable and save energy inside. For example, you can determine where the prevailing winds come from and use that information to locate outdoor rooms in calmer areas, develop windbreak plantings to improve overall conditions on the property, and perhaps even funnel summer winds onto your land for natural cooling.

An important application for climate data is in selecting plants that will survive and thrive. This consideration is so critical that all gardening and landscaping literature, sustainably oriented or not, addresses it in detail. One of the most important pieces of information about any given plant is its *hardiness,* which is how well it tolerates cold. (Despite the connotations of the term, it isn't about overall toughness.) Every plant used in horticulture is ranked for its hardiness, using *hardiness zone maps* to indicate what degree of cold it tolerates. You can locate your community on the map, see which zone you're in, and then pick plants that work for you.

The most common hardiness zone map in the U.S. comes from the United States Department of Agriculture (USDA); you can find it find online at `www.usna.usda.gov/Hardzone/ushzmap.html`. Canadians can use the one at `nlwis-snite1.agr.gc.ca/plant00/index.phtml`. You can find similar maps for many other parts of the world.

One special map system is the Sunset zone system. It's more sophisticated than the USDA map because it incorporates data on rainfall, high and low temperatures, humidity, and growing seasons. Many gardeners in the U.S. and parts of Canada depend on it. To find a map for your area, go to `www.sunset.com` and search for "zone map."

Deciding What You Want from Your Property

After you've surveyed your property and its surroundings, it's time to look inward to the needs and desires of yourself and your family. If your design takes the environment into account but ignores your personal needs, it's a failure. In this section, you get to be selfish (in an altruistic and sustainable way, of course).

Don't forget to involve the other family members, including kids. Assuming they're willing, everyone will probably enjoy the process, you'll like the company, and the eventual outcome will be better suited to everyone because they've played a role in it. Besides, you won't have to take *all* the blame when something goes haywire.

It's all about you: Identifying your needs

To get a design that suits you, you simply have to ask what you want from it. For example, maybe you want your landscape to include gardens for growing food, a wildlife viewing area, compost areas, nap zones, and so on.

Make a list that's just right for you. If you don't know what you want, you'll probably never get it, and you'll be missing out on some great experiences. To make your list, draw a line down the center of a piece of paper and write your needs and desires on the left side of the page. Then to the right of each entry, write down the kind of physical features you think could meet them and indicate where they may go on the property.

Don't worry if you don't have all the answers. You're in the midst of going from the general to the specific, and it's okay not to know everything yet. The design process takes time. Allow yourself to think freely and dream big, as if you had all the money and resources in the world. You can pare things down at a later stage. Whatever you do, don't cripple your imagination by assuming you could never do or afford some particular element.

Out of my way: Identifying and overcoming problems and limitations

After you've had a chance to get to know your property, you'll probably have a list of problems as well as a list of dreams. For example, you may have found that the chickens next door make too much noise. This is a problem because you were planning to put a patio nearby, and there's something about all that clucking that just drives you nuts. You know you won't be happy with the noise, but you don't see another place in your yard where the patio will work. Limitations like this one crop up on every project.

Solving project problems and limitations can be tricky and often involves tradeoffs, such as living with the chicken clucking or tolerating a patio in a less-than-ideal location. However, a little outside-the-box thinking can sometimes provide you with a solution that offers unexpected benefits, so inventory your possible workarounds. For instance, you may put in a fountain that's pleasantly loud enough to mask the chicken noise, with the added benefits of cooling off the otherwise warm patio, being a lovely focal point, and providing habitat for dragonflies, fish, and birds. Another approach may be to build a solid, noise-blocking masonry wall on that side of the yard. Combine the wall with the fountain and the patio, and you have a very fine outdoor room that's better than your original design thanks to those darn chickens. Whatever the source of your problem, see whether you can find a solution that leaves you with more than just an end to the problem.

Determining how much maintenance work to create with your design

A sustainable garden is by definition undemanding. But any living system requires some care, and you need to consider this important fact now, not later, when poor design decisions have left you with a mess that forces you to spend way more time and money on maintenance than you ever intended. I talk more about the specifics of maintenance in Chapter 20, but for now it's important to realize that the amount of care that your landscaping requires is a direct result of design.

Plants that are too big for their allotted space attempt to grow to their genetically programmed height and width forever. They don't stop just because their roots are growing into your foundation. Plants don't know what you think they're supposed to do, and they don't give a hoot about you and your silly little landscaping problems. This is just one example of the many ways poor design can give you grief.

By designing your landscape properly, you short-circuit many of the most common problems that go disguised as normal garden care. So during the site analysis phase, be sure to answer the following questions:

- ✔ **Are you a gardener?** What role do you want to play in the ongoing care of your garden? Do you love to get out and work in the yard? Are you at home when planting things and then nurturing, pruning, and watching them grow? Or are you a lazybones who loves to enjoy her garden from the hammock or from the recliner in the living room?

   There's no right answer, but if you like to garden, you'll be unhappy if you end up with a static, severely low-maintenance landscape that offers no place to putter. On the other hand, there's nothing worse than a long to-do list if you can't stand working in the yard. Answer this question at the site analysis phase so you can tune your design to your anticipated role in future stewardship.

- ✔ **Will you hire a gardener?** Perhaps you have too many things on your calendar, and the last thing you need is a set of repetitive tasks to further overload you. That's okay. More and more people are hiring gardening services to care for their yards. Gardeners can be a great way to take some of the pressure off. Decide now whether you want to have help with garden care, and then approach your design accordingly. (Turn to Chapter 3 for more on gardeners.)

Chapter 5

Brushing Up on Design Basics

In This Chapter

▶ Examining the elements of design

▶ Picking up design secrets from the pros

▶ Considering special design situations

▶ Designing a safe landscape

Sustainable or otherwise, a proper landscape has to look beautiful. And to make it look beautiful, you have to rely on the elements of design. You may be intimidated by the design aspect of your landscaping project, thinking that artsy stuff isn't your thing. But not only is design easy; it's also a lot of fun. After you get the hang of it, you may find yourself looking for design projects everywhere.

In this chapter, I show you some of the age-old principles of design that apply to all gardens, and I also provide you with the inside story on some tricks that landscape architects use to bring magic to the places they design. (Keep in mind that this is a very basic introduction to the complex world of design.)

You'd be correct to ask what all this design info has to do with sustainability. Just remember that this chapter is about the visual and aesthetic side of design, not so much about how the landscape functions. When you partner the principles of sustainable design covered elsewhere in the book with the techniques of making beautiful spaces that I discuss here, you'll end up with the beautiful, functional, sustainable landscape that's the ideal.

Getting an Introduction to Design

Every landscape designer has a "toolbox" of sorts. Inside that toolbox are things like color and texture and balance. Each item in the toolbox is a way of looking at the arrangement and character of a landscape. These items are the elements of design, and if you take them into consideration, your project will be that much better for it.

Chances are that you already understand good design on some level. For instance, if you've ever arranged furniture in a room, you were using design principles to make everything look and work right. You may not have been able to state the principles, but you knew them instinctively and acted on them. It's not that large a leap from appreciating a well-designed landscape to creating one. Apply the principles that I introduce in the following sections to your project, and you can soon see a wonderful garden emerge.

Making your landscape safe is a part of good design that you shouldn't overlook. You can avoid, eliminate, or prepare for common problems such as killer plants and slick sidewalks caused by a poorly-designed irrigation system. Be sure to ponder the potential for mayhem when you design, and keep an eye out for developing problems as the landscape matures.

Be sure to plan for any special accessibility needs. By eliminating steps and creating wide and gently sloping paths made of smooth, solid material, people at many ability levels can get around easily. Specially designed raised beds and planters and unique enabling tools and equipment can make gardening possible for folks with all sorts of disabilities, even for those in a wheelchair.

Unity: All the pieces working together

Nothing is more disconcerting than a garden that's a chaotic mishmash of all sorts of plants, ten different paving materials, and too many colors. These types of gardens look as if the nursery truck tipped over on its way somewhere else and the plants took root wherever they fell.

A space with *unity* — one that's composed of harmonious elements and a consistent and comprehensible color scheme — is pleasing to both the eye and the mind, and it makes for a place where you want to linger.

How do you create unity? First refer to Figure 5-1 to compare a garden plan with good unity to a garden plan with bad unity. Then follow these steps:

1. **Decide on a style for your garden.**

   Will your garden be formal, natural, geometric, curvy, rectilinear? You can choose whatever style you like and whatever is appropriate to the surroundings. I discuss shape and formality in some of the upcoming sections, and you can find out more about style in the later section titled "Considering style."

2. **Choose harmonious plants and hardscape elements.**

   Make sure the plants and hardscape elements all look good together. Then use them repeatedly throughout the design — in the foreground and the background to create a sense of depth.

3. **Choose a suitable color scheme.**

    You wouldn't wear a hot pink shirt with bright orange pants unless you were headed to a Halloween party, right? Well, similarly, being careful to coordinate the colors of your plantings, hardscape elements, and house helps everything to look attractively harmonious. That's unity in action. (For more on color, turn to the section titled "Color: Letting your landscape's true colors shine through," later in this chapter).

TIP

Unless you're a master of design, keep the number of elements in your plan fairly minimal — a few kinds of plants, one or two hardscape materials, and not too many precious geegaws. Having too many elements in one composition drives the mind to distraction, blowing unity to bits.

Balance: Formal versus informal

Balance means maintaining a sense of proportion in your design. In a formal garden, you achieve balance through right-left symmetry arranged along a central axis. In other words, if you plant one lilac on the left, you have to plant an identical lilac on the right. In an informal garden, balance is asymmetrical, with differing elements arranged without a formal axis. Instead, this type of garden relies on a more subtle equilibrium of their *overall mass.* Have a look at the two plans in Figure 5-2 to see the difference between formal and informal gardens.

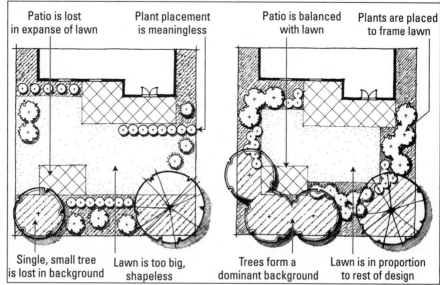

Figure 5-1: Landscaping plans showing bad (left) and good uses of unity.

Patio is lost in expanse of lawn

Plant placement is meaningless

Patio is balanced with lawn

Plants are placed to frame lawn

Single, small tree is lost in background

Lawn is too big, shapeless

Trees form a dominant background

Lawn is in proportion to rest of design

A sustainable landscape can be formal or informal — you don't have to give up your design aesthetic to go the sustainable route.

Repetition: Following nature's lead

Don't be afraid to repeat design elements in your garden; repetition makes the design that much stronger. Think of a forest with thousands of the same kind of tree, each with the same vegetation underneath. A forest like this beautiful, yet most people seem timid about using repetition in their landscaping.

Repetition carried too far creates a tedious scene, but a lack of repetition works hard against unity. One daylily gets lost in a planting that's made up of 100 varieties of plants, but an acre of daylilies is boring. If you strew clusters of daylilies throughout your garden, repeating them like a musical refrain, they gain energy and contribute to the continuity of the planting. If you do that with many elements, both plants and hardscape features, your design will be strong and good-looking. Check out Figure 5-3 to see examples of poor repetition and strong repetition.

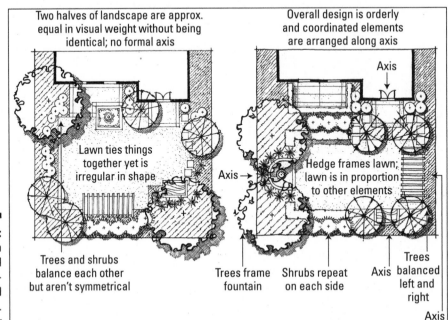

Figure 5-2:
Plans with symmetrical and asymmetrical balance.

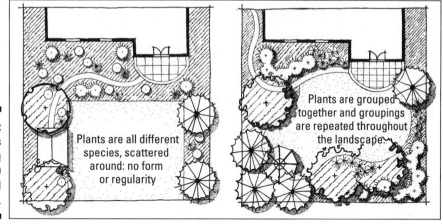

Figure 5-3:
Plans
showing
bad (left)
and good
repetition.

Plants are all different
species, scattered
around: no form
or regularity

Plants are grouped
together and groupings
are repeated throughout
the landscape.

Contrast and variety: The spice of life

The dance between repetition and variety in landscape design is a delicate
one. After all, repetition is important for unity, but including elements that
contrast with one another in color, form, shape, and overall character can
add a lot of life to the composition. For instance, if you want to create a lively
scene, plant light-colored foliage against a dark background, place rough
natural stones against refined smooth concrete, and use trees or overhead
structures to produce patterns of sun and shade. These are just a few ways
to add variety to your design.

Shape and form: One big happy family

I think of *shape* as being the two-dimensional arrangement of the elements
of the landscape when viewed from above, whereas *form* is the three-dimen-
sional space that things occupy when viewed from ground level. Both are
important elements of garden design.

Getting into shape

Decide on a shape family for your landscape layout. You can choose among
the many different families, including rectilinear, curvilinear, angular, or free-
form. A landscape made up of strongly geometric shapes can be very formal
(if it's symmetrical) or elegantly restful (such as a Japanese garden).

On the other end of the spectrum, a free-form approach is best suited to the naturalistic garden. But even the free-form is not free of form; the form is just more subtle. Study wild natural areas to see how trees, rocks, and streams are arranged very beautifully yet without apparent geometry — they're products of the natural forces in the system. If you can do that in your yard, you'll really achieve something great.

Whatever you do, make your shape family consistent and relate it to other shapes that may be present on the site. Pair round shapes with rolling hills and rectangles with a boxy modern house, or contrast them for a different look. Figure 5-4 shows bad and good uses of shape.

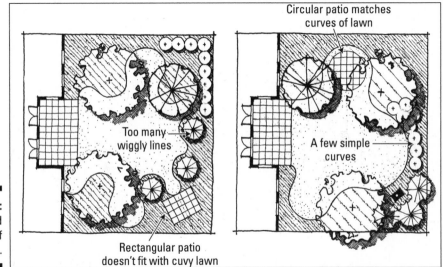

Circular patio matches curves of lawn

Too many wiggly lines

A few simple curves

Figure 5-4: Good and bad uses of shape.

Rectangular patio doesn't fit with cuvy lawn

In good form

Closely related to shape is the form, or 3D outline, of plants and other features. A sheared boxwood hedge has a strict rectilinear form, whereas an Italian cypress or poplar tree has an upright, column-like form. And a spreading oak tree grows in the form of a broad canopy. Each form has a particular role to play. The boxwood leads you along a path, the upright cypress is like a giant exclamation point, and the oak embraces and shelters the area beneath it.

Include some plants with strap-shaped leaves such as Iris or some boldly-shaped succulents like Agaves in your plantings. They act as points of emphasis in the design, and the contrast they make with the leafier textures and shrubbier forms pleases the eye and is enlivening.

Line of sight: Getting all your ducks in a row

Plantings, hardscape, and other landscaping features create lines of sight. Lines of sight can be explicit, such as elements arranged strictly along an imaginary central line called an *axis* or perhaps an *allée* (a long double row) of trees, or it can be subtle, such as a gently curving path. Lines lead the eye through the scene and help make sense of the elements it contains. Have a look at Figure 5-5 to see what works and what doesn't.

Lines can run parallel to or at right angles to buildings and other existing structural elements, or you can place them at 30-degree, 45-degree, or 60-degree angles. The angular approach usually has more visual energy and creates a feeling of movement and depth in the overall composition. It's especially useful in making small spaces seem bigger. Curves are also quite lively and can make for a delightful sense of movement.

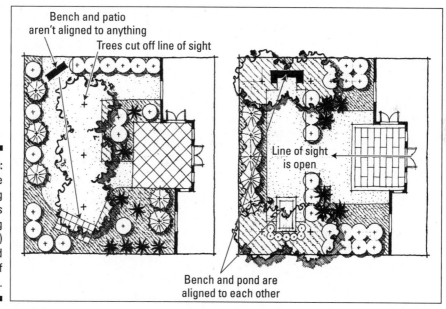

Bench and patio aren't aligned to anything
Trees cut off line of sight

Line of sight is open

Figure 5-5: Sample landscaping plans showing bad (left) and good uses of lines.

Bench and pond are aligned to each other

Focal points and vantage points: Grabbing people's attention

Imagine sitting out in your backyard on a balmy summer's evening, watching the water dance in your fountain. Or picture yourself coming around a corner and seeing a gorgeous persimmon tree laden with fruit, the leaves starting to turn color. Those attention-grabbing elements are called *focal points*. Any strong and striking visual element, such as a piece of sculpture or a particularly stunning plant, can be a focal point in your composition.

Focal points are often placed on axes (long, straight lines of sight) with other features. You may, for example, put a bold fountain in line with a set of French doors. Focal points are also effective when placed in corners, where they provide an endpoint for the view and give the area a feeling of depth and energy. Without good focal points, your eye searches in vain for a place to rest, which leads you to feel a sense of incompleteness.

Every focal point has at least one *vantage point* (a place from which it is viewed). This can be your patio, the living room sofa, or a bench. Sometimes it works to have several vantage points. For instance, you may have a fountain that's visible from several places in the garden. When you put together your landscape design, the creation of focal points and vantage points should be one of the first things you consider. Refer to Figure 5-6 to see how vantage points work in landscape plans.

Don't have too many focal points. If you have more than three in any given area, you weaken the design and create the same confusion as having none at all — the eye has no place to land.

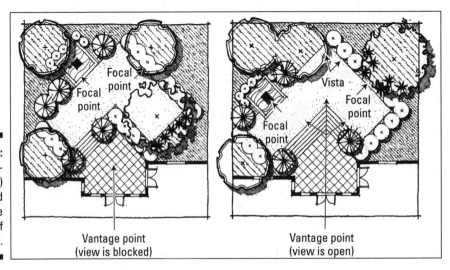

Figure 5-6:
Plans showing bad (left) and good vantage points of focal points.

Vantage point
(view is blocked)

Vantage point
(view is open)

Texture: Feeling your way around

Designers contrast plant textures for appealing combinations. They play coarse against fine and then repeat the play of textures using different plants. When skillfully combined with nicely-partnered colors, textures are a key element in what makes plantings work well. A tropical Philodendron with leaves 6 feet across is said to have a *coarse* texture. A tiny-leaved thyme plant, on the other hand, has a *fine* texture.

This rule of texture also applies to hardscape. For instance, sometimes a surface made of large tiles looks great in a small space because the texture is unexpected and it makes the area seem roomier than it is. The texture of paving, walls, woodwork, and other man-made elements contributes greatly to the overall effect of the landscape.

You can use texture to create a sense of depth by placing finer textures in the background, or you can create drama by purposefully placing a coarse-textured plant in an unexpected location.

Color: Letting your landscape's true colors shine through

The color of your plantings as well as your hardscape features works to create many different effects. Use color to generate a look and mood that's appropriate to your particular situation. For instance, I like to use plantings in bright yellows, oranges, and reds in front yards to create a cheerful and welcoming atmosphere. A single bold red plant can really liven up a portion of your landscape. And something *variegated* (with multicolored leaves), such as a spider plant, can brighten a shady area under a tree where it's difficult to get flowers to grow. You can use these simple strategies in many contexts with many kinds of plants.

Foliage colors other than green play a strong role in design, too, adding lively, year-round interest. Don't overlook seasonal changes in leaf color — they can be incredibly rewarding. Match the fresh green leaves of spring with brightly colored flowers, and then later in the year, match the autumn foliage to more somber autumn colors by using fall-blooming plants. The tricks you can play are endless.

Use the plant lists in gardening books such as *Gardening All-in-One For Dummies* (Wiley) to plan out your color schemes by season. Looking at images of the plants and putting them together into a collage helps you see how the planting will look. Visit nurseries and gardens to see real plants in bloom, and don't overlook seeing mature plants growing in real places.

Your hardscape needs to have a color scheme, too. Hardscape colors are usually more subtle than those of flowers, but sometimes it's really fun to use an outrageous bright red, purple, or yellow piece of art in a focal point where it will have a stunning impact amid the more demure colors of the plantings. (See the earlier section "Focal points and vantage points: Grabbing people's attention" for details.)

From a sustainability perspective, the color of pavement can affect the livability of the area you're landscaping. The relative reflectivity (or *albedo* as we fancy-pants landscape architects like to call it) of a surface can make it literally hot or cool. And very few people enjoy having to sit or walk on a surface that's too hot.

Picking Up On the Design Secrets of the Pros

We landscape designers have all kinds of design secrets up our sleeves, and in this section, I spill a few of them. Read on for some pretty cool tricks of the trade that you may not think of on your own — tricks that can help you achieve a really striking landscape design. Why settle for an ordinary landscape? By being innovative and by asking new questions about the possibilities, you give yourself a chance to come up with something special that fits your needs.

Controlling people's feelings and behaviors with your design

I always say that designers are the dictators of feelings and behavior. They can make people experience certain emotions and even act in predictable ways simply through design choices. Of course, the benevolent dictator uses this power only to do good.

For an idea of how design can affect your emotions and behaviors, picture yourself sitting on a bench in a public park. The bench is out in the open, and behind you is a large expanse of lawn. If you're like most people, you'll soon notice a certain discomfort setting in. It's because we're genetically programmed to watch our backs. (Thank our ancestors, who were constantly getting eaten by saber-toothed tigers, for this built-in surveillance system.) However, if you move that bench up against a sun-warmed wall, you'll likely have created a situation that makes you want to linger because you feel safe (and toasty warm).

The bottom line is that people respond strongly to design and to how it's carried out in the actual landscape. So if you make a place that's unsettling, nobody will want to use it. No doubt you've seen and visited places like this. In fact, your backyard may be one of them. On the other hand, you can use design to create a place that evokes positive feelings, such as safety, calm, curiosity, peace, or delight. As a designer, you have incredible control over how people feel and behave. Use your power wisely, and your landscape will be a source of joy for years to come.

Designing outside the box

Fresh ideas can be difficult to come up with. Even seasoned landscape professionals can fall into the trap of plugging in the same old ideas: living space in the back, patio directly outside the house, and so on. A key part of the design process is asking the right questions to get inspiration. What if you put the living space in the front of your house? Suppose you place the patio farther back in the yard — how would that look? Ask questions that help break your mind out of what it thinks are limits.

A little unconventional thinking can lead to stunning results. For example, you may decide to mix vegetable plants with ornamental plants in a more gardenesque arrangement, or you may devote your front yard to an orchard or native garden instead of a less useful lawn, or you may even lower your lighting to illuminate the paths only, removing the hot spots and urban light pollution generated by bright light fixtures traditionally located on the porch next to the door. Designers know they need to think beyond normal practices, particularly when they're stumped. If you aren't sure what to do with your design, turn everything you know on its head and approach things from a totally different perspective.

Keep in mind that unconventional thinking can go too far when it violates design principles. And remember that someday, you may want or need to sell your house. Consider the effect of your landscaping on marketability and property value; don't make things so weird that you can't sell the place.

Don't just design for the eye. Use all your senses. Take into account sound, fragrance, and the tactile qualities of plants and surfaces. You can even consider the taste of things (like the succulent blueberries I just grazed off the bush — yum!).

Paying attention to the sequential experience of the landscape

One of my very favorite design principles is what I call the *sequential experience of the landscape.* It may sound complicated, but believe me, it's easy to understand and put into practice. First, think of a garden setting where you can see everything in the whole place at the same time. In this type of setting, you can stand and scan from one end of the place to the other in 30 seconds. Then it's time to go back inside because you've seen all there is to see. The landscape offers no excitement and no sense of depth, and nothing very intriguing is going on.

But if you were to create some subtle divisions within that space — such as a shrub that partially conceals a portion of the garden — your mind would start to work on it and you'd become curious about what's going on behind the shrub. So take on the role of the benevolent design dictator and run a curvy pathway around that shrub, creating the possibility of access. (See the earlier section "Controlling people's feelings and behaviors with your design" for more on becoming a design dictator.) Put something really cool behind that shrub, such as a secluded bench or a pond full of rubber duckies, and you've created a feeling of mystery — of being invited into a special, secret world. By doing so, you've made the process of moving through the landscape an adventure. Check out Figure 5-7 for a sample landscaping plan that shows this design principle.

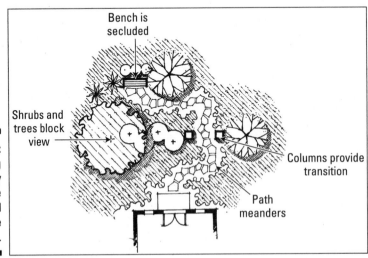

Figure 5-7:
Creating
mystery
with the
sequential
experience
technique.

Bench is secluded

Shrubs and trees block view

Columns provide transition

Path meanders

When you create this type of subtle separation in your yard, you've also created what some people call an *away place.* Imagine the difference between having a cool drink at the end of the day on the patio just outside the kitchen door and taking it back to that secret spot to visit your rubber duckies. One location makes you feel like you're still on the hamster wheel, and the other feels like a mini-vacation because you've disappeared for a little while. You can create away places for one person or for a whole crowd. When you get to your away place, you literally see the world, and your garden, from a totally different perspective. How refreshing is that?

Landscape design is about creating places that not only look good and work right but also make you feel good. You might say that's the winning combination: beautiful, sustainable, and emotionally satisfying.

Considering style

Most garden design literature is about style. In fact, you can find entire books on just about any style: Southwest Style, Thai Style, Kankakee Style, and so on. These books generally don't address sustainability issues, but they do offer an important lesson: Every place has a certain indigenous quality. This lesson is less true as the world becomes more homogenous, but elemental factors, such as climate, can give rise to certain architectural responses. For example, depending on the weather in your area, you may need a peaked or flat roof, and you'll likely have different types of plants than someone in an opposite clime. Climate also impacts whether you have a rack for surfboards or snowshoes on the back porch.

Here's a fancy landscape architect's word that will really impress your friends: *genius loci.* It means the "spirit of place." When you capture the genius loci of your property, you'll be better able to come up with a fitting design. For example, suppose you live in a desert climate. The proper response to that environment is to plant desert plants, not tuberous begonias. That response matters from a sustainability perspective, of course, but it also matters because the genius loci demands it. Responding to genius loci is what style is on a deep level.

Styles can be derived from culture (formal, modern, Victorian, urban), from regional sources (Thai, Mexican, English), or from the natural world (desert, tropical, alpine).

Take local style into account during your design adventure. After all, your region, your town or neighborhood, and of course your house all have a style, and the landscape you create will make a lot more sense if you fit it carefully into its surroundings. Remember that traditional styles arose as a sustainable response to the realities of the environment, so by respecting that ancient wisdom you also bring environmental sensibility to your design.

Sticking with your garden over time

It's easy to forget that gardens aren't static like furniture or pictures hanging on the wall. A garden is a living ecosystem, and even the most stable, sustainable landscape is changing all the time. Your garden will look very different 1 month, 1 year, 10 years, and 50 years after you create it. By planning for those stages, you develop a landscape that endures, and there's nothing more sustainable than that.

For example, in your plantings, the annual plants will be around for the first year; the perennials and groundcovers, for the first 10 years; and the trees, for 50 years or longer. Over time, the trees will alter the environment, and the plants beneath the trees will change. The wise designer looks ahead and plans for the inevitable and desirable transitions so the project keeps working over the long haul.

Chapter 6

Plotting Your Sustainable Landscape

Designing a landscape that looks great and also works well (that's the *sustainable* part) can seem intimidating and mysterious if you haven't done it before. But if you follow the steps in this chapter, you shouldn't have any trouble putting together a beautiful, sustainable landscape.

If you get stuck, remember that there's no shame in running your ideas by a landscape architect for feedback. The price of a consultation (usually $100 to $300) is a tiny fraction of the overall cost of the project, and it can save you much grief later.

Deciding What Plans You Need

You wouldn't think of building a house by gathering up some lumber, concrete, and roofing materials and then making the house up as you went along. First you need a plan to direct the course of the work and ensure a satisfactory outcome. Landscaping is no different. In fact, the landscape, especially the sustainable landscape, is complex, and it demands a great deal of thought if you want to end up with something that works well *and* looks good.

When most people think of a landscape design, they imagine a set of plan drawings showing where everything is going to be located — the trees and shrubs, the patio, the paths, and all the rest. When you hire someone to design your landscaping for you, this is one of the things you get for your money. Plan drawings are handy to have, and they can be a great tool if you're doing your own design. But it's entirely possible to develop a great design without ever drawing a plan. Take a minute to consider two equally valid approaches to design:

- ✔ **Sticking to the bubble diagram/field design approach:** If you have a small-scale plan in mind (for instance, you want to change some plantings in the back flower beds and switch your lawn to a more sustainable meadow) or if you have a fairly clear vision for some more major changes, drawing detailed plans may not be necessary. You may need only to sketch a bubble diagram and spend some time outside marking off the edges of beds with a garden hose or rope or staking out the location of a new patio with wood stakes and builder's twine. This marking and staking is referred to as *field design.* (Check out the next section to find out more about bubble diagrams and field design.) This hands-on approach helps you experiment with designs until you find the one that's best.

- ✔ **Drawing full-blown landscape plans:** If you'll be laying out an entirely new landscape, with paving, retaining walls, outdoor rooms of various kinds, and lots of details, draw it all to scale using the techniques and plans I describe throughout this chapter. Include the *concept plan,* a simpler version of the detailed landscape plan a professional landscape architect might develop for you. A detailed concept plan helps you make sure everything in your new landscape fits and works well together, and it provides a clear roadmap for installing your own landscaping.

Be sure you do all the designing you need to in order to have a well-planned landscape that takes all the issues of function, appearance, cost, legality, and environmental suitability into account. What counts in the end is not the quality of the pretty pictures you draw but the quality of your thinking and planning.

Making the Fundamental Decisions

Design goes from the general to the specific. Whether you end up with a formal set of plan drawings or not, the first step in the design process is to write down, in a very informal way, the general ideas you've had during your site analysis and initial design work, which I cover in Chapters 4 and 5. The second step is to take your design outside, where you mark it all out on the ground to get a feeling for how it'll look when you do it for real. In this section, I introduce you to bubble diagrams and field design.

Creating a bubble diagram

When you're ready to write down your landscape design ideas, make a rough sketch of your property on a sheet of paper. This rough sketch, or *bubble diagram,* doesn't have to be to scale at this point, but try to make it reasonably accurate. Then start writing words and phrases in appropriate locations: "new patio," "remove tree," "dog run," "vegetable garden," and so on. The ideas you write down can include anything from problems, opportunities, and needs to desires and specific features you know you like. Encircle each feature with a simple oval. Now isn't the time for fancy graphics — your bubble diagram just needs to be useful, much like the simple diagram in Figure 6-1.

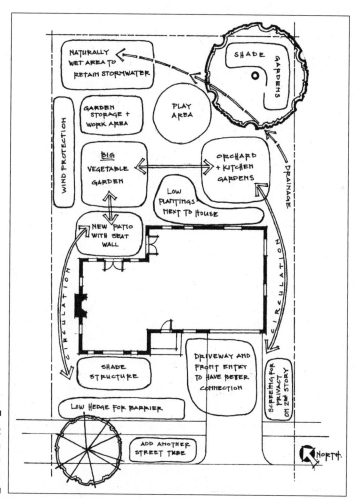

Figure 6-1:
An example bubble diagram.

After you finish your bubble diagram, take it outside and sit with it. You want to be sure it all makes sense. You may even want to make two or more bubble diagrams to explore different approaches (for example, with the patio here versus the patio there). This step opens your mind to all the possibilities; right now you're still exploring, and you don't want to miss a thing.

Move around your property and imagine how it'll look when it's done. Picture the shade of the new trees, the size and shape of the flower beds, the changed landforms, and everything else. Visualize everything as best you can before you act on your decisions. After all, landscaping your yard two or three times isn't sustainable.

Laying it out on the ground: Field design

If you have a difficult time visualizing the changes you wrote down in your bubble diagram (see the preceding section), mocking up the landscape can be a wonderful way to make them more realistic. Here are a number of handy techniques you can use to accomplish this mock-up, which is referred to as *field design:*

- ✔ **Mark out the boundaries of planter beds, patios, pathways, and so on with lines of powdered gypsum or lime.** These materials are available in bulk at nurseries, and you can apply them by hand. Colored spray paint is great for color-coding the different features, but it isn't very good for the environment. And isn't sustainability the whole point of this project?

   Use a garden hose or a flexible nylon rope to temporarily delineate curves; then apply the gypsum or lime along the lines you've created.

- ✔ **Stake the corners of structures with 1"-x-2" wooden stakes and then use builder's twine to connect them.** This reveals the footprint of the completed work.

- ✔ **Map out your trees and other tall features.** Use *pin flags* (small flags available at building supply places), or even long pipes stood on end, to indicate tall site features, such as tree trunks or light posts.

- ✔ **Place big wads of crumpled newspaper where boulders or shrubs will be.** The wads of paper should be close to the realistic size of the feature; that way you can get a good idea of how everything will look when finished.

- ✔ **Construct fake fences and walls with corrugated cardboard or sheets of plywood.** Stake the temporary structures in place with steel T-posts.

Materials from your mock-up can come from the waste stream, of course. Buying them new and using them once would be the antithesis of what sustainable landscaping is all about, so use what you have or look to neighbors or local businesses. Dumpster diving is no shame. Oh, and that gypsum or lime is good for the soil, so no harm done there.

Observe the "finished" landscape from every angle. Walk the "paths" and sit on the "patio" with a cool drink. See how you like it. Live with it for a few days (or longer), and make changes as necessary. Give this decisive moment your best thought before you proceed to the next level of commitment.

Making a bubble diagram and testing it through field design doesn't answer all your questions. Whether you go to the trouble of making a formal landscape plan or simply get on with the process of constructing your new landscaping, be aware that you have plenty more details to resolve. Even if you won't be drawing a concept plan, be sure to read the rest of this chapter to understand how to go from the general ideas you have at this stage to the specifics of exactly what you'll be doing. You definitely don't want to miss the "Remaining within the Law: Considering Legal Issues" section!

Taking Your Plan Drawing to the Next Level

Sometimes a project is just too big or complex to design on the ground. That's when it's time to do some detailed planning on paper, just like the pros. This planning involves measuring the site and developing what's called a *base sheet* (a drawing of your property with all the existing features on it, such as the house, trees, and property lines), and then developing a concept plan on top of that base. The following sections guide you through this process.

Measuring your site the easy way

To design a more complex landscape, you have to draw plans to scale. And to do that, you need reasonably accurate measurements of your site. After you've gathered your measurements, you transfer them to paper. Assuming your property is relatively flat, not too big, and fairly limited in complexity, you can easily measure the site yourself.

If your property is complex or if you need more-detailed information (for your own use or to fulfill requirements of agencies that you may be submitting your plans to), hire a licensed land surveyor. These professionals aren't cheap, but they work to a much higher degree of accuracy than you (or I) ever will.

Follow these steps, and in just an hour or so, you'll have a fairly accurate set of measurements:

1. **Gather your tools.**

   You need a 20-foot tape measure (the 1-inch wide ones are nicely rigid and easy to work with), a 100-foot tape measure, a clipboard, paper, pencil, and the usual Indiana Jones hat, chaps, rattlesnake boots, and machete.

2. **Start by measuring your house.**

   Begin at an easy point, such as one of the front corners. Measure from the corner of the house to the first window. Stop there and measure the width of the window. Then measure from the window to the door, and so forth, working around the house until you come back to your starting point.

3. **Measure from the house out to the property lines.**

   Run your tape from all the house corners perpendicularly out to the fences or other assumed property lines. On an ordinary suburban lot, this step is no big deal; on larger or thickly-vegetated properties, this measurement can get a little gnarly. (That's why you're wearing the Indiana Jones gear.)

   If you plan to install any fencing or make any other changes along your property lines, be sure you know where the legal boundaries are, because you'll be responsible for any encroachments. A professional boundary survey is well worth the price.

4. **Measure any other buildings on your property and any hardscape features.**

   Use the same simple linear technique here that you used on the house. Leave no detail unmeasured. This includes seemingly unimportant things like downspouts, light fixtures, drains, and so forth. Be nitpicky.

5. **Measure planter beds and major plants.**

   Include the length and width of the beds, the approximate canopy spread of the trees, the depth of the hedges, and the locations of tree trunks.

6. **Measure the spaces between features.**

   Measuring how far apart things are will enable you to place features in accurate relationship to one another.

Engineers use triangles to brace things like bridges and buildings because the triangle is rigid. That rigidity works in measuring, too; it helps you place seemingly random site features — such as tree trunks, sheds, and kiddie pools — on your map with a high degree of precision. To use the secret art of *triangulation,* simply measure to, say, a tree trunk, from at least two points on a fixed feature, such as two corners of your house. When you transfer these measurements to paper, your tree will be in exactly the right location. Figure 6-2 shows how all this looks on your field notes.

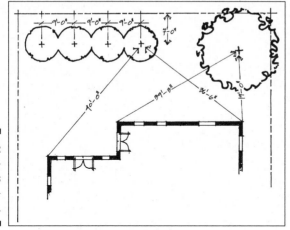

Figure 6-2:
Site measurements with triangulation.

Triangulation goes much more smoothly with a helper, but if you don't have one, no problem. Just add one more tool to your kit: a screwdriver. Use it to pin the end of the 100-foot tape to the ground (such as by a corner of your house) when you take your long measurements. Pivot to all the distant points you'll be measuring before you move to the next location.

Using your measurements to create a base sheet

After you take all the measurements of your property, you get to go inside where it's cool and comfortable. There you can settle down to the task of transferring your measurements to paper. To tackle this task, you need the following tools: gridded drafting paper, an architect's scale, a T-square, a triangle, a compass, and a drawing board. Chapter 3 describes these tools and where to get them.

After gathering your tools, tape a sheet of drafting paper onto your drawing board and follow these steps to transfer your measurements to paper and create your base sheet:

1. **Add up your measurements to determine the overall length and width of your property.**

   Total all the measurements in each direction: the length of the property lines if you measured them or the sum of the width of the house plus the spaces between the house and the boundaries.

2. **Using the architect's scale, transfer the overall dimensions to your paper, arranging the lot so that it fits comfortably on the paper.**

First lay out the shape of the lot so that it's reasonably centered on the page. Start with one corner and measure out in both directions to the farthest extent of the property boundaries. Make adjustments as needed to provide adequate margins around the drawing.

When drawing the lot, it's great if you can use an existing survey or house plot plan that you have on hand from when the house was built or remodeled. Then you can simply trace this onto your base sheet and you're done with this step. If it's not drawn at the right scale, take it to a blueprint or copy shop and have them use their fancy equipment to blow it up to the scale you need.

When transferring, choose the scale that produces the largest drawing possible so you have room to include all the details without crowding. For an ordinary-size suburban lot, usually a scale of $1/4$ inch to 1 foot is fine. In other words, each $1/4$ inch on paper represents 1 foot in the real world. If the lot is too big to fit comfortably on the paper at that scale, go to $1/8$ inch to 1 foot, which cuts your drawing size in half.

Don't forget to locate north and mark it with an arrow on your base sheet; this tells you where the sun goes every day, which is essential to designing plantings and virtually every other sustainable landscape feature so that it's all well-adapted to the sun and shade patterns on your property.

3. **Using your property line and triangulation measurements, accurately locate and place the major features on your drafting paper.**

   Here's how to place the triangulations, which you measure in the preceding section:

   1. **Set a compass to one of the distances you measured.**

      Place the needle point of the compass on the zero mark of the architect's scale and then adjust the compass so that the drawing end lines up with the distance you want to strike off on the paper (this matches the measurement you took outside in the real world).

   2. **Draw an arc on your paper.**

      Place the needle of the compass on the paper at the point where you took the measurement in the field, such as at the corner of your house. Being careful not to adjust the compass, draw an arc on the paper.

   3. **Repeat the first two steps for your other triangulation measurement and mark where the two arcs cross.**

      Where the arcs meet is the point you measured. Make a pencil mark there and identify it as "oak tree" or whatever.

Accuracy is important because if, for instance, the oak tree is a couple feet away from where you show it on the plans, whatever you put in that area will have to be changed later when you start your construction work. Inaccuracies can also affect how many materials you order and the overall cost of the job.

4. **Gradually add in the little details, such as doors, windows, gates, and so on.**

   Make little tick marks for each measurement; you can go back later and draw them in more detail so that your finished drawing is clear and readable.

   Include *setback lines* (internal boundaries on your property that determine where you can and can't put certain kinds of improvements, such as overhead structures that aren't allowed to be right next to a property line), easements, overhead and underground utilities, and any other critical elements. Show the tops and *toes* (a fancy word for bottoms) of any slopes. Mark drainage patterns with arrows pointing to the downhill flow of water.

5. **Turn your rough layout into a tidy finished base sheet.**

   Trace over the base sheet onto another sheet of paper (drafting paper is semi-transparent). Use Figure 6-3 as a base sheet model. You use this base sheet as a template for the actual plans: concept plan, planting plan, irrigation plan, and so on.

If drawing a base sheet is a bit much for you, you do have other options. You can hire a surveyor or landscape architect to create your base sheet. You may also look into landscape design software (check out www.landscaping-software-review.toptenreviews.com for software recommendations). You'll still have to go through all the measuring and plotting, though, so those programs don't really keep you from having to do that work.

Creating a concept plan

After you measure your site, use a bubble diagram and your best thinking to explore the options, and create a base sheet (see the preceding section), you're ready to create a concept plan like the one in Figure 6-4.

Creating a concept plan for any major changes you're planning is a good idea because it makes you think about the details of what you're doing. A *concept plan* is a way of showing the general elements that make up your project, such as patios, walks, trees, and water features. You don't know precisely what material the patios and walks will be made of or what kind of trees you'll use, but at this stage, you'll understand the placement, size, and purpose of each element of the finished landscape.

Creating a concept plan is an important stage of the design process because you make overall decisions about how the landscape will look and function.

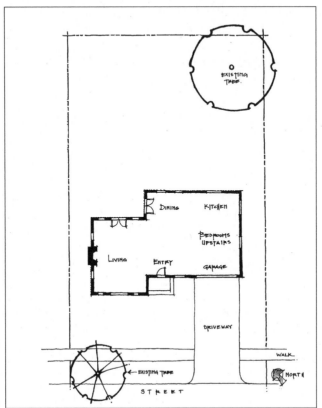

Figure 6-3:
A base
sheet.

The details that you fill in later will be built on the strong foundation you create at the concept plan stage.

When creating a concept plan, ask yourself questions like the following:

- How wide will the front walk be?
- Where will the raised veggie beds be located?
- Is there really space for a small patio outside the master bedroom?
- Will the hardscape be rectilinear, curvilinear, angular, or free-form?

These questions aren't specific to your situation, but they give you an idea of the types of questions to ask. You need to ask such questions to flush out hidden problems, to develop the overall function of the elements of the project, and to make sure everything that needs to be there is present and in the proper place.

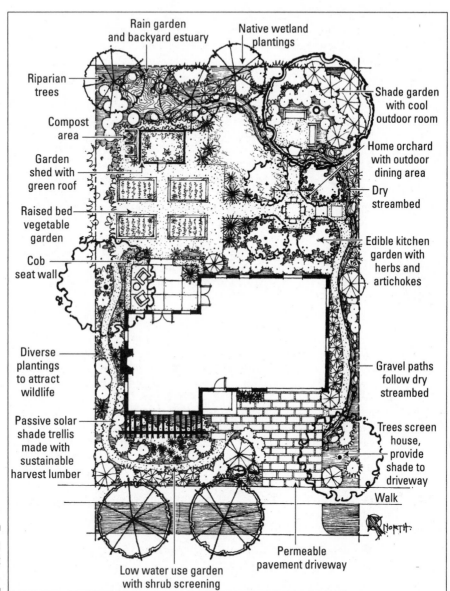

Rain garden
and backyard estuary

Native wetland
plantings

Riparian
trees

Shade garden
with cool
outdoor room

Compost
area

Home orchard
with outdoor
dining area

Garden
shed with
green roof

Dry
streambed

Raised bed
vegetable
garden

Edible kitchen
garden with
herbs and
artichokes

Cob
seat wall

Diverse
plantings
to attract
wildlife

Gravel paths
follow dry
streambed

Passive solar
shade trellis
made with
sustainable
harvest lumber

Trees screen
house,
provide
shade to
driveway

Walk

Figure 6-4:
A concept
plan.

Low water use garden
with shrub screening

Permeable
pavement driveway

Fine-tuning the site: Space planning

One aspect of planning at this conceptual stage is making sure everything fits. Have you ever rearranged your living room furniture and found that it fit better in one arrangement than it did in another? In addition to injuring your back, you were doing *space planning* — the art and science of making everything go together in a way that not only fits but also looks like it really belongs there and meets your needs.

From a sustainability perspective, the better things work, the fewer resources you'll use to create and maintain them. Space planning can highlight areas where you can downsize lawns or reshape flower beds to make maintenance easier, for instance.

Space planning is a process where a scale drawing really pays off. Place a sheet of clean tracing paper over the base sheet that you create in the earlier section "Using your measurements to create a base sheet." Begin drawing in the elements of your design as precisely as you can. For instance, you may have decided that your patio will be 12 x 18 feet, will be rectilinear and parallel with the house, and will be located in the far left corner of the back yard. Draw that on the tracing paper. Continue drawing in paths, turf or meadow areas, raised beds, planter beds and borders, major trees and shrubs, and whatever else is on your bubble diagram and in your mind (see the earlier section "Creating a bubble diagram"). At this stage, don't worry about what materials or plants you'll use in your landscape.

Cut out pieces of paper to scale for major features and physically move them around on the base sheet so you can see how the different placements will work.

You can do space planning electronically, too, using one of the many landscape design programs that help you visualize your future landscape. These programs can even go into 3-D mode and zoom around your property, showing you how the completed project will look from different angles. Check out www.landscaping-software-review.toptenreviews.com for software recommendations.

As you're adding features, be prepared to make a lot of changes. Work in pencil at first, and try different approaches. Head outside to check your ideas often. Don't get discouraged when your favorite idea doesn't work the way you dreamed it would. Just keep trying things until it all seems to lock into place.

Color in your final concept plan to better separate elements and to get a better idea of how the landscape may really look.

Pondering your plant and materials palettes

The next step in developing your concept plan is to begin to explore what materials are available for you to use. You make final decisions later in the process when you have a clearer picture of precisely how things will go together, but now is when you see what's out there. Think of it as window-shopping. (In fact, you get to go window-shopping for real at this point.)

Visit building materials suppliers, nurseries, and other vendors. And consider scouring the waste stream by checking out Craigslist (www.craigslist.com), eBay (www.ebay.com), and other sources of used stuff. Check your local dumpsters and garage sales, too. Oh, and don't forget to inventory what you already have on site, including soil, boulders, or even the opportunity to grow something like bamboo to be used in your construction projects. That's about as sustainable as it gets.

Start off with the plants and develop a *plant palette,* a list of candidate plants to fill the roles you've already defined in your concept plan. For example, you may have decided to plant a 20-foot-tall deciduous tree with a broad canopy to shade the driveway. The tree's shade will keep your car cool and reduce the evaporative losses from the fuel tank. Now you're thinking sustainably!

If you don't know what types of plants thrive in your area, do some research. Chapters 16, 17, and 18 provide advice on selecting plants, trees, and shrubs that are appropriate for your climate and yard space. Gardening books and the Internet can help you become familiar with your plant choices as well. Also, if you have the time, visit real plants in real places — see how they behave, how big they get, how they smell, and everything else about them.

Now develop a menu of paving materials, lighting fixtures, furniture, and any other materials you think you may need for your project. This list serves as your *materials palette.* See Chapters 2, 12, and 13 for details on choosing sustainable materials.

Narrowing down the possibilities

After you create your concept plan and plant and materials palettes, you may feel overwhelmed by the possibilities. Congratulations! This is a sign that you've done a great job of gathering information. It's time to shift gears and begin eliminating the landscape features that don't really fit. You've developed an extensive list of possibilities, and you'll never be able to use them all. This narrowing process may seem intimidating, but don't worry. Here's how to whittle your way to a cohesive set of appropriate materials and wise choices:

- ✔ **Screen your choices for availability.** Check to be sure your preferred materials are available, preferably from local sources. Drop anything that's difficult to find from your materials and plant palettes.

- ✔ **Check each item for sustainability.** Be sure that the materials and plants you choose meet reasonable sustainability standards. Check all your materials, plants, and other inputs for their impacts on the environment (both on your property and off-site as well).

- ✔ **Be sure your choices will work the way you want them to.** Ask yourself a few questions: Will those plants really thrive in my yard? Will the patio materials stand up to my cold winters? Will that drip system work with my sandy soils?

- ✔ **Check costs.** Eliminate anything that will take the project over budget. You did create a budget before you started, didn't you? See Chapters 1 and 3 for details.

✔ **Make sure the feature fits style you already have.** A formal fountain looks great with a traditional style house, but I doubt you'll be happy if you pair one with Japanese architecture. Cut anything that doesn't match the style of existing features.

✔ **Dump what you don't like.** Your personal preferences count here, too. Drop stuff that you haven't really warmed up to.

If you heeded my advice from the preceding list, you probably narrowed your choices down pretty well. Do you have a compatible set of elements? If so, you're well on your way to a lovely, coherent design. If you're still feeling uneasy, you may want to get an expert opinion by running your design past a professional landscape architect.

Polishing off the concept plan

By now you should be pretty clear about what elements will go into your new landscape and how they'll be arranged. You can modify things on the fly at any point in the process — even during construction — but the more you figure out now, the easier the rest of the job will be.

Consider drawing a fresh version of your concept plan. By doing so, you give yourself an opportunity to rethink everything and fine tune your layout. Plus you'll have a new, clean copy that's easier to read.

Generally speaking, for a residential job, you don't need to develop *working drawings,* which show every last detail in the exact form it will be in after it's built. However, under certain circumstances, developing an exact landscape plan is best. You may need a landscape architect for this. Find out about working drawings in the next section.

Planning for Particular Needs

If you're required to submit formal landscape plans (also known as *working drawings*) to the city or other agencies in order to get a building permit, if you're planning to put your project out to contractors to bid, or if you just want to take the design process to the next level of detail for your own use, the following sections provide a summary of what's involved.

Working drawings include tons more detail than a concept plan, and they may even run to several pages, with separate pages for planting, grading and drainage, irrigation, hardscape, and other aspects of the job. Considering the intricacies involved, a full set of working drawings suitable for submitting to agencies or contractors is really a job for a landscape architect. But if you're ambitious, you can tackle a simplified version. Just be sure to include adequate detail to spell out exactly what's to be done. The following sections provide some example plans.

Grading and drainage plans

A *grading and drainage plan* shows where the water goes. A simplified plan shows where to put *swales* (long, shallow ditches) and drainage systems to move, capture, and disburse the water on your property (see Chapter 7 for examples of some water-harvesting systems). At the other end of the spectrum is a full-blown engineering plan that's highly detailed and that will be of considerable use to your contractor should you choose to hire one.

A good contractor often can get the grading right without a drawn plan. Invest in a plan if you need this level of detail or if an agency requires it; otherwise, just be sure you're in the hands of experienced professionals if your drainage situation is in any way tricky. See Part III of this book for complete information on sustainable grading and drainage.

Planting plans

A *planting plan* is simple. After you know exactly which plants you want to use (check out Chapters 16, 17, and 18 for ideas), you draw them to scale.

The planting plan accomplishes three things. First, it helps you to see how many plants you'll need to purchase. Second, it helps you visualize the final planting design. And third, it becomes a reference that you can use at planting time to remember exactly what you had in mind. Oh, and if you're getting a permit for your landscaping, you need a planting plan to submit to the agency.

To draw a planting plan, get out a piece of tissue paper, place it over your base sheet, and draw a final planting plan like the one shown in Figure 6-5. (If you haven't created a base sheet, check out the earlier section "Using your measurements to create a base sheet.") Use a circle template or a compass to draw each plant to scale at its mature size.

For example, say you want to put three *Philadelphus* 'Buckley's Quill' in the back corner of the backyard. Your gardening book says they grow to 5 feet tall and 5 feet wide. If you're working at a 1/4-inch scale, 5 feet in diameter would equal 5 quarters on your scale, which is 1 1/4 inches. Choose that size opening on the circle template, place it where the plants will go, and pencil in the three circles. Repeat for all the plants you'll be using, layering as necessary for low-growing plants that are placed under taller ones.

With a little practice and a bit of creativity, you can turn these circles into lovely symbols like the ones in Figure 6-5. Or you can just leave them plain, with labels showing the name of the plant and the quantity in that grouping.

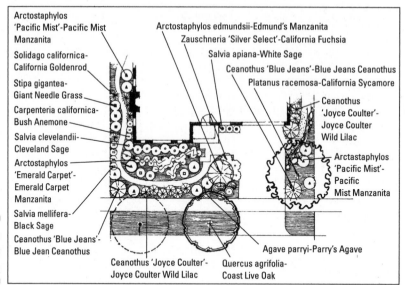

Figure 6-5:
Planting
plan.

Arctostaphylos 'Pacific Mist'-Pacific Mist Manzanita

Solidago californica-California Goldenrod

Stipa gigantea-Giant Needle Grass

Carpenteria californica-Bush Anemone

Salvia clevelandii-Cleveland Sage

Arctostaphylos 'Emerald Carpet'-Emerald Carpet Manzanita

Salvia mellifera-Black Sage

Ceanothus 'Blue Jeans'-Blue Jean Ceanothus

Ceanothus 'Joyce Coulter'-Joyce Coulter Wild Lilac

Arctostaphylos edmundsii-Edmund's Manzanita
Zauschneria 'Silver Select'-California Fuchsia
Salvia apiana-White Sage
Ceanothus 'Blue Jeans'-Blue Jeans Ceanothus
Platanus racemosa-California Sycamore

Ceanothus 'Joyce Coulter'-Joyce Coulter Wild Lilac

Arctastaphylos 'Pacific Mist'-Pacific Mist Manzanita

Agave parryi-Parry's Agave

Quercus agrifolia-Coast Live Oak

Irrigation plans

The most sustainable irrigation approach of all is a water-harvesting system. You don't really need to draw plans for that part of the project. However, you do need to understand how it all works and how to create a system on your property. I cover that thoroughly in Chapter 8.

If you decide to install a permanent irrigation system, there are a couple of ways to determine how it all goes together. For most small systems, an understanding of basic irrigation design principles and a little time out in the yard can be adequate. If your system is large or complex, or if you'll be hiring someone to install it, you may want to draw a detailed irrigation plan or hire a pro to do it for you.

I don't have room in this book to coach you through a short course in irrigation design, but fortunately there's an alternative. All the major irrigation manufacturers have handy design and installation tutorials on their Web sites, and some of them can even create a design for you at a very modest cost. How cool is that? So if you were worried you'd have to become an instant engineer, chill. But just to get your bearings, look at Figure 6-6, which shows you what a finished irrigation plan looks like.

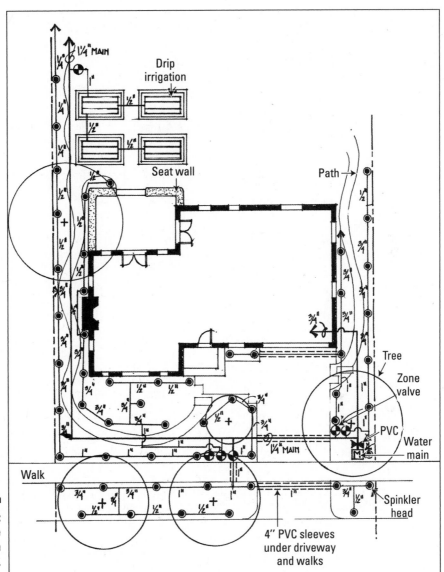

Figure 6-6:
An example
irrigation
plan.

Getting Down to the Nitty-Gritty with Construction Details

Construction detail drawings are images of the guts of a piece of work, laid out like an X-ray so you can see exactly what to do. Nearly anything from tree staking to electric valves to patios can be the subject of construction details. See Figure 6-7 for two examples.

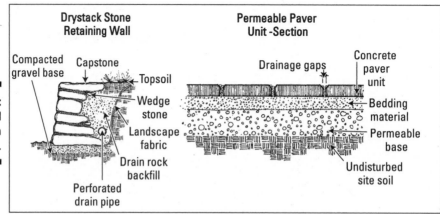

Figure 6-7: Typical construction detail.

Details are partnered with *specifications,* which are written instructions that cover what can't be drawn, such as how soon to water plants after installation, the type of tile to be used on the patio, how much fertilizer to use on the plants, and so forth.

As with formal plan drawings, you don't need formally drawn details and carefully written specifications unless you need them for permitting reasons or if you'll be putting the project out to bid. This is really the work of the landscape architect, and you may want to hire one if you need this level of detail. But it's good to know how all this works if you're in a position to need it.

As with everything in landscaping, the little things matter. How much rebar goes into a concrete footing influences how strong it is. The kind of wood in a deck helps determine its longevity. Details are everything; they drive the outcome of the project in so many ways. They determine how a project looks, how safe it is, and how durable and sustainable it is.

Landscaping For Dummies, by Phillip Giroux, Bob Beckstrom, Lance Wallheim, and the Editors of the National Gardening Association (Wiley), has basic details for many common construction projects, such as steps, walls, fences, and others. You can also find details in many homeowner-oriented how-to books on landscaping. These books can give you an idea of how to build common landscape structures.

When using other books, remember to substitute sustainable materials and practices using the information in this book.

For details of truly sustainable landscape construction projects, look for books on specific topics such as cob building, water harvesting, or other subjects. There's plenty to pick from these days. *Green Building & Remodeling For Dummies,* by Eric Corey Freed (Wiley), is a great place to start. And don't forget the Internet, which is crawling with information on how to build sustainable landscape features. Even though there's no one-stop source of sustainable landscaping help, you can search on a particular subject, such as "cob walls" or "rain gardens" and get lots of good information.

Remaining within the Law: Considering Legal Issues

The long arm of the law doesn't reach as far into landscaping as is does into other aspects of modern life. But you certainly need to consider specific legal issues when planning your sustainable landscape. Here are a few of the most important issues to keep in mind:

- ✔ **Architectural review boards:** A major landscaping project may require community approval to be sure its appearance is consistent with neighboring features. Check with your community's building or zoning department for specifics.

- ✔ **Building permits:** Permit requirements vary from place to place, of course. But generally speaking, you need a building permit — and perhaps other approvals — to do any kind of major construction, such as working on decks, retaining walls, fences, electrical work (other than low-voltage lighting), certain portions of your irrigation system, and most anything else that affects public safety. In most areas, you don't need a building permit to do planting, minor grading, or other horticulturally oriented projects.

  The best strategy is to call your city building department and ask which permits are required.

- ✔ **Covenants, conditions, and restrictions (CC&Rs):** These are the legal constraints describing what you may and may not do on your property. Check your title documents to see how CC&Rs work on your property.

- ✔ **Easements:** An *easement* is a legal right of others to enter or work on your property. For instance, a utility company, a government entity, or another public interest may have access to your property to run power lines, grant beach access, or work on a sewer main. Construction in these areas may be restricted if it would get in the way of that access. You may find easements in your community as well. The introduction of tall trees and other view-blocking features may be controlled on these pieces of land. Start by checking the title documents to your property and follow up with a call to the county records office and possibly the utility companies that serve your area.

✔ **Legal liability:** Take care not to create trip hazards, slippery surfaces, and other nuisances for which you could be sued if someone hurts himself. Similarly, don't plant poisonous, treacherously thorny, or highly fire-prone plants.

✔ **Neighbors:** Many bitter conflicts over landscaping have destroyed relationships between neighbors. To avoid such a situation, inform your neighbors about your project and apologize in advance for the noise and hubbub that will accompany it. Respect your neighbors' rights to the preservation of views, privacy, and sunshine. In other words, don't plant invasive plants or tall trees that will affect the environment of others without getting permission first. Similarly, don't direct storm water onto neighboring property (that's illegal) and don't destabilize soil on slopes.

If you're part of a homeowner's association or other neighborhood group, your project may have to be approved by that group. However, even if you have a great deal of freedom to do what you want in your community, it often isn't good politics to exercise that freedom to its fullest extent.

Work *with* your neighbors to create a sustainable neighborhood. Coordinate food production, develop local water-harvesting systems that span property boundaries, and cooperate on safety issues, such fire protection. Why let sustainability stop at your property lines? Get the whole community involved!

✔ **Property lines:** Have all property lines surveyed before doing any construction. That way you'll be sure that you aren't encroaching on your neighbor's property. Otherwise, you may be faced with costly repairs or legal bills. Call a licensed land surveyor for help.

✔ **Zoning and setbacks:** Nearly every community has zoning restrictions that govern how you can and can't use your property. This restriction controls the presence of livestock, the use of land for commercial purposes, and many other things. *Setbacks* are invisible, internal boundaries within your property in which your freedom to build certain types of structures is limited. For example, you probably aren't allowed to build a tall arbor right on your property line where it could affect neighbors. Similarly, many communities restrict the height of fences in the front yard. Regulations vary from community to community, so check with the zoning department at city hall.

Part III

Water, Water, Everywhere: Water-Conserving Irrigation and Drainage

The 5th Wave   By Rich Tennant

"It's my husband's idea of a drip irrigation system."

In this part . . .

Unless you live in a very wet climate, you probably need to water your landscaping. Yes, even sustainable plantings need some irrigation now and then. Landscape water use has a huge effect on the environment, especially in arid zones. But it doesn't have to be that way.

In this part, you see how to minimize your need for imported water by harvesting the rain that falls on your property and allowing it to soak into the land or by storing it for use during the dry season. You also see how to design, build, and maintain an efficient irrigation system that makes the most of the water you do buy, with minimum waste. You even discover fancy gadgets, such as controllers, that manage water from outer space — amazing but true. Finally, you find out about some simple ways to manage your watering, with or without a fancy irrigation system. That way you apply only the water the landscape really needs.

Chapter 7

Surveying Your Watering Options

*T*he science of sustainable landscaping isn't a closed book. We're still learning, and some problems are harder to solve than others. Irrigation is a tough one, because unless you live in a wet climate or want to carry water up from the river in your hat, you may have to depend on some kind of technology. Even sustainable landscapes need some supplemental irrigation, if only to get plants established. Most plants, even native ones, perform better with optimal watering, and if nature doesn't provide it, it's your job to take up the slack.

As always, the first step is to build a landscape that follows the rules of nature. Choose low water–use plants where possible so that irrigation becomes a minor task. Use mulch to help conserve water. Make your garden more like a wild system, and you won't need much water.

Second, develop your land so that it holds as much rainwater as possible. Water harvesting is the most sustainable way to get water to your plants with a minimum of consumption and fuss. This chapter gets you up to speed on these systems.

Finally, if you have to purchase and distribute municipal water, I show you how to do it as efficiently as possible. You have to weigh the benefits and drawbacks to decide whether a conventional high-tech plastic irrigation system is right for your sustainable landscape — and, if so, what kind.

This chapter introduces watering systems and and helps you weigh your options. When you're ready to get your hands dirty (or wet), check out Chapter 8 for info on harvesting water and installing irrigation systems.

Relying on Mother Nature: The Fully Adapted Landscape

The most sustainable option is the landscape that's so well adapted to your conditions that it requires no irrigation system at all. The fully sustainable landscape, like wild natural systems, thrives on natural rainfall only. A completely sustainable landscape certainly is possible anywhere on this planet. Lovely native plants grow pretty much everywhere, and nobody waters wilderness; rainfall is sufficient for the most beautiful places on earth. Check out Chapter 9 and Part V for advice on creating a no-water native landscape.

Even native landscapes require supplemental irrigation to get them established. This may be as simple as hand-watering if there aren't too many plants involved and you're careful to apply enough water to irrigate the entire root zone. For larger plantings, consider a temporary drip system with an emitter or two at each plant (see "Drip irrigation: A smarter way to water"). You can use this temporary system during the first year or two and then remove it. Be sure to save it to use another time or pass it along to others.

Some people opt for a permanent irrigation system in case of drought — even native plants suffer when faced with inadequate rainfall. It's your choice, but remember that an irrigation system comes with unavoidable environmental impacts (see "Deciding Whether to Use a Permanent Irrigation System"). If you can get by without one, so much the better.

Saving Your Own Rainwater: Harvested Water Systems

One of the key strategies in a sustainable landscape is making use of what you have to work with on the site. Irrigation is no exception. Harvesting the rainwater that falls onto your land is the primary means of ensuring that your plantings have the water they need. Using water from the sky has several benefits: It's relatively pure, it picks up nitrogen from the atmosphere on the way down, and it's free. Instead of developing a drainage system that efficiently throws all the rain away, as most landscapes do (see Figure 7-1), develop your landscape to conserve that water.

In the following sections, I discuss several water-harvesting methods: non-storage, storage, and graywater. Visit Chapter 8 for information on developing your own harvesting system.

Figure 7-1:
A landscape that allows its valuable water resources to drain away.

Nonstorage systems

The conventional landscape is often flat or mounded in shape, which causes it to spill water rather than absorb it. A water-harvesting landscape is concave (bowl-shaped), with plenty of low points to hold valuable rainwater on the site and keep it out of the streets, where it can cause flooding and wash pollution into nearby bodies of water. This type of landscape is well suited to a nonstorage water-harvesting system. *Nonstorage water harvesting* involves making your landscape as absorbent as possible so that water soaks into the ground instead of running off. Figure 7-2 shows a system that uses gutters and downspouts to direct water toward plants and a concave terrain that holds water naturally.

Figure 7-2:
A concave landscape works like a sponge to catch and hold water.

A nonstorage system is the cheapest and easiest way to make use of rainfall, and therefore it should be your first choice if you're looking to use rainwater without investing in a costly cistern or other storage system. You may even be able to develop a *zero-runoff landscape,* which sheds water only during the biggest storms.

A nonstorage water-harvesting landscape can include the following features:

✓ **Swales, dry streambeds, and bioswales:** A *swale* is a shallow ditch with gently sloping sides that runs very gradually downhill in the direction in which you want water to flow. It allows rainwater to soak in as it goes. You can incorporate rounded boulders to create a naturalistic *dry streambed* or plan the swale so that the plants and soil purify the runoff water using natural biological processes (this is called a *bioswale;* see Figure 7-3).

✓ **Percolation chamber:** Underneath your swale or at any appropriate, stable low point on your property, you can dig a percolation chamber (see Figure 7-4). Water drops into the chamber and continues to percolate down into the soil, recharging the groundwater. The water goes below the roots of most plants but stays out of the street — and out of trouble.

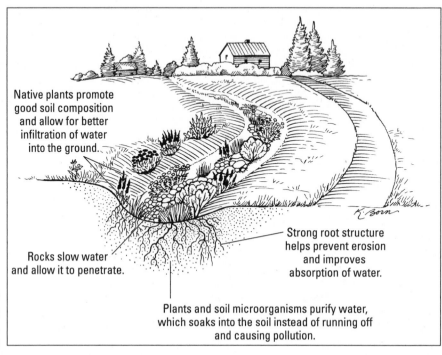

Native plants promote good soil composition and allow for better infiltration of water into the ground.

Rocks slow water and allow it to penetrate.

Strong root structure helps prevent erosion and improves absorption of water.

Figure 7-3: A bioswale.

Plants and soil microorganisms purify water, which soaks into the soil instead of running off and causing pollution.

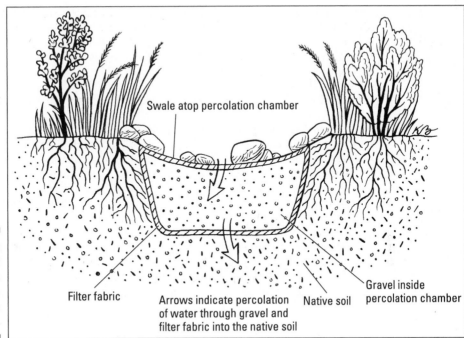

Swale atop percolation chamber

Filter fabric

Arrows indicate percolation of water through gravel and filter fabric into the native soil

Native soil

Gravel inside percolation chamber

Figure 7-4:
A typical swale atop a percolation chamber.

Even when water isn't running, dry streambeds and bioswales in particular are lovely additions to any landscape. But doing water harvesting the wrong way involves risks, so be sure to read more about these systems in Chapter 8.

Storage systems

Storing harvested water for use during dry periods is a sustainable way to water. Storage systems capture rainwater from the roof and pipe it to a nearby tank; when it's needed, the water is pumped out of the tank into an irrigation system. (Better yet, you can allow gravity to do the job, which eliminates electricity use and a layer of technology.)

The advantage of storing rainwater is that you can use it during the dry season, when the plants need it most. Because of the cost of the tank and related equipment, the storage method is costlier than the nonstorage method in the preceding section. Water storage isn't for everyone. Choose to store water if you can afford to, if you have the space for a tank, and if you're willing to do a bit of maintenance to keep the system operating (see Chapter 10).

The storage method centers on a *cistern,* an aboveground or underground tank made of brick, concrete, or plastic (see Figure 7-5). A cistern is connected to the roof drains of the house and other buildings. It incorporates screens to keep the vermin out, an overflow line for excess water, and sometimes a *first-flush system* to divert the dirty water from the first rains away from the cistern. Water is then gravity fed or pumped into a drip or other distribution system.

You can store a bit of rainwater in salvaged 55-gallon drums placed beneath your downspouts, of course, but that quantity of water doesn't go very far when you're irrigating an entire landscape. Similarly, you can store water in open ponds, an old swimming pool, or your kid's red wagon — but shoot, I'm talking about a real system here, one that will serve your needs and last a long time.

I strongly recommend that you do a lot of research on cisterns before you jump in (figuratively, I mean). Any number of things can contaminate stored water, so the type of cistern system I describe in this section is *not* meant to supply water for personal use such as drinking, cooking, and bathing; the water is intended for the landscape only. Other wicked little hazards include people drowning because the lid wasn't locked, poorly made or incorrectly installed tanks collapsing, and flooding due to tank or component failure.

Graywater systems

Graywater is the wastewater from washing machines, showers, and sinks (not toilets). You can use graywater to irrigate ornamental plants and fruit trees as long as (for health reasons) the water doesn't come to the surface of the ground.

Graywater systems range from simple gravity-fed pipelines that drain into porous soak zones at the base of plants to complex high-tech contraptions. Figure 7-6 gives you an idea of how a simple graywater system works.

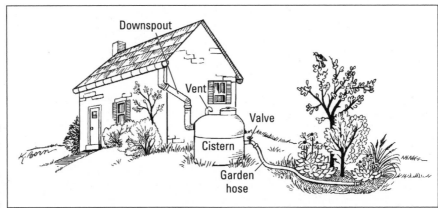

Figure 7-5:
A basic cistern system.

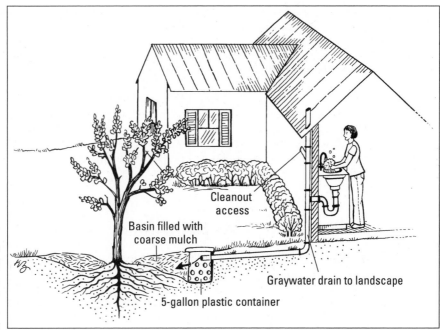

Figure 7-6:
A basic graywater system.

Cleanout access

Basin filled with coarse mulch

Graywater drain to landscape

5-gallon plastic container

Develop a graywater system if you have plants that can use frequent watering and if your household generates enough graywater to have an impact on your water use. Also be sure your house plumbing is suited to the task of sending graywater into the garden. See Chapter 8 for details.

Considering Other Sustainable Ways to Water

You don't necessarily need to invest in a permanent irrigation system. Consider two classic methods: watering with a hose and using portable sprinklers. Relying on bare-bones watering technology has many benefits: it's simple, it's cheap, it has a much lower environmental impact than a full-blown irrigation system, and it's adequate for a small or low water–use landscape. (For details on when and how to water, turn to Chapter 9.)

Watering by hand

A 1999 survey conducted by the American Water Works Association (AWWA) found that hand watering uses 33 percent less water than a sprinkler system.

When properly done, hand watering can be very efficient — but it also has some downsides. For one, you're applying the water so fast that you risk runoff in heavy soils or on slopes. Also, if you have both a big property and a life, hand watering with a hose just isn't an option — you may find it tough to stand there long enough to get the water to really soak in.

If you're going to stand at the end of a hose, you may want to invest in a fancy nozzle. My favorite nozzles are the pistol types with a wheel that you can use to select the watering pattern: stream, shower, mist, flood, deluge, and so on. If you want to save money but still apply water fast, skip the fancy nozzle and simply block part of the open end of the hose with your thumb. Works like a charm.

Using portable sprinklers

Select portable sprinklers for even coverage. I like oscillating sprinklers because they apply water slowly but in larger streams that don't blow away easily. Sprinklers with old-fashioned impact-type heads *(tssh-tssh-tssh-tik-tik-tik-tik-tik)* are fun to watch and easy to adjust for distance of throw. I've never tried the sprinklers that walk around the yard on their own; they kind of scare me.

If you set out portable sprinklers, move them around periodically to get good coverage, and time the application so you don't waste water. Check out Chapter 9 for more info about watering wisely.

Deciding Whether to Use a Permanent Irrigation System

If you find yourself seduced by the charms of a permanent irrigation system, don't feel bad. Although there's clearly a negative impact to using that much plastic and other materials, and despite the decidedly unnatural presence of a life support system of this kind, irrigation systems do a good job of keeping your plantings well-watered and vigorous.

In fact, there are plenty of times when an irrigation system is the only reasonable option. If you live in a climate with long dry spells during the growing season, or if your property is large, nothing will keep things going quite like a drip or sprinkler system. The same is true if your soils are very sandy and require frequent watering or if they're heavy clay that's slow to absorb water, making hand watering problematic.

Considering the pros of irrigation systems

When well designed and properly used, an irrigation system works on behalf of the environment and offers the following benefits:

- ✔ **Marginal land brought into cultivation:** Turning a barren corner of your property into a green space that's generating oxygen, sequestering carbon dioxide, providing habitat for wild things, or growing food for you is a wonderful thing to accomplish. Even if the change takes a little supplemental water and an irrigation system, the situation is better than the way things were.

- ✔ **Time savings:** Use the time you would've spent watering to work on behalf of endangered species or some other cause.

- ✔ **Health of the plants:** Hand-watering methods often leave a lot to be desired in terms of coverage and penetration. You may think that you've watered adequately, only to find dry soil an inch below ground. An irrigation system can solve this problem.

- ✔ **Potential efficiency:** Because you can operate an irrigation system to virtually eliminate runoff, it can deliver water with little or no waste.

- ✔ **Potential water conservation:** Using water efficiently means using less of it. Delivering water to the plants (and only to the plants) in the exact quantities required uses the least water possible.

- ✔ **Watershed protection:** Runoff of landscape water and leaching of nutrients and garden chemicals can damage streams, rivers, lakes, and oceans. An irrigation system keeps water on site, where it belongs.

Weighing the cons of irrigation systems

Lifetime water savings and overall garden health may not adequately offset the materials and energy consumed by an irrigation system. No one really knows for sure. Here are some potential negative environmental effects to consider:

- ✔ **Plastics use:** Nearly all plastics are made from fossil fuels, which are nonrenewable, dwindling, and extracted from the earth in ways that cause massive environmental and social damage. Until someone figures out how to make durable plastic out of soybeans or old coffee grounds, we're stuck with the petroleum-based kind.

- ✔ **PVC pipe:** PVC pipe is arguably the very worst aspect of an irrigation system. The plastic used to make the rigid pipe and fittings, as well as much of the other hardware in an irrigation system, is an environmental nightmare for several reasons: It's made from petroleum; its manufacture causes the release of massive amounts of *dioxin,* one of the most toxic manmade materials in existence; making the chlorine that goes into PVC requires a lot of energy (in fact, it requires an amount equivalent to that produced by eight nuclear power plants); the solvents used to fasten the pipe and fittings are hazardous to installers; and currently, the pipe isn't recyclable.

Alternatives to PVC pipe are available. *Drip tubing* is made of polyethylene, which also comes from petroleum but is nontoxic, isn't cemented together, and is at least theoretically recyclable. A pipe called *cross-linked polyethylene* works for pressure lines, eliminating PVC almost entirely. Cross-linked polyethylene has been used in Europe for quite a while now; it's reliable and easy to work with.

✔ **Possible overwatering:** Overwatering kills plants. You can prevent overwatering easily enough by using some simple management tips (see Chapter 9). But remember that an irrigation system can be an efficient plant-murdering device.

✔ **Potential waste of water:** A perfect irrigation system can still waste tons of water if it's managed poorly. The American Water Works Association found that in-ground sprinkler systems use 35 percent more water and that drip systems use 16 percent more than properties without a system. This difference isn't due to deficiencies in the systems themselves but in the ways they're managed. The worst offenders can be automatic controllers, which I cover at the end of this chapter.

Choosing a Permanent Irrigation System

After you've decided to invest in a permanent irrigation system, you have to decide what kind to get. Unfortunately, irrigation systems don't come in a nice tidy box with all the parts and instructions and special tools, as if you were buying a piece of furniture. Instead, you have to design the system to fit your particular situation, and then you have to build it from hundreds of parts gathered up from bins at the irrigation supply store. It's challenging, but anyone can do it. Your first step is to figure out where you'll be using sprinklers and where a drip system would be a better choice. In the following sections, I give you the ins and outs of the different approaches.

Sprinkler systems: Spritzing water everywhere

Sprinklers are generally more wasteful than drip systems (which I cover in the next section) because they apply water in less efficient ways. However, they still have a place in the sustainable landscape. Overhead sprinkler systems are designed primarily for watering lawns, which need even, shallow water delivery. They're also used for ground covers, flower beds, and similar large areas of relatively shallow-rooted plants. (***Note:*** A permanent sprinkler system is buried in the ground. The term *overhead* refers to the fact that sprinklers spray water into the air rather than applying it directly to the soil, as a drip system does.)

Sprinkling by design

A typical permanent sprinkler system consists of heads that either pop up from the ground or are fixed on plastic risers. The heads are connected by an underground network of pipe and are controlled by a manual or electric valve. When the system is in operation, arcs of water squirt out of each head, spraying the irrigated area from several directions for better coverage.

Benefits and drawbacks

The following are some advantages of permanent overhead sprinklers:

- ✔ Water application is visible (and quite attractive to watch).
- ✔ Foliage gets washed off during irrigation.
- ✔ You can use the system to wash fertilizer into the soil.

Here are some disadvantages of permanent overhead sprinklers:

- ✔ They're susceptible to wind drift, runoff, evaporative loss, and misting, all of which waste water.
- ✔ Coverage is about 70 percent accurate at best, resulting in overwatering to compensate for dry spots, which wastes water.
- ✔ Sidewalks, driveways, houses, cars, slow-moving pedestrians, and domestic animals often get watered too. They seldom benefit.
- ✔ Runoff wastes water and can make pavement dangerously slippery.
- ✔ Overhead watering brings up lots of weeds.
- ✔ Impact-type heads can be noisy.
- ✔ Sprinkler heads can be trip hazards if they're installed near traffic areas.

Drip irrigation: A smarter way to water

Permanent sprinklers are being displaced more and more by drip systems, which greatly reduce water use. A *drip system* is made up of flexible polyethylene pipe, usually installed on the surface of the ground and covered by mulch, with small drip emitters that are either plugged into holes punched in the tubing or molded directly into it. (The latter type is much more durable and easier to install.)

Drip irrigation is controlled with a manual or automatic control valve the same way as an overhead sprinkler system. But it has two additions: a small filter to prevent dirt and other particulate matter from plugging the emitters and a small pressure regulator to reduce the pressure, which prevents the tubing from blowing apart. Chapter 8 provides info on designing an efficient drip system.

To drip, or not to drip: The good and the bad

Here are the advantages of a drip system:

- ✔ Direct application of water into the soil results in little or no runoff, no spray drift, and consequently no wasted water or safety problems.
- ✔ Drip systems are nearly 100 percent efficient, delivering all the water to the root zone of the plants in an even pattern throughout the area.
- ✔ Because most of the soil surface remains dry, you'll have fewer weeds.
- ✔ Most plants really love being drip-irrigated and respond with strong, healthy growth; sturdy root systems; and reduced disease problems.
- ✔ The system is invisible and silent when it's in operation.
- ✔ No trenching is required to install a drip system.
- ✔ Costs of materials and installation are comparable to (or lower than) those of a sprinkler system, and your water bill will be smaller.

These are the disadvantages of a drip system:

- ✔ Drip tubing can be damaged by careless digging, rodents, vandalism, and foot traffic.
- ✔ You can't see or hear a drip system working, so you can easily forget to turn it off if you have a manually operated system. You can set a timer to remind you, of course, or automate your system (see the section on automatic irrigation controllers later in this chapter).
- ✔ A drip system won't wash fertilizer into the soil. Instead, when you apply fertilizer, you have to water it by hand or with a portable overhead sprinkler, or you can apply it just before a good soaking rain.
- ✔ Drippers don't wash off foliage or keep mulch moist. It's a good idea to supplement drip irrigation with an occasional overhead watering, if only to keep things clean. Cleanliness isn't just for the sake of appearance; photosynthesis works better when plant leaves are free of dust and dirt.

Misconceptions about drip

If you talk to enough people in the landscaping business, sooner or later you'll run across an anti-drip zealot who jumps up and down about how bad drip systems are. No offense to these well-meaning people, but they're very wrong about drip. They usually don't understand how drip works, or they've installed systems poorly and have suffered the consequences.

Here are some of the misconceptions about drip and why they're wrong:

- **Drip doesn't last.** Poorly installed systems of any kind don't last. But drip tubing is made of polyethylene, which will endure far longer than us, our gardens, and probably civilization itself. Unless it's damaged, your drip system won't have longevity problems.

- **The emitters plug up.** If you've installed a proper filter, the tiny particles that get through it will also get through the emitters, because their openings are bigger than the openings in the filter. If you keep your filters in good shape by periodically cleaning them and replacing damaged inserts, you'll never have a problem with plugging.

  The one exception is the nasty problem called *bacterial iron slime,* which can grow in emitters and quickly plug them. See Chapter 8 for info about identifying bacterial iron slime.

- **Drip doesn't cover properly.** Use the grid system to water entire root zones. This method is the solution to the coverage problem, and it really works. I cover this concept in detail in Chapter 8.

Shying away from soaker hoses and mini-sprinklers

I've never been too fond of soaker hoses or mini-sprinklers. Here's why:

- *Soaker hoses* are long tubes made of plastic or recycled rubber tires, connected to a faucet. Allegedly, they emit water along their entire length, saturating the soil directly beneath them. I've found, however, that all the water comes out in one or two places, usually in low spots. This happens because soaker hoses provide no internal control over the distribution of the water as drip systems do so well.

- *Mini-sprinklers* are tiny sprinkler heads that are installed on drip tubing. Mini-sprinklers are fine for specialized applications, such as potted plants, some vegetable plantings, and very small areas. However, the mist they deliver is very fine, so it tends to blow away or evaporate before it reaches the soil. Also, the heads are fragile and easy to knock off kilter, resulting in uneven coverage.

Adding an automatic irrigation controller

The busy folks at the American Water Works Association found that installing an automatic controller on a manual system increases water use by 47 percent. This statistic seems to indict controllers as being very nonsustainable. But when properly used, controllers really can save lots of water.

Don't assume you *need* a controller. It isn't a requisite component of a good irrigation system, and there's no shame in having a manually operated system that you turn on and off yourself. Still, if you have heavy soils or a large property, or you're disabled, busy, or just lazy, a controller may be the solution.

Advantages and disadvantages of an automatic system

Here are some benefits of using automated irrigation controllers:

- ✔ You can cycle the controller to prevent runoff in tight soils and on slopes. For instance, you can set it to water for 5 minutes at a time, repeating the cycle every hour so the water has a chance to soak in.

- ✔ Most controllers are easy to operate. Smart controllers (which I cover later in this chapter) are a little more difficult to program, but you only have to set them up once.

- ✔ You get exact control of your watering program and don't have to depend on your memory or walk around with a stopwatch.

- ✔ A controller works even when you aren't there.

- ✔ Standard controllers require adjustment only for seasonal changes and extreme weather conditions. Smart controllers don't have to be adjusted at all.

The following are some drawbacks of using automated irrigation controllers:

- ✔ They aren't totally automatic. Unless you have a smart controller (see the next section), making them work efficiently is up to you.

- ✔ They have to be programmed carefully. If they're programmed to overwater, for example, they continue to do so for as long as you pay your water and electric bills.

- ✔ You have to make seasonal adjustments to the program to get sustainable results.

Smart versus dumb controllers — and why it matters

A traditional controller is just a timer. For example, you set it to turn on valves 1, 3, and 7 for 20 minutes each at 6 a.m. on Tuesdays and Fridays. The controller does this until you tell it differently, because it's ignorant of outside conditions. Unfortunately, conditions change constantly. And when you think about it, time has nothing to do with water need. The conditions that regulate water demand — temperature, wind, cloud cover, humidity, precipitation, and of course, the seasons — are in a constant state of flux.

Smart controllers are different. They're keyed in to actual conditions, getting data from local weather stations and translating that data into an ever-changing program that's sent to your controller by satellite. (Some smart controllers come with their own weather station that lives right in your backyard; others use "historical" weather data for your area, which isn't nearly as accurate as real-time information.)

A system with a smart controller, which some people call "watering from outer space," works really well and can reduce your water use by 20 to 50 percent or more. Smart controllers cost more than conventional ones, but you recoup that cost quickly in water savings.

To use a smart controller, you program it one time (when you install it), fine-tune it a bit during the first few weeks, and then never touch it again. The controller asks you for soil type, kinds of plants, slope, exposure (sun or shade, for example), and other facts about the environmental conditions in each zone. It uses this information to modify the incoming schedule for each zone.

Chapter 8

The Nuts and Bolts of Water Harvesting, Irrigation, and Drainage

In This Chapter

▶ Designing a rainwater-friendly landscape

▶ Irrigating the natural way with storage and nonstorage irrigation

▶ Using graywater in an irrigation system

▶ Installing permanent systems and making them more sustainable

▶ Facilitating drainage without damage

This chapter provides the basics of how water harvesting, permanent irrigation, and drainage systems are put together and what makes them tick. If you aren't the nuts-and-bolts type, you may be tempted to skip this chapter. Please consider, however, the importance of water to all landscapes, and remember your role in creating an appropriate, sustainable water system for your property. Chances are that your land was set up to drain water away as quickly as possible. In most cases, that kind of design isn't sustainable and needs to be changed.

 To get the most out of your landscaping and to be a responsible water manager, you need to understand how these systems work, even if you plan to hire someone to install one. Take the time to educate yourself to make sure that you get a truly sustainable water system.

You can find that information right here. Read on for info on setting up a water system.

Making Your Property a Home for Rainwater

In Chapter 7, I cover the basic principles of harvesting rainwater. In this section, I provide some tips on how to make it happen on your property. Some water-harvesting strategies are good do-it-yourself projects; others should be done by professionals. I alert you when you need to hire someone.

Water harvesting is a big subject. If you'd like more information, check out the *Rainwater Harvesting* series (Volumes I–II), by Brad Lancaster (Rainsource Press). Or refer to any of several books on these various strategies by Art Ludwig (www.oasisdesign.net) or Robert Kourik (www.robertkourik.com).

Follow the water

Your first task is to look hard at your site to determine where the water comes from and where you can intercept it. The main idea behind a water-harvesting system is to collect water from as many places as possible and deliver it to as many places as possible. So you need to identify collection and delivery points. Start at the high points of your land and follow the path of the water as it flows across the ground, running along low points in the terrain; also follow the water as it runs off your roof into gutters and downspouts. Perform the water-flow check while it's raining so you see what really happens, not what you think *might* happen.

Picture the possibilities

Imagine the shape of your land in light of your objective: slowing the moving water and giving it as many opportunities as possible to soak in and irrigate your proposed plantings. Also look at sources of graywater, such as washing machines and sinks; you may be able to use that water to irrigate fruit trees or other plantings. Finally, consider where you can install a cistern, either above or below ground, to capture roof runoff for use during the dry season.

It's also important to consider how and where you'll dispose of runoff beyond what your water-harvesting system can handle. In other words, if the rain falls hard and long enough, at some point it will fill your cistern and saturate your soil. All the rain that falls after that point has to be removed from the property safely. That's the job of your conventional drainage system — a topic that I cover at the end of this chapter.

Think safety

Be sure to take safety, legality, and the integrity of your land into account when developing a water-harvesting system. The following considerations can keep you out of trouble:

- ✔ If you live where rainfall is more or less continuous during part of the year, or if your soil is heavy clay or has a hardpan layer that holds water, be careful not to create concave areas that drown plants.

- ✔ If your property is on a hillside or has potentially unstable soil, check with a geologist before you attempt to increase the amount of water that soaks into your land. When improperly handled, water harvesting can cause a major landslide.

- ✔ Make sure all ponding areas are lower than your house and other structures; otherwise, they may flood.

Be wise: Hire a professional if you have even the slightest concern. The consequences of a badly designed water harvesting system can be catastrophic. Whatever you do, don't get in over your head.

Make a sketch and check it twice

Make a quick sketch of your re-engineered watershed (or catchment area), showing the proposed new path of the water, including all swales (shallow ditches), ponding zones, and other features. (I explain these terms in the later section "Factoring in the right features.")

Double-check your plans to be sure that water goes where you want it to and that excess water leaves quietly. Your plan should look like Figure 7-2 (see Chapter 7). If, with your plan, you'll turn your property into a big sponge, with no appreciable runoff other than excess water, congratulations! You're on your way to a truly sustainable landscape that operates mostly on natural inputs and that keeps stormwater from damaging the environment.

Creating a Nonstorage Water-Harvesting System

Nonstorage irrigation systems use the land itself to hold water, mimicking the way natural watersheds function. By contouring the land to create flow lines for the water to slowly travel along and low spots where it can soak in, you accomplish your goal without purchasing materials, and you expend little or no extra effort in the process (assuming you were going to grade the land anyway).

Nonstorage water harvesting can be done on any geologically stable site but preferably not on a hillside, where saturated soil can cause problems. Check with a geologist if you aren't sure about your site's stability.

How much water can you save with a nonstorage irrigation system? Well, an inch of water falling on 2,500 square feet of land — about the size of the footprint of an average tract house — makes 1,400 gallons of water available to your plants. That's 1,400 gallons of water you don't have to buy and 1,400 gallons less impact on the environment. Multiply that figure by the inches of rainfall you get annually, and you'll see that water harvesting amounts to a major benefit. Don't you wonder why you've been throwing water away all this time?

Grading your property

To develop your property into a water-harvesting system, grade the land so that it has low spots to soak up water. Also make sure that paved areas are *pervious* (they allow water to pass through them into the soil) or that they shed the water that falls on them into an adjacent vegetated area.

If you have an underground drainage system to take away excess water, set the tops of your catch basins 2 to 4 inches above grade so that water pools around them (see the section on drainage systems at the end of this chapter).

You may be required to get a grading permit if your system is a large one with lots of soil being moved around. Check with your local building department to be sure.

Be sure to keep all water away from your house and other buildings. Your water-harvesting zones should begin at least 10 feet out from the foundations. Also test your soil to make sure it percolates adequately for the water to soak in. Doing so is important because standing water breeds mosquitoes. And never, ever mess with natural streams or other watercourses; modifying them is illegal, and you may cause erosion or other serious problems. Besides, real streams often carry a lot of water, and your hard work could simply wash away in the next rain.

Factoring in the right features

A safe, effective nonstorage system incorporates some or all of the following features:

- ✔ **Swales:** *Swales* are shallow, low ditches through which water moves from high to low points. Locate your swales on gentle slopes, not steep ones, where they could cause erosion problems.

  Swales can swerve back and forth artistically across your land, becoming giant earth sculptures that also happen to be habitats for plants. See Chapter 7 for more on swales.

- ✔ **Ponding zones:** Shallow depressions (10 to 20 inches deep) called *ponding zones* are located at low points where the water can soak into the ground. These low points are good places to plant trees to use the captured water. However, note that the trees go next to the ponding zone, not in the bottom, where they could drown.

  Ponding zones should be located to the side of drainage paths, out of the direct path of the strongest flow. They're filled by the swales above them, and excess water moves along through more swales on the low side of the ponding zones. Keep ponding zones away from septic systems and leach fields, and make sure they won't back up and cause flooding where you don't want it.

- ✔ **Percolation chambers:** Closely related to ponding zones are *percolation chambers,* which are underground gravel-filled pits that hold lots of water. Roots use the water that these chambers collect. See Chapter 7 for more on percolation chambers.

- ✔ **Terraces:** You can use terraces on hillsides to slow and hold water but only if you're sure that they won't affect the stability of the land. On gentle slopes, your terraces can be simple contours made of the earth itself. On steeper slopes, use retaining walls to hold soil in place; talk to a civil engineer about this type of project.

- ✔ **Dutch drain:** A *Dutch drain* is an underground polyethylene drainage pipe that's perforated with holes so the water leaks out. It's placed over a gravel-filled trench.

  One end of the drain can be connected to the downspout that takes water from your roof. The other end can emerge from the soil (or it can *daylight,* as we say in the business) at a safe location. Excess water is removed from the area safely, while the bulk of the water leaks out of the pipe into the porous gravel and then into the soil, where roots will find it.

✔ **Pervious pavement:** Using pervious pavement is a great strategy for keeping water on your property. If your paving isn't pervious (or if pervious paving isn't an option for you because of unsuitable soil or geological conditions), use conventional nonpervious paving as a catchment feature that drains water into nearby swales and ponding zones. Read about pervious paving choices in Chapter 12.

I discuss how to install most of these features in the later section "Working your plan."

Planning your work

Like any sustainable landscaping project, water harvesting benefits from careful observation of the site and meticulous planning. Because it's so difficult to fix mistakes in major, underlying changes like grading and landform, and because the consequences of bad planning are potentially serious, it's important to pay attention to what you're doing.

I can't go into all the depth you need here, so plan on honing your skills with some of the books and Web sites I mention throughout this section. And as always, work with a pro if you aren't completely sure of what you're doing.

Planning for a water-harvesting system is best done out on site, not at a drawing board. In this case, planning and implementation are both physical acts. You may want to sketch out your design on paper, but don't consider it to be of primary importance.

A wonderful first step in the planning process is to visit a real creek or stream to get the idea of how nature makes irrigation work. Notice how the water flows, where it erodes banks, where and how it pools, how the stones look, and where the plants grow. The more your system is like nature, the better it's going to work.

After your visit to the creek, come home and consider how you can implement the principles you observed in nature on your own land. You won't be replicating what you saw of course, but you will be making your land work in a natural way. Make sure that your strategy relates to existing and proposed vegetation and to any hardscape features you already have or plan to construct.

To get your ideas going, follow these steps:

1. **Starting at the top of your property, use a band of powdered gypsum or lime to lay out the approximate path of the water from top to bottom.**

2. **Develop a system of swales to move the water back and forth across the land, and add basins and ponding zones at frequent intervals so water slows down enough to soak in.**

Vary both the depth and width of your swales for a more natural and more absorbent outcome. Getting the overall layout correct is critical. If the swales are too steep, the water will run off, possibly picking up enough speed to cause erosion. If the swales are too gradual or don't go downhill at all, water may back up where you don't want it.

Checking these features by eye can be difficult. You need to check the elevations throughout the system by using a *sighting level* or *transit* (surveying devices that measure the elevations of the land) to be sure that your swales run downhill. If you don't have a lot of surveying experience, you may want to work with a landscape professional.

3. **At the lowest points in the system, determine your overflow routes where excess water should go, and put spillways at those points.**

A *spillway* is a slightly lowered portion of the bank that forms the swale; it creates a path for water to get out. Use multiple spillways, if possible, to distribute the water evenly (concentrated flows of water can cause erosion problems). Make sure the spillways drain into safe places and won't flood neighboring properties, cause erosion, or present safety hazards.

The volume and velocity of the water at this point can be very high, so stabilize your spillways with heavy boulders or other structures. Either add plants and mulch or put boulders in all vulnerable points in the system — wherever water flow could erode soil.

Working your plan

The physical act of creating a nonstorage irrigation system isn't complicated. The tools aren't complicated, either: You need a pick or mattock (which is like a pickaxe with a flat blade), maybe a digging bar, a shovel, and a rake. You know what I'm going to tell you next. Yup. Start digging.

Swales

Create each swale by making a shallow ditch. Place the soil from your ditch on the downhill side of the swale, creating a bank like a little levee (or put the soil on both sides, where the land on both sides of the swale is equally high). Be sure to leave extra soil on the outside of turns, where potential for erosion and blowouts is greater.

If you'll be adding boulders to the swale to make it into a dry streambed, choose rounded rock forms, not angular or broken pieces. Vary the sizes, being sure to include some big boulders — as large as you can safely move.

Bury at least one-third of each large boulder so that it isn't just sitting on the surface. To make things look more natural, place a few boulders on top of others, as though rushing water tossed them there. Make sure that your boulders are big enough that they won't wash away. And, finally, never use gravel in the bottom of the swale where the water runs; it'll be gone in the first good storm.

Ponding zones

Mark off the borders of your ponding zones with gypsum or lime. (You can make the ponds interesting shapes, if you like.) Adjust the depth so you won't have standing water for more than 12 hours after a rain; if your soil drains quickly, you can make your ponding zones as much as 18 inches deep. Surround your ponding zone with a *berm* (a low mound made of the earth you remove from the basin of the ponding zone itself) that's at least 2 feet wide so the zone lasts a long time.

The bottom of each basin should be flat and level so the water spreads out as much as possible. If the soil is compacted, break it up with a pick. Plant and mulch your basins for stability.

You can make swales and ponding zones deep and visible or so shallow that nobody but you knows they exist; this decision is an aesthetic one that's up to you. The basins will eventually fill with mulch and plants, anyway, becoming less apparent than they were when they were new.

Percolation chambers

To make a percolation chamber, follow these steps:

1. **Dig a hole at least 4 feet wide and 2 feet deep.**

2. **Rough up the bottom of the hole with a pick or digging bar.**

3. **Line the bottom and sides of the hole with synthetic filter fabric.**

   Filter fabric is an environmentally less-than-perfect (but in this case useful) material that keeps soil and roots from filling the voids between the rocks.

4. **Dump 1- to 2-inch rounded gravel or crushed rock into the pit, up to about 6 inches below the surface of the soil.**

5. **Cover the pit with another piece of filter fabric.**

6. **Top it off with your swale or dry streambed.**

   You can also run pipes from your downspouts or from your underground drainage system into the percolation chamber.

Before you dig, check for any utilities in the area, and make sure you aren't digging on top of a septic system or any other underground structures. See Chapter 11 for details on who to call before you start work.

Terraces

If you're going to build terraces, first check with a civil engineer or a geologist to ensure that it's safe to do so. They can also help you develop a design that will hold up to the forces of gravity. You may need to get a building permit for your retaining walls.

On shallow ground with less than a 3:1 slope (1 foot of elevation change for every 3 feet of horizontal distance), you probably can get away without installing retaining walls. On steeper slopes, make walls from *urbanite* (salvaged broken concrete), wooden timbers or logs, natural stone, or a reusable segmental retaining wall system. (See Chapter 14 for information on building retaining walls.)

If you aren't building retaining walls, follow the procedure in the earlier "Swales" section to make your terraces. Excavate earth and form it into a berm on the downhill side, creating a level area behind the berm. If your topsoil layer is thin, remove it, grade the soil underneath, and replace the topsoil when you're done. Compact and stabilize the berm by stomping on it. Prevent erosion by planting sturdy plants with good root systems and by covering the soil with a 3- to 4-inch layer of organic mulch such as wood chips.

Dutch drains

In its simplest form, a Dutch drain is a ditch filled with coarse gravel. Water runs into it from surrounding areas and soaks into the soil, where plants can take advantage of it. That system works fine, but more sophisticated approaches can make it last longer and work better.

To construct a first-class Dutch drain, follow these steps:

1. **Dig a ditch at least 1 foot deep and 10 inches wide.**

2. **Drape a large piece of filter fabric down into the bottom of the ditch and up the sides.**

   Make sure that the material extends far enough onto the ground on each side of the trench so you can fold the material over to cover the top of the system after you're done installing the gravel (and pipe, if used).

3. **Place a layer of 1- to 2-inch diameter gravel or crushed rock or any similar porous material — even rubble — in the ditch, leaving room for the pipe (if you'll be using one).**

4. **Install the pipe (if you're using one) on top of the gravel.**

   Use 4-inch corrugated polyethylene perforated drainpipe wrapped in a special filter fabric "sock", which you can purchase at any irrigation supply store. (The staff will know exactly what you need.) Hook the pipe to your downspout. Run the end of the pipe up and out of the trench, and extend it to a safe place where the excess water can drain away without causing erosion, leaving the end of the pipe open. Place a 1- to 3-inch deep layer of rock over the pipe to cover it.

5. **Flop the two edges of the filter fabric over the whole mess as if you're rolling up a burrito.**

6. **Cover with topsoil, stomp on it to compact it, and then smooth it off with a rake.**

Storing Harvested Water

A rainwater storage system uses a tank called a *cistern* to hold the water. The most common source of water is the roof. You deliver water from the roof to the cistern by connecting the downspout from your gutters to the cistern with a pipe. Water is held in the cistern until the dry season, when it's pumped or gravity-fed into your swales or a ditch or it's delivered by a hose or drip system. See Chapter 7 for more on cistern systems.

Assembling the components

Standard components of a cistern system include the following:

- A way for the water to enter the tank and a way for it to leave
- A drain that's used for periodic cleanouts
- An overflow pipe that allows excess water to leave the system in a controlled way
- A vent that allows air to come and go as the tank empties and fills
- An access door at the top that allows a worker to get inside to do servicing work
- Devices to keep animals from entering the tank

As for the tank itself, it can be made of steel, plastic, masonry, concrete, wood, or other materials. Composition is where sustainability goes a little sideways, because all these materials have significant environmental impacts. To boil a complex discussion down to the basics, avoid PVC tanks. High-density polyethylene (HDPE) is the most popular tank material; it's fairly nontoxic as far as anyone knows, and it has the lowest impact of any suitable plastic. It's relatively inexpensive, but it's also totally butt-ugly, so plan to camouflage this sucker with plants or fencing. Sometimes, you can find a used HDPE or steel tank for cheap.

Developing a cistern system

Creating a cistern system is a field day for techie types. On the other hand, it's probably not such a great experience if your idea of doing plumbing is changing the washer in a leaky faucet. But if you're ready for the challenge, creating a cistern system can be a fun project. The following sections show you the story, in a nutshell, of how to complete the project. *Remember:* If you lack confidence in your plumbing abilities, work with a licensed plumber who's experienced in cisterns.

Get tanked

Before you do anything else, decide where you'll place your tank and whether it'll be aboveground (less expensive, uglier, but preferable overall) or underground (more expensive and subject to collapsing and floating out of the ground). I proceed on the assumption that your tank will be aboveground.

In the ideal scenario, your house is on top of a hill, and the landscaping is downhill from the house. The tank should be located next to the house so that it can gravity-feed into the yard. If the tank is lower, count on using a small electric pump to send the water uphill.

Keep these points in mind:

- ✔ Make sure your tank is located on undisturbed, stable soil (*not* fill soil). After all, 1,000 gallons of water weighs as much as two cars.

- ✔ Leave enough room to walk around your tank for servicing.

- ✔ Make sure the surrounding soil slopes away from the tank in all directions.

Size up your storage

After you know where you want to house your cistern, decide how much water you want to store. There's a whole science to sizing cisterns, but an easy rule of thumb is to keep it to a maximum of 5,000 gallons. How far through the dry season that amount will take you depends on the size of your garden, the water needs of your plants, the climate, the soil, and other factors. It's a safe bet that you'll still have to buy water, which is why I include information on conventional irrigation systems in this book (see Chapters 7 and 10).

Install the cistern

How you install your cistern depends on what it's made of. Count on at least getting help from some strong friends, and know that you may even need heavy equipment to move this big boy. Here are some general guidelines to keep in mind for each type of cistern:

- ✔ **Plastic:** Place a plastic tank on a smooth, 1- to 2-inch-thick layer of compacted fine pea gravel (the rounded kind) or sand (but make sure it won't wash away).

- ✔ **Steel:** If your tank is steel, place it on a bed of compacted coarse gravel, which keeps the bottom of the tank dry and postpones the inevitable rusting.

- ✔ **Concrete:** If you'll be installing a concrete or other type of tank, work with a qualified contractor.

Distribute the water

If you have enough elevation change to depend on gravity to send the water out to your plants, use a hose or possibly a drip system to distribute it (making sure to filter that drip system). If you're using a pump, you can apply the water with a hose, a drip system, or even sprinklers.

When setting up a cistern, some subtle but important details are involved in connecting the inlet, outlet, drain, and other pipes to the tank. For example, the inlet has to have an air gap between it and the high-water mark so the water can't siphon out of the tank, and the drain pipe has to be carefully located to make cleaning sludge out of the bottom relatively easy instead of having to mop it up and haul it out through the top in buckets. I don't have the space to detail the connections and the many other complexities of tank design and installation here. If you'll be doing the work yourself, I recommend that you get a copy of *Water Storage: Tanks, Cisterns, Aquifers, and Ponds,* by Art Ludwig (Oasis Design).

Recycling Water with a Graywater System

A *graywater* system uses secondhand water from your washing machine, sinks, and possibly tubs and showers (never toilets). The water is collected with a system of pipes throughout the house and delivered to landscape plantings.

Graywater isn't for everybody or every situation. You must have the following:

✔ Accessible plumbing

✔ A normal soil type

✔ Moderate climate (neither too wet nor too cold)

✔ An attitude that allows you to put up with a bit of work and tinkering to keep your system going (see Chapter 10)

Graywater isn't legal everywhere, and even in areas where it is, certain systems can get you in trouble. In some areas, a building permit is required for a legal graywater system.

You can irrigate fruit trees as well as ornamentals with graywater, but for health reasons, don't use it on vegetables or other edible crops. Even though experts claim that there are no documented cases of anyone becoming sick from contact with graywater, you shouldn't ignore potential health risks. Because of the potential for problems, graywater can't be allowed to appear on the surface of the ground and can't be applied through overhead sprinklers or garden hoses.

Also, when using a graywater system, be careful what you put down the drain. Use only natural and graywater-compatible cleaning products. If you wash diapers, send the rinse water into the regular sewer system. And don't flush meds or other potentially harmful substances into the sink and out to your garden.

Choosing a graywater system

You can find many kinds of graywater systems, from a simple pipe or hose that empties a sink or the washing machine into a flowerbed to a highly complex computerized system that costs thousands of dollars. The consensus seems to be that a simpler system is best. The one I describe in this section was developed by graywater expert Art Ludwig after decades of experimentation. I agree with him that it's the best way to go for many situations.

Figure 7-6 (in Chapter 7) shows you how this system looks. A pipe taps into the drain from the bathroom sink and leads out to a mulch-filled basin with some useful plants growing in it — no filters, tanks, pumps, valves, controllers, or space-age gadgetry involved. The system is incredibly simple to build and maintain. You can start with something simple like this and later expand into a slightly more complex system, such as the *branched drain system*. If you'd like, you can read more about this complex system in Ludwig's book, *Create an Oasis with Greywater* (Oasis Design). Visit www.oasisdesign.net for details on this book.

Building a graywater system

Here's how to make a simple graywater system (check out Figure 7-6 in Chapter 7 for a visual):

1. **Locate a good source of graywater.**

   In this case, say it's a bathroom sink.

2. **Drill a hole in the wall next to the water source (watch for hidden plumbing or electrical wires) and install a drainpipe**

3. **Outside, run the drainpipe to a tree or other plant that's downhill.**

4. **Dig a hole in the ground and then invert a 5-gallon plastic planting container in the bottom of the basin.**

5. **Cut some holes in the container and run the pipe that comes from the sink into another hole in the top of the container.**

   The container acts as a surge tank, leaking water out into the basin.

6. **Fill the basin with coarse mulch.**

7. **Install a tight-fitting screen on the outlet end of the drainpipe to keep critters from crawling into your bathroom.**

If one basin won't handle all the water, you can hook up more of them via a more complex branched drain system that distributes the graywater to several locations using a system of carefully-leveled pipes. Refer to the earlier section "Choosing a graywater system" for more on complex systems.

The previous steps are a quickie version of real instructions; I recommend that you do your homework before tackling a job like this. I'm not saying that a simple system like this is beyond the skills of a handy homeowner. But if you get into anything more complex, you need a resource devoted to the subject or the help of an expert.

Getting a Bird's-Eye View of a Permanent Irrigation System

You may find, as many people do, that you need to use water from the tap to supplement rainfall. That means developing a permanent irrigation system. You don't need to fear the complexities of an irrigation system; it's just a bunch of valves, pipes, sprinkler heads, and drip lines. This section gets you up to speed on the parts and pieces and how they fit together (see Figure 8-1 for an overview).

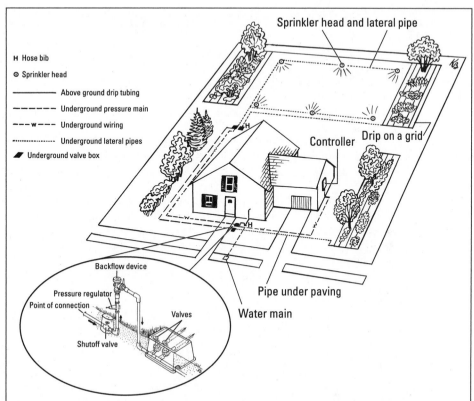

Figure 8-1:
Irrigation
system
overview.

When shopping for irrigation equipment, buy only the very best available. Shop at irrigation supply stores — where the pros shop — not at places that sell to homeowners, where merchandise is often inferior. The equipment may cost a bit more, but the system will last a lot longer — a very sustainable way to go if you must have a permanent system.

Hooking up: Point of connection

The place where you tap into your water main is called the *point of connection*. In most cases, you saw the pipe in two and install a tee to connect your pressure main.

Choose a point of connection that's as close to the water meter or city water main as possible so you get the maximum volume and pressure. Don't try to run a system off a hose bibb (outdoor faucet) that comes out the back wall of the house or from a soft-water line.

Tapping into the water main can be tricky business and is best left to a pro, even if you plan to install the rest of the system on your own.

Keeping it clean: Filtration

If your water supply is particularly dirty, grit and junk can end up in the system, causing valves to stick and heads to plug up. Check with your water purveyor about whether you need a filter at the head of the system. Most municipal systems are fairly clean, but well water and small private systems are notoriously dirty.

Bacterial iron slime (also known as *iron bacteria*) is present in some water sources and can cause real problems with irrigation equipment, particularly drip systems. Even though it isn't toxic to people, bacterial iron slime is difficult to treat and can't be filtered out. If you have colored, smelly, or iron-flavored water, or if you see slimy stuff inside your pipes and fixtures, check with your water purveyor to see whether you have this problem.

Delivering the goods: Pressure mains and hose bibbs

The *pressure main* is the underground pipe that supplies water to your control valves. Unlike lateral pipes that are downstream from the control valves, pressure mains are under continuous pressure. Pressure mains should be at least ¾ inch in diameter; 1 inch or larger is better, though, because you're going to need a lot of water.

Pressure mains usually are buried at least 18 inches below ground — deeper in cold climates. Heavy-walled Schedule 40 PVC is the usual choice for pipe, but PVC is an environmental nightmare. Consider a more sustainable alternative such as cross-linked polyethylene pipe.

Put *hose bibbs* (those are the faucets you hook your garden hoses up to) near control valves and anywhere else you need to have running water.

For safety and durability, the *riser* — the pipe that comes aboveground to supply the hose bibb — needs to be metal, not plastic. (This is true of any situation in which pipe is exposed.) Stake the hose bibb to a 4-x-4 wooden post or attach it firmly to a fixed object, such as your house, so it won't break off when you tug on the hose.

Keeping it safe: Backflow prevention devices

To prevent contaminated irrigation water from entering the domestic water supply, the law in most places requires you to have an approved backflow prevention device permanently installed on your system. A *backflow prevention device* is simply a one-way valve that lets water through but doesn't let it turn around and go the other way.

Some backflow preventers are located at the point of connection (which I discuss earlier in this chapter). These devices are called *pressure vacuum breakers, reduced pressure devices,* or *double check valves.* Other backflow preventers are installed at each valve; these devices are called *atmospheric vacuum breakers.* The latter are easier to install than the other kinds, and they can be less costly if you have only a few valves.

Without getting into all the gory details, I can tell you that each type of backflow device offers a particular level of protection, so you need to talk to your local building department about what kind to use. In most communities, you need a building permit for your backflow device; you may or may not need a permit for the rest of the system. You also need to have the device tested annually by a certified backflow test technician.

Reducing your pressure: Regulators

A *pressure regulator* is a simple mechanical device that's installed on the water main to, well, regulate water pressure. If your incoming pressure is higher than 80 to 100 pounds per square inch (psi), install a pressure regulator at the point of connection to avoid damaging the system. Excess pressure can cause heads to blow off and drip emitters to pop off the tubing. And, of course, poor system operation leads to water waste.

Gaining control: Zone valves

A *zone* is a particular physical area of your landscape, served by its own separate zone valve that turns it on and off. Zone valves can be operated manually or automatically by a controller that sends 24 volts of electricity to the valves via underground wires. Valves are grouped in *manifolds* (branched pipes) in one or more locations throughout the landscape. Manual valves are installed aboveground so they can be operated conveniently; automatic valves are placed underground in plastic valve boxes.

Zones exist for several reasons:

> ✔ **Water use:** You can separate the system (and the plantings themselves) into *hydrozones* that contain plants with similar water needs, each controlled by its own valve. That way, you don't over- or underwater plants.
>
> ✔ **Exposure:** You can provide separate valves for sunny and shady areas, windy areas, or areas under trees that may need more or less water.
>
> ✔ **Hydraulics:** When any area is too big to be served by one valve because of limitations in the water supply, you can break the area into smaller parts and have multiple valves come on one after another, in sequence.

Sending water to the sprinklers: Lateral pipes

The underground pipes that send water from the valves to the sprinkler heads or drip lines are called *laterals*. As with pressure mains, the conventional pipe choice is PVC, but cross-linked polyethylene is much more sustainable if you can find it. Laterals don't carry as much pressure as mains, so the pipe doesn't have to be as strong. Laterals can be buried a foot deep.

Applying the water: Sprinkler and drip systems

Sprinkler heads and drip emitters are the end of the line for the system; they deliver water to your plants. Sprinklers spray water overhead and are supplied by a system of underground pipes. Drip emitters apply water very slowly, fed by tubing that's installed between the soil and the mulch. I explain both in the following sections. Refer to the later section, "Applying Sustainable Watering Concepts to Your Permanent Irrigation System" for more on how to sustainably use sprinkler and drip systems.

Sprinkler systems

Even though sprinklers are inefficient compared to drip, they do a good job of watering a lawn or meadow or large areas of low ground cover (although a sustainable landscape wouldn't take this approach in the first place). In these cases, do everything you can to make the sprinkler system as efficient as it can be.

Select a type of sprinkler head that's appropriate for the circumstances. Note that heads come in aboveground and pop-up versions. Here are some popular types of sprinkler heads and how they're used:

> ✔ **Spray heads:** Small areas are best served by spray heads, which cover up to a 15-foot radius from the head. The spray head has a fixed nozzle that delivers a fan-shaped arc of water in a circular pattern.

- ✔ **Rotor heads:** Rotor heads have a gear-drive mechanism that delivers water via rotating streams, putting the water down more slowly and evenly than spray heads do. The coarse streams are less apt to blow around in wind. Rotors are used for larger areas because they shoot water over longer distances — a radius of 20 to 40 feet or more.

- ✔ **Impact heads:** Impact heads use a swinging arm to break a stream of water into a wider pattern. This old-fashioned design is quite efficient, though rather noisy. (A sustainable garden should be a quiet garden.) Impact heads are used the same way as rotor heads.

Never mix different types of heads on one valve, because coverage patterns and precipitation rates can vary considerably.

Drip systems

A well-designed, properly installed drip system can be one of the most sustainable features of your landscape, saving lots of water and making the plants truly thrive. Consider the following:

- ✔ Drip systems apply water via *emitters,* which are small, precisely engineered openings that keep the flow consistent from one emitter to the next.

- ✔ Emitters can be installed on or molded right into polyethylene drip tubing; the latter arrangement is better because the emitters stay put.

- ✔ Each emitter dribbles out water at a very slow rate — usually ½ to 2 gallons per hour — and the water soaks straight into the soil without being sprayed into the air.

- ✔ Filtration is essential to the longevity of the system, because even tiny bits of grit in the water can plug the small openings in the emitters. *Wye-type filters* with 150-mesh screens are the best. (Certain types of water can clog emitters even with proper filtering, so check with your water district to be sure that drip will work with your water.)

- ✔ Drip systems operate at 20 to 30 pounds per square inch (psi) of pressure. Because this pressure is much lower than the incoming pressure for most water systems, small pressure regulators especially made for drip systems are required at each valve.

- ✔ Elevation changes can affect the accuracy of delivery, resulting in more water going to low spots. If you have more than 3 to 5 feet of elevation change within the area served by one zone valve, either split the system into high and low sections or use pressure-compensating emitters, which handle elevation changes better than standard emitters do.

- ✔ Drip tubing usually is installed on the surface of the ground and covered with mulch, but some types can be buried beneath the soil surface. Tubing is fastened to the soil with drip staples, which should be installed every 3 feet to prevent the tubing from popping up through the mulch.

Timing it right: Irrigation controllers

If you have an automatic system, you can install the controller in the garage or another protected but accessible location. You can also place it outdoors where your gardener or others can get to it when you're not home. For detailed information on smart versus dumb controllers and on how to choose a controller, refer to Chapter 7. I strongly suggest that you consider a smart controller; it really works, and it saves a lot of water and money.

Installing a *rain sensor* — a little cup located in an open area that catches rain and shuts off the system until the weather dries out — isn't a bad idea. Nothing is sillier or more wasteful than sprinklers coming on in the rain.

Applying Sustainable Watering Concepts to Your Permanent Irrigation System

I've looked at a lot of irrigation systems in my time, and most of them have been subpar in terms of design and performance. That's a shame, because putting together a really good system — one that irrigates instead of irritates — doesn't take much knowledge. Start with the principles that drive the design of a system, which I cover in the upcoming sections.

Sprinkler distribution uniformity

Here's a paradox: Try getting even coverage by watering a square area with circular arcs of water. One look at the geometry of the situation makes it clear that sprinkler coverage — or *distribution uniformity* (DU), as we irrigation pros say — can never be perfect with this kind of setup.

Given the impossible geometry, we allow ourselves to be satisfied with 70 percent DU, meaning that a fairly large part of the area isn't getting adequate water. To keep those drier areas irrigated properly, you'd have to increase watering time to the point that the rest of the area is being overwatered. This system isn't very sustainable, which is why I like drip so much; the DU for it is 100 percent for all intents and purposes.

To get optimal DU, place your sprinkler heads so that each head shoots over to all its neighbors, as you see in Figure 8-2, where the dots represent sprinkler heads and the numbers note the number of heads hitting each area of the yard. That arrangement is called *head-to-head coverage,* and it's essential to proper performance of the system. Without it, you get dry spots, wasted water, and sickly plants.

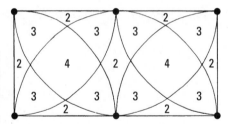

Figure 8-2:
Distribution
uniformity.

Drip on a grid versus drip at the plant

Putting one or two drip emitters at the base of each newly planted plant is no way to build a drip system. The crown of a plant, especially a drought-tolerant one, is the last place you want water, because water there encourages pathogens that could ultimately kill the plant. Also, if you don't have emitters elsewhere throughout the mature root system of the plants, they'll never get enough water (see Figure 9-1 in Chapter 9 to understand where roots really are).

The proper way to create a drip system is to make a grid of emitters, using tubing with molded-in emitters. Space the emitters a set distance apart (usually 12 to 24 inches) and install parallel lines of tubing throughout the entire planted area, wherever roots may roam (see Figure 8-3). That way, the wetting pattern is more like rain — even and consistent.

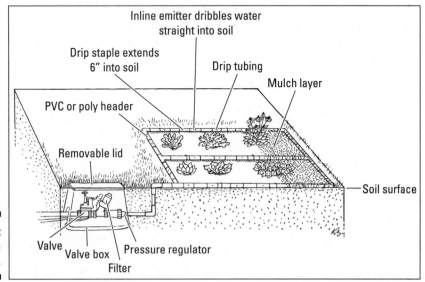

Figure 8-3:
Drip on a
grid.

Including Sustainable Drainage Systems

Water-harvesting systems hold rainwater on the land; drainage systems take it away. Sounds kind of crazy, doesn't it? Well, the traditional drainage system, without the earth-friendly water-harvesting element, *is* pretty crazy. Somewhere along the line, rainwater became a waste product in people's minds, and drainage systems went far beyond the admirable task of keeping your house from flooding. Instead, they went on to become water-squandering, street-flooding devices that cause more problems than they solve.

The conventional drainage system consists of site grading that runs all water to low points away from the house and catch basins that capture it and deliver it to the street in underground pipes. When it's in the street, the water contributes to urban flooding and also washes pollution into streams, lakes, and other bodies of water. This system is a great way to deal with excess water that could do real damage to your property, but it takes all the water away before it can do any good.

Nonetheless, most landscapes need a drainage system of some kind to prevent catastrophic or nuisance flooding. So if you're going to include a drainage system, make sure you design one that's sustainable. I show you how in the following sections.

Designing your drainage system

Keeping in mind the dual purposes of drainage in a sustainable landscape (to keep water on site as much as is practical and to prevent excess stormwater from doing damage), here are the steps in designing a drainage system:

1. **Find out where the water is coming from.**

   Survey your site to see where stormwater is coming from. Review the section "Follow the water" earlier in this chapter. This time you should be looking at rainwater as a potential problem, not a resource, but the principles are still the same. Talk to neighbors if you aren't familiar with storm behavior and drainage patterns in your neighborhood.

2. **Find out where the water is going.**

   See where the exit points are on your property and note any low spots where water backs up. The low spots could be troublesome if they cause damage or oversaturate an unstable slope, but they're welcome if they act as ponding zones to keep water on your land. (Refer to "Factoring in the right features," earlier in this chapter, for more information on ponding zones.)

3. **Consider locations for water-harvesting strategies.**

   See Chapter 7 and the first part of this chapter for specific ways to keep water on the land.

4. **Identify any safety problems.**

   Make sure your property is geologically stable (check with a consulting geologist on this). Discharge water onto pavement or stable ground to avoid erosion problems. Plan good overflow paths for heavy flows.

5. **Coordinate your drainage design with the overall landscape plan.**

   Think about where plants that will use the water will be placed and how the drainage patterns will affect patios, paths, lawns, and other areas.

6. **Try to drain the property without using pipes.**

   When pipes plug up, the water backs up and you have a flood. If you can grade your property so that floodwaters run harmlessly across the surface of the ground, you'll be a lot better off in most cases. When you solve the problem with grading, you have no pipes to plug up, and your only responsibility is maintaining an adequate cover of vegetation so the soil doesn't wash away. In cold climates, freezing weather can wreak havoc on drainage systems by clogging pipes and intakes with ice. In such places, surface drainage is almost always preferable.

7. **Place catch basins at low points and connect them to a suitable discharge location with an underground drainpipe.**

   Make sure that your low points are at least 10 feet from the house — preferably as far out on your property as practical. Plan pipe runs to avoid tree roots, and try not to dig trenches straight down slopes, because they could wash out in a storm. Set the top rims of all catch basins a couple inches higher than the surrounding grade to form shallow ponding areas where water can soak in. Make double-sure that the rims are well below the floor height of your house and other buildings. Where catch basins are located away from traffic areas, use domed *atrium grates* rather than flat-topped ones so that leaves won't plug them up.

8. **Evaluate your design in the field before you build it.**

   Unlike surface features of your landscape, grading and drainage are final. They're nearly impossible to change after they're in. If you have the slightest doubt about the wisdom, safety, or legality of what you're doing, have it looked at by a qualified professional.

Don't forget to include French drains behind retaining walls and anywhere you have groundwater getting into the house. A *French drain* is a ditch with a perforated drainpipe in the bottom — an upside-down version of the Dutch drain I introduce earlier in this chapter. Like the Dutch drain, the French drain is lined with filter fabric to keep soil out but let water in; it's filled with coarse crushed rock to create a porous zone that attracts water from the surrounding area. Water goes down into the pipe and can be sent to a suitable place for safe use. (In short, French drains absorb troublesome water and take it away, whereas Dutch drains take water from somewhere else and let it soak in.)

Installing and maintaining your drainage system

As long as you're careful to set the grades correctly, the installation of a drainage system isn't complicated — just a lot of hard work. Consider the following tasks:

- ✔ The drainpipes need to be buried, which of course means a lot of trenching and backfilling.

- ✔ You need to keep the pipes going downhill consistently, at a slope adequate for them to empty thoroughly (at least $1/8$ inch of drop per foot of pipe). Therefore, you need to check the slope with a level as you go.

- ✔ You must minimize standing water. I like to drill a hole in the bottom of catch basins and put a layer of gravel under them to eliminate tiny ponds where mosquitoes can breed.

- ✔ You must provide cleanout fittings so you can flush out the system before the rainy season.

Use rigid, smooth-walled pipe wherever you can; it's easier to keep clean than the corrugated kind.

You have very little to do to keep a drainage system working properly. An annual flushing keeps things flowing. Plus be sure to keep the area around the catch basins free of litter and leaves to prevent clogging. Check the exit point of your pipes every now and then to make sure that the water isn't causing erosion.

Chapter 9

Managing Water: The Other Half of the Irrigation Equation

In This Chapter
▶ Planning a water-conserving landscape
▶ Figuring out the best irrigation schedule
▶ Following some easy tips for managing water

*I*t isn't enough to build a water-conserving irrigation system if you still water every day. The other half of the equation is behavior. Savvy water management isn't complicated, and it can save you big bucks while you do the sustainable thing for the environment. Keep in mind, too, that water management isn't just for folks with a fancy irrigation system; it's just as important for those who water by hand.

Unless you've set up a landscape that never needs supplemental watering, you have to apply water to make up the difference between what the weather brings and what your plants need. To do that efficiently, you need to apply a few principles to your irrigation practices, making good decisions about when and how much to water.

The first step is to develop a landscape that doesn't need much water in the first place. Then, if appropriate, incorporate water-harvesting strategies so you don't have to buy as much water (see Chapter 8). Next, if you have an irrigation system, design it so that it incorporates as much drip as possible, efficient sprinkler heads, and a smart controller. (Chapters 7 and 8 can help with all your irrigation needs.) Finally, find out how to be a savvy water manager.

Developing a Water-Wise Landscape

By using plants that are adapted to your particular conditions, covering the soil with a protective layer of mulch, and developing water-harvesting systems to make use of rainfall, you've set the stage for water conservation. You've also given yourself tools to work with as a water manager.

Picking climate-compatible plants

You can choose to create a sustainable landscape that needs no irrigation system and no water management. First, evaluate the native plant communities in your area (hint: take a hike) and decide whether they meet your property's needs. If they do, you may be on your way to achieving the deepest level of sustainability: the no-water native landscape.

Visit a local botanic garden or ask professionals about the feasibility of bringing nature into your garden. If it looks like this plan will work for you, forget about installing an irrigation system and get to planting!

Your landscape doesn't have to be strictly native to do well without watering. Plants from any region of the world where the climate is similar to yours can work. Choose your plants carefully; Chapters 16, 17, and 18 can help.

Thinking long and hard about plant placement

After choosing appropriate plants for your climate, you also have to determine the best places to put those plants. Group your plantings into *hydro-zones* — those handy groups of plants with similar water needs. In other words, plan your landscape so that higher and lower water-using plants are in separate areas and on separate irrigation valves. Don't mix plants with different water requirements; otherwise you'll always be overwatering or underwatering certain plants.

Considering turf and mulch

Lawns use tons of water and create other problems as well. In fact, lawns are the most consumptive of all landscaping features. If you can't eliminate your lawn, make it smaller. And if you can't make it smaller, at least manage watering well. Aerate your lawn and remove thatch once or twice a year to allow water to penetrate.

Don't forget the water-saving qualities of mulch. A 3- to 4-inch-thick layer of organic mulch covering the surface of the soil can reduce water use by 50 percent or more. Mulching has many other advantages as well; see Chapter 16 for the lowdown.

Creating a Watering Plan or Schedule

In order to be a savvy water manager, you have to create a watering plan for your landscape. The watering plan spells out which plants need watering and when. Your watering plan delivers water where it's needed, without excessive runoff or spray drift, and in adequate quantities for the needs of the plants.

This section helps you figure out your landscape's water requirements; put together a watering schedule that meets those requirements; and then tweak that schedule based on seasons, soil conditions, and other factors.

Discover the truth about roots

The first task is to understand what you'll be watering. You may be surprised to find that the root systems of plants aren't where your junior-high science teacher said they were. You may remember a lecture about the roots of a tree: The teacher may have said that the roots go about as deep into the ground as the tree is tall and that they extend out about as far as the tree canopy is wide. My teacher drew a dumbbell-shaped tree on the blackboard, complete with a tidily symmetrical root system. At the time I was pretty impressed, but it turns out she made it all up.

As you see in Figure 9-1, the roots of a tree (and for that matter, the roots of a shrub or perennial) extend much farther than the canopy, and they're mostly within the top 18 inches of soil. There are exceptions to this rule, of course; some trees actually do the dumbbell thing, and unusual soil or weather conditions can send roots down rather than out. But overall, Figure 9-1 shows the way things happen underground.

The implications for irrigation (and for many other landscaping practices) are significant. If you've been deep-soaking your yard, you may have been wasting a lot of water or recharging the groundwater at your own considerable expense. If you water only at the base of plants and ignore the soil out in the open, you've been doing the plants a terrible disservice. Effective watering covers the entire root system and goes no deeper than the roots do. That means wide, relatively shallow coverage, which can be done with sprinklers, drip on a grid, or hand watering.

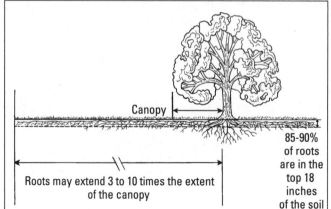

Figure 9-1:
What root
systems
really look
like.

Canopy

85-90%
of roots
are in the
top 18
inches
of the soil

Roots may extend 3 to 10 times the extent
of the canopy

Figuring out how much water your landscape needs

People are nurturers, and because watering feels like nurturing, it's the part of gardening that most people love. But combine love of nurturing with lack of knowledge about watering decisions, and you have the ingredients for water waste and unhealthy plants.

How much you water depends on the root depth of your plants, the soil type you have, and the application rate of whatever delivers your water, whether it be sprinklers, drip, or you standing at the business end of a garden hose. The frequency and quantity of watering depends on many factors as well; try a good watering followed by a waiting period to see when it's time to water again. Then use this result as your base schedule for the season (refer to the following section to see how to read plants for signs of water need).

Observing your plants

You don't have to gather a lot of data and crunch a lot of numbers to see that plants need water. Some simple signs in the weather, in the soil, and in the plants themselves will tell you most of what you need to know about when to water.

Watch plants for symptoms of drought stress, such as loss of shine on leaves, slowing of growth, and dropping of older (that is, lower) leaves. If you see any of these signs, check your soil. If the soil is dry 6 to 12 inches down, water the plants, and adjust your controller (or the calendar in your mind) to water more often. If plants show stress and the soil is moist, reduce the frequency of watering. (Oddly enough, the symptoms of too much water and too little water are the same.)

Also pay attention to the weather. If it's windy, hot, or dry, go see whether your plants need a drink. In fact, if you're thirsty, your plants may be thirsty too.

Don't let plants dry out to the point where they wilt. Wilting is hard on them.

Using evapotranspiration to your advantage

Evapotranspiration (also known as *ET*) is the combination of evaporation of water from the soil and the transpiration of water through the leaves of your plants. It's a way of indicating how much water your landscaping is using in any given weather situation. Many things affect ET, including temperature, humidity, wind, cloud cover, size/age/condition of plants, and time of year.

You can save a lot of water by matching your irrigation to the *ET*. You can access current ET data by calling your water purveyor for a local resource. Then you can reprogram your controller to match the watering times to the current ET. If the ET for the past week was 1.2 inches, for example, you can use the scheduling data you develop in your water audit (refer to the later section "Perform a water audit") to adjust your watering time to replace the 1.2 inches — no more. I show you how to do this in the next section.

If you get a smart controller, of course, you can ignore this section; the controller itself will make the adjustment, using data from local weather stations.

Soil conditions: Precipitation rate versus infiltration rate

Each soil type absorbs water at a particular speed known as the *infiltration rate*. Clay soils, which are made up of tiny, tightly packed particles, are the slowest to absorb water. Sandy soils, with their big chunky particles and numerous air spaces, drink up water fast. Water goes straight down in sandy soil rather than spreading out as it does in a clay soil. Loam soils are in the middle. Table 9-1 shows the differences in infiltration rates.

Table 9-1	Infiltration Rates of Soil Types
Soil Type	*Infiltration Rate (Inches per Hour)*
Clay	0.2 to 0.4
Loam	0.5 to 1.0
Sandy	1.0 to 2.0

Your irrigation system delivers water to the soil at a particular speed known as the *precipitation rate*. As you may guess, the precipitation rate needs to be slower than the infiltration rate of your soil; otherwise, you'll have runoff.

If you use sprinklers, keep these figures in mind:

✔ Spray heads apply 1 to 4 inches per hour.

✔ Rotor and impact heads deliver 0.2 to 1.0 inches per hour. (These heads are better for heavier soils because they apply water much more slowly.)

To prevent runoff, design your system so that its precipitation rate is lower than or equal to the infiltration rate of the soil. It isn't the end of the world if you can't, however; you simply can use your automatic controller to apply water in short bursts, with rest periods in between to allow the water to soak in. (The precipitation rate of drip systems is low enough that they won't create runoff in even the heaviest soils.)

Paying attention to water holding capacity

Soils also differ in how much water they hold and in how fast they dry out (which is referred to as *water holding capacity*). In sandy soil, you need to water every 2 to 7 days, depending on the type of plants you have and the weather conditions; in loam soil, the interval is 3 to 11 days; and in clay soil, it could be 3 to 15 days.

Performing a water audit

The basic idea of a *water audit* is to determine whether your irrigation system is operating at peak efficiency and to figure out what improvements or adjustments you need to make to fine-tune the system. Then you make those changes and develop a schedule for operating the system so it keeps the plants healthy without wasting any water. You can get help from your local water purveyor or perform a water audit yourself.

A simple, effective water audit will take you about an hour to complete. The audit can be used for a permanent sprinkler system or with a low-tech system like a sprinkler at the end of a hose.

1. **Evaluate landscape water use.**

   Compare water use (found on your water bill) from a hot period, such as August, with one from winter when you aren't watering at all. The difference between the two amounts is your approximate landscape water use.

2. **Evaluate the overall landscape.**

   See whether you can eliminate turf or high-water-use plants in some areas, incorporate water-harvesting features, or cover planter beds with mulch. Each of these measures can reduce water use significantly.

3. **Check the system for leaks, overspray, tilted heads, and missing or broken nozzles or drip emitters; then make any necessary repairs.**

   See Chapter 10 for details on how to accomplish this task.

4. **Do a catch-can test on your sprinkler system.**

   Set some tuna cans out on your lawn (take the tuna out first). Use about eight cans for an average-size lawn, placing some at sprinkler heads and some in the spaces between heads. Run the system for exactly 15 minutes. Then use a ruler to measure how much water is in each can. If the water depth differs by more than 30 percent, change the sprinkler-head spacing to improve coverage; double-check your repair work; repeat the catch-can test; and measure the depth of water in each can. Add the depths, divide by the number of cans to get the average, and then multiply by 4 to get the precipitation rate in inches per hour. Use this figure to develop a watering schedule (see the next section).

5. **Check your controller (if you have one), and write down the schedule for each zone.**

6. **Program a new watering schedule into your controller or modify your manual watering schedule to account for what you've discovered.**

7. **Next time you get a water bill, compare water use to see how much you've saved.**

Setting the watering schedule

Use your precipitation information and current ET data to develop a watering schedule; then use the schedule to reprogram your controller or to water by hand. The discussion here assumes you'll be using a controller, but if you're watering manually then simply write the schedule down and follow it.

To truly save water, reprogram your controller at least four times a year, when the seasons change. Ideally, you adjust the watering schedule every time a significant weather change occurs. Smart controllers make those adjustments automatically; you could skip this section and go buy a smart controller. But assuming that you have a conventional timer, here's help for you:

1. **Find your precipitation rate.**

   For details, refer to Step 4 of "Performing a water audit," earlier in this chapter.

2. **Develop a base schedule for your turf areas, which generally use the most water of any part of the landscape.**

3. **Program this base schedule into your controller.**

4. **Adjust the program as you observe the actual response of your lawn to the irrigation cycle.**

The base schedule accounts for average water use but is only a starting point for irrigation management. Your job is to reprogram the controller every time the weather changes significantly; wind, temperature, sun or clouds, rainfall, and other factors all affect actual water needs. Table 9-2 provides a handy chart to work with.

Table 9-2	Base Schedule Controller Settings for Turf		
Precipitation Rate (in./hr.)	Spring (0.90 in./wk.) Minutes per Irrigation	Summer (1.20 in./wk.) Minutes per Irrigation	Fall (0.60 in./wk.) Minutes per Irrigation
0.5	35	46	23
1.0	18	24	10
1.5	12	16	8
2.0	9	12	6
2.5	7	10	5
3.0	6	8	4
4.0	5	6	3

Program the numbers in Table 9-2 into the watering time or station time of each lawn valve station on your controller (or water this long by hand). Set the days to three per week (Monday, Wednesday, and Friday, for example). Change the numbers as the seasons change. That's it.

Note: This information assumes that you program for three watering cycles per week, which is ideal for most lawn types. In other words, water for the times indicated three times per week. If you water more or less often, set your watering times to deliver the *total* number of inches per week (listed in the table column heads) for whatever season you're in. You may need more or less water in your particular climate; check the ET via your local water purveyor.

For flowerbeds, ground covers, and other non-turf areas that are irrigated with sprinklers, determine whether they need more or less water than your lawns. Then you can adjust your base schedule accordingly. Keep an eye on the condition of your plants; dig into your soil periodically to determine actual soil moisture, and then make adjustments based on what's really going on.

Some communities have permanent watering restrictions designed to conserve water year round; others have restrictions only during certain seasons or times of drought. Typical restrictions include limiting watering to certain hours (usually prohibiting watering during the heat of day) or certain days of the week, dictating the kind of watering equipment you can use, and prohibiting watering of turf or high-water-use plants. Check with your local water utility for specific information.

Watering Wisely: Some General Tips

Here are some tips for making sure your watering efforts are as effective as possible. Stick them on your fridge or hang them in the garden shed.

- ✔ Early morning is the best time to water, because there's less evaporative loss due to heat, less wind, and better water pressure. Morning watering also supplies plants with the moisture they need to get through the day. Finally, the foliage has a chance to dry out, which reduces the likelihood of diseases arising from nighttime wetness.

- ✔ Check soil moisture with a soil probe or trowel before watering.

- ✔ Don't water when it's windy.

- ✔ Put a rain sensor on your controller so it doesn't water in the rain.

- ✔ Don't hose off your pavement unless the water will run into an area that needs to be watered.

- ✔ Look for particular plants that show drought stress first; use them as indicators that you need to water the area they're growing in.

- ✔ Keep weeds down; they use water too.

- ✔ Go easy on the fertilizer. Plants that are growing fast and loose use more water than ones that are more sedate.

Community resources for water conservation

Most communities, especially in hot dry climates, offer a wealth of information on landscape water conservation. Check your water utility's Web site, or call to see whether the company offers on-site water audits, free water conservation tools (such as catch-cans for water audits, soil moisture probes, and low-cost recycled mulch), educational materials, classes, or demonstration gardens.

Chapter 10

Maintaining Water-Harvesting and Irrigation Systems

In This Chapter

▶ Taking care of your water-harvesting system

▶ Keeping permanent irrigation systems up to snuff

▶ Handling special irrigation problems

*W*ell-designed and properly built water harvesting and irrigation systems require little care. But ignoring maintenance tasks can result in wasted water and ruined landscaping. You don't need to make maintenance a frequent part of your regimen, but even a perfect system needs attention now and then as this chapter explains — nothing too complex. Promise.

Keeping Your Water-Harvesting System in Shape

Low maintenance is one of the side benefits of a water harvesting strategy. Compared to the work needed to keep a hi-tech irrigation system in good condition, there's little to take care of. However, some parts of this system do call for a bit of upkeep. In the following sections, I give you some tips on what to do with each particular type of system.

Taking care of nonstorage systems

A *nonstorage system* consists of earthworks, such as swales, dry streambeds, percolation zones, and other naturalistic features. One important maintenance task to take care of for this type of system is checking all the parts after (or during) each significant rainstorm to make sure they haven't collapsed or filled with silt. Ensure that the water is going where it's supposed to, and make any repairs immediately by regrading and compacting failed areas or by using rocks to stabilize weak points.

This task is especially important with new systems, because you may need to tweak the contours of the soil so that water flows the way you intended. However, even an established system can use adjustment now and then; gopher or ground squirrel activity or gradual changes in soil levels due to siltation can affect your system. If your swales are planted, keep the plants in good condition so they hold the soil together, preventing erosion.

Checking out storage systems

Storage-type water harvesting systems consist of a cistern or tank, along with a delivery system for the water. Storing lots of water comes with a responsibility to prevent it from becoming a problem. So check for sediment periodically, and clean the bottom of the tank as needed. Maintain critter-exclusion devices to keep mosquitoes and other vermin from coming to live in the system. Keep lids and access ports locked so nobody gets inside and drowns.

Keep in mind that tanks can eventually leak or even fail catastrophically. Inspect them at least once a year for leaks, rust spots (metal tanks), cracks (ferrocement or masonry tanks), undermining of the tank foundations, or any other signs of failure. Be sure to check all components after an earthquake.

Monitoring graywater systems

Simple *graywater systems*, consisting of pipes that deliver water from the source (such as your washing machine) to plants by means of gravity, rarely need service as long as they don't introduce a lot of gunk into the lines (and assuming that you have consistent downhill flow into soak zones). The system will let you know when it needs to be serviced by backing up into, say, your laundry room.

By law, you can't allow graywater to come to the surface of the ground. If it does, it may be a sign that you're delivering too much water for the ground to absorb. Or it may mean that excess rainfall is saturating the soil. Consider expanding the distribution for added capacity, or at least divert water to the regular sewer until things dry out a bit.

Many simple graywater systems drain into mulch-filled underground basins, which need to be cleaned out and refilled annually. Systems need occasional flushing with clean water, and sometimes you have to backflush the pipes by shoving a hose up an outlet to release plugging. No stinky smells should be coming from your system; foul odors indicate gunk in the lines or a backup. If you suspect a backup, flush the lines.

Keep an eye on the health of plants watered by the system, and irrigate them with fresh water now and then if the graywater seems to be adding too much crud for them to keep up with. Your plants will let you know if this is the case by developing dead tips on the leaves (indicating that salts are building up in the soil) or by showing signs of stress or reduced vigor.

Even though there are apparently no documented cases of anyone ever having become ill from contact with graywater, cleaning a graywater system exposes you to bacteria and many potential health risks. Wear protective gear, and wash up (in fresh water, please) after you're done.

Inspecting and Maintaining Your Permanent Irrigation System

The following sections help you evaluate the condition of each part of your irrigation system — sprinklers, drip, and other related components — and make repairs. Spending a pleasant hour with your system two or three times during the growing season can make a big difference in its performance, in your water bills, in the health of your landscaping, and in the environmental benefits that accrue from not wasting water. With the exception of maintaining backflow prevention devices, which should be done by a licensed technician, none of the servicing is complicated.

Start your inspection by looking for excessively dry or wet areas, poorly performing plants, or other signs of misbehavior. Refer to the related subsection of this chapter for detailed service procedures on specific components.

Turn off the water when working on any pressurized part of the system (that is, any part that's before the lateral lines and drip tubing). And be careful to keep dirt out of objects that you're working on; dirt only makes things worse.

Backflow prevention devices

The backflow preventer is the one-way valve that keeps your water supply safe. Often it's a single device at the beginning of your system called a *pressure vacuum breaker,* a *reduced pressure device,* or a *double check valve.* If you have a centrally located device, the law says it has to be serviced annually by a licensed backflow test technician. Call your community's building department for a list of approved companies. If you have atmospheric vacuum breakers at each valve, they generally require no service.

Pressure regulators

The *pressure regulator* is located at the head of the system along with the backflow prevention device; it's the gadget that controls the water pressure. If your sprinkler heads are generating more mist than spray, or if your heads or drip emitters are constantly blowing off, perhaps your regulator has gone wonky on you. Regulators usually last for decades, but if the incoming water is gritty, you may run into problems. Sometimes age takes its toll, too.

Attach a pressure gauge to a hose bib to test the pressure, and adjust the regulator if necessary by turning the adjustment screw (which is easy to find, because it's the only adjustable thing on the unit). If the pressure doesn't adjust properly, purchase a rebuild kit from your local plumbing or irrigation supply store.

Zone valves

Zone valves are the individual electrically or manually controlled valves that operate the sprinklers or drip. You have one valve per *zone* (the system of sprinkler heads or drip lines that are controlled by the valve). Valves are located aboveground (manual and some electric valves) or underground in valve boxes (electric valves only).

For underground installations, the valve box should be dry inside; if it's flooded, check for leaks. Occasionally, an electric valve sticks open — usually due to grit lodging in the solenoid port. Piece of cake to fix. First, turn off the water. Then remove the *solenoid* (the thing with the wires attached to it) and gently rinse any grit out of the port located in the valve body. The other thing that could cause a valve to stick is a punctured diaphragm (no birth-control jokes, please). Remove the top of the valve, inspect the rubber diaphragm for holes or tears, and replace it if it's defective.

Every now and then a solenoid goes bad. You can test for trouble by removing the solenoid and applying 24 volts from the transformer of your controller (*not* high voltage at an outlet!) to see whether it clicks on. Replace it if it doesn't. (If electrical stuff makes you nervous, call an irrigation company to do this test for you.)

If ground squirrels or gophers have filled the valve box with soil, clean it out. While you're in there, turn the valve on (use the *manual bleed control* that's on the valve, which is a little lever or screw), and then adjust the flow control (usually a cross-shaped handle on top of the valve) so that the sprinklers are getting enough water. Flow controls usually are set to wide open, but in some cases, you may want to adjust them down to reduce flow over the whole zone.

Another part of the system that sometimes causes problems is the wiring that connects the valve solenoid to the controller. The weak points are the waterproof connectors that join the control wires coming from the controller (these wires come into the valve box from underground) to the solenoid wires. If the connectors fail — or if the connection is made improperly with electrical tape, wire nuts, or duct tape — replace with proper connectors.

Sometimes underground wiring is damaged due to careless digging or burrowing animals; both can be a serious problem. (You'll know when you have this problem, because one or more valves won't turn on from the controller.) Unless you see suspicious activity aboveground, such as a gopher mound or recent digging, finding the problem can be mighty challenging. Instead of tearing up the whole yard, call an irrigation company that can locate the fault with special electronic equipment.

Controller

Very few things go wrong with modern controllers. The vast majority of "broken" controllers are just programmed incorrectly. (The program, by the way, consists of the time settings and other information you enter into the unit with all those dials and buttons. You did this when you put the controller in, right?) If the system isn't coming on automatically, the best thing you can do is get out the instruction book for the controller and reprogram it. If reprogramming doesn't do the trick, take the unit in to a dealer for repair.

Power outages lasting a few hours or more may cause the backup battery to run down, in which case you lose the program. The remedy is simple: Replace the battery and reenter the program. (You did keep a hard copy of the program, didn't you?)

Adjusting the program at least four times a year to account for seasonal changes in water demand is one of your most important jobs in the sustainable landscape. Refer to the water management information in Chapter 9. (If you have a smart controller, you're off the hook.)

Sometimes a problem looks like a controller malfunction but is actually a short in the wiring or is a bad control valve. If at least one valve doesn't come on, use a voltmeter to measure the voltage at the terminal strip inside the controller; it should be delivering 24 volts to whatever valve is set to come on. If it is, but the valve still isn't working, measure the voltage at the valve. If the valve is getting power, you've got a bad solenoid or a defective valve; if the valve isn't getting power, you likely have bad wiring.

A *rain sensor,* which is a little cup located on the eaves of the house or at some other location that's exposed to rainfall, turns off the controller temporarily in the event of rain. Once in a while, a rain sensor can cause an overall system malfunction. Disconnect the rain sensor at the terminal strip inside the controller; if the system works, the sensor is bad. Some rain sensors can get filled with leaves, so clean them out now and then.

Never hook up a controller to an electrical circuit that also serves a washing machine, compressor, or other piece of equipment that has a large power draw. Power surges resulting when the equipment starts up can throw the delicate electronics of your controller into a permanent snit.

Drip filters and regulators

Each of your drip irrigation zones is equipped with a *drip setup* located at the valve for that zone. The drip setup consists of a small regulator to reduce incoming water pressure and a filter that screens junk out of the water so that it can't plug the emitters. Drip regulators don't need service. However, regular cleaning of drip filters is essential, especially if your water is on the dirty side. Unscrew the canister using your hands. Carefully remove the cartridge, keeping dirt from falling into the open filter body. Wash the cartridge at a nearby hose bib, using a toothbrush if necessary to gently remove gunk. Rinse the cartridge and canister, reinstall the whole business being careful not to overtighten, and turn the valve on and look for leaks.

Drip tubing and emitters

The *drip emitters* that supply water to your plants are installed on or molded into black plastic tubing called *drip tubing*. The tubing usually sits on top of the soil and beneath the mulch. In that position, the tubing is vulnerable to physical damage from weeding, foot traffic, and animal activity.

To inspect your drip lines and emitters, turn the system on and look for any funny business. You may find tiny geysers squirting festively into the air; in that case, check to see whether any emitters have come off. If an emitter pops off, put a new one in the same hole. Or close off the hole with a *goof plug* (see your dealer for this item) and make a new hole nearby for the replacement emitter. If a critter has noshed on the tubing, remove the damaged section and patch a new piece in, using two drip couplers that are friction-fitted on, just like other fittings on the system. (Be very careful to keep dirt from finding its way into the tubing while it's open and vulnerable.)

Every once in a while, despite adequate filtration, an emitter stops working. A dead or dying plant will tell you that you have a clogged emitter. Some emitters can be cleaned if they plug up; others have to be replaced. (The best ones are self-cleaning.) If the emitters are mounted on the drip tubing, pull off the stopped-up one and install a new one. (Keep a supply of emitters on hand for moments like these.) If the emitters are molded into the tubing, you can simply make a hole in the tubing next to the dead emitter and install a tubing-mounted emitter in the hole.

After a few years, the drip tubing will disappear under the soil. You can pull it back to the surface or leave it there (especially if you have in-line emitters that are approved for burial). As tree roots grow, they sometimes put a crimp in the drip tubing; replace the crimped part with a small new section of tubing, connecting it to the ends of the old tubing with drip coupler fittings. Give it some slack to account for the next few years' growth.

Sprinkler systems

Choose a sunny day when you need to work on your sprinkler system and don your swimsuit and flip-flops because you're going to get wet. Turn on one valve at a time, looking for broken heads or nozzles, tilted heads, misaimed heads, overspray, underspray, or otherwise out-of-whack heads. Use the adjuster screws on top of the heads to fine-tune the distance of throw.

Rotor heads sometimes have nonintuitive ways of adjusting the arc; refer to the manufacturer's catalog for instructions. Set all heads so the bodies are straight up; they depend on being plumb to deliver an accurate pattern.

You can unthread and remove the nozzles for cleaning or replacement. While you're in there, remove and clean the strainer basket that's usually located underneath the nozzle. If water leaks out of the head while it's in operation (other than where it's supposed to, that is), you may need to clean or replace the seal in the threaded cap that holds the head together. If water constantly leaks out of the lowest head in the zone, check for a leaky control valve; if that's okay, you probably just have water draining out of the pipes for a while after the zone shuts off. To remedy, install a check valve on that head.

Winterizing your irrigation system

Ever notice that the ice cubes are bigger than the amount of water you put in the trays? It's not your imagination. Unlike most materials, water expands when it's frozen. It does that in your irrigation system too. So if you live where winters are cold, you need to drain the water out of the system at the end of the season to avoid damaging pipes and other equipment.

All the pipes in a good cold-weather system slope to drain valves located at low points, making it easy to open the valves and empty the lines quickly — that is, unless it's already starting to freeze. If your system doesn't have drain valves, use a compressor to blow the water out of the lines. Either way, make sure that the lines are completely empty before freezing weather comes along. After you've removed all the water from the lines, turn off the main valve at the beginning of the entire system, and then set your automatic controller to the rain-off position.

When plants grow up, they can block sprinkler heads, leaving dry spots on the lee side of the plant. In fact, sprinklers work best when plants aren't around. Don't remove them, though; just cut back the offending foliage.

When you're done checking your sprinkler system, use catch-cans to do a water audit to ensure that you got things right. Chapter 9 shows you how.

Coping with Special Irrigation Situations

Most people have fairly simple systems that are served by municipal water. But sustainability often takes us in odd directions. In the following sections, I provide some tips on managing special circumstances and equipment.

Caring for wells and treatment systems

If your water comes from a private well, you probably have a well expert to care for all the problems that come up. Similarly, you should contact a knowledgeable professional to treat problem water; he or she will have special equipment for this job.

Treating special water problems

Bacterial iron slime is an organism that inhabits some water supplies. It grows inside pipes, valves, sprinklers, drip emitters, and other parts of the system. If your pipes have greenish-brown slippery stuff inside them, chances are you've been slimed. Treatment isn't easy or practical. The best thing to do is to stick with sprinklers, avoiding drip systems and mini-sprinklers, which can easily become plugged.

Hard water can affect irrigation equipment, but not as often as you may think. Because the insides of the equipment don't dry out very often, the minerals that are present in hard water stay in solution and ride on through. Still, if water is hard enough, you may find yourself replacing equipment regularly. Treatment of the water usually isn't practical for irrigation because of the volume of water used.

Dirty water can make a mess of the best systems. Installing a prefilter at the point of connection can help; talk to your supplier about options. Clean the filter regularly, and be sure to choose contamination-resistant valves (also called *dirty water valves*) that are better suited to passing lots of gunk.

Part IV

Hardscaping Made Easy: Creating Awesome Features without Wrecking the Environment

The 5th Wave   By Rich Tennant

"I wanted a gazebo."

In this part . . .

*H*ardscaping is a fancy landscape architect's term for the nonliving elements of the landscape: patios, decks, retaining walls, walkways, and so on. One thing that makes a landscape sustainable is an emphasis on living systems, but every property needs some hardscape.

Just as the title suggests, in this part I show you how to create great hardscape features without messing up the environment. I cover paving, fences and walls, retaining structures, woodwork such as arbors and decks, and even fun stuff like water features and art. What's more, I show you how to assemble all these elements into beautiful, functional outdoor rooms that will serve your family's needs for decades to come. I also discuss how to prepare your site, and how to maintain the finished product.

Chapter 11

Preparing Your Site

. . . .

In This Chapter

▶ Staying safe on the job

▶ Steering clear of utilities

▶ Making your demolition derby sustainable

▶ Working the land: grading and drainage

▶ Fighting weeds the sustainable way

. . . .

*I*f you've taken the time to design a truly sustainable landscape (see the chapters in Part II), you probably thought you'd never get around to actually building it. Well, it's time to get dirty and build up calluses on those hands — or to hire a professional to do the whole job. Either way, the goal now is making sure that you know what to do at each stage of the site prep part of your project. Even if you'll be hiring someone to ready your site, knowing how things work will make you a more informed consumer of services and keep you out of trouble. Okay, slip on those boots. Here we go.

Safety First and Nobody Gets Hurt

Landscape construction is heavy work involving tools and equipment that are often much bigger, harder, sharper, and more powerful than you. Because you'll be doing your landscaping sustainably, you won't be using toxic chemicals, so that problem's out of the way. But you have to deal with numerous other considerations to stay in one piece and to keep your family and others safe:

> ✔ **Keep the place clean.** Make sure that all pathways, all work areas, and the site in general are tidy at all times. Don't leave materials stacked precariously, sharp tools left in harm's way, or open trenches unmarked. Keep in mind that kids and possibly the public may find their way onto your property during construction. Make daily inspections.

✔ **Wear proper clothing and safety gear.** Heavy boots (no flip-flops or tennies), sturdy clothing, gloves, safety goggles, a back brace for lifting, and a dust mask — all these items are essential to keeping you safe.

✔ **Lift with your legs, not your back.** In other words, squat (keeping your back straight) to lift instead of bending over. And don't be macho; get help with heavy stuff.

✔ **Know how to use your tools.** Read instruction manuals that come with the equipment you're using. And get a lesson on operating any heavy equipment you rent.

✔ **Keep tools and equipment in good condition.** Make sure that safety guards are in place. Watch for frayed power cords, loose blades, and dull cutting tools (sharp ones are actually safer).

✔ **Use a GFCI.** That's a *ground fault circuit interrupter* — a safety device for electrical equipment that cuts off power before it can hurt you in the event of a short circuit.

✔ **Never refuel gas-powered equipment while it's running or hot.** Also, be sure to store fuel in approved containers in a safe location.

✔ **Stay out of wet concrete.** Contact with skin can cause cement poisoning. So be sure to wear rubber boots and gloves when working with concrete.

✔ **Stay out of trees, too.** Leave tree climbing to experts and squirrels. It's a long way down.

✔ **If you're working around dry grasses and weeds, keep a fire extinguisher on hand.** Avoid using steel tools that can spark against rocks.

✔ **Keep a first-aid kit handy at all times.** Know emergency contact numbers, and let family members know if you'll be doing something risky.

✔ **Keep kids and pets out of the way.** They don't understand the dangers.

✔ **Watch your contractors.** Not all contractors provide safety training for their workers. Keep an eye on them.

✔ **Do only what you're comfortable with.** It's always better to hire a professional than to get hurt.

Locating Utilities before You Dig

Utilities come into your property underground as well as overhead. Before you start digging, you need to determine the exact locations of gas and water mains, power lines, telephone and television cables, sewer pipes, and any other utilities serving the site. You also may have *utility easements* (legal access to the use of your property by others, often utility companies) running through your property. You may have transmission lines or pipes within those easements.

You must locate utilities on your property before you work, because finding them accidentally could get you injured or even killed. What's more, it would cost you (or your next of kin) a lot to fix damaged utilities — and to pay the fines for not following the law that says you have to find your utilities with something other than a backhoe or pickaxe. Lots of nice folks have blown themselves up hitting gas lines, fried themselves poking into underground electric wires, disrupted phone service to whole neighborhoods, and had other highly humbling misadventures. Don't be one of them.

After you have everything flagged and marked on the ground, take a little time to draw a map of your property showing the exact locations of everything, because it's only a matter of time before the markings disappear during construction.

Calling your state's locating service

Be sure to arrange for utility location at least a few days before you start digging. Call 811 to arrange for the service; this number serves the entire U.S. (Visit www.call811.com for more details.) After you call 811, your local One Call Center will contact all the utility providers serving your property and arrange for them to come out and flag everything. You'll have to mark the area first so they know where to look for utilities; the 811 operators will explain how to do this when you make the call. Within a couple of days after calling 811, all your utilities should be identified, and you then can dig with confidence. One Call service is free — and required by law.

Tracking down private utilities

You may have to locate where the utilities, such as water and gas lines and other underground lines, run inside your property, as the One Call service usually covers only up to the property lines. Many companies have cool equipment to do this job for a relatively modest fee, and they save you the trouble of digging the yard up looking for things.

Getting Down and Dirty with Demolition

The landscaper's first task is to make a wreck of the place — in other words, demolish it. This part can be a lot of fun, and the clean slate that you end up with can be invigorating. Often, demolition is completed with heavy equipment, such as a tractor. If your project is large, that's the way to go, but for smaller jobs consider giving the environment a break by using hand tools as much as possible.

Practicing sustainable disposal

The old-school approach to demolition was to push the old yard into a trash bin and send it away to the landfill. Now we realize that nothing ever really goes "away" and that everything we dispose of causes problems somewhere else.

Instead of treating the unwanted parts of your existing landscaping as waste, see whether anything could be useful in constructing your new landscaping: soil, trees, broken concrete, bricks from your old patio, useful plants, or artsy junk. Set these reusable castoffs aside for later use.

Also be sure to recycle where appropriate. For example, send green waste to the local composting operation instead of mixing it with other materials in a trash bin (call your local trash hauler or municipal solid waste department to find out about the options that are available in your area). Separate recyclable metals, concrete, and soil, all of which may be of value to others even if you can't use them. Craigslist, Freecycle.com, and the local classifieds and bulletin boards are ways to find homes for these useful castoffs.

Protecting existing land and vegetation

Keep nature safe as you demolish your existing landscape. One way to do that is to mark off the *drip line* (the outermost extent of the tree's foliage) of your existing trees with a ring of flags or better yet with temporary fencing. This marked line alerts workers about the importance of not grading or compacting the soil with vehicles, equipment, or foot traffic during construction. Also avoid placing building materials under trees.

Similarly, get your big trees in shape before you do any landscaping. The project will be easier and cheaper if the tree-care workers don't have to pussyfoot through new plantings. You can do tree work any time in the early stages of the project.

Choose your tree-care company carefully. A hundred years of growth can be destroyed in minutes by improper care.

Also, protect against erosion by installing *straw wattles* or *silt fencing* (see Chapter 14 for information on these and other erosion control strategies) at the base of piles of soil that rain could wash away (a precaution that's required by federal law). Avoid working in wildlife habitat or nesting sites. And keep soil out of waterways.

Making the Grade: Doing Your Earthwork

One of the most important elements of your sustainable landscape is the underlying earth. How you grade your property determines how long water remains on the land; how it travels across the surface; and whether it soaks usefully into the ground or runs off to cause erosion, flooding, and pollution. Grading keeps your house safe from flooding, creates usable areas, and sculpts dull terrain into elegant sensual forms.

You grade your land only once — and you have to do it properly, because you can't change it after the plants are in. For that reason, understanding how grading works is important. I walk you through the details of grading and drainage in Chapter 8. And see how to create grading and drainage plans in Chapter 6.

Grading the ground sustainably

The sustainable approach to grading is to do as little as possible (because soil is damaged by moving it around) and to have specific reasons to grade, such as conserving water on site, preventing erosion, or keeping the house from flooding. Here are some basic grading principles:

- ✔ Check all existing grades with a sighting level or have the area surveyed; then plan a grading strategy to accomplish your objectives.

- ✔ Talk to a geologist if you have any potentially unstable areas. Never use terracing or water-harvesting strategies on unstable slopes. (You can find information on terracing and water harvesting in Chapter 8.)

- ✔ Evaluate the site for desirable features, such as trees or native ecosystems, and grade to protect those features. Fence off protected areas.

- ✔ Follow or restore the natural landform where possible, or use the information in Chapter 7 to develop a water-harvesting strategy for your land. Water harvesting modifies the terrain so it soaks up water.

- ✔ Avoid rototilling, which destroys soil structure. Similarly, avoid compacting the soil with heavy equipment if grading by hand is feasible. And never work soil when it's wet, because you can severely damage it. Instead, wait until dry weather.

- ✔ Never add sand to clay soils unless you're planning to build walls with the resulting glop.

- ✔ Talk to an arborist before grading around mature trees.

✔ Don't add amendments except in special circumstances. Do add small amounts of living compost and mycorrhizal fungi to planted areas at planting time, not during grading. (See Chapter 16 for more information on soil preparation.)

✔ For major grade changes, remove the topsoil, regrade the subsoil, and then replace the topsoil. This practice will make a big difference in plant growth.

Importing and exporting soil

Sometimes, you can't avoid moving soil off your site. If that's the case for you, try to find a good home for it. Make sure it will be used to repair a damaged site rather than create new problems. And if you need to import soil, ask about its source — perhaps even requesting a complete soil test as a condition of purchase. (You probably won't get far with this tactic, but it's worth a try.)

Having said all that, do avoid bringing soil in or taking it away, if you can. Both practices can disrupt off-site locations and involve the usual pollution and fossil-fuel dependency of trucks and heavy equipment. In addition, when you import topsoil, you run the risk of also importing new kinds of weeds, diseases, and even toxic substances.

When an area needs to be leveled, try to *balance cut and fill* to avoid importing or exporting soil. In other words, remove soil in one area and use it to fill another so it comes out even. You can do this when creating a level pad for a patio, for example. Be careful not to undermine unstable slopes, expose or smother tree roots, unbury utility lines, or change natural drainage patterns.

Outsmarting the Weeds on Your Site the Organic Way

Pretty much every site has weeds. Weeds are difficult to control because they evolved to be aggressive, sneaky, virile, and just plain annoying. If you don't get the weeds under control before you install your landscaping, they'll come right through and make a mess of your lovely work. *Annual weeds* will come back from seed, and *perennial weeds* will poke up from old root systems.

The easiest and best way to tackle a weed problem is to get 'em during the site prep stage. Beating weeds early saves time and effort; you won't have to fight them after your landscaping is in place. Just remember that herbicides damage the environment, so you want to practice sustainable weed control instead. I explain everything you need to know in the following sections.

Understanding why you should avoid herbicides

I won't mention any names, but certain herbicides have been applied to our poor, suffering planet for decades now, yet there seem to be just as many weeds as ever. Seems like we're losing the battle despite all the poisons — just another example of how conventional methods really don't work.

Commonly used herbicides have significant effects on the environment, such as toxicity to wildlife, especially amphibians and fish. Toxicity to humans is also a considerable problem; instances of acute and chronic health problems are numerous and well documented. Finally, some weeds are developing resistance to herbicides, becoming superweeds that nothing can control. Because good alternatives are available, you have little or no reason to use herbicides any longer.

Practicing sustainable weed control

Facing a weed-infested site can be intimidating, especially if you've chosen to forego the herbicides. It's tempting to bend your ethics just this one little time. After all, who wants to spend all summer hoeing and pulling? Fortunately, smart sustainable gardeners have come up with some safe alternatives that don't break your back (or hurt the environment).

Use horticultural vinegar

Horticultural vinegar is a keen way to kill weeds without nasty chemicals. It doesn't kill every weed in the book, but it's pretty effective on many, especially the young ones.

Horticultural vinegar is stronger than ordinary vinegar, so treat it with care (as you would any other strong acid). Weeds sprayed with this substance often die within a couple of hours. Your yard will smell like a salad for a bit; otherwise, the vinegar is environmentally benign. Some nurseries carry horticultural vinegar, and a few of the mail-order garden supply places also offer it.

As of this writing there's some controversy over horticultural vinegar's registration with the EPA as an herbicide; hopefully this issue will be resolved by the time you read this book.

Smother weeds with sheet mulching

Sheet mulching is the practice of killing weeds by smothering them. Hoe out any surface weeds, cover the soil with two or three layers of corrugated cardboard salvaged from the waste stream (buy it from recyclers or gather it up from dumpsters behind stores). Overlap the cardboard and wet it down thoroughly, and then cover the whole funny-looking mess with at least 4 inches of organic mulch (wood chips, for example). Leave everything in place for a few months, if you can. Sheet mulching has proved to be more effective than herbicides, which can also take months to kill weeds fully. See Chapter 16 for an illustration of sheet mulching.

Rent a goat or try some other weed control methods

In some progressive communities you can rent a goat or a whole herd to gobble up your weeds while you sit on the porch sipping lemonade and watching the show. This method may sound crazy if you live in the suburbs, but animals have been eating weeds for millennia. If you're out in the country, getting a goat (or for that matter some sheep, horses, or cattle) should be even easier. A bonus is that they fertilize at the same time.

Other weed control methods include burning weeds (please talk to the fire department first!) or killing them with special steam or heating tools (search for "flame weeders" with your favorite online search engine). And yes, there's always chopping and hoeing.

Chapter 12

Exploring Basic Hardscape Elements and Outdoor Rooms

*E*very garden needs basic *hardscape* features: places to sit and entertain, and safe steps, paths, and enclosures. However, conventional hardscape can be entropic, high maintenance, and troublesome. It's made up of materials that are taken from the planet and that can be toxic, nonrenewable, high in embodied energy, and transported from far away by means of climate-wrecking fossil fuels. Their operation and upkeep can require toxic finishing substances and energy-intensive processes.

Sustainable hardscape, on the other hand, emphasizes plants and biological elements over industrial elements made of concrete, steel, plastic, and other manmade materials. Even hardscape at its most sustainable is a "less-bad" solution to the problem of environmental impact. For that reason, you should try to use the least amount of hardscape that serves your needs. The good news is that many alternative materials and methods minimize negative effects; you can use them to create some truly beautiful and useful additions to your project.

This chapter covers some popular hardscape options that can add both visual appeal and function to the landscape. With the right approach and materials, you can have great hardscape features without all the environmental problems.

Getting Floored: Surveying the Many Flooring Options

Landscapers design gardens in terms of the base plane, or floor. Think about it: A landscape plan is a diagram of how the floor is arranged. Laying out the floor — whether it's a patio, deck, or other surface — is a great starting point for developing your overall hardscape. In the following sections, I lay down the foundations of good floor design and show you some creative, sustainable options. (Check out Chapter 14 for tips on constructing floors of all kinds.)

Floors should be beautiful; ugliness isn't a requirement of sustainability. You'll have no trouble finding something that complements your landscaping, is compatible with the architecture of your house, and is easy on the environment.

Floors 101: The basics

Unlike the other elements of the hardscape system, floors need to withstand traffic. You have a wide range of serviceable materials to choose from (many of which won't lay waste to the planet).

From a sustainability point of view, many flooring materials have unacceptable negative effects. The off-site impacts of getting the materials in the first place can be extreme: strip mining, clear-cutting forests, dredging riverbeds, or drilling for oil. The processes used to turn raw materials into finished products can be energy-intensive, toxic, climate-changing, and hazardous to workers. Installation can involve heavy equipment, fossil-fuel use, and lots of noise. Surfaces that require periodic maintenance can make unreasonable demands for chemicals and energy.

You'll also find some sustainable imposters — materials that have questionable or fraudulent environmental credentials. These materials include plastic lumber, phony plastic lawns, and mulch made from ground-up tires. Plastic lumber isn't all bad, but the phony lawns and mulch are environmental nightmares.

Stick with materials that are as close to a state of nature as possible and that require minimal processing and maintenance. And, build things so they last; durability is a supremely sustainable strategy, because it divides the initial inputs over many decades of use.

Concrete versus cement

There's a difference between concrete and cement. Even professionals don't always understand this, so if you do, you'll be among the initiates into the Mysteries of the Cementitious Realm. Here's the scoop:

✔ **Concrete** is a mixture of *aggregate* (crushed rock), sand, portland cement, and water.

✔ **Cement** is one of the ingredients of concrete. One adds cement to aggregate, sand, and water to make concrete for a patio. However, one does not make a cement patio (or, for fans of *The Beverly Hillbillies*, a ceeement pond). Now you know.

The manufacturing of cement for concrete production is incredibly energy-intensive, and it generates 5 to 10 percent of the world's carbon dioxide emissions, but improvements in the processes used are lowering that figure dramatically. New technologies such as *nano-concrete* (made with a special kind of cement that has a much lower environmental impact) are very promising. And believe it or not, a new type of *photocatalytic concrete* (using a technology called *TX Active*) actually absorbs air pollution.

Because rainfall runs off of solid paving, it can be an unfriendly part of the watershed, causing flooding and stream pollution when the water spills into the street and carries contaminants into waterways. Choosing pervious surfaces is one way to deal with that concern, but you can also purposely choose impervious surfaces to act as water catchment zones that spill their captured water into bioswales, planted areas, or other spots where it will be put to use. (See the later section "Using safe, sustainable materials" for more information on pervious materials, and refer to Chapter 8 for details on water harvesting.)

Using safe, sustainable materials

The following sections show some flooring surfaces that your enviro-side can feel good about. None of these is perfect, but each gives you a floor with less negative impact.

Poured concrete

The poured concrete patio is the classic solution for flat surfaces outdoors. Concrete can be colored, textured, imprinted, seeded with pebbles, and generally dolled up in many ways. Use concrete where you want a relatively inexpensive and very durable surface. But keep in mind all that strip mining and carbon dioxide production, and consider alternatives before you make the knee-jerk choice of concrete.

Fly ash (a waste product of coal-burning power plants) makes concrete stronger and it looks and acts like regular concrete. Not only does it use a waste product, it also reduces carbon dioxide production.

Paver blocks

Paver blocks aren't permeable, but specially-designed ones leave openings that absorb rainfall at the rate of about 1 inch per hour. Because they can be reused, pavers are the quintessential heritage material. (Refer to Chapter 2 for more on heritage materials.) Pavers are ideal for driveways, paths, and patios.

Pervious concrete

Pervious concrete is regular concrete without the sand — just crushed rock, portland cement, and water. It comes out looking like a giant rice cake. The voids between the bits of rock slurp up water at a rate of up to 350 inches per hour, which — take it from me — is beyond biblical.

Pervious concrete can take plenty of weight, so it's great for driveways, and other heavy-traffic surfaces. It can be colored, and the top can be ground for a smoother, more attractive surface.

For more information on this material, visit the Pervious Concrete Web site (www.perviouspavement.org) or ConcreteNetwork.com (www.concrete network.com).

Urbanite

This newly discovered "mineral" is nothing more than old, broken concrete paving, used like flagstones to make what the British call *crazy paving*.

Urbanite is the ultimate waste-stream material, with no environmental impact other than transport. It can be stained or used as is, and it makes a lovely surface. Urbanite is available nearly everywhere; look for demolition projects in your neighborhood or call contractors to find out who's planning to generate some waste concrete.

Living ground cover

Making a living floor is a biological solution. Living ground covers include low-growing plants like thyme, chamomile, and yarrow as well as a conventional lawn. Unmowed, these plants make a gorgeous natural meadow; mowed, they form turf that you can walk and play on. Nearly all ground covers require some watering and fertilizing, but most are less needy than turf.

Plants won't take the kind of abuse that a harder surface will, and they can be troublesome to walk on when wet. Reserve them for low-traffic and play areas.

Wood decking

Wood decking is a renewable natural material, and its embodied energy is fairly low. Be sure that the wood you use is certified as sustainably harvested by the Forest Stewardship Council in the United States (www.fscus.org) or the Programme for the Endorsement of Forest Certification (PEFC) globally (www.pefc.org).

Plastic lumber

Plastic lumber is a decking material that's made from soda containers, grocery bags, and wood waste. It looks more or less like wood. Plastic wood can smell on hot days (and it can be hot underfoot if the wood is dark).

Alternative woods

You may be able to find local, sustainably produced wood for your deck. For instance, black locust is a weedy tree that can be harvested and milled into durable lumber that's a nontoxic substitute for pressure-treated wood. Local *sawyers* (people who turn trees into boards) can generate the lumber. Black locust is a very hard wood and can be challenging, but by no means impossible, to work with. Reclaimed and salvaged lumber is another possibility.

Mulch

Mulch has to be the daddy of all sustainable surfaces — so natural that it could have come from your own backyard (and if you got the chips from tree trimming, perhaps it did). It's biodegradable, low in embodied energy, beneficial for the soil and plants, attractive to look at, fragrant, pervious to water, and good at keeping the weeds down and the roots of your plants happy. Mulch is a great surface for informal areas, and it's cheap as anything you can imagine. It's simple to install, too: just dump it and rake it around.

Mulch isn't the best for putting chairs on, as the legs can sink into moist soil, and it isn't so great for handicapped access. Also remember that because it slowly decomposes, adding valuable organic matter and nutrients to your soil, mulch gets thinner over time. So you have to top it off with a new layer every couple of years.

Gravel or crushed rock

Taken from riverbeds or quarries, gravel or crushed rock carries an environmental price. Plus rock-covered surfaces attract weeds that can be difficult to control. Use these surfaces sparingly, where their simplicity, perviousness, and nice crunchy sound underfoot are welcome.

Considering maintenance

Paved surfaces require little maintenance unless you make the mistake of painting them. Don't waste your money on sealers and stains, which often contain toxic and air polluting ingredients. Instead, leave surfaces to age naturally and gracefully. If you must use a finish, choose nontoxic, low VOC materials (*VOCs* are air-polluting chemicals that evaporate from many finishes as they cure).

Ground covers require weeding, watering, and other normal plant care. Choose species that are adapted to your area, and research their needs before making your decision.

Concrete patios just need a sweeping every now and then. Wood decks can be a little more demanding; they need periodic power-washing, sanding, and refinishing. Plastic lumber decks just need power washing.

Choosing between a patio and a deck

If you have a steep slope, consider a deck. If you have more or less level, stable ground, stick with a patio. A patio made of nearly anything is cheaper and easier to build and more durable than a deck. The rub comes when you have a hillside that has to be leveled and stabilized before it can support the weight of a patio, which can mean a very costly retaining wall system and still more environmental impact. In this situation, a deck starts to look good.

If you live in a high fire hazard area, check with local authorities about special regulations for decks, which can be fire magnets if they aren't built properly. (For more on firescaping your yard, check out the appendix.)

Dividing Space Using Walls, Fences, and Other Barriers

The vertical plane, or walls, in your landscape can be made of plants or manufactured materials. A wall may be connected to a floor and a ceiling of some sort to create an outdoor room, which I discuss in "Using Sustainable Hardscape Features to Build an Outdoor Room," later in this chapter. Walls don't have to be restricted to the outer boundaries of your property. Use interior walls to create outdoor rooms and break the space into interesting subspaces.

Use walls or fences to block views of neighbors or to create an enclosed courtyard or walled garden. For complete privacy, make your enclosure solid and at least 6 feet high.

Solid enclosures change the microclimate. They create shade on one side and sun on the other, block or channel winds, and sometimes absorb or reflect heat. When handled properly, these characteristics can be desirable, but if you aren't aware of the changes you'll be creating, you could end up with trouble.

Keeping people and animals in or out of your property requires sturdy barriers. The most sustainable of these barriers are thorny or otherwise impenetrable shrubs. However, small or determined interlopers can still make their way through these barriers. For complete security, choose a solid masonry or adobe wall, or consider chain-link fencing made of recyclable steel. This section introduces the types of walls and fences that you can incorporate into your hardscape. Chapter 14 provides some pointers on building sustainable walls.

Free-standing walls

Free-standing walls enclose space to create privacy, make an area secure, or improve the microclimate. For minimal environmental impact, build an earth wall. Earth (aka soil) can be shaped into adobe blocks that are then stacked to form a wall, tamped between temporary wooden forms to make rammed earth, or simply plopped into a free-form wall of *cob* (fancy language for blobs of mud and straw). For a higher-tech and more formal-looking wall, look into new soil-cement blocks that are coming onto the market. They're made from natural materials, have a high recycled content, and require much less energy to manufacture than the conventional concrete blocks they replace. And don't forget the usefulness of living hedges and vines in creating privacy.

Of course, you can use more traditional materials such as wood, metal, or *masonry* (brick, stone, concrete block, or plaster) to build a wall. Masonry walls are durable and handsome, but they're also more expensive and often higher in environmental impacts than the other types. A traditional masonry wall, made almost entirely of cement-like materials has all the drawbacks inherent to that material: strip mining, carbon dioxide production, and embodied energy. If you decide to build a wall with one of these materials, build it so it will last for decades — maybe even centuries. Spread the inputs over the lifespan, and you'll have a very sustainable structure. Using high-volume fly ash concrete for the footings will help as well.

Retaining walls

Retaining walls hold back slopes and can be used to increase the usable space on your property. Retaining walls 2 feet or less in height are easy and usually safe to build, but because taller retaining walls support impressive loads, they need to be treated as structural elements as well as visual and functional ones and are more complicated to install.

Sustainable materials for short retaining walls include dry-stacked urbanite, rubble, or stones from your site or a nearby site. The newer mortarless individual stacking block systems, called *segmental retaining walls* (see Figure 12-1), are made from concrete but can be reused, making them good heritage materials. Adobe can be used for very low walls with little pressure on them, but keep in mind that holding back soil with more soil isn't much better than having no wall at all.

Some taller types of retaining walls can also be fashioned from wooden timbers, landscape ties, reclaimed wood, and logs. If you use treated wood, choose the kind that's free of arsenic.

For taller walls, and where you have a *surcharge* above the wall (a slope rather than level ground), you need to use a *cantilever wall,* consisting of a base and a stem. For any wall taller than 4 feet (including the base), or where you have a surcharge of soil behind the wall, hire a civil engineer to design the wall. Look into building-permit requirements, too.

Figure 12-1:
A segmental retaining wall.

Courtesy of Rockwood Retaining Walls, Inc.

Breaking wind like the pros

Windy sites call for something to intercept or divert the wind away from use areas. A windbreak not only increases comfort, but also can reduce heating and cooling needs inside the house. Trees and shrubs are good at breaking wind because they absorb energy efficiently.

Solid fences and walls can actually worsen wind on the lee side by creating an eddy effect. Slatted or louvered fencing does a better job, as does a fence with an angled top to change the flow characteristics. Earthen berms or mounds can also direct wind.

Fences and other barriers

Like walls, fences enclose space to create privacy and make an area secure. Your most sustainable fence material option is living plants, which do wonders to create privacy. Hedges and vines are inexpensive, tagger-proof, and offer all the environmental benefits of any biological solution.

If you need a more solid solution, sustainable wooden fences made from certified sustainably harvested wood, nontoxic treated posts, and high fly ash content concrete to fill the post holes are an option. Unfortunately, certified fence lumber can be difficult to find. If you have to buy noncertified wood, at least it's a natural material and not the worst thing you can choose.

Modern wooden fence posts are pressure-treated with a nontoxic chemical called *alkaline copper quaternary* (ACQ). It's much safer than old arsenic-treated wood, but there are concerns about corrosion of fasteners in contact with ACQ. Be sure to use only ACQ-compatible fasteners and hardware; otherwise, the fence may fail prematurely, which isn't sustainable at all.

If you're replacing an existing wooden fence, see if you can salvage the fence boards, which are often still in excellent condition, and just replace the posts and any other rotten wood. Consider using steel posts, which last a lot longer than wood ones.

Chain link or other steel fences are common, inexpensive, and pretty sustainable too. Steel has a high embodied energy, but the material itself is usually recycled and also recyclable, so you'll know that your new fence will be turned into something useful when it's finally old. Avoid vinyl-coated chain link, though.

Topping Off Your Hardscape with a Ceiling

Ceilings, living or manmade, offer shelter, shade, enclosure, privacy, architectural interest, and a place to hang your wind chimes. One of my favorite memories of my youth is of an intimate little patio tucked into the back fence line of an old house, enclosed on all sides but the front, sheltered from rain by a solid roof, and furnished with an old-fashioned glider with thick, comfy cushions and a couple of big armchairs. It was nothing fancy, but I vividly recall sitting there for hours in a state of complete peace. Thinking back on it in later years, I realized that if you took away any of the sides — especially the roof — the cozy magic would be lost.

Like floors and walls, ceilings may be part of an outdoor room (see "Using Sustainable Hardscape Features to Build an Outdoor Room," later in this chapter). This section explains the ins and outs of outdoor ceilings.

Constructed ceilings

The sky is a nice ceiling: It's time-tested, colorful, attractive, durable, and made from local materials; it goes well with nearly any architectural style; and it's free. Still, sometimes the sky isn't quite what you want in an overhead structure. It doesn't keep out the sun or rain, and it doesn't modify the microclimate. And it also doesn't give you that cozy, snuggly feeling of being sheltered by a room-height ceiling. That's when you turn to the alternatives.

Attractive sustainable overhead structures can be made of salvaged wood, driftwood, tree branches, canvas, or metal (the latter is especially good in high fire hazard areas). Unlike trees, constructed ceilings require some skill to design and build, and usually they're subject to building codes to make them safe.

One type of constructed ceiling is sometimes called a *pergola* (see Figure 12-2). A pergola may be just what you need to provide shade while at the same time letting in air and light.

Take into consideration the following factors when pondering whether to include a constructed ceiling in your plans:

- ✔ **Be sure you really need one.** A very cool or foggy climate calls for openness to let light and heat in, not a shade-casting overhead.

- ✔ **Choose a rainproof roof if you live in a wet climate or enjoy being outside during wet weather.** Remember that fully-roofed structures have to be built to withstand wind; check with a builder or landscape architect for details.

✓ **Determine how much shade you want.** The density of the structure can result in anywhere from 10 to 100 percent shade. If you use parallel louvers to cast shade, place them perpendicular to the rays of the sun. Take the path of the sun into account when placing your structure, and don't forget to estimate where the sun will be at different times of the year. Well-cast shade can make the patio and house more comfortable and can save energy.

✓ **Set the height of your ceiling so that it's in scale with surrounding elements and creates the feeling you want.** Tall ceilings feel open; low ones, cozy.

✓ **Don't paint overhead structures.** Painting costs money and uses resources. Worst of all, repainting is a huge pain when the time comes, especially if you have to remove a covering of mature vines first. Penetrating stains are okay; so is natural unfinished wood.

✓ **If you want a vine on your overhead, choose well.** Most vines carry a lot of dead stuff beneath them; choose something that looks good from below. Make sure that the vine won't drop litter on your dinner. Use a deciduous vine if you want the sunlight to penetrate in winter. Try edible vines such as grapes to get more use out of the structure.

Check local zoning ordinances to be sure you don't put an overhead structure in a location on your property where it isn't permitted, and ask whether you need a building permit for your structure.

Figure 12-2:
A patio with a pergola ceiling.

Courtesy of Butte Fence, Inc.

Living ceilings: Trees

What's more sustainable, durable, or beautiful than a tree? Name another overhead that creates oxygen, sequesters carbon, cools by evaporation, operates by solar power, costs practically nothing, provides habitat for birds and other organisms, lasts for centuries, is fun to climb, and makes flowers and fruit.

Plant trees around your patio or other hardscape elements to provide shade, or construct your deck or patio underneath existing trees for immediate results.

 Avoid messy or weak-wooded trees, ones that might blow over, and certainly ones with root systems that lift pavement. As with all plantings, be sure that the tree you choose is adapted to your climate, soil, and other conditions, and place it carefully so that it casts shade where you want it. Take size into account.

Deciduous trees (ones that lose their leaves in winter) automatically provide shade during summer and allow sunlight to penetrate in winter — one of the most considerate things about trees. Evergreen trees can make a good overhead, too, as long as you can use the shade all year.

The living ecoroof

One of the coolest sustainable landscape elements is the living *ecoroof,* also known as the *green roof* (see Figure 12-3). Made of drought-tolerant plants growing in a shallow layer of lightweight soil held in place by a waterproof membrane and supporting structure, or planted in individual recycled plastic bins, the ecoroof turns your roof into a beautiful living ecosystem. Ecoroofs are showing up all over the place, from tiny sheds covered in succulents to the world's largest (more than 10 acres) covering a Ford Motor Co. plant in Michigan. Tax credits are available for ecoroofs in some places.

Ecoroofs offer a number of environmental advantages in addition to their special quirky charm. They

- ✔ Absorb rainwater and pollutants, keeping it off the streets
- ✔ Produce oxygen and sequester carbon
- ✔ Cool the climate both inside and out
- ✔ Increase the life of the roof
- ✔ Produce food as well as ornamental plants
- ✔ Create beautiful living surfaces

Figure 12-3:
An example
of an
ecoroof.

Courtesy of Bryan Gaier

Before you go dragging a bunch of plants up to your roof, here are some important considerations:

 Ecoroofs aren't do-it-yourself projects. Hire an expert to help you.

✔ Ecoroofs are heavy, so first you need to be sure that your house can handle the extra weight. A structural engineer can help. Don't scrimp on this step, because nothing will spoil your day like a squashed house, especially if you're in it. If significant strengthening is required to support the ecoroof, it may be beyond a reasonable budget.

✔ Ecoroofs can slide off if they aren't properly anchored. A slide-off isn't quite as bad as a squashed house, but it's still no picnic.

✔ You, too, can slide off your roof, especially if you step back to admire your work or trip on a pumpkin vine.

Ecoroofs are pricey and challenging, but they offer great benefits to you and the environment. Besides, what's more fun than having the neighbors decide that you're definitely insane? To decide whether an ecoroof is for you, and to find qualified ecoroof professionals in your area, visit Green Roofs for Healthy Cities (www.greenroofs.org) and Greenroofs.com (www.greenroofs.com).

Moving Around Your Landscape with Paths and Steps

Moving from one part of the landscape to another should be as close to effortless as possible. Paths can be exciting hardscape elements, leading you on a journey that's full of interesting focal points and discoveries. This section helps you sort out how to use paths and steps and what materials are most sustainable. (Refer to Chapter 14 for construction information.)

Striding along sustainable paths

Paths get people from one place to another comfortably and safely. They lead the eye and the mind, too, as a visual element. Paths are indispensable.

Practical paths can be straight or gently curved, and should be as level as possible. Locate paths along natural lines of travel so that passage is comfortable and so that people don't cut corners. For high-traffic areas, choose solid, wear-resistant paving; for secondary and occasionally used paths, select something inexpensive and organic like wood-chip mulch.

Of all places to throw sustainability to the wind, the pathway is perhaps the most forgivable. The pavement here must be durable and free of hazards, which means you need a solid, smooth path of a permanent hard-wearing surface such as concrete, brick, tile, or grouted flagstone.

To reduce the environmental impact of your pathway, use bricks or paver blocks securely set on sand (so that they can be reused) or high-volume fly ash concrete (which uses a waste-stream product and reduces production of carbon dioxide). For low-traffic paths, consider stepping stones made from *urbanite* (salvaged concrete). For more information, refer to "Using safe, sustainable materials," earlier in this chapter.

Use light-emitting-diode (LED) path lights, which use a fraction of the energy of high- or low-voltage lights. (For more on outdoor lighting, turn to Chapter 13.) Getting to your front door is an important daily act for your family and others. The experience should be comfortable, safe, and welcoming. Provide a pathway that leads unambiguously to the house; one that's wide enough to accommodate two people walking side by side (at least 4/2 feet); and that's smooth, safe, and well lit.

Level changes: Sustainable steps and ramps

Steps are used where the terrain is too steep to walk on; they provide a controlled way to move up and down. Ramps are handy when the slope is gentle enough that steps aren't necessary. They make it easy to wheel things in and out, and they're safer than steps because there's nothing to trip on.

Steps and ramps should be wide, even, and well marked with edges defined by stones or other edging. They should also have handrails for safety. Because the ground isn't level, safety is the most important consideration. However, you don't have to use unsustainable approaches. As long as they aren't a hazard, natural materials often fit the bill just as well as high-tech ones.

In the old days, we built steps (and walls) of railroad ties. They were a waste-stream product, having been removed from railroad tracks when they became split or just old. Railroad ties have downsides, though. They're heavy and difficult to cut; and even worse, they're soaked with creosote, which is a health hazard. Their overall nastiness makes railroad ties a bad choice.

Better options include steps made of

- **Urbanite,** which is flat, usually around 4 inches thick, easy to stack up, and quite handsome. Turning your old patio into steps is ultrasustainable (assuming that you don't need your patio anymore, of course).

- **Landscape ties,** which aren't perfect but provide choices including pressure-treated wood, recycled plastic, melted plastic from automobiles, and rot-resistant wood timber made from sustainably harvested or urban trees. Of the bunch, this last choice, made from trees such as black locust, white oak, cedar, or cypress, is a sustainable choice because these ties tend to be local, are possibly a waste-stream item, aren't chemically treated, and aren't plastic.

- **Stone from on-site or nearby.** Stone is natural, has a low embodied energy, is nontoxic, and is mighty easy on the eyes.

- **Concrete,** which can be lower in its impact if you choose high-volume fly ash content concrete. Or perhaps try a new carbon-sequestering or even pollution-absorbing concrete, which may be on the market by the time you read this.

As you can see, no one option is perfect but there are some excellent choices.

Using Sustainable Hardscape Features to Build an Outdoor Room

Hardscape features combine with plantings to create *outdoor rooms,* places that serve particular functions similar to indoor rooms: eating, entertaining, working, and so on. The idea of the outdoor room goes far back in the history of landscape design. Cro-Magnon caveowners in the Paleolithic Era had spacious outdoor rooms that they used for eviscerating woolly mammoths and entertaining visiting troglodytes. Over time, the idea evolved into the modern outdoor room equipped with 50 square feet of barbecue-grill surface, two convection ovens, a big-screen television set, spa, fitness center, and maid's quarters. Somewhere between these two extremes lies the sensible, sustainable outdoor room of the future. You can see a plan for an outdoor room in Figure 12-4.

Many outdoor rooms are more versatile than indoor ones, combining functions that you'd never pair up indoors, such as providing a place for lounge chairs, bouncing light into the house, and soaking up rainwater. *Permaculture,* a methodology of holistic design, calls this multiple-use approach *stacking functions,* and it's a hallmark of sustainable design.

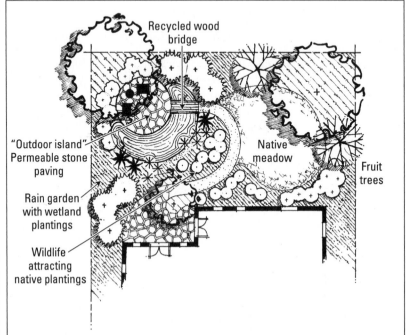

Figure 12-4: Typical outdoor room plan.

Recycled wood bridge

"Outdoor island" Permeable stone paving

Native meadow

Fruit trees

Rain garden with wetland plantings

Wildlife attracting native plantings

Keeping the cars happy: Outdoor parking

The automobile is with us for the foreseeable future, and both yours and those of your guests need to be parked somewhere. Ponder the possibilities of making parking space smaller and more environmentally friendly. Here are some tips:

✔ **Make your driveway permeable.** Runoff from driveways causes flooding and pollution. Use pervious concrete or pervious paver blocks so that water soaks in and is used by plants rather than going into the gutter.

Another cool option made of a honeycomb of recycled plastic panels is a vegetated paving system. They make your driveway look totally rad. Check out Chapter 14 to see how the system is put together.

✔ **Pave with mulch or gravel.** Both are permeable and much lower-impact than concrete or other formal paving. Just keep in mind that gravel attracts weeds.

Like indoor rooms, outdoor ones are made up of floors, walls, ceilings, and paths. But outdoor rooms usually are less rigidly defined than those in the house, with partially transparent walls, less privacy, and few or no doors to subdivide the space emphatically.

Materials used for outdoor rooms vary widely and can be quite different from materials that are used for indoor rooms. However, some continuity can be achieved by taking weather-tolerant indoor flooring or wall elements outside.

The ideal outdoor room should feel like part of nature. An overabundance of manmade structures and appliances is not only environmentally unsound, but it also creates a setting that's too much like the indoors. The whole appeal of having landscaping in the first place is to be closer to natural things, so why muck it up with a lot of hardware? After all, the Garden of Eden didn't have a spa and an eight-burner barbecue.

Many outdoor rooms serve the same functions as indoor ones. A patio is a type of outdoor living/dining room combination. A lawn is like a playroom. A veggie garden or orchard is the pantry. A potting bench is the garden's workbench. The following sections offer the lowdown on some of the most common outdoor rooms.

Living and entertaining space

Outdoor living and entertaining space is likely to be located on a patio or deck, which usually is the heart of the garden — the locus of individual, family, and group activities. As with an indoor living room, the outdoor living room can serve many purposes. It can be enclosed and intimate or open and expansive.

Here are some tips for creating a successful, environmentally-friendly and beautiful outdoor living room:

- ✔ **Accommodate whatever size group will be using it frequently.** Small is sustainable. Make the space big enough for regular use, not infrequent parties. A family-size outdoor living room should be around 12 feet on each side.

- ✔ **Create a retreat.** Think about making the main room an "away" place, somewhat distant from the house so you feel like you're more immersed in the garden and less connected to the hubbub of indoor life.

- ✔ **Think about microclimate.** Evaluate your planned use and the micro-environments around the house; then place living spaces where they'll be best adapted. If you'll be using the space mainly on hot afternoons, place your room on the north or east side of the house, away from the scalding sun. If the room is to be used for breakfast, put it on the east side where morning sun will warm chilly bones.

- ✔ **Evaluate wind conditions.** Locate your room in the lee of existing structures or vegetation or add fences, walls, or plantings to provide a windbreak.

- ✔ **Consider proximity to neighbors, street noise, odor, traffic patterns, and immediate and distant views.** If you're surrounded by unpleasant sights, sounds, and smells, you'll be less inclined to use your outdoor room.

- ✔ **Take the relationship to indoor rooms into account.** Locate the dining patio fairly close to the kitchen and not so close to the bedrooms, for example.

The outdoor kitchen

Traditional cultures have been cooking outdoors for millennia, using simple equipment. Western culture has made outdoor cooking the domain of the male of the species, bravely directing the immolation of animal parts on the outdoor grill. Recently, entire modern kitchens have been appearing in the yards of well-to-do homeowners, complete with nearly everything an indoor kitchen would have.

Outdoor cooking is fun, keeps the real kitchen cleaner, and may even use less energy. If you're going to include a kitchen in your hardscape, here are some points to consider:

✔ Keep it simple. A modest kitchen area with low-impact fixtures and appliances is sustainable.

✔ Consider cooking with charcoal instead of gas; it isn't a no-impact approach but it's somewhat better. An even better idea would be to incorporate a solar cooker; visit www.solarcooking.org for hot ideas on this subject.

✔ If you have a sink, let the graywater irrigate your landscape. See Chapter 8 for the lowdown on graywater.

✔ Add solar lighting so you can see whether your tofu is burning.

✔ Use natural materials like cob, adobe, and stone.

✔ Place the outdoor kitchen close to the indoor kitchen. Don't make yourself carry ingredients, tools, and finished meals all the way across the yard.

✔ Locate cooking areas where prevailing winds will blow smoke and odors away from living areas.

✔ Allow room for socializing. People tend to congregate in outdoor kitchens the same way they do in indoor ones.

✔ Don't cook under overhanging trees or structures that could catch fire.

Recreation and sports

Kids, adults, and pets all need rec spaces. Generally, these facilities should be on level ground, with safe surfaces, and should be located away from quiet spaces or fragile plantings. Lawn is the traditional recreational surface, and there's no denying its safety, durability and usefulness. But meadows made of yarrow, sedges, or native grasses can stand up to a decent amount of play activity too, so consider them for a more sustainable alternative.

Informal lawn sports like volleyball and badminton require pretty large areas (80 x 45 feet and 60 x 30 feet, respectively). Formal recreation courts (tennis, racquetball, and so on) aren't terribly sustainable; they use up lots of resources, and they require impervious surfaces and regular maintenance. Similarly, swimming pools are pretty over the top, with their immense demands for energy and water. Why not save yourself big bucks by enjoying the local public facilities and use your yard to grow food instead?

Personal spaces

Personal spaces can be used for meditation, relaxing in a hot tub, reading, or sleeping. Needless to say, they should be private, serene, and very beautiful. They can be softer and more natural than more formal areas and less dependent on technology. A mulched space surrounded by especially elegant plants is quite nice and very sustainable. Think about including some food plants for easy snacking while relaxing.

Chapter 13

Spicing Up Your Hardscape with Other Fun and Functional Elements

- -

In This Chapter

▶ Crafting a relaxing space with sustainable furniture

▶ Shining sustainable light

▶ Working with ponds, streams, and other water elements

▶ Adding workspaces and storage facilities

▶ Introducing livestock hardscaping to your landscape system

- -

This chapter picks up where Chapter 12 left off, introducing more exciting hardscape options. After all, sustainable landscaping isn't supposed to be grim or sacrificial. The trick is figuring out how to have fun without ruining the planet. A little restraint combined with a few sustainable hardscape strategies can add playfulness and beauty to your landscaping.

Including Fine Furniture Without Felling Forests

Gardens are places for lingering, and it's difficult to linger unless you have a comfortable place to sit or lie down. So you'll probably want to include some furniture in your landscape.

Furniture Rule Number One is this: You aren't going to buy yard furniture made from rainforest woods, built by cowering slave children, and shipped halfway around the world in exhaust-belching cargo ships. You're simply not going to go there. Fortunately, you don't have to; the good green people of the world have come up with many guilt-free alternatives. Here are some of them:

✔ **Make your own furniture from stuff you already have.** Suppose you have to take down a tree for some reason. Don't send it to the chipper if you can use the wood to make a bench or other furnishings. If milling logs is a little beyond your talents, think about growing your own bamboo or saving trimmings from your fruit trees.

As an alternative, construct built-in furniture from local stone or fashion furniture from cob, which is basically just soil slapped into the form of a bench and coated with a natural mixture of cooked white flour, soil, and straw. Adobe blocks and rammed earth can be made from soil that's on your site. For more information, see the nearby sidebar "An earth-building primer."

✔ **Buy used furniture.** Find a bench or chairs with character at a garage sale, antique store, or thrift store. Enjoy their funky patina, or restore them with a couple coats of nontoxic paint.

✔ **Use ultra-low-impact materials.** Straw bales, wood from urban trees, and salvaged or reclaimed lumber are all commonly available, sometimes with a little sleuthing. Stack up some straw bales and cover them with earthen plaster for a great outdoor sofa. Create nearly any style of furniture from salvaged wood. Look for furniture made from these materials by local craftsmen. (Supporting local businesses is part of the sustainable way.)

✔ **Purchase commercially available green furniture.** Many manufacturers now offer well-designed, carefully built sustainable garden furniture of all kinds — and at reasonable prices. Spend a little time on the Internet to uncover all sorts of possibilities.

Keeping Lighting Environmentally Friendly

Why bother lighting your property? Lighting uses energy and involves a lot of high-tech gadgetry. Certainly, you don't *need* to do any lighting at all. It's supposed to be dark at night; that's why the sun goes down. Still, a bit of lighting can be very nice at times.

Lighting used frivolously is not so good, but a fixture used to illuminate a level change and keep people from tripping is a justifiable expenditure of resources. So is lighting for security, provided that it comes on only when needed. The keys to lighting a sustainable landscape are powering up your lighting the proper way and using just enough lighting (not more than is necessary).

An earth-building primer

Making walls, benches, and even houses from soil is an ancient art going back to the dawn of civilization. It appeals to the caveman (and cavewoman) in all of us. Soil is the most available material anywhere (why do you think they call it Planet Earth?). It's right underneath your feet, is easy to form into any shape, requires no outside energy other than human labor, and is as close to a state of nature as you can get. And when it's the end of the line for your earth-made bench or toolshed, it can just melt back into the ground it came from. With some protection from the elements (this is especially important in wet climates) and the use of an organic sealer, earthen structures will outlast you.

Here are a few variations on the theme:

✔ *Cob* is soil, straw, and water that's hand-formed into nearly any shape. It's the simplest and most versatile of earthen materials, easily made into free-form and rectilinear shapes.

✔ *Adobe* is the same material as cob, but it's formed into large brick-shaped units and then stacked and mortared together.

✔ *Superadobe* is a special technique that uses long flexible tubes to contain the earthen material, forming it into sausages; then the sausages are stacked to form retaining walls, buildings, and other structures.

✔ *Rammed earth* is soil that has been firmly compacted between two temporary wooden forms. When the forms are removed, the smooth, straight walls stand on their own.

✔ *Straw-bale* construction uses a core of baled straw covered by earthen or other plaster. Strictly speaking, it isn't an earth-building technique, but it's a close relative.

You can use any of these methods to build free-standing walls, benches, chairs, small garden buildings, and sculptures. You can find a wealth of information out there to help: books, Web sites, workshops, and demonstration projects.

From an eco-friendly point of view, the two best ways to power garden lights are using a transformer to drop voltage to a safe, energy-efficient 12 volts, and using solar lights or powering the system from your home's solar panels.

Solar is the most environmentally friendly lighting method, but the solar fixtures currently on the market don't deliver much light, especially if you place them in areas that don't get much sunlight during the day. As a result, low-voltage systems make sense for most people.

In addition to a transformer, a low-voltage system consists of some type of control to turn lights on and off, underground wiring to send power to the fixtures, and the fixtures themselves (see Figure 13-1). The transformer is installed indoors or outdoors in an out-of-the-way location that's central to the fixtures it serves.

The system controller can be a manual switch in the house (call an electrician to install it), a timer on the transformer that turns the lights on and off at set times, or a photocell that turns them on at dusk and off at sunrise. If you want to automate the system, try a combination of a photocell and a timer. This hybrid approach fires up the lights at dusk no matter how long or short the days are, making seasonal reprogramming unnecessary. And the timer can be set to shut things down at bedtime, eliminating the problem of lights staying on all night. This saves energy.

You can make many permutations on basic landscape lighting themes (think uplighting trees or downlighting pools of soft light from overhead), but path lighting and safety and security lighting get the stamp of approval from the sustainability gods.

You can accomplish safety and security lighting with solar-powered motion-sensing lights mounted on the house. Just avoid placing big spotlights where they could come on during outdoor activities and spoil the ambience by creating hot spots; they can also disrupt the natural cycles of local wildlife.

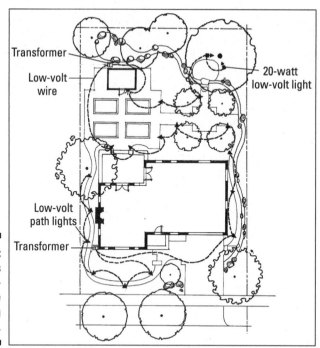

Figure 13-1:
Components of a low-voltage lighting system.

Junk or art? Using waste-stream materials in your garden

The most sustainable way to bring art into the garden is to turn to the waste stream. So much great material goes to the landfill every day that you'll have no shortage of ingredients for your own amazing sculpture or decorative addition to walls, paving, or other structures. Here are a few zesty art pieces made from junk that I've seen in my travels:

✔ Pathway edging made from bowling balls

✔ A decorative planter made out of old car headlights mortared together

✔ Paving embedded with found objects

✔ Elegant bonsai pots made from old truck brake drums

✔ Plants growing in old work boots (size 13D, if I recall correctly)

✔ Totems assembled from coffee cans, doll heads, toys, and plastic fruit

With imagination, nearly anything can become art. To find materials, try thrift stores, garage sales, or dumpster diving. There are even stores and community workshops devoted to transforming society's castoffs into masterpieces; they often teach classes and sell materials from the waste stream. Consider the creative possibilities for every piece of junk you come across. If you lack the talent to come up with your own art, press your kids into service, or look around the community for local artists doing cool stuff with junk.

The two negative environmental impacts of outdoor lighting systems are energy use and light pollution. *Light pollution* is the leakage of manmade light into the night sky, hiding the stars from astronomers, disrupting ecosystems, and possibly causing health problems. Fortunately, neither problem is all that difficult to solve. Here's the skinny:

✔ Select low-voltage LED (light-emitting diode) fixtures, which use a fraction of the power of conventional fixtures. Try solar fixtures where you don't need strong light, because they tend to produce a feeble display. Switch lights on only when you need them, and don't keep them burning all night. Or consider a timer and photocell as described earlier in this section. Of course, if your house is solar powered, you're home free.

✔ The International Dark-Sky Association (IDA) has developed guidelines for outdoor lighting and makes recommendations on the best fixtures; visit www.darksky.org for details. Keep wattages down, avoid directing light upward, use shields on all fixtures to keep the light pointed downward, and turn lights off when they aren't in use.

Find out more about developing a landscape lighting system in *Landscaping For Dummies,* by Phillip Giroux, Bob Beckstrom, Lance Walheim, and The Editors of the National Gardening Association (Wiley).

Water Features: Ponds, Streambeds, Waterfalls

People gravitate to water. Maybe it's because our lives depend on it. Maybe it's because we ourselves are mostly water. Or perhaps it's just because it's so darn beautiful. Whatever the reason, adding a water element to your garden, no matter how small, creates an instant feeling of rightness. Nothing can really substitute for water in the garden, and my feeling is that no garden should be without a bit of refreshing water somewhere, even if it's just a birdbath.

Water features use resources for their construction, require regular top-offs with fresh water (at about the same rate as a lawn), and consume electricity for pumping. Water features may seem like unsustainable indulgences, but if they're incorporated properly, they produce real benefits to the environment that compensate for at least some of the negative effects.

For example, in neighborhoods utterly devoid of natural water sources, I've encountered backyard ponds and running streams that were hubs of life, teeming with bees, birds, frogs, and countless insects (many of them beneficial). I think that a world of diminishing habitats and relentless urbanization argues for more water in gardens, not less.

Elements of sustainable water features

You need a vessel of some kind to hold the water: a birdbath, a fountain, a ceramic pot, a prefab or custom in-ground pond made of concrete or plastic (I prefer concrete), or a running streambed. Some water features are kept free of plants and fish, but the sustainable garden is about nurturing life, so consider populating your water feature. Plants and fish provide for one another and keep the system in balance so that it requires little input from you.

Water features can be formal or informal, manmade-looking or naturalistic, simple or complex. A bubbling spring can spill into a small stream that runs down into a pond reflecting the sky and overhanging tree branches. A waterfall can create pleasant sounds to screen noise. A tiered fountain can be the centerpiece of a courtyard. The possibilities are endless.

Passive versus active water features

A *passive water feature* is still and pumpless, such as a lovely urn with standing water and a plant or two. Because they use no energy, passive water features are the more environmentally friendly choice; they create a serene mood with no negative impacts and cost very little money.

An *active water feature* is one that uses a pump to move water for filtration purposes or for the beauty of sound and movement of the water. The most effective filter for an active water feature is a 10-inch-deep layer of coarse (1- to 2-inch-diameter) gravel on the bottom of the pond (see Figure 13-2), with a set of PVC-pipe suction lines at the very bottom to draw water down through the gravel and return it to the pond via a jet of water or a waterfall. (Yes, I know, PVC piping is a no-no. But landscaping isn't perfect. Other types of piping just aren't possible for this project.) Bacteria come to live in the gravel — good bacteria that eat pond gunk for breakfast and will keep the water nice and clear. (Check out *Landscaping For Dummies* for specific information on creating an active water feature.)

To keep the bacteria in your active water feature alive, you should use a small, low-volume, high-efficiency pump; and you should run it all the time. Naturally, a pump uses some electricity, but a 50- to 100-watt pump usually moves enough water for a small pond. Larger ponds and thundering water-falls require larger pumps, of course, which is a good reason to keep your pond small. The benefits are the same at any size.

Ideally, you'll use solar power so that operating the pump doesn't cause a drain on the power grid. You can find small pumps that have their own solar panels built in; these devices are okay for moving tiny quantities of water but not for running an under-gravel filter or powering a rushing stream.

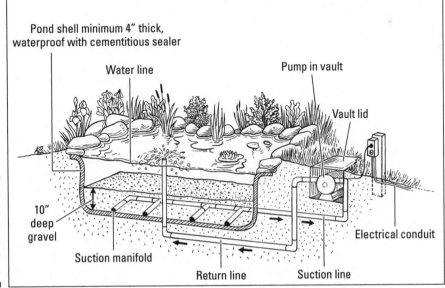

Figure 13-2: A small garden pond with an under-gravel filter.

Pond shell minimum 4" thick, waterproof with cementitious sealer

Water line

Pump in vault

Vault lid

10" deep gravel

Suction manifold

Return line

Suction line

Electrical conduit

Caring for your water feature

Bringing a new water feature into balance takes a little time. High nutrient levels and alkalis leaching from the pond shell must dissipate before you introduce permanent organisms. You'll have a big algae bloom at first, but it should diminish with time.

Start with some water hyacinths, which grow very quickly and absorb nutrients and contaminants. After the growth of these plants has slowed, remove them and bring in the permanent residents. You have many plant species to choose from. Be sure to include some mosquito fish or goldfish to keep the mosquitoes from breeding. This natural approach to mosquito control means that you don't have to treat your water feature with chemicals. Over time, your little ecosystem will become nearly self-reliant.

Ongoing maintenance consists of topping off the water (and replacing about half of it once a year), cleaning out the worst of the junk, feeding the goldfish in summer perhaps, and keeping an eye on the pump. The under-gravel filter will work for years with no care whatsoever, but even the best pumps last only a couple of years, so plan on replacing yours as needed.

Discouraging critters from checking out your water features

Out here in California the raccoon has become one of the dominant suburban species — and boy, do raccoons love water features. They brazenly turn over pots, trash delicate plants, eat thousand-dollar koi, and generally raise hell. I wish I had a perfect solution for their nightly predations, but I don't. However, here are a few tips for mitigation:

- ✔ **Avoid small, easily tipped pots.** Use big heavy ones that critters can't overturn.

- ✔ **Make a hidey hole for the fish.** A big clay pipe lying on the bottom works; so does a cave of bricks with a heavy pot set on top. An over-hanging ledge prevents animals from reaching into the water, too.

- ✔ **Get dark-colored fish.** I suggest this because they're less visible. Cheap feeder goldfish from the pet store are more than adequate for your pond; just be sure to pick the dark ones. Or call your local mosquito abatement district for some (usually free) mosquito fish, which are nearly invisible.

- ✔ **Try a little technology.** You could use motion-sensing sprinkler heads, electric fencing, or plastic bird netting suspended over the water.

> ✓ **Place little vials of coyote or other predator urine in the area.** Or use your own, for that matter. (Do this after dark if neighbors can see you. And don't pee *in* the pond; go *next* to it.) Don't try to collect predator urine on your own either; you can buy it online or at some nurseries.

Birds of prey, such as great blue herons, may visit your pond on fishing expeditions. You'll enjoy these visits until you see a huge bird fly off with your prized koi. Hawks and owls may also see your pond as a resource — but that's not all bad, especially given the loss of wetlands and other habitats that drives these creatures into our backyards.

Birds of prey are protected by law, so don't even think of taking a potshot at them. Instead, use netting, motion-sensing sprinkler heads, and the family dog as bird deterrents. Herons can sometimes be fooled by decoys. Or try an alligator. (Ha-ha. Just kidding. A grown alligator won't actually fit in a small pond.)

Working with and around natural water features

If you're fortunate enough to have a real stream or pond on your property, you have some special responsibilities. It's usually against federal and local laws to modify, pollute, excavate, harass, fold, bend, spindle, or mutilate natural bodies of water and the life in them. Be content with enjoying them as they are.

If a natural waterway has been damaged and you want to restore it (hats off to you!), first check with your local flood control agency to see what regulations apply. You'll probably have to work with numerous agencies, such as the state department of fish and game and the U.S. Army Corps of Engineers (bet you didn't know they were looking after your little creek!), your local flood control agency as well as biologists and other professionals. Sometimes the government will even help pay for restoration work.

The bottom line is that natural waterways are delicate but complex and deserve the very best of care. Take advantage of your awareness to do the job right.

Incorporating Storage Spaces and Work Places

In the excitement of planning a new landscape, you can easily overlook boring, practical things like potting benches, trash cans, and garden tools. For the avid gardener, these hardscape elements can be central to the experience of the garden. For those who don't garden often, these elements are accessed as needed and can be in an out-of-the-way location. Either way, make sure you plan for the useful areas of your landscape.

The coolest toolshed I ever saw was a curvaceous cob structure with a flamboyant ecoroof covered in luscious plants. It was unique, sensual, and beautiful, and made from materials mostly found on site, and other than the labor required to build this unique shed, it was . . . well, dirt cheap.

You can create the same type of building. With all the information available on cob construction, getting up to speed on dirt building is easy. Remember, cob isn't your only choice; you can create a small building out of any earthen material: adobe, superadobe, straw bale, or rammed earth. (Refer to the sidebar "An earth-building primer," earlier in this chapter, for explanations of these materials.) Alternatively, try reclaimed wood, used metal siding, or whatever else is available that fits into your overall scheme.

Make sure that flooring surfaces in work areas are level, smooth, and solid. (If you've ever lost a small but important screw in gravel, you know what I'm talking about.) Also, be sure to keep these areas away from living areas and neighbors if they'll be sources of noise.

An 8- by 10-foot storage shed is wonderful, but if you don't have that kind of room on your property, look for other places to sneak storage in: along fence lines, under eaves, or in idle corners. A narrow storage cabinet is ideal for garden tools and most small supplies. Be sure to allow at least 3 to 4 feet in front for access, and check local zoning laws to be sure you aren't putting your storage in a forbidden location.

Garden work areas such as potting benches, cold frames, and small greenhouses can assist your efforts to propagate plants and grow useful food. These structures, which can be made from scrap, make great weekend projects. Consider including a salvaged kitchen sink that drains into the garden, for washing veggies and pots and watering the garden at the same time (assuming that you won't be using any toxic substances).

Animal Plan-It: Chicken Coops, Rabbit Hutches, and the Like

Incorporating small livestock into your landscape system may sound outrageous, but it makes sense to balance the extraction of food crops with the input of animal-based nutrients such as chicken manure. This arrangement replicates ancient agricultural systems and is one of the core principles of permaculture. On this planet, plants and animals support one another;

leaving the animals out of your system forces you to import expensive (and inferior) fertilizers to make up the difference. But when you add animals to your sustainable landscape, you get to enjoy the benefits of both plant and animal productivity.

Poultry in motion: The chicken tractor

Chickens are multipurpose garden elements, providing cultivation, weeding, pest control, fertilizer, eggs, and cuteness all in one feathery, clucking package. Three or four hens will keep a family well supplied with eggs. (Roosters will get you busted in most places, though.) A classic henhouse — around 4 by 8 feet, made *very* sturdily to keep predators out — is a wonderful addition to the sustainable garden. But another approach is even more sustainable because it performs more tasks than a henhouse. Stand back — here comes the chicken tractor.

A *chicken tractor* is essentially a portable coop with four walls and a roof covered in (what else?) chicken wire; it also has a somewhat enclosed roosting area. What makes this contraption unique is that the bottom is open to the ground. Imagine your little cluckers happily munching away on the weeds and depositing valuable nutrients on the soil. Now imagine rolling the whole shebang, chickens and all, to a fresh spot every couple of weeks. That would be a chicken tractor — a cozy, predatorproof, attractive way to get some help with the needs of your garden. Figure 13-3 shows how it may look.

Figure 13-3:
A typical chicken tractor.

Doin' the bunny hop

Rabbits aren't as productive as poultry, because they haven't invented bunny eggs (despite what you'd think at Easter). But rabbit poo makes pretty good fertilizer, and the bunnies are adorable!

A rabbit hutch usually is a single room, with all sides including the bottom made of 1- by 2-inch heavy-gauge wire (smaller for the bottom, according to some experts), a rainproof roof, and legs to keep it 3 to 4 feet off the ground as protection from predators. Avoid using wood where the bunnies can reach it; wood can be harmful to them if chewed, especially if it's painted.

Other oddball animal habitats

People keep all sorts of animals in their yards, including edible fish in plastic garbage cans, allegedly edible snails in aquariums, and the latest trend: *cowpooling*. This trend involves keeping a community cow on a lot in the neighborhood to supply everyone with milk. Go figure.

Chapter 14

Sustainable Hardscape Construction

*B*uilding sustainably means reducing your use of power equipment, buying locally or not at all, vetting all your materials for their environmental impacts, protecting existing site features, and building things that last. Upholding these commitments isn't difficult (except maybe giving up labor-saving power equipment), but it takes care and attention. Your rewards? A beautiful, wholesome landscape; hardscape free of contaminants and planet-bashing effects; and big-time fitness from doing all that hard work.

In this chapter, I introduce the sustainable aspects of various elements of landscape and hardscape construction, particularly site management, paving, and wall building. I cover some variations in the construction process to make it more sustainable and eco-friendly. Consult Chapter 12 for sustainable material options, and check out *Landscaping For Dummies* by Phillip Giroux, Bob Beckstrom, Lance Walheim, and the Editors of the National Gardening Association (Wiley) for general hardscape construction techniques and details.

Fossil-Free Construction: Forgoing the Heavy Equipment

Tractors are fun. I admit that. I also admit that using heavy equipment to move heavy things like soil and rocks saves a lot of work and gets things done really fast. Unfortunately, tractors, skid-steer loaders, trenchers, and other heavy-duty landscaping tools are hard on the environment, and they really aren't very efficient when you factor in the effects and costs of making, buying or renting, fueling, repairing, and disposing of them.

In their landmark book *Sustainable Landscape Construction: A Guide to Green Building Outdoors* (Island Press, 2007), J. William Thompson and Kim Sorvig point out that an earthmover can move 20 cubic yards of soil 600 feet in less than 2 minutes — a task that would take eight workers using hand tools a whole day. But the machine's energy consumption is four times that of the laborers, and food to fuel the workers is renewable, whereas fuel for the machine is not. Workers generally don't spew diesel smoke or make a big racket, either.

With power tools you also have to consider pollution (running a chain saw for 2 hours produces more pollution than driving a car 2,500 miles); noise; damage to soil from the weight of the machines; and the effects of tractor factories, gas stations, repair shops, and junkyards, to mention just a few. Add this all up and you can see why it makes sense to minimize the use of power equipment.

Electric tools like chain saws and mowers are much more efficient than ones that operate on gas or diesel fuel. And if you must use heavy equipment, there's some solace in knowing that smaller machines are much more efficient.

The bottom line? Do things by hand whenever possible. It's better for you and for the planet. It'll take longer, but hey, what's the hurry? Hand tools often do a great job in the hands of a skilled user. A skinny old man in a town near mine used to hire himself out to dig huge pits with just a shovel and a digging bar. If he could do it, so can you.

Managing Your Site

Many construction sites look like they're being managed by a 14-year-old, but they don't have to be ugly, messy, and dangerous. A little housekeeping and common sense goes a long way toward protecting the environment, being respectful of neighbors, and making the work go more smoothly because you know where everything is.

Storing materials and equipment safely

First off, let's agree that you won't bring any toxic materials onto your construction site. I don't need to tell you that, right? Not inviting rude guests to the party is the first rule. Still, even nontoxic materials can be hazardous under certain conditions. Follow these guidelines:

✔ Keep fertilizers, paints, and chemicals away from waterways.

✔ Be especially careful with tools; they can hurt. Keep them locked up or at least safely stored in one central location.

✔ Take the keys out of heavy equipment when you're not around.

✔ To the degree that it's practicable, place equipment, vehicles, and piles of materials in a part of the property that's paved. That way the ground pressure doesn't compact the soil or damage tree roots.

Noise and dust control

I live near (not in) one of the wealthiest communities in the world. People are continually remodeling, both inside and out. You can hardly find a quiet place; so loud is the din of tools, equipment, and music coming from tiny radios. During the rare intervals when they aren't being worked on, most of the fine homes are surrounded by the racket of their neighbors' projects. It's a good lesson in just how noisy most construction activity is.

Noise disrupts wildlife. In nature, noise is a sign of danger, and animals (including humans) respond to noise with anxiety and preparedness for fight or flight. The solution is to avoid using power tools wherever you can; when you do use them, stay within your community's guidelines on hours of use.

Dust is another nuisance that really isn't difficult to control. Avoid working very dry soil; avoid using equipment like rototillers, which stir up a lot of dust (and which damage soil anyway); and use the dust-suppression attachments that come with most masonry saws and similar equipment.

Erosion Protection during Construction and Beyond

Does your soil have big parallel cracks in it? Are utility poles and trees tilting at crazy angles? Is your land riddled with gulleys? Does rainwater concentrate in one big soil-stripping torrent? Is your house missing its gutters? You could be sitting on a soil erosion time bomb. When the rains come, it's too late to do anything about these problems, so tackle them now.

First, get acquainted with the two types of erosion:

✔ **Surface erosion,** which occurs when water carries the topsoil away

✔ **Landslides,** in which huge chunks of a hillside cut loose and plop down on the land (or house) below

Both types of erosion are potentially very big trouble. Each kind has its own set of strategies for control.

The early stages of your hardscape project probably will involve laying bare large areas of soil. Protecting against soil runoff from your property during construction is mandated by federal law, and the penalties can run up to $5,000 per day for anyone caught with mud slithering across property lines into streets and waterways.

After the job is done, your attention will turn to preventing erosion in the established landscape. Hopefully the way you develop the landscape will put the problem to rest once and for all, but if you live on unstable soil, erosion protection will be an ongoing task. This section helps you handle erosion problems, both short term and over the long haul.

Controlling surface erosion

During the course of your project, you need to manage your site with soil protection in mind. For many reasons, you want to expose the least amount of soil possible. Naked soil can easily wash away, blow away, or become a slippery, muddy mess. When major grading is inevitable, here are some strategies you can use (see Figure 14-1 for an overview):

- Make sure that all grading, whether temporary or permanent, directs water where it can be controlled.
- Maintain natural landforms where possible.
- Avoid concentrating water in one big stream. Spread water out, and look downstream to pinpoint where your water is going.
- Filter runoff with erosion control fabric, straw wattles, silt fencing, and other strategies so that only clear, clean water leaves the site. (I explain these strategies in the following sections.)
- If you expect slopes to go through a rainy season before permanent landscaping is established, seed or hydroseed them with suitable temporary plantings, or mulch them with straw or hay. (For more information, see the section on hydroseeding later in this chapter.)

Where the risk of runoff problems is low (stable soil and gentle slopes, for example), a 3- to 4-inch layer of ordinary recycled organic mulch, available from local recyclers or municipalities, can be spread on the area and simply left in place after planting is done.

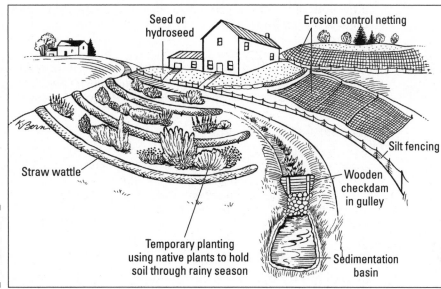

Seed or hydroseed

Erosion control netting

Silt fencing

Straw wattle

K.Born

Wooden checkdam in gulley

Figure 14-1:
Erosion control strategies.

Temporary planting using native plants to hold soil through rainy season

Sedimentation basin

Erosion control fabric

Roll erosion control blankets made from jute, coconut fiber, straw, or other natural materials onto exposed soil to protect it from surface runoff during rains. You can use this material on slopes or wherever runoff poses a risk of erosion. It lasts a couple of years, decomposing into soil-improving organic matter. By that time, your plantings should be well-established.

Installation is simple. Grade the area; dig a shallow trench at the top of the slope; bury the ends of the material in the trench; and unroll the fabric down the slope, overlapping sections for good coverage. Metal soil staples (the same ones used to hold drip irrigation tubing in place) fasten the fabric to the soil.

Straw wattles and other runoff control strategies

Straw wattles are one of the cool new ways of intercepting and filtering water that sheets off slopes. A straw wattle is a long sausage-like tube about 10 inches in diameter. It's filled with rice straw, compost, or other organic material. You install it by partially burying it in a shallow trench (about 3 inches deep). Place the wattles perpendicular to the slope and in parallel rows every 10 to 20 feet down the slope, following the contours of the slope so the wattles are level; then secure them with wooden stakes driven into the soil. Dirty surface water runs through the wattles and is filtered clean by the straw. Reusable *sediment tubes* work the same way but can be used more than once.

At the bottom of a slope, use silt fencing as the final line of defense against runoff. A *silt fence* is a long, low ribbon of tightly woven synthetic fabric partially buried in a trench and held up with wooden stakes. Should soil move downhill, the silt fence traps it. Silt fence is generally not reusable. *Checkdams* are wooden boards or other small obstructions placed across gulleys to slow the flow of runoff. *Sedimentation basins* are pits dug at the bottoms of slopes to capture mud-laden runoff before it escapes.

Hydroseeding

Hydroseeding is a process of applying seed to a *slurry* of wood fiber, fertilizer, and binding agents via a huge truck-mounted contraption that shoots the mixture up to 50 feet through a hose. The slurry protects the seed and the slope. Hydroseeding is fun to watch, and if you choose species of seeds that are appropriate to your site conditions, the technique can be a quick and inexpensive solution.

Plants that keep the soil in place

The best erosion control devices are sturdy plants with extensive roots to knit the soil together. That's how nature does things; everything else is just a temporary solution until the plants grow in.

The best erosion control plants provide a dense canopy of foliage that breaks the force of the rainwater and an extensive root system to hold soil in place. Provide your new plants proper irrigation using a drip or overhead sprinkler system. (See Chapter 7 for information on these systems.)

Preventing landslides

Some land is especially prone to landslides. If you suspect you're on such land, call a geologist for a consultation.

Preventing landslides in some geologic conditions is nearly impossible, but you can do the following things to prevent catastrophic losses in basically stable soils:

- ✔ Avoid terracing slopes so that they catch rainwater (terracing can be a great strategy in stable soils but disastrous in fragile situations).

- ✔ Use a drainage system to catch roof water and site runoff and take it well away from the slope.

- ✔ Don't build structures or retaining walls without professional advice.

- ✔ Avoid planting the slope with grasses, which have large numbers of stem penetrations (as opposed to individual shrubs with only one stem each). Grass blades are little funnels that direct water into the soil and supersaturate it, making it more likely to cut loose.

Creating Paved Surfaces for Patios, Paths, and More

Paving (or *flatwork,* as we call it in the biz) will be essential to hardscapes until humans learn to levitate. Until that day comes, we need safe, durable surfaces. Biological solutions such as ground covers are great up to a point, but there comes a time when everyone recognizes the need for something more substantial. So it's good to know that you have sustainable choices. Refer to Chapter 12 for more about hardscape material options.

Making a concrete patio

Without going into a whole short course on concrete work, here's some critical information on creating a patio. I recommend that you have a professional handle this work, but if you're determined to do it yourself, keep these tips in mind:

- ✔ **Safety first!** Avoid all skin contact with wet concrete, which can be toxic.

- ✔ **Prepare your soil.** If your soil is expansive or unstable, place a layer of sand or base material under the slab to isolate it. In any case, install your patio on undisturbed or well-compacted soil so it doesn't settle.

- ✔ **Set your forms carefully.** Make sure you have at least ¼ inch of slope per foot of run so water drains away from structures. Stake forms carefully so they don't shift during the pour.

- ✔ **Buy ready-mixed concrete instead of mixing your own.** Purchasing ready-mix saves a lot of work. You won't have time to mix, pour, and finish if you're working by yourself or with only one helper.

- ✔ **Don't try to finish concrete yourself.** *Finishing* is the art of making a nice smooth surface; it's a whole lot trickier than you might think and isn't something for beginners to tackle. If you haven't finished concrete before, hire a finisher even if you do the rest of the work yourself.

Placing unit pavers on a subslab

Where you need a stable, permanent pavement, one solution is to mortar individual *unit pavers* (or simply *pavers*) such as brick, paver blocks, flagstone, or tile over a subslab of poured concrete. However, this method increases your cost and also the environmental impact because that concrete has to come from somewhere. Plus, once you mortar those puppies down they can't easily be reused in the future.

Make your subslab 4 inches thick, and give it a rough broom finish that you'll stick the pavers to with thin-set mortar mix. If you're pouring onto an expansive soil (gooey clay that moves in response to changes in soil moisture), use a sand subgrade under the subslab, and install a grid of #3 steel *rebar* (steel rod used to strengthen) at 24 inches on center to keep the subslab from cracking.

If your soil is stable, you could leave the rebar out, which would make the subslab reusable as urbanite if the pavement is ever taken up (rebar makes reuse nearly impossible). Without the rebar, you may get some cracking, but perhaps that's a small price to pay to improve the integrity of the project.

Positioning unit pavers on sand

Positioning unit pavers on sand is cheaper than installing a subslab, and it allows the pavers to be reused. Water will penetrate through the cracks in the pavers and into the soil, reducing runoff. The downside is that over time, the pavers can settle, causing unevenness that can make the surface difficult to walk on and possibly even hazardous. However, it's easy to reset sunken areas. You simply lift the pavers, add a little more sand, and replace them.

A 3- to 4-inch-deep layer of builder's sand is usually adequate. If you want a firmer base, add portland cement to the sand (up to 10 percent by volume), along with enough water to make the mixture moist but not wet. (The pavers can be reused because they don't stick to the sand/cement base.)

Installing vegetated paving systems

Vegetated paving systems help make your driveway and other areas permeable so that water soaks in and is used by plants rather than going into the gutter. These systems were designed to be used with lawn grasses, but no law says you can't plant them with native plants, wildflowers, or even broccoli. (Well, because the systems are made to be driven on, maybe broccoli isn't such a great idea.) You can see how a typical system is put together in Figure 14-2.

Numerous vegetated paving products are on the market, and each manufacturer has its own specifications for installation. The general idea is to excavate down a foot or more; replace the native soil with a base material like crushed rock that will support the weight of vehicles; add a layer of good soil; place the plastic or concrete support material on the graded soil; add more soil (or sand, in some cases); and then sod or plant it from seed.

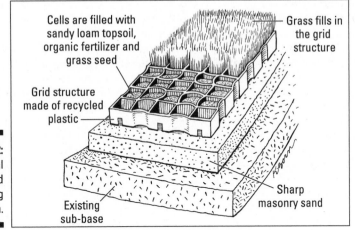

Cells are filled with sandy loam topsoil, organic fertilizer and grass seed

Grass fills in the grid structure

Grid structure made of recycled plastic

Figure 14-2: Typical vegetated paving system.

Existing sub-base

Sharp masonry sand

You may want to incorporate a sprinkler system if you'll be planting something that needs regular watering. It's better, though, to choose plants that thrive on natural rainfall.

Spreading loose paving materials

If you want a paved surface that's easy to install, loose paving materials, such as gravel or *decomposed granite* (*d.g.,* as we affectionately refer to it in the business), are the way to go. However, don't apply loose materials to slopes where they can slide downhill and be dangerous to walk on; they're only meant for level or nearly level ground.

Many people put a layer of weed control fabric under the gravel. This practice isn't such a great idea because weeds come in from the top, their roots grow through the fabric, and they become impossible to pull out, making spraying with herbicides necessary. Also, gravel dust can change your soil chemistry enough to harm plants. Wash the gravel off before using it. Do this on a paved area where the sediment can be trapped within a ring of straw wattles and swept up when dry for safe disposal. Be sure that only clean water runs off the area.

To construct your paved surface, prepare your subgrade, paying attention to where the water will go during rains. Then place your gravel or d.g. on the subgrade. For gravel or crushed rock, use no more than a 1-inch-thick layer in most cases; deeper gravel can be difficult to walk on.

Decomposed granite goes on 3 to 4 inches deep. Excavate the soil to accommodate the material or install header boards made of recycled plastic lumber so that the d.g. is entirely or partially above grade. Place the d.g. and grade it level with a rake, then wet it with a hose and compact it with a water-filled lawn roller so it will stay in place. Unlike gravel, d.g. forms a pretty solid surface. Many people mix portland cement or special stabilizing agents with the loose d.g. before they place and compact it; this technique helps it last longer but also makes it impracticable to reuse the material.

Opting for mulch

A 3- to 4-inch-thick layer of wood chips or other organic mulch is fine for areas with light foot traffic. Even though it's last in this list, make it your first choice when you don't need the durability of a hard surface.

Mulch is simple to install; just dump it and rake it around. But before placing the mulch, lower the soil 3 inches along the edges of pavement so that the mulch won't spill onto the paved area. Don't put anything down under the mulch; weed control fabrics make weeding even harder and plastic sheeting interrupts the movement of water into the soil. If you have serious weed problems, put three to four layers of corrugated cardboard on the surface of the soil before you place the mulch.

Tips for Constructing Steps Sustainably

Landscaping, like life, has its ups and downs — literally, in the case of steps. Negotiating the journey safely and comfortably doesn't mean throwing environmental considerations out the window, however. First refer to Chapter 12 to pick out the sustainable material you want to use, and then head to *Landscaping For Dummies,* which tells you how to build garden steps out of stone or timber. Here I provide tips for putting steps together safely and sustainably:

- ✔ If you make steps from stone, set larger stones directly into the soil without any use of concrete (making them a reusable heritage material).

- ✔ If you use smaller, less stable stones, make sure the steps are tied together with strong concrete footings containing plenty of steel so they don't crack or move independently.

- ✔ Placing rebar in a set of steps is a good idea, because steps are subject to movement and cracking. Adding rebar means that your steps won't be as easy to recycle at the end of their life, but they'll last longer.

Raising Earthen Garden Walls

Chapter 12 helps you select materials for fences and walls (garden as well as masonry), and *Landscaping For Dummies* tells you how to build them. So here I focus on a more unique yet sustainable construction project: building earthen garden walls.

Earthen walls come in many forms. In the following sections, I include general instructions and tips for building the three most popular kinds of earthen walls. This is a basic treatment of a complex subject; for more information visit www.greenhomebuilding.com. Or get a copy of the excellent book *The Hand-Sculpted House* by Ianto Evans, Michael G. Smith, and Linda Smiley (Chelsea Green Publishing Company).

Getting the soil right

The soil for earthen structures should be a sandy loam, not expansive (which means that it won't swell and shrink to the point of cracking), with a low organic-matter content. The National Bureau of Standards (NBS), which ought to know about these things, recommends a mix of 17 percent clay, 25 percent silt, 19 percent coarse sand, and 42 percent fine sand. (***Note:*** Those NBS folks may be real smart, but they sure can't add. Still, their advice makes sense as long as you adjust the numbers a little bit to come out to 100 percent. Don't exceed 100 percent; if you do, you may experience structural problems.) Straw is often added to the soil mixture to improve its strength. Water content should be around 10 percent (7 percent for rammed earth).

Use soil from your site if it can be taken without damaging the environment; soil can come from a spot where you'll be building a structure. Using on-site soil is the most sustainable way to go. Whatever the source, choose your soil carefully.

Waterproof the soil by mixing *asphaltic emulsion* (a bad petroleum-based product) at 4 percent by volume into the mud when making the bricks; they'll last a lot longer. You can also add portland cement (up to 6 percent of the total volume) to waterproof and strengthen the material. Keep in mind that these adulterants make the wall less recyclable. However, it will still have a much lower impact than a concrete block or other conventional wall.

It's a good idea to do a test block to be sure your soil mixture won't crack excessively. Adjust the clay/sand ratio of your soil if you have problems. Add clay if the soil is too crumbly and sand if it cracks too much.

Building a solid foundation

The long-term stability of your wall depends on a solid foundation, or *footing* as it's often called. In a stable soil that has the strength to support a lot of weight (and that doesn't expand and contract with changes in moisture content) you have some latitude in the kind and size of footing you use. Less favorable soils may require the help of an engineer to design a solid footing for a long-lasting wall.

Earthen walls are often put on a conventional concrete footing, but they can also be built on stone or other more natural waterproof materials. The foundation should go below the frost line in cold climates and must be strong enough to hold the wall. For a wall under 2 feet in height, a foundation 12 to 18 inches wide and 8 to 12 inches deep is usually adequate. But soil conditions may require larger footings in some cases; consult with a civil engineer if you aren't sure. Also be sure to check local building codes for requirements in your area.

Plastering your wall

An earthen wall isn't naturally waterproof, but covering it with a natural plaster (not a conventional cement-based plaster that can cause moisture problems and eventual failure) can make it last much longer. You can also cover earthen walls with a projecting protective tile or wooden cap to keep them from melting in the rain. This is especially important in wet climates.

Many recipes are available for plasters that are friendly to earthen walls (and the environment). They contain earth and other elements, such as sand, straw, cooked flour paste, and various kinds of feces; they generally don't contain cement-based materials or anything that would seal the wall up. Like humans, earthen structures need to breathe; if they can't, they eventually fall apart. For good info on earthen plasters, check out the book *The Hand-Sculpted House,* which I mention earlier. Or pick up *The Natural Plaster Book* by Cedar Rose Guelberth and Dan Chiras (New Society Publishers.)

Putting your wall together

If you're ready to put your wall together, you've come to the right place. In this section, I provide a rundown of techniques that are specific to the many different kinds of walls.

Adobe block

Adobe is soil formed into large, unfired bricks and dried until quite solid. You can buy adobe bricks in many areas, especially the Southwest, or you can make your own. Here's how:

1. **Prepare a level, open area of bare ground where you can make the blocks and leave them to dry in the sun.**

   If you'll be buying soil, be sure the site is accessible by truck. If you can, choose a spot that's close to where the bricks will be used (carrying is hard work). Make blocks in warm, dry weather so they cure properly.

2. **Create shallow wooden forms made from four 2 x 4s nailed into an 8-x-16-inch rectangle.**

   Blocks should be around 8 inches wide and 16 inches long for most landscaping applications. Anything larger is too heavy to carry. However, a 4-inch-thick block offers strength.

3. **Mix soil with water into a dough-like consistency.**

   Each 8-x-16-x-4-inch block uses about one third of a cubic foot of soil, so you'll get about 80 blocks out of a cubic yard of soil. You'll also need about 65 to 75 gallons of water to mix with each cubic yard of dry soil.

4. **Place the forms on level ground and lightly wet them. Then place the soil in them.**

   Place a thin layer of sand on the bottom of the form to prevent the blocks from sticking to the ground.

5. **Tamp the soil well to exclude air pockets, and then let it set up for an hour or so before gently lifting the form from the block.**

6. **Allow the blocks to cure for at least three days or until they can be moved without breakage.**

   Stand them on edge next to each other to save space. However, be sure to leave air space around the blocks so they dry properly.

Allow the blocks to dry in hot sun for at least two weeks before using.

When your bricks are ready, follow these general steps to build a non-retaining wall under 2 feet tall. First build a foundation (see the earlier section "Building a solid foundation"). Then drive two tall wooden stakes into the ground at the two ends of your foundation. Stretch a level string between them, right near where you're laying blocks; the string will give you something to measure to so your wall ends up straight and level. Lay the blocks in an overlapping pattern like bricks.

Now mortar the blocks in place. You can use regular cement mortar, or for an ultra-sustainable wall, use earthen mortar of the same material that the blocks are made of. (Sift the dry soil you'll use to make the mortar so rocks and trash are removed.) The mortar joints should be ½- to ¾-inch thick. Place a single piece of #3 rebar horizontally in the mortar between *courses* (layers) of blocks. If you use a concrete foundation, install vertical rebars every 4 feet, running from inside the concrete up through the wall (you'll have to drill holes in the blocks so that the rebar can pass through them).

Rammed earth

Rammed-earth walls are truly lovely. Here are brief instructions for building a wall with this material. First build a foundation (see the earlier section "Building a solid foundation"). Then set up two low, very strong wooden forms parallel to each other on top of the foundation. Use 2- x 12-inch wooden boards for the forms, placing them horizontally on top of the founda- tion. Limit the height of your form to 24 inches (to build a higher wall, move the forms upward on the finished portion of the wall). Fasten the forms together by screwing them to vertical 2 x 4s placed every 4 feet along the outside of the horizontal forms. Brace the forms using 2 x 4s set at 45 degree angles from the ground up to the top of the horizontal form boards; there should be a brace every 2 to 3 feet. Secure the braces to the ground with strong stakes driven into the soil. Your forms have to be sturdy to resist the forces of tamping.

Next, place earth in the forms and compact it by hand (very sustainable, hard work) or with a pneumatic tamper. (In ancient China, people whacked it with giant baseball bats.) Be sure the corners get compacted, but avoid hitting the sides of the forms. Compaction is adequate when the tool bounces off the soil surface. Let the soil sit for 24 hours before removing the forms.

Finally, raise the forms on the finished section of the wall and repeat the process until the wall reaches the desired height. You can add layers of different colored earth for a striated, geological effect.

Cob

A *cob* wall (see Figure 14-3) is made of chunks of mud slapped into place on top of one another and then smooshed into whatever size and shape you want the wall to be. This technique makes for a lot of artistic freedom, so cob walls tend to be curvaceous, interesting, and often embellished with bas-relief dragons and lizards, embedded bottles, and other handmade artsy touches.

The first step in making cob is to mix the earth, straw, and water. One traditional approach is to place the materials into a pit and then stomp on them. Often this is done by several people who link arms, chant, and make a dance out of it. All very festive. You also can mix on a tarp, concrete slab, or sheet of plywood. To mix, add water to the soil, working it until it's a doughy mass and not too wet. Then start adding straw (a total of about 2 pounds of straw per cubic foot of soil) and stomping it in. When the mix is stiff, and it's difficult to pull a chunk away from the larger mass, it's ready to use.

Figure 14-3:
An example
of a cob
wall.

Now you can knead "loaves" of the wet soil and plop them on top of one another to form the wall. Make the loaves small enough that you can carry them to and from the mixing location to the wall. To get a good bond between layers of cob, use a cobber's thumb to punch the newly-applied loaf into the ones below it, stitching the layers together into one single mass of soil. (A *cobber's thumb* is a stubby wooden rod with a ball at the end that's just big enough to fit in the palm of your hand. In a pinch, a broom handle or wooden dowel will do.)

As you go, eliminate any seams, gaps, or voids, which can weaken the structure. Place yourself above the work to avoid muscle strain and to use the weight of your body to compress the cobs into a single mass. Don't work the wall too much, though, because excessive pressure can make it turn to jelly and lose strength. Allow the finished surface of the wall to be somewhat rough so it dries properly; a smooth surface will seal moisture inside. (Your earthen plaster coat will cover the roughness.) Don't let the surface dry out as you're working; otherwise you'll weaken the bonds between the layers of cob. If the surface does dry out, be sure to rewet it before adding any more cobs. If the wall starts to bulge out from the weight of the material, trim off the excess and slow the process down to allow the soil to partially solidify.

Wally's World

It's truly amazing how much weight you can move around safely if you know what you're doing. A guy in Michigan can move and raise stone blocks of almost 10 tons by himself — without any heavy equipment. He's replicating Stonehenge in his backyard. Search YouTube (www.youtube.com) for *Wally Wallington* to see an amazing sight. But *you're* not Wally, and you'd better learn what you're doing before you start heaving rocks around.

Holding Back: Retaining Structures

You retain soil for a variety of reasons, the most common being to create level ground where you once had a slope. You have to build retaining walls correctly, though, or you'll have a world of trouble. Your backyard could end up sleeping in your bedroom.

If you'll be building a retaining wall taller than 4 feet from the bottom of the footing (foundation) to the top of the wall, or if you have a slope behind the wall (called a *surcharge*), do yourself a favor: Talk to a civil engineer first. Remember, too, that taller walls require building permits.

Living solutions to retaining challenges

Look first at biological solutions for holding slopes back. If your slope is gradual enough that deep-rooted ground covers (or better yet, tall shrubs) will hold it in place, you score big in the sustainability and tightwad departments. Bully for you.

Choose climate-appropriate plants that also have recognized potential for erosion control. Generally, these plants have roots that are deeper and stronger than those of average plants, can thrive on little or no supplemental watering beyond what nature delivers, and are long-lived and dependable. How do you find such plants? Your best bet is to talk to a local horticulturist or landscape professional who's knowledgeable about such situations. Gardening books help, of course, and so does the Internet, but there's really no substitute for local experience.

Piling up stone retaining walls

Lucky is the property owner who has an abundance of good solid stones on the land. Stones are useful for many landscaping applications, especially for retaining slopes. Even if you don't have stone on your land, local stone is low in embodied energy and delivers a durable result at little environmental cost. (Speaking of cost, stone can often be had for the hauling, especially from farmers' fields and construction sites.)

If your soil is stable and your wall isn't too tall, start with a base course of stone buried in the soil. In unstable situations use a poured concrete foundation (and get help from a civil engineer when designing your wall). Make your base deeper in colder climates to allow for the freeze-thaw cycle that can heave shallow footings and ruin walls. The lowest-impact wall is the *dry-laid stone wall,* which is fitted together without mortar. Dry-laid walls are leaned back into the slope (this very particular lean is called *batter*) at a ratio of 1 foot of lean for every 3 to 6 feet of wall height, depending on the soil conditions and type of stone you're using.

Refer to *Landscaping For Dummies* for further directions on building a great stone wall.

Keep in mind that this project is not only dangerous but challenging, both physically (you *will* be tired) and in terms of the skills needed to do a truly decent job. But it's a great do-it-yourself project for very fit homeowners (or for those who aspire to be fit). As always, check local building codes, and get professional help if you aren't sure what to do.

Assembling block retaining walls

The conventional *concrete block* wall (which is also known as a *cinder block* wall) on a poured concrete footing is an undertaking even for professionals or very skilled amateurs. Luckily, over the past couple of decades, the popularity of *segmental retaining wall systems* (SRWs), using blocks that fit together without mortar (like Lincoln logs), has increased greatly (check out Figure 12-1 in Chapter 12 for a visual). SRWs are easier to put together than conventional block walls, and most important, they're easy to dismantle and use again and again, making them a heritage material. The SRW is a preengineered and very strong wall that any able-bodied do-it-yourselfer can build.

SRWs don't require a foundation. They're stacked on a shallow *leveling pad,* which is a 6-inch deep by 30-inch wide layer of crushed rock placed in a trench. It's important to get this layer very level so the wall itself is level. Lay your base course of block on top of the leveling pad, using a level string line attached to two stakes driven into the ground to keep the wall straight.

You don't use any mortar with an SRW and you don't fill the interior cells of the blocks with concrete as you do with a conventional block wall.

Lay additional courses of block on top of your base course. Cap the wall with matching cap pieces, and backfill behind the wall with gravel. Depending on the type of wall, it may be necessary to install a French drain (see Chapter 8 for details) behind the wall to carry excess water away.

For more on building a segmental retaining wall, search for "segmental retaining walls" at www.concretenetwork.com.

Building earthen retaining walls

Generally speaking, using earth to hold up more earth is not the smartest thing to do. You need something stronger. Yes, you can make a low wall out of any earthen materials, but keep it 18 inches tall or less, preferably without a *surcharge* (a slope above the wall). Refer to the earlier section "Raising Earthen Garden Walls" for more on creating earthen walls.

One pretty amazing earth technology called *superadobe* really works for retaining walls, however. Visionary architect Nader Khalili developed a method of filling long fabric tubes with soil and arranging the tubes like a coil pot to make retaining or freestanding walls and buildings. The walls are plastered so the tubes don't show. The strength and longevity of this material are excellent. Visit the Cal-Earth Web site (www.calearth.org) for the lowdown on this extraordinary approach.

Erecting wood and timber retaining walls

Timber walls, properly installed, can be quite strong and very handsome. They don't require a concrete footing — just a first course of timbers laid *below grade* (that is, below the surface of the ground). Leave the timbers long and stack them one layer on the next, overlapping them halfway with courses above and below as though you were laying bricks. The best way to connect them is to drill through two or three courses and drive #4 steel rebar or galvanized steel pipe down through them. This all-but-invisible reinforcement creates incredible strength.

For taller walls, it's a good idea to install some vertical posts of the same material, buried at least 2 feet (preferably 3 feet or more) into the ground in front of the wall, spaced 4 to 8 feet apart. Another strategy is to use *deadmen*, which are long ties that extend back into the slope to add tremendous strength. You can even make a freestanding vertically oriented wall by digging a trench and standing ties up in it, fastening the ties together with rebar.

You can create many variations on the basic theme; a little imagination can produce walls with built-in seating, arbors overhead, steps integrated into the walls, and many more features.

Depending on the material you use and on how well they're constructed, timber walls can last 10 to 20 years. If you backfill your wall with gravel to keep soil away from the wood, you can make it last longer.

Chapter 15

Hardscape Maintenance

A well-built and intelligently designed sustainable hardscape pretty much takes care of itself because it's made properly of stuff that lasts a long time with little or no care. Not that this idea is a new one, mind you: Consider the maintenance requirements of the Giza pyramids, the Roman aqueducts, or Stonehenge. Okay, I know that they're going to rack and ruin, but slowly, over thousands of years. In the meantime they require very little care because they were built properly in the first place.

This chapter tells you what kind of maintenance you can expect to perform on your well-designed sustainable hardscape.

Sustainable Surface Care: One Big Secret

Here's the story: Don't paint, seal, stain, or otherwise coat anything. Ever. Well, okay, there are a couple exceptions. Cob construction, for example, needs to be sealed with natural coatings to protect it from the weather. It's also okay to use a penetrating natural stain to color wood or concrete and then let it weather naturally. The key is to avoid toxic materials and labor-intensive processes. Use materials that have an integral finish — such as stone, wood, concrete, brick, and tile — and then leave them alone to age naturally. These materials look good just as they are. If you start applying finishes, you'll find no end to the scraping, sanding, sandblasting, priming, painting, and related chores that you'll have to do.

Maybe you don't give a hoot about the environment. Maybe you *hate* the environment. Fine. Just suppose that you never have to do any of this tedious work again. That's okay even though it's good for the environment, right? So lay off the finishes, and enjoy being lazy.

Hosing, Blowing, and Sweeping: Keeping Things Clean

The prevailing wisdom out my way is that hosing off surfaces is a very bad, antisocial, wasteful, totally uncool thing to do. Mostly, that wisdom is true: Hosing wastes water, and sweeping or raking gets the job done without consuming anything. But exceptions exist.

Studies show that people who hand-water their landscapes, using a hose, use less water than those who have an automatic irrigation system. Suppose that you're one of those people, and your flower beds need watering. Using the water to wash off the adjacent walkways, allowing the water to run usefully into the beds, is actually better than sweeping or blowing the walkways, because it uses the water twice: once to clean and once to irrigate. Don't tell my sustainable friends, but I do this at home. They'd be horrified and might not understand the logic, but it works. The other good thing about washing the place down is that keeping foliage dust free helps it photosynthesize better, because more light is reaching the leaves. It also knocks down pests.

On the other hand, if your wash water is going down a drain or the beds really didn't need watering, yes, you're bad, very bad, and totally uncool in the very worst way. Like most decisions, the wash/no wash choice is complex; each situation needs to be evaluated in its own light.

Sweeping, of course, is classic cleanup m.o. and good exercise, too. What's more ancient and time-tested than a broom? Or hey, forget the broom — an old gardener in my town used palm fronds to sweep sidewalks and other paving. That trick is kind of hard to pull off in Minnesota, on account of the relatively few palm trees growing there, but where you can find a natural tool that works, you're way ahead of the curve.

The real bad boy of garden care is the power blower. Most landscaping professionals continue to insist that mechanical blowers are essential to their survival. Nonsense. The blower sucks in dinosaur juice (also known as fossil fuels) and spits out noise and exhaust fumes while stirring up potentially toxic dust and blowing it into the neighbor's yard. This situation is completely crazy. Don't own one of these fiendish contraptions, and if you catch your gardener using one, fire him. (Blowers are illegal in many progressive communities, but in my little town, there's virtually no enforcement. One local curmudgeon snatched the blower off an offending gardener's back and smashed it on the ground. He got arrested, but many of the residents secretly considered him to be a hero.)

What's Noshing on My Deck?

If it weren't for the fact that sometimes, nothing but a deck will get you level space at a reasonable cost, I'd recommend that nobody ever put in a deck. Still, the United States has 30 million decks, so they clearly meet a need for many people, such as those whose homes are on very steep terrain.

However, wood decks are notoriously vulnerable to attack by various pests and pathogens as well as to the general ravages of weather, sun, and time. Alternative decking materials, such as plastic lumber (see Chapter 12), are much easier to live with and require no maintenance other than periodic cleaning. But they're usually used in combination with natural wood framing, which has its own problems.

Termites

In many climates, termites are the bane of every homeowner's existence, constantly noshing on the house and any other wood that's handy. Decks are no exceptions; in fact, they're particularly vulnerable because they're hanging out there like tempting slabs of chocolate layer cake. In the old days, termite remedies were toxic to more than just the termites and didn't always work so well. Nowadays, safe, effective new control methods are available. I explain everything you need to know in the following sections.

Practicing your best defense: Prevention

The first line of termite defense is prevention. All the eradication techniques are useless if your deck is vulnerable in the first place. So follow these prevention tips:

- ✓ **Termites love moisture, so keeping things dry is a good start at controlling them.** Direct sprinklers away from the deck. Plant drought-tolerant plants nearby, but keep *all* plant parts at least 24 inches away from the deck. Direct runoff away from the area. Don't let water from potted plants soak through to the deck; use waterproof saucers that drain clear of all decking.

✔ **Build your deck properly, with an eye toward making it less vulnerable.** Contact between soil and wood is a good way to call up a termite infestation, for example. Set posts on concrete footings, and put the posts in special metal anchors that hold the ends up in the air.

✔ **Never store wood or allow wood scraps to be left in the vicinity of the deck.** Termites often feed on these canapés before moving on to the structure entree.

Calling in the pros

Unfortunately, prevention sometimes doesn't cut it, and your deck may be attacked despite great housekeeping. For severe infestations, call a licensed structural pest-control professional who understands and uses the least toxic methods. No matter what you do, however, remember that the termites will be back. You need to make at least annual inspections of all wood and treat it for termites as necessary. Look for entry holes, mud tubes, hollowed-out wood, and piles of *fecal pellets* (a fancy term for termite poop, which looks a bit like sand). Dogs are sometimes used to detect termites (probably not your dog, though).

Knowing your termites

These wood-eating pests fall into two categories: *subterranean termites,* which are quite widespread, and *drywood termites,* which live in warm climates. (The Southern United States and California are at highest risk for both kinds of termites.) Within these categories are a number of species, each with its specific behavior patterns. Check with local organic pest-control professionals for details on what works against the termites in your area.

Controlling subterranean termites

Subterranean termites generally are controlled with in-ground bait stations, but some nontoxic approaches are slowly moving out of the experimental category. A *sand barrier,* for example, is a mechanical deterrent that involves surrounding vulnerable wood with a 4-inch-deep by 24-inch-wide moat of sand or ground cinders. You can't use just any sand, though. You need a specific size, called *16 grit,* that's too big for the termites to move around and too small for them to use as substrate for building the protective tunnels (known as *mud tubes* or *shelter tubes*) they need to get to your deck posts.

You can also clad posts and other vulnerable wood with metal flashing or special termiteproof stainless steel mesh. You need to install this material with the utmost care, though, because termites can pass through a 1/64-inch opening.

Other defenses include treatment with nematodes, boric acid, or desiccants such as diatomaceous earth. There's also the simple act of finding and destroying the underground nest.

Fungus with powers for good

An eccentric, utterly credible, and brilliant scientist named Paul Stamets, up in the state of Washington, is working on a special fungus that poisons termites. Stamets claims that he can eradicate termites permanently at a cost of about $1 per treatment. Visit his Web site at `www.fungi.com`.

Controlling drywood termites

Drywood termites enter wood from the air, not the ground. After they enter a piece of wood, they can be impossible to detect until something collapses from the effects of their feeding. According to independent authorities, no homeowner-applied treatments are effective on drywood termites; professionals should be called in at the first sign of infestation.

Nontoxic treatments include heating the wood with big space heaters (difficult to do on a deck, though), using localized heat guns, chilling them out with liquid nitrogen, zapping them with electricity, and sending microwaves into the wood.

Tenting and fumigation — the most widespread control method — is toxic and dangerous, and apparently doesn't work as well as its proponents claim.

Dry rot

Dry rot is a fungus that, despite its name, occurs in the presence of moisture. Why it's called dry rot is anybody's guess. It can spread through a deck like cancer, turning it to powder in seemingly no time at all. Many a homeowner has stepped through his deck one sunny Saturday afternoon. It's easy to poke at your deck with an awl or screwdriver to find rotted portions, but the deck usually has concealed damage as well.

All the methods of keeping a deck dry to protect it from termites are also effective against dry rot, so start by eliminating sources of moisture. Remove leaves and junk from between deck boards, get those pots off the surface, and make sure the roof isn't dumping water on the deck. If you have dry rot, remove and replace all the affected wood immediately.

Using pressure-treated wood is the best approach for preventing dry rot from coming back. People make claims for various toxic chemicals and sealants, but these products are dubious both environmentally and in terms of effectiveness.

Other deck-care issues

Even if you don't have any pests or pathogens dining on your deck, you do need to give it a little attention from time to time. Add these tasks to your deck-care checklist:

✔ Clean your deck periodically, using a pressure washer and a mild solution of biodegradable laundry soap.

✔ Follow up the cleaning with a light sanding of natural wood (not plastic or composite materials) and a sealer if you absolutely must (though sealers generally aren't as effective as their makers claim).

✔ Use a biodegradable mildew remover as needed.

✔ Inspect the entire deck at least annually, looking for termites, dry rot, failing fasteners, soil contact, splinters, and broken or sagging wood.

Caring For Other Hardscape Elements

The caretaking chores that you put on your Saturday morning to-do list depend on the hardscape elements you include in your space. This section looks at some of the most common tasks to give you an idea of the required regular maintenance for various features of your hardscape.

Weeding pavers

Weeds come up in between pavers, especially ones with open joints that make them more pervious. Naturally, you'll be tempted to spray the joints with herbicides, but instead, you can spray something quite innocent on young weeds to kill them.

The secret, believe it or not, is vinegar. I'm not talking about just any vinegar (although the grocery-store kind will kill very young weeds pretty well). I'm talking about horticultural vinegar. *Horticultural vinegar* is an ultrastrong version of the culinary kind; because of its potency and acidity, it needs to be handled with care. But it's environmentally benign and knocks down many types of weeds if you get them when they're young. Let them mature, and you're looking at some time on your knees with a weeding tool. Your yard will smell like a salad for a couple of hours; otherwise, you won't encounter any bad side effects. (Though you still should keep pets inside until the spray dries.) Note that as of this writing, horticultural vinegar is awaiting EPA approval for use as an herbicide.

Sweeping and recompacting decomposed granite

Decomposed granite (also known as *d.g.*) is a compacted granular material that develops loose particles on the surface. For safety's sake and to avoid tracking the particles into the house (where they can do a number on hardwood floors), it's a good idea to sweep the particles off.

An alternative method is to recompact the surface periodically with a lawn roller filled with water or with a vibratory place compactor. This compactor is, as you might guess, a big vibrating metal plate, the sole purpose of which is to squash things flat. You walk behind one of these devices the way you walk behind a lawn mower.

Prevent water from running across d.g., because it can wash out little gulleys pretty quickly, especially if the material isn't treated with a stabilizer. Loosen, regrade, and recompact d.g. if the surface gets too gnarly for safety.

Testing lighting systems

Check your lighting system now and then for burned-out bulbs, fixtures knocked off kilter by clumsy kids and flying newspapers, and funky wiring. Don't forget to reset the timer (if you have one) twice a year when the time changes (unless you live in one of the few areas that doesn't observe Daylight Saving Time). You can find more about hardscape lighting systems in Chapter 13.

Cleaning and maintaining drainage and erosion control features

One of the most important hardscape maintenance tasks is keeping storm water from doing harm. So before every rainy season, grit your teeth, get out your ladder, and clean the gutters. When you're safely back on the ground, run a hose down your catch basins to dislodge any trash, rat carcasses, sidewinders, or small kids from the drain pipes. Check your surface drainage and make any corrections, remembering that the grades you carefully set up when you put in your landscaping may have changed due to intentional or accidental soil movement, sedimentation, settling, plant growth, trash buildup, or other causes. Look at erosion control blankets, wattles, check dams, and other erosion control structures to make sure they're still in place and working properly. It sure is difficult to work on this stuff when it's pouring rain.

Staying Safe: The Site Inspection

Landscaping slowly changes — without any help from you — in ways that sometimes result in the creation of new hazards. Develop the habit of keeping an eye on things from a safety perspective. Here are some items for your checklist:

✔ **Trash:** Look for debris piles that can attract vermin, create a fire hazard, or endanger children.

✔ **Fire:** Clear out dead or overgrown vegetation, low-hanging tree limbs, flammable fuels, and other materials that are just lying around.

✔ **Trip hazards:** Paving settles, sprinkler heads seem to emerge from the ground, and foliage hangs over walks — all these situations can create things to trip over. Make adjustments as needed.

✔ **Tree safety:** Leave this one to the pros. Get an annual inspection by a certified arborist, who will look for weak or broken limbs, heart rot, decay, and root problems that could cause part or all of the tree to fall onto structures, power lines, or people.

✔ **Plumbing problems:** Look for leaks, runoff that could make sidewalks slippery, sprinkler heads sticking up where someone could trip over them, and loose drip tubing. Have your backflow prevention device checked annually, as required by law, by a licensed backflow test technician. (Call your county health department for a list of names.) Turn to Chapter 10 for full coverage of irrigation system maintenance.

✔ **Play equipment and child safety:** Check for loose or protruding fasteners, sharp edges, broken parts, splinters, cracks, and peeling paint. Clear the area of beehives, animal feces, broken glass, and thorny or toxic plants. Also make sure that self-latching gates are working properly, especially around pools and ponds.

Part V
Great Greenery for a Green Garden

The 5th Wave   By Rich Tennant

"I just think it's ironic that someone with a face lift, an eye job, implants, and a hair weave, should all of a sudden become Miss Sustainable Landscaper."

In this part . . .

The sustainable landscape is a living system that's dependent on plants and all the other elements of a living ecology. Plants don't just look pretty; they also do stuff that actually matters, like making food, preventing erosion, reducing energy demand inside your house, attracting beneficial insects, and a whole lot more. Of course they're pretty too, aren't they? There's nothing unsustainable about that!

This part shows you how to use plants effectively, create beautiful plantings that demand little upkeep, and even design a lawn that requires very infrequent mowing and watering. You see how to care for your soil and the life within it. You also discover how to buy good plants (including trees and shrubs), how to plant them, and how to care for them using the most sustainable approaches, new and ancient. The basics of organic pest, disease, and weed control are in this part too.

Chapter 16

Planting the Seed: Sustainable Plant Basics

The huge variety of plants, the complexities of soil and fertilizer, and the mysteries of creating and managing the living portion of the landscape can be overwhelming. This chapter introduces you to the world of living systems and gives you the confidence to get to work on your own sustainable paradise.

Because so much of the wasted effort and materials in the landscape result from poor planting choices, discovering how to use plants properly will greatly improve the environmental performance of your project and will also save you lots of trouble over the years.

Making Sustainable Plant Choices

If you pick plants well and combine them skillfully (two of the most important sustainability concepts), they'll be an asset and a delight for decades and even centuries. Choose poorly, and they'll torment you forever, growing too large, becoming invasive or hazardous, or suffering from poor growing conditions. So give the selection of trees, shrubs, and smaller plants your utmost attention. The following sections detail some practical matters to be aware of. (Check out Chapters 5 and 6 for plant, tree, and shrub design considerations.)

Discovering which plants are sustainable and why

A number of factors make any given plant sustainable in a particular application and setting. A plant that's sustainable in one place would be dreadful in another. Here are some general guidelines to consider when choosing plants sustainably:

- ✔ Learn all you can about each location on your property, and match plants carefully to the light, soil conditions, and other factors.

- ✔ Choose plants that are adapted to your climate.

- ✔ Pick long-lived plants so you don't have to replace them often.

- ✔ Choose plants that are resistant to pests and diseases. Often one cultivar will do better than another in your area.

- ✔ Where appropriate, emphasize local native plants because they've had millions of years to adapt to local conditions. But realize that many exotic plants from similar climates will be just as successful as natives.

- ✔ Avoid invasive or troublesome species. There are often official lists of problematic exotic plants in your area; take these seriously.

- ✔ Consider the need for inputs like water and fertilizer. Tough plants don't need much of either.

- ✔ Screen your prospective plants for drawbacks, such as susceptibility to wind, high flammability, and thorns to name a few. Avoid trees that may crack your pavement with their extensive root systems, drop sap or seeds, or poison the neighborhood kids.

Loading up on plant information

Information on plants is everywhere. Because gardening is one of the most popular leisure-time activities, ample advice is just waiting for you to find it. However, as with most things, some of that advice is bad, so choose well-established sources. The following are some great ways to learn about plants:

- ✔ **Look at mature specimens.** Visit real plants in real places, not in pots at the nursery where they all look pretty much the same and there's no hint that one plant will grow to 100 feet tall while another will stay a foot or so.

   Botanic gardens offer mature plantings in well thought-out combinations, with good labels and lots of chipper staff to answer your questions. Public parks often contain a remarkable variety of species as well. Walk around neighborhoods, especially your own, to see which plants are doing well. Go on garden tours.

✔ **Seek out gardening books that address your region.** Nothing is quite like a good plant encyclopedia to get you up to speed on an unfamiliar species.

✔ **Take advantage of the Internet.** Many wholesale growers and retail nurseries have great Web sites. So may the cooperative extension service or ornamental horticulture department of your state university. Search for the scientific name of a plant.

✔ **Be sociable.** Gardeners love to talk. Strike up conversations in nurseries and at public gardens, or pester people working in their front yards. Tap the (free!) wisdom that's all around you.

Size does matter: Giving plants room to grow

Plants aren't just pretty things to put around the yard; they're living organisms with their own way of getting along in the world. They have a very specific destiny — a set of genetic instructions that determine their height, width, growth rate, and many other characteristics. Plants are indifferent to your needs. This concept is difficult for a plant lover to accept, but it's true. Plants don't give a hoot about you and your landscaping. Sorry.

This means that your job as a landscaper is to figure out what plants need and then make sure they get it. Suppose you put a 20-foot wide shrub where you want a 4-foot one. The shrub, in its blissful ignorance, will keep trying to grow to 20 feet wide, and you'll have to keep cutting it back. A plant can't be trained as if it were a dog, and your relationship with that plant will go on unchanged, with much labor on your part, until you finally take it out and put in something that grows to the proper size.

The implications of not giving plants room to grow are many:

✔ **You work harder, finding yourself in a constant battle with your yard.** The battle gets bloodier the more oversized plants you have.

✔ **The plants suffer from the abuse necessary to keep them in bounds.** They look cut-back rather than natural, and some may never flower.

✔ **Your green waste container is always full of clippings.** *Green waste* is the plant parts you remove in the course of pruning work.

✔ **Pruning is bothersome and wastes energy.** The energy use and noise from using power tools and hauling clippings away is bad news.

I call this strategy *adversarial horticulture,* and believe me, it's an epidemic. In some gardens, 80 percent of the work consists of cutting plants back all the time. It's unnecessary and is a sign of terrible, unsustainable planning.

The remedy, of course, is simple. Believe the gardening books when they list sizes. Choose plants that grow to the size you want for any given application. Then enjoy watching the garden develop into a graceful state of equilibrium, getting easier to live with rather than harder.

Starting off on the right root: Choosing healthy plants

Suppose you had to choose between three plants at the nursery — all the same variety and all in the same sized containers. One is huge and in luscious bloom, the second is mid-sized, and the third hasn't even grown out to the edges of the pot. Which would you pick?

Most people would pick the first one, thinking it was the better deal because it was already fully grown. That would be the very worst choice in most cases, because it's probably *root-bound*. Roots that circle in the pot, as they do when confined for too long, continue to circle in the ground and never grow out into the soil. The plant that looked so great at the nursery will slowly decline, and when you pull it out after a couple of years, you'll find little or no root development.

The best choice in most cases would be the mid-size plant. If you were to carefully remove such a plant from its container, you'd find roots that are just beginning to emerge from the root ball and touch the sides of the container. The soil would be solidly knitted together with no circling roots, and it wouldn't fall apart as would a younger plant.

Here are a few other things to keep an eye out for:

- Look at the *crown* of the plant, which is where the stem enters the soil. You shouldn't see any circling roots there either.

- Beware of plants with roots growing out of the drainage holes in the bottom of the pot; those guys belong on the compost heap.

- Check the above-ground parts of the plant, looking for good structure. You don't want any broken, crossing, or rubbing branches, and the overall shape of the plant should be roughly symmetrical in most cases. Look for an abundance of growth buds, indicating vigor.

- Be sure no pests or diseases are evident, and watch for yellowing of the tissue between the veins or any other abnormal coloration that may indicate nutrient deficiencies or other problems.

Of course every plant is different, so these are only very general rules. Don't assume that every plant offered for sale is in good condition. Check each one carefully.

Selecting plants that naturally thrive in your area

Choose varieties that are strong and well adapted to your growing conditions. Some species (and even entire genera) of plants are going to be weaklings, either because they're so far out of their element in your climate that they can't possibly thrive or because they've been hybridized for appearance at the expense of performance.

Make sure the backbone plants in your yard are survivors. Walk your neighborhood to see what does well and talk to local nursery staff and others who really know plants. Don't give yourself an uphill battle by choosing plants that will never thrive. That's not sustainable; it's just pointless.

Getting to know the natives

Natives are plants that have evolved in place and, in the case of North America and other colonized areas of the world, were present prior to European settlement. They weren't introduced or dispersed by humans; they developed on their own.

A native species doesn't exist in a vacuum; it's part of a *plant community* of interconnected species that have all grown up together. In turn, the plant community is part of a larger, highly complex *ecosystem* made up of plants, animals, insects, bacteria, fungi, bodies of water, soil, and even weather patterns and other nonmaterial influences. Native plants are highly adapted to local conditions, so much so that they often grow in a very specific part of the local ecosystem, such as a wet spot or on a sunny slope.

Because of their specificity to a particular environment, native plants may be touchy about being moved to different environments. They thrive under proper conditions with little or no supplemental watering, fertilization, or other special treatment. This is important in developing a sustainable landscape because sustainability is all about minimizing inputs.

The constant destruction of ecosystems today makes it important to restore as much as possible. Therefore, using natives in a landscape setting will help bring things back into balance. Native plants provide food for native animals and insects, so inviting those plants into your garden will benefit many species. In fact, an all-native garden can be an excellent option. Well-placed natives will make gardening much easier than using ill-adapted nonnative (aka *exotic*) plants.

On the other hand, in an urban or suburban area, feel free to mix in well-adapted plants from regions with climates similar to yours. They can add diversity and interest to the plant community you're creating. Exotics are also handy for filling niches that native plants can't tolerate. Don't forget that most of our food plants aren't native, and yet they deserve a place in our sustainable gardens.

Myths about native plants

Some folks have peculiar notions about native plants. Here are some of them:

- **Natives require zero maintenance.** This notion may be true in some cases, especially if you're okay with the unkempt appearance of wild places. Natural ecosystems depend on dead plant material, thickets, and fallen leaves to provide cover, food, nesting materials, and other necessities for the native wildlife. Your garden can do the same. But if you want your property to look a little more respectable, be prepared to groom those natives a bit. And of course, dead stuff can attract undesirable critters and become a fire hazard.

- **Natives never get pests or diseases.** Native plants have their own complement of native insects and ills. The difference is that in most cases beneficial insects and other natural controls keep problems in check.

- **All natives are drought tolerant.** Consider a plant that's native to a local wetland. It's certainly not drought tolerant, so don't put it in an area that can't meet its considerable need for water. If you're concerned about saving water, pick drought-tolerant species, whether native or not.

- **Natives are easier/harder to grow than other plants.** Growing difficulty depends on the plant and how well suited it is to where you place it. Plants that are out of place suffer and are difficult to live with; this is especially true of natives. But put a native where it wants to be and chances are you'll have a happy, easy-care plant for a long time.

Working with native plants

If you're considering natives, do your research first. Visit a local botanic garden that features natives, take a class in native plants, read up on natives, or join a native plant society. Above all else, spend time in truly wild places in your region to understand what a native plant community is, what makes it tick, what plants are associated with one another, and whether these plants are really something you want on your property.

After you've done your homework, check to be sure that the conditions on your property are right for the plants you're considering. Soils, exposure, water, and other elements often have to be just so, and not all sites are suitable for natives. If you aren't sure how to proceed, consult with a professional who specializes in native landscaping.

When you plant natives, do so in the proper season (which is often fall, but it varies depending on location), and be careful to avoid fertilizers, soil amendments, and other modifications unless you know that the plants you've chosen really need them. During the establishment period, keep an eye on watering and other care, because even native plants need a little babying when they're pups. Over the long haul, avoid killing your natives with kindness, keeping in mind that they're quite happy with what nature delivers.

If you live near wild land, be careful about introducing natives that aren't present in the immediately local plant community. If your plants are genetically similar to the truly local natives, they can hybridize with the locals and cause genetic pollution.

Never dig plants from wild places, even on private property, unless you're sure you aren't disrupting a native ecosystem or if you're saving the plants from approaching bulldozers. Buy from reputable growers who can guarantee that they aren't dug in the wild.

Avoiding invasive plants

Some plants are so nasty that they should never show up in your garden. A particular species may be just fine in its native habitat (where competition, browsing animals, or insects keep it under control), but taken elsewhere, it runs everything else out of town. Every location has its outlaws, and you may already know (and curse) the names of your local botanical hoodlums. People have been moving plants around the globe for centuries, and even though most introductions are benign, quite a few have made a mess of things. They out-compete native plants, increase fire danger, destabilize slopes, ruin the habitat for indigenous animals, and more.

Look to your local native plant society, botanic garden, or university or visit www.usna.usda.gov/Gardens/invasives.html for information on troublesome plants in your area.

Some invasive species are still sold at nurseries. Just because you see a plant for sale doesn't mean that it behaves itself. Know which species are invasive and never plant them, no matter how cute they look in the container.

Developing a plant palette

A *plant palette* is a list of plants that might be suitable for your project. You'll pick from the palette to develop your planting design, narrowing down the list to the most compatible and desirable varieties. For now, this is an opportunity to expand your awareness of plants that will work for you and for the environment. Here's how to develop a plant palette:

1. **Begin investigating the possibilities for your plant palette.**

   Make a menu of choices that fits your criteria for each spot in the landscape. Start with plants you know and like. List them by type of plant (perennial, shrub, tree, and so on), by size, by potential location in the landscape (shade tree for the back patio, ground cover for the back slope), or whatever other considerations are important to you. Make the same kind of list for each type of plant that you need.

2. **Go visit the plants.**

   Visit places that have full-size plants. Go where you can see how plants behave, how big they get, how they smell, and everything else about them. See "Loading up on plant information" earlier in this chapter for more details.

   Ultimate size is one of the most important considerations when viewing plants. When you see a mature plant, you can really understand its ultimate size.

3. **Prioritize your list.**

   While all the plants are fresh in your mind, make little happy faces by your strong favorites, and cross out ones that just don't fit for whatever reason (wrong size, wrong color, spouse hates it, or whatever).

You won't be able to use all the plants you've listed on your plant palette, and for reasons of good design you'll want to select a reasonable number of varieties for the final design. You'll need to pare down your list in order to develop a final design.

Here are some tips for narrowing down your plant palette:

- **Choose compatible colors, textures, and forms.** Use the design skills I provide in Chapter 5 to pick combinations of plants that work well together visually. Sure, sustainability is about how things work, but it's also about how things look.

- **Select plants based on their watering needs.** Choose plants that you can group together according to water need — into *hydrozones*. Place medium water-use plants together in one area, low water-use plants in another, and so on. Then develop your irrigation system so that each hydrozone has its own separately-valved system that can be controlled independently of the others. This way you're sure that you aren't drowning your drought-tolerant plants in order to give the higher water-use ones the water they need, or vice versa. (Chapter 9 provides more information on water management.)

- **Only keep those plants that fit the spaces you have.** If you give plants room to grow you'll be about 40 percent of the way toward a sustainable landscape — even if you do everything else wrong. Why? Because so much effort, time, energy, and money are spent cutting back plants that have grown too big for the space they're in. Pruning to control size is a sign of design failure. By checking the ultimate size of all your plants at the design stage, you'll be nipping this problem in the bud. Refer to the earlier section "Size does matter: Giving plants room to grow" for more on choosing plants based on their sizes.

✔ **Eliminate problem plants.** Do not for one minute believe that your plants will be free of the shortcomings described in the gardening books. Your ivy *will* creep under the siding of your house just the same as anybody else's. Ivy doesn't know that you're special. So, ruthlessly remove problem plants from your palette. There may be no bad dogs, but I'm here to tell you that there are definitely some very bad plants. Each region has its own collection of them, and gardeners will know what they are. Ask, and then act accordingly.

The Secret's in the Soil

Dirt is the stuff you wash off your clothes. *Soil* is the living layer of minerals, organic matter, air, and microorganisms that makes up the root zone of your yard. Surprisingly, about 50 percent of a healthy topsoil is air; most of the other half is made of minerals, with only about 5 percent organic matter, such as decaying leaves, roots, and other former and current plant parts.

Microorganisms also are an immensely important element of living soil. The billions of beneficial bacteria, fungi, insects, and other critters that live in just a handful of soil are responsible for the health of both the soil and the plants. Protecting and nurturing these microorganisms turns out to be one of the most essential tasks of sustainable landscaping. Nothing is better than vital, living soil to make plants grow well.

Soils are divided into three main categories:

✔ **Clay soil:** *Clay soils,* which gardeners usually detest, are composed of very fine particles. They're often sticky and difficult to work with, and they retain water for long periods of time. These soils tend to be fertile, but sometimes they can have trouble releasing nutrients to the plants. Clay soil isn't the end of the world, but it requires special consideration.

✔ **Sandy soil:** *Sandy soils* are made up of relatively large particles, and they have trouble holding water and nutrients. As with clay soils, if you have sandy soils, it's best to pick plants that are adapted to them rather than committing yourself to a lifetime of constant watering and fertilization.

✔ **Loam soil:** *Loam soils* are just right. They're a mixture of clay, sand, and organic matter, among other things. If your soil is loamy, you're a very lucky gardener because you get the best of both worlds — good drainage and water holding capacity, decent fertility, and no particular problems. You can plant almost anything you want.

To determine your soil texture, moisten a small handful of soil (not too wet, please) and make a wiener-shaped gob. Close your hand around it, and squeeze it out between your thumb and index finger. Pay attention to the feel of it, and to how long a ribbon you can get to extend into the air before it breaks off. Then use the following descriptions to determine what type of soil you have:

- **Clay:** Eeew! This type of soil is all sticky and slippery and gooey! It makes a piece in the air at least 1 to 2 inches long.

- **Clay loam:** This soil is kind of sticky, but the air piece will be an inch or so long.

- **Sandy loam:** The sand makes this soil feel somewhat gritty; the clay and silt make it feel a little gooey. It hangs together but won't form a ribbon in the air like the clay soils.

- **Sandy:** This type of soil is loose and gritty; not at all sticky. It would never form a ribbon. Instead, it just falls apart.

Soil management myths and misunderstandings

First of all, there are no "bad" soils other than those contaminated by human activity. Soils are classified by texture — whether they're sandy, loam, or clay (with some variations on those themes). Plants grow in all kinds of soils, but most growers consider loam ideal. So what if yours happens to be sand or clay? Should you try to convert it to a loam? The answer is no; most attempts at changing soil are about as successful as getting your chain-smoking uncle to give up cigarettes.

Myth 1: You need to improve your soil with amendments

One of the persistent myths of gardening is that you need to "improve" soil by adding organic matter (*soil amendment*). This practice actually makes the situation worse in most cases because it reduces water holding capacity and fertility (unless your soil is very sandy), makes the soil dry out faster, and attracts rainwater, causing the plants to drown.

The only proper way to add amendments is if you incorporate them into the entire root zone of the mature plant, which isn't very practical except in the case of very small plants. Even then, amendments seem to do more harm than good in most cases. You *do* need to add a good living mix of organic nutrients and beneficial soil microorganisms, especially *mycorrhizal fungus*. (See the nearby sidebar "Mike O'Who???") These microorganisms are applied in small quantities as inoculums that will boost the living element in the soil.

The sustainable strategy for dealing with less than desirable soil is to pick plants that like the soil you have. This approach reduces maintenance and improves performance.

Myth 2: Soil polymers help you save water

Another myth is that magical *soil polymers* (chemical soil additives) help you save water. This isn't necessarily true. Polymers have been proven to be ineffective much of the time and can actually be harmful in some situations.

No polymer (or anything else for that matter) can change the inherent water requirements of a plant any more than adding something to your gas will boost the mileage of your car. In theory polymers hold water, releasing it to the plants when they need it. Nice idea, but they often don't let go of that water, so it's unavailable to your plants. Plus, the effectiveness of polymers is often compromised by fertilization and other changes in the soil. They don't last very long either, and some of them are made from wicked chemicals.

Myth 3: Clay soils can be "fixed"

You can add *gypsum* to clay soils to help break them up, but that's only effective if the soil has a high sodium content. So have your soil tested first. Sand added to clay can turn it to concrete, but if you use at least 30 percent sand by volume you can successfully lighten some clay soils. Adding organic matter to clay soils provides no long-term benefit. Maintaining a cover of mulch might help over years or decades, but it won't do you any good in the short term. The best way to handle clay soils is to choose plants that tolerate it. Gardening books don't typically list clay-tolerant plants, so look around your neighborhood to see what's doing well.

The soil food web: Bringing life to your soil

Sustainable gardeners talk about soil not just as a physical and chemical medium but as a living *soil food web:* beneficial fungi, bacteria, earthworms, insects, and other organisms that partner up with plants to make them thrive. All these critters build soil structure and work to retain nutrients and convert them into forms plants can use. Without life in the soil, plants barely survive. Check out Figure 16-1 for a visual.

Your job as the sustainable gardener is to create the conditions for the soil food web to thrive. You also must reinoculate damaged soils with the life they need. Do this by incorporating living *compost, mycorrhizal fungus, beneficial soil bacteria,* and *humic acids* into the soil at planting time. How? Look for a good organic fertilizer that lists these elements on the label. Any good nursery carries at least one brand. Also recognize that common activities such as grading, fertilizing with chemicals, and using herbicides and pesticides have a toxic effect on soil organisms, so use them sparingly (if at all).

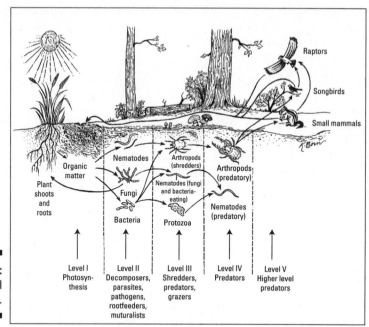

Figure 16-1:
The soil
food web.

Soil testing: Chemistry versus biology

In order to grow plants successfully, you need to know what kind of soil you're working with. The best way to do this is by sending a sample of your soil into a lab for a *landscape suitability analysis* (LSA). Like a blood test, the LSA tells you a lot about the chemistry of your soil: *pH* (whether it's *acid* [technically anything with lots of hydrogen ions and a pH below 7.0] or *alkaline* [low in hydrogen ions and with a pH above 7.0]), nutrient content, salinity, and a number of other factors.

In some states, the agriculture department or cooperative extension service does soil testing; in other places you have to use a private lab. Take a sample of soil from where the roots will grow; anything between 6 inches and 12 inches deep is usually adequate. Mail it to the lab, and in a week or so you get back a complete readout of your soil and specific treatment recommendations. Ask the lab for *organic recommendations* rather than chemical ones, since you won't be using chemical fertilizers.

Mike O'Who???

Most people think of fungi as bad things that eat your plants or cause athlete's foot. But not all fungi are bad, and *mycorrhizal fungus* is among the best. It attaches to the roots of many kinds of plants and acts as a souped-up accessory root system to greatly increase the uptake of nutrients and water, improving the health of plants and reducing the need for supplemental feeding and watering. Though mycorrhizae occur naturally in most soils, grading, chemical fertilizers, and pesticides can destroy them. The good news is that you can easily reintroduce them by using fertilizers that contain them or by adding them in granular or liquid form either at planting time or in the established landscape. They make a huge difference in your garden.

An LSA doesn't tell you anything about the condition of the soil food web. For that, you need another set of tests done by special labs that focus on biology rather than chemistry. Unless you have a special problem, the addition of a good organic fertilizer should jump-start your soil's living element without the expense of biological testing.

The LSA also doesn't tell you anything about the presence of toxic substances. If you suspect that pollutants are causing problems, talk to your lab about ways to test specifically for them.

Diagnosing internal soil drainage

Dig a hole a foot deep and a foot wide and fill it with water. Come back in a few hours. If the hole is still full of water, your soil has an internal drainage problem. Choose plants that are okay with wet feet (many gardening books provide lists of plants suited to poorly drained soils).

If you must grow plants that want good drainage, take steps to improve it: Dig a deep posthole to punch through the clay layer (if that's the problem) and fill it with gravel so that water drains out, or run drain pipes underground to draw water away from the area. You can also plant on mounds or in raised beds, ignoring the bad drainage altogether.

Fertilizers 101: Opting for organic

Plants need *macronutrients* (nitrogen, phosphorous, and potassium, which most plants use in large quantities), *secondary nutrients* (calcium, magnesium, and sulfur) and *micronutrients* (iron, magnesium, zinc, boron, and others). Soils vary in their natural fertility, so you may need to add nutrients if your plants need more than what your soil has to give. Nutrient deficiencies lead to slow growth, increased susceptibility to pests and diseases, and symptoms such as *chlorosis* (yellowing of leaf tissue).

Organic fertilizers come from plant and animal sources such as manure, kelp, blood, feathers, cottonseed, and alfalfa; they nourish the soil food web. Chemical fertilizers are made from fossil fuels and mineral salts; they deplete nonrenewable resources, kill the life in the soil, burn plants if applied too generously, and leach into ground and surface water.

Organic fertilizers are better for plants and soil because they're gentler, slower-acting, come from natural renewable sources, are low in salt content, don't leach into groundwater, and work in harmony with microorganisms to improve the soil. In fact, organic fertilizers need soil organisms to convert their nutrients to forms your plants can use.

The occasional (2 or 3 times per year) application of a good-quality organic fertilizer is adequate for most kinds of plants. Fertilize plants with special needs (such as acid-loving species or fruit trees) with specially-formulated organic fertilizers.

Break It Down: Composting Plant Tissue

Compost is the other end of the cycle of birth and death: it's plant tissue broken down by natural forces into nutrients that other plants need to grow. Compost returns nutrients to the system in their most natural form, improves soil structure, stabilizes soil chemistry, makes plants more drought tolerant, nourishes beneficial soil microorganisms, suppresses diseases, neutralizes contaminants, increases soil permeability, and reduces runoff. Compost is essential, sustainable, and beautiful.

Reasons to compost (and reasons not to)

The sustainable landscape is cyclical, not linear; nothing goes to waste in a sustainable system. Nowhere is this truer than in the dance between living plants and compost. You have the opportunity to take part in one of the great cycles of life, and the payoff for you is healthier plants, lower fertilizer bills, richer soil, and less green waste being hauled away by noisy diesel-spewing trucks. This benefit is reason enough to compost, but when you finally harvest your finished compost and run the silky, fragrant stuff through your hands, you finally understand what it means to be a truly sustainable gardener.

Some circumstances may make composting impractical or unnecessary. One is lack of space for a compost pile, but that's a pretty lame excuse since some compost containers take up a tiny 2 x 2 foot area. You can even use worm composters in the kitchen. A more legit reason to not have a composting system is that your landscaping doesn't generate enough green waste to supply it. That can happen if you've done a bang-up job of choosing the right plants; then nothing really ever needs to be cut back.

Small quantities of clippings should be cut up and left as an offering at the base of the plant they came from. This practice is called the *chop and drop method,* and it can absorb virtually all the plant parts in a well-balanced garden. (Flip to Chapter 20 for more on this method.)

Fancy-pants composting technology and the supplies you really need

You don't really need much technology to be a gardener, and composting is no exception. An old-fashioned compost pile works fine, as it has for eons. You simply find a suitable spot and heap up some stuff, using the simple formula in the next section. Then cover the pile to keep the heat in. Turn it now and then if you want it to break down faster (see Figure 16-2). Squirt some water on it every week or so. Harvest ripe compost. That's it.

If you must buy composting bin, look for a simple bin made of recycled plastic (Figure 16-2 also shows an upright compost bin). The bigger the better; piles around 3 x 3 feet heat up better than smaller ones. Throw plant parts in the top and periodically pull finished compost out the little door in the bottom. No muss, no fuss, no turning. Or get a tumbler-type bin and give it a spin once in a while. You can also build a series of bins out of concrete block, scrap wood, or other sturdy material for the dividers. You want to turn the compost in a bin system; a concrete floor makes that easier.

Figure 16-2:
A compost pile (a) and a compost bin (b).

a

b

Composting step by step

Composting is simple. Even though you find many subtleties and various approaches, getting things to rot isn't really that mysterious. Follow these simple steps and you're on your way:

1. **Make a pile of the right stuff — half green, half brown.**

   Gather up some green stuff and some brown stuff. They can be lawn clippings (green) and dry leaves (brown), freshly cut hedge clippings and wood chips, or any similar mixture of materials. The greens supply the nitrogen and the browns kick down the carbon. The right combination, which turns out to be about half of each, makes for a good, hot pile that breaks down quickly. Using too much green material makes the pile stinky, and using too much brown material slows the activity in the pile to a crawl. The more you chop up the material, the faster it composts. Using food scraps is okay if you cover them with leaves or shredded paper to keep the flies out; meat and other animal parts attract vermin and are best left out. For sure don't add dog or cat poo; they can harbor wicked diseases.

    Don't waste your money on "compost starters" or other gimmicks that purport to make the process happen faster. The heavy lifting in the composting process is accomplished by a crack team of bacteria, fungi, enzymes, and earthworms; most of them are present in the material you feed into the pile. If you want to speed the process, add a few handfuls of topsoil, manure, finished compost, fireplace ashes, bloodmeal, or bonemeal.

2. **Add water to your pile.**

   Once a week, soak the pile down until it's moist but not saturated. Cover the pile with a tarp or close the lid on the composter to keep the heat and moisture in.

3. **Turn the pile weekly.**

   Turning with a pitchfork speeds up the decomposition process.

4. **Harvest your compost when it's dark brown, looks kind of like coffee grounds, and has a wonderful sweet/earthy fragrance.**

   You can screen it to sift out any coarse pieces or just use it as is.

5. **Use your compost at your next planting.**

   Dig a handful of compost into the soil when planting a new plant (you don't need much). Spread it on the surface of planter beds as a combination mulch and fertilizer (the nutrients leach into the soil during overhead watering or when it rains). Incorporate it into potting soil.

Solving compost nuisances and problems

If you follow the recommendations in the previous sections, you shouldn't have any trouble with composting. But if things go sideways on you, here are some tips:

- **It stinks!** You have too much green stuff or water in your mix. Turn the pile and add some browns.

- **It's too cold!** Make your pile bigger, water it, turn it, or add some greens. Insulate the pile with straw if air temperature is low.

- **It's too hot!** The pile is supposed to be quite hot, especially during the early stages. But a pile that's too big or not well ventilated can overheat, killing the microorganisms that are there to help. Turn the pile and divide it if necessary to reduce the size.

- **It's overrun with critters!** No meat in the pile, okay? It attracts raccoons, skunks, rats, and other meat-eaters. And cover those kitchen scraps, which attract fruit flies. If you see a large furry paw rising up out of the pile, run like crazy.

Giving a New Plant a Good Home: Planting Basics

No matter what you're planting, what you do when you put it in the ground can affect the well-being of the plant for its entire life. Digging a hole and shoving a plant into it is only the beginning. As with many aspects of horticulture, some of the common knowledge about planting is wrong. Here's how to do it right, step by step (check out Figure 16-3):

1. **Dig the hole.**

   Plants like to be planted a little high, so make your hole about 1 inch *shallower* than the depth of the root ball (2 inches shallower for larger plants) and twice as wide as the root ball. Don't overexcavate and then refill the bottom of the hole with loose soil; put your plant directly on undisturbed soil. Beat up the sides of the hole so the roots can get out into the surrounding soil; a smooth-sided hole creates circling roots. If you're planting on a slope, make the hole perpendicular to the face of the slope, as shown in Figure 16-3; this technique prevents upslope soil from collapsing onto the plant.

2. **Prepare the *backfill soil* (soil that will fill the hole).**

   Refer to the soils section earlier in this chapter for information on amending and improving soils. Add any appropriate materials as necessary and gently mix them in, being careful not to overwork the soil and destroy its structure. In most cases, you don't need to add soil amendments other than perhaps a bit of compost.

3. **Remove the plant from its container.**

   For plants in nursery pots, turn the plant upside down, holding the soil in place with your hand. Give the rim a downward tap; the plant should slide out of the pot. For larger containers, place the plant on its side and gently pull it from the pot. Cut the container off if necessary, but don't break the root ball. Place *balled and burlapped* plants (plants wrapped in burlap instead of being in a pot) in the hole and then uncover the top half of the root ball, allowing the burlap to remain in the soil, where it eventually decomposes.

4. **Examine the root ball.**

   If the plant has circling roots, gently dislodge them and spread them out. For a normal root ball with roots just touching the outside, no action is necessary, though you can stimulate root development by lightly scratching the ball with your hands. Discard or return any plant that's seriously *root bound,* with many circling roots; it will never succeed.

5. **Put the plant into the hole.**

   Check the depth, remembering to plant a little bit high. Center the plant in the hole. For bare root plants, spread the roots out on a cone of soil you've made in the center of the hole. Place the backfill soil about halfway up the root ball and gently compact it to eliminate any air pockets. Add some water to soak the backfill soil. Backfill and compact more soil the rest of the way to the surface, and use the remaining soil to make a small, temporary basin around the plant so you can flood it with water a few times.

6. **Apply mulch.**

   Place mulch around the plant as shown in the illustration. See the later section "Mulching: The Sustainable Garden Miracle" for information on the benefits of mulch.

Even the toughest plants need babying when they're first planted. Pay close attention to watering, keeping the soil (especially the root ball) constantly moist but not soggy. Poke a finger into the soil to test for moisture. As the plants mature, water longer and less frequently, because the root system will be more extensive.

Don't try to hurry plants along with strong doses of fertilizer; allow them to develop in their own time. Watch for pests and diseases, and take action immediately, knowing that young plants have few reserves to protect them. Maintain a good cover of mulch to keep moisture in and weeds down. Finally, get after those weeds pronto, because they can outcompete your plants quickly.

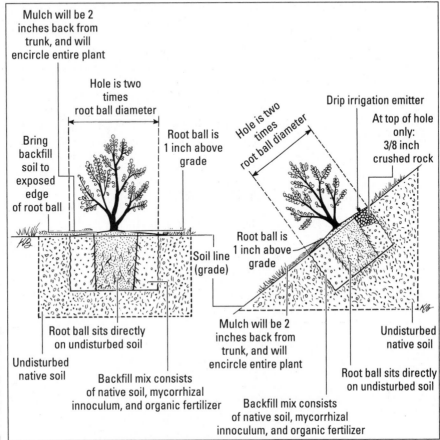

Mulch will be 2 inches back from trunk, and will encircle entire plant

Hole is two times root ball diameter

Bring backfill soil to exposed edge of root ball

Root ball is 1 inch above grade

Hole is two times root ball diameter

Drip irrigation emitter

At top of hole only: 3/8 inch crushed rock

Root ball is 1 inch above grade

Soil line (grade)

Root ball sits directly on undisturbed soil

Undisturbed native soil

Backfill mix consists of native soil, mycorrhizal innoculum, and organic fertilizer

Mulch will be 2 inches back from trunk, and will encircle entire plant

Backfill mix consists of native soil, mycorrhizal innoculum, and organic fertilizer

Undisturbed native soil

Root ball sits directly on undisturbed soil

Figure 16-3: Planting small plants on slopes and level ground.

Mulching: The Sustainable Garden Miracle

Back in the old, unsustainable days, everyone used to rake up the leaf litter from flower beds and lawns and cast it into the trash, leaving soil exposed to sun, wind, rain, and footfall. It sounded good at the time — keep the place tidy, avoid harboring pests and diseases, get your property looking all suburban and respectable, and let the magic truck take the bad stuff out of your life forever.

"Good" homeowners acted that way, and many still do. Just one problem: The castoffs weren't litter, and there was no "away." What people were really doing was squandering precious nutrients, water, and fossil fuels; causing pollution; harming their plants; supporting a destructive chemical fertilizer industry; increasing weed and pest problems; destroying their soil; and short-circuiting one of the handiest nutrient loops in the garden system.

Modern sustainable landscapers know better. They treat every molecule of organic matter with the utmost care, knowing that it's essential to the long-term health of their personal ecosystems. That's where mulch comes in. *Mulch* is a blanket of organic (or sometimes inorganic) material that sits on the surface of the soil. (It's not the same as soil amendment, which you dig into the soil.)

Mulch serves many functions in the landscape system, as the following sections show. If I had to pick the top two or three most essential elements in the sustainable landscape, mulch would surely be one.

Mulch ado about mulch: Benefits of mulching

Mulch is an expert at *stacking functions* (multitasking). Here are a few ways that mulch benefits your sustainable landscape:

- ✔ **Saves water:** A couple of inches of mulch can cut your water use by at least half and greatly increase the intervals between waterings. Note that mulch must be coarser-textured than the soil beneath it in order to get the full water-saving benefits.

- ✔ **Reduces plant stress:** Mulch insulates roots from heat and cold in addition to adding and retaining nutrients.

- ✔ **Keeps weeds down:** Weeds can't get a foothold in mulched soil, and the few weeds that do come up are weak and easy to pull out.

- ✔ **Protects the soil:** Mulch eliminates compaction and crusting of the valuable topsoil layer. Beneficial soil microorganisms get what they need under a cover of organic matter.

- ✔ **Improves the soil:** As organic mulches slowly decompose, they release their nutrients into the system. They also harbor beneficial soil fungi whose *mycelium* (a structure similar to a root system) helps open the soil and improve its structure.

- ✔ **Eliminates damaging soil cultivation:** Tilling, digging, and violent weeding become things of the past, which allows soil structure to develop unmolested as it should.

- ✔ **Improves water penetration:** Because the soil is open, it accepts water much more easily. Roots get more of the water because less of it runs into the street.

- ✔ **Eliminates surface erosion:** Soil can't wash away in a rainstorm if it's snuggled under mulch. It stays where it belongs.

- ✔ **Prevents soil splashing:** Mud that splatters up onto plants often carries diseases. Mulch keeps it in place.

- ✔ **Creates a mud-free, dust-free, walkable surface:** No more slogging through the muck after a rain with gobs of earth sticking to your shoes. No more dirt tracked into the house by kids, dogs, and husbands. And no more dust storms on windy days.

- ✔ **Hides drip tubing:** Drip irrigation is great, but frankly even I think it's pretty unattractive. Mulch makes it disappear.

- ✔ **Makes the yard pretty.** Just as making the bed is the easiest way to straighten up a bedroom, mulching instantly dresses your garden up.

Surveying the types of mulch

Mulches fall into two general categories: organic and inorganic. In this usage, organic has nothing to do with purity or pesticides; it refers to the nature of the material. *Organic* mulches come from living sources; *inorganic* ones come from minerals or other nonliving origins.

Organic mulches

Organic mulching materials include tree chips, shredded bark, pine needles, leaves, straw, nut shells, and compost. Organic mulches are the best way to go because they're part of the living cycle of nutrients. Organic mulches mimic the natural *duff layer* in a wild ecosystem; *duff* (the stuff that falls off plants) is just mulch by another name.

This brings up an important point: Your plants will mulch themselves by dropping leaves and other parts when they're no longer useful or at the end of the season. Nature's way is to allow that organic matter to decompose in place, returning the valuable nutrients to the soil. Gardeners make a big mistake in raking all this stuff up and sending it off to the landfill. Why waste the very best thing your plants need? You're supposed to let plant matter remain where it falls.

Never allow organic matter, however groovy it may be, to become a fire hazard. Keep mulch no more than 4 inches deep. Thicker mulches may ignite through spontaneous combustion or as the result of a carelessly discarded cigarette.

Inorganic mulches

Inorganic mulches include gravel, crushed rock, cinders (also known as *pumice*), decomposed granite, brick chips, plastic sheeting, *geotextile fabrics* (woven or non-woven synthetic cloth), *crumb rubber* (ground up car tires), and recycled broken glass (tumbled to remove sharp edges).

Inorganic mulches last much longer than organic ones because they don't break down very fast. But they also don't improve the soil like organics do, and some of them are problematic (check out the next section). Inorganic mulches also don't provide the insulating qualities of organics because they have little or no *loft,* the fluffy quality that makes sleeping bags warm and keeps root systems cozy. Inorganics are okay in cactus gardens where organic mulch would look unnatural and in specialized plantings where effect is more important than horticultural perfection (but keep these to a minimum for sustainability's sake).

Mulches to avoid

Some mulches have too many problems to recommend them, and a few are downright dangerous. For instance:

- ✓ **Stay away from highly flammable materials,** such as loose leaves or fine-textured coconut fiber that can spontaneously ignite on a very hot day or that may be toxic to pets (cocoa hulls can poison animals).

- ✓ **Avoid dyed mulches,** which have potential problems with the dye. Also avoid crumb rubber mulches, which are one of the worst mulch materials; see Chapter 2 for the grisly details.

- ✓ **Never place plastic sheeting under a layer of mulch;** it prevents water from soaking into the soil and gases from escaping. *Geotextile fabrics* allow water and gases to pass through, but weed seeds germinate on top of them and then root through the fabric into the soil, making physical removal impossible and necessitating the use of herbicides.

- ✓ **If you use a gravel mulch, wash it first,** because dust particles may change soil chemistry for the worse.

A lesson in mulching

Mulching demands little brain power, and requires the simplest of tools. Here's how to apply an organic mulch, step by step:

1. **Finish grade the area to be mulched.**

   To *finish grade,* smooth the soil, remove any surface rocks and debris, and make any adjustments to the terrain so that water goes where you want it when it rains (no point in flooding the house, right?).

   Dig along the edges of walks and patios, lowering soil about 3 inches below the top of the pavement. Slope the soil gradually back into the adjacent grade so it doesn't drop off abruptly. This practice provides a lip to catch the mulch so it doesn't spill all over the pavement.

2. **Murder the weeds.**

   Remove any weeds, including the roots. If your weeds are *perennial* (meaning the kind that come back from the roots), dig out as much of the root system as you can and proceed to Step 2a; otherwise skip to Step 3.

2a. **Smother perennial weeds with sheet mulching.**

   Sheet mulching (shown in Figure 16-4) is the process of covering the soil with a layer of cardboard and mulch to kill stubborn weeds. It works better than herbicides and at a much lower cost to the environment.

   Cover the soil with two to three layers of corrugated cardboard (old appliance boxes or any kind of heavy corrugated packaging). Overlap the cardboard pieces by at least 6 inches so that no weeds come up through the cracks. Wet the cardboard and move to Step 3. (***Note:*** You don't have to remove the cardboard; it decomposes in place, adding valuable organic matter to the soil. When the time comes to plant, usually a few months after sheet mulching, just make a slit in what's left of the cardboard and plant as usual.)

   In this era of recycling, cardboard has become difficult to find because supermarkets no longer give it away. Try waylaying someone on the way to the recycling center with a truckload of cardboard by offering them some money to dump it at your house. Or offer to buy it from the recycler.

3. **Dump on the mulch.**

   Make an even layer 4 inches thick; it will settle to 2 to 3 inches over time. You need about 13 cubic yards of mulch to cover each 1,000 square feet. Be careful not to squash your plants, and lift trailing branches up so they're on top of the mulch.

Figure 16-4:
Sheet
mulching.

Courtesy of Joan Z. Rough

Keep mulch 6 inches away from the trunks of trees and shrubs. Contact between mulch and trunks can harbor pathogens and possibly harm the plants. Wet down the mulch to settle the dust and kill water-repelling fungus spores that can make mulch shed water like a duck.

It's important to keep mulch away from your house. Contact between organic matter and a building can create perfect conditions for the development of *Meruliporia incrassata,* or "house-eating fungus." This bad boy, rare but potent, can turn your home into a shell of rotten wood before you know what happened. It's caused by moisture in contact with wood; mulch can initiate the problem.

4. **Maintain mulch thickness.**

Remember that mulch breaks down, which lets the nutrients and organic matter in the mulch improve the soil. But it's bad because the thinner the mulch gets, the more easily weeds can pop through. Once a year or so, add mulch wherever there's no plant cover, maintaining the 3-inch optimum cover.

Dealing with mulch problems

Other problems with mulch tend to be inconsequential. Here are a few items that may come up:

- ✔ **Fungus amongus:** Organic mulches and decomposing organisms go hand in hand. Most of them are utterly harmless, but some, like *dog vomit fungus* and various *slime molds,* can be alarming to look at. And then you have *artillery fungus,* which spritzes little flecks of goo on walls and anything else that's nearby. Fortunately, none of these buggers causes any real damage, and they're all passing phenomena hitching a ride on your mulch when it's at a particular stage of decomposition. Once that stage passes, so do the fungi.

- ✔ **Sour smell:** This too is a product of the decomposition process that will go away after a few days in most cases.

- ✔ **Trash in recycled mulch:** Because recycled organic mulch is made from green waste, it often contains bits of drip tubing, plastic pots, and other debris that has to be picked out. It's a small price to pay for the sustainable benefits of recycling green waste and saving lots of money.

- ✔ **Weed seeds:** I once covered a property with cypress mulch; I drove by a couple of years later and found that our landscaping had been swallowed in a forest of cypress trees. If seeds germinate, just pull them out.

- ✔ **Pests and diseases:** The concern that mulch may be a carrier for pathogens and insects appears to be unfounded, but some unwanted pestilence may possibly get a foothold. If that happens, follow the pest management recommendations in Chapter 21.

Chapter 17

Introducing Beneficial Trees and Shrubs to Your Landscape

*T*rees and shrubs form the basic structure of the landscape. Smaller plants come and go, but woody plants can live for decades or even centuries. As the biggest living things in the garden, trees and shrubs can demand more than their share of attention and resources if they're ill-suited to your growing conditions, too big for the space they've been given, or susceptible to problems. Choose trees and shrubs carefully, give them a good home, and provide the minimum care they need to thrive. They'll reward you with an abundance of valuable services.

In this chapter, I go into the environmental benefits of trees and shrubs, show you how to choose trees and get them off to a good start, and explain how to care for them in youth and in age.

Appreciating the Many Benefits of Trees

Aside from their obvious beauty, trees offer so many benefits that it's difficult to imagine how we'd ever get by without them. Bet you didn't realize that trees affect all of the following:

✔ **Environment:** According to the esteemed International Society of Arboriculture (www.treesaregood.com), an acre of mature trees generates enough oxygen to meet the needs of 18 people and *sequesters* (absorbs from the atmosphere and holds in its tissue) 2.6 tons of carbon per year — equal to the amount generated by driving a car 8,700 miles. Carbon sequestration is particularly important because the more carbon we can take out of the atmosphere, the lower the threat of global warming. The same acre of trees sucks up other pollutants as well, including ozone and sulfur dioxide.

✔ **Ecosystem:** Trees play a key role in the natural environment, hosting birds, insects, and animals as well as providing shade for understory plants. They also increase available water by improving absorption into the soil, and their dense canopies and extensive root systems protect the soil from erosion and landslides.

✔ **Garden value:** Trees provide privacy, screen out undesirable views, frame attractive views, and absorb noise. A tree canopy provides shade and reduces glare. Also, many trees make fruits, nuts, and other foodstuffs.

✔ **Microclimate:** A bank of *evergreen trees* (trees that hold onto their leaves all year, such as pines or live oaks) planted about 50 feet from your house on the windward side, protects your land and home from damage, and improves the microclimate in your garden. The sheltering effect of trees also protects against frost, allowing you to grow a wider range of plants.

✔ **Your home:** Placing *deciduous trees* (trees that lose their leaves in winter, such as maples or plane trees) on the east and west sides (and in some cases the south side) of your house keeps it cooler in summer and warmer in winter, lowering utility bills, saving energy, and reducing global warming. Trees also cool the environment around them by an average of 20 percent compared with adjacent treeless areas.

Trees make pavement and cars last longer by providing shade that keeps them cooler. The shade also reduces off-gassing from vinyl and other materials inside your car, so you aren't stepping into a toxic cloud every time you hop into the driver's seat.

✔ **Economics:** A study in the 1990s placed a net value of the services provided by a typical mature tree in California at $48 to $63 per year. Benefits included savings in electricity and natural gas used for heating and cooling (a savings of $2.1 billion a year in the United States alone), reductions in pollutants such as carbon dioxide and ozone, rainfall interception resulting in a reduction in stormwater runoff, and aesthetic benefits. The study also found that a mature tree in the front yard of a residence increased the sales price by around 1 percent. Keep in mind that the dollar amounts would be much higher today. Check out Figure 17-1 to see how this impact looks in the real world.

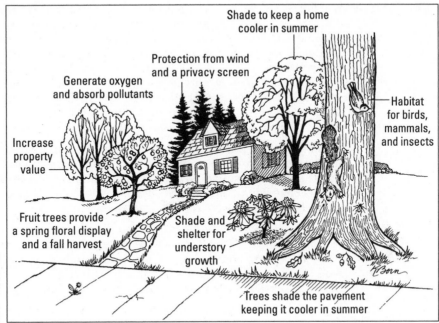

Shade to keep a home
cooler in summer

Protection from wind
and a privacy screen

Generate oxygen
and absorb pollutants

Habitat
for birds,
mammals,
and insects

Increase
property
value

Fruit trees provide
a spring floral display
and a fall harvest

Shade and
shelter for
understory
growth

Trees shade the pavement
keeping it cooler in summer

Figure 17-1:
The value of
trees.

Determining Which Trees Meet Your Needs

The right tree is one of the most essential and sustainable elements in a typical landscape. But before you hustle down to the nursery and get a whole bunch of trees, you need to do your homework.

First, compile a list of candidate trees. Read up on trees in a good gardening book, check out the mature trees in a local botanic garden, or visit `http://selectree.calpoly.edu` for great information on choosing the right tree. Then ask yourself the following questions about your candidate trees to help bring matters into focus:

- ✔ **What's it gonna do?** As always, the sustainable question is "What's the purpose of your tree?" You may be looking for shade, wildlife habitat, flower or foliage color, wind protection, food, all those functions, or even more. Pick a tree that meets your needs.

- ✔ **Where's it gonna go?** Pick a location where shade will be desirable, and where the tree has room to grow. Check for compatibility with other plants in the area and with the style of your house.

✔ **What's it gonna mess up?** Check for adequate clearance from power lines, underground utilities, pavement, and foundations. Avoid placing trees with aggressive roots anywhere near any plumbing, pavement, or buildings. Don't plant a tree that drops a lot of leaves, flowers, and fruits over pavement, especially if it creates a hazard. Think about the effect of the tree on your view and on the views your neighbors enjoy; some communities outlaw trees that grow into a neighbor's view. Avoid trees that are poisonous, highly flammable, short-lived, brittle, unstable, invasive, weedy, or particularly susceptible to pests and diseases.

Criminey! It sounds like all trees cause problems, but that's not the case. Many trees are almost problem-free, and even ones with drawbacks will be fine in the right situation. But be realistic about problems and don't let love blind you to the realities (remember that you might live with this tree longer than you live with your spouse).

✔ **What's it gonna look like?** Ponder the many shapes of trees: broad crown, spreading, narrow crown, pyramidal, vase, and columnar, not to mention the distinctive shape of palm trees. Imagine how these shapes would fit in your yard. Think about foliage texture and color, flower color and season, branching habit, and even wind movement.

✔ **What's it gonna need?** Consider the water requirements of the tree as well as the soil, food, and weather conditions it needs, its requirements for pruning and other professional care, and its resistance to pests and diseases.

Giving New Trees a Solid Start

Proper selection, correct planting, and good follow-up care are essential to success with trees. If you bollix up an annual or perennial, starting over is no big deal. However, messing up a tree means years of lost time or a permanently disfigured or inappropriate (and very large) element in the landscape. Choose, plant, and care for your trees with the utmost loving attention. I show you how in the following sections.

Selecting the right-size tree

Unless you have a genuine need for instant shade and a huge budget, plant a relatively small tree. Trees come in all sizes, and costs run from a few dollars to thousands.

A smaller tree will be the fastest-growing and most rewarding way to go. Those big specimen trees are way past the age for travel; their roots are old and set in their ways. In many cases, a big tree sulks, showing little vigor and displaying little growth. But a young tree in, say, a 15-gallon container, will take off and grow like a puppy, rooting vigorously into the soil.

The sustainable home orchard

Fruit trees are among the most sustainable plants you can grow. Most fruit-bearing trees require relatively little care and can actually be fun to husband. If you choose varieties with a history of success in your area, you'll be able to harvest organically grown, local food for decades to come.

To develop a home orchard, list the fruits and nuts that you like to eat. Check with local food-growing experts and your neighbors — especially old-timers — to learn which varieties work best in your area. (Nurseries, especially the big chains, often buy whatever's on the market and rely on the ignorance of their customers to make the sale. If you expect to get good yields and tasty fruit, exact varieties matter. Choose carefully.)

Next, plan how to incorporate the trees into your landscaping. Place the most attractive trees (such as persimmons, citrus, apricots, pears, apples, figs, cherries, and many nut crops) in prominent locations, keeping the less charismatic varieties out of sight. (Peaches, for example, can be homely, especially if they get leaf curl.) Make sure that soil conditions are suitable by testing as described in Chapter 16. Plant your trees where they'll get full sun all day long.

You can pack fruit trees in tightly, but avoid doing so if you have plenty of room. Don't forget that many kinds of fruit trees can be *espaliered* (trained into a flat panel-like shape to save space) against a sunny wall. You can also plant dwarf fruit trees that take up lots less room.

Finding a healthy specimen

Choosing a quality tree is vital to its long-term performance. In this section, I show you what to look for in a tree and how to avoid some of the pitfalls you may not know about until it's too late.

Tree packages

Trees are grown several different ways, with regional differences based on climate and custom. There's no "right" kind of package; here are a few of the most common types:

- **Containers:** Trees are often planted in plastic pots of varying sizes, expressed in gallons. Sizes range from 1 to 15 gallons. In terms of the actual size of the tree, and depending on the species, a "one" (as it's called in the biz) generally is 1 or 2 feet tall, not too impressive at the start but a good way to go if you want fast growth and low cost. A "fifteen" is 5 to 8 feet tall with a *caliper* (diameter of the trunk) of 1½ to 2 inches; it's a great choice for a reasonable-size, fairly inexpensive tree.

  Larger trees are contained in tapered wooden boxes running 24 to 72 inches wide and even bigger. The biggest boxed trees need to be planted with heavy equipment and are stunningly expensive. A 24-inch tree isn't a bad way to go, planting out at 12 to 15 feet tall and still young enough to establish well.

✔ **Balled-and-burlapped:** In many regions, trees are grown in the ground and dug up at the time of sale; the root ball is swathed in burlap and fastened with twine or cradled in a wire basket. These *balled-and-burlapped* (B&B) trees come in various sizes. B&B trees are most often the deciduous kind, dug in the *dormant season* when they're leafless; plant them as soon as possible after purchase.

✔ **Bare root:** Deciduous fruit and ornamental trees are often sold as *bare-root* trees in winter, when they're dormant and leafless. Because their roots are exposed, they need to be planted quickly. They tend to be small (6 to 8 feet tall), lightweight, and easy to plant; they're also a snap to evaluate for condition because you can see everything.

✔ **Transplanted:** Established trees can be dug from one place and planted in another with implements ranging from ordinary hand tools to tractor-mounted tree spades. It's best to dig around part of the root system 6 months to 1 year in advance, to allow new roots to develop within the future root ball. Transplanted trees are at high risk for loss but can be a good way to go if you have a good tree in a bad location.

Tree features

Most commercially available trees are grown too tall and skinny; placed too close together in the nursery; and trained to be top-heavy, with lots of canopy on a feeble trunk. Bare-root and B&B trees (see the previous section) tend to be better than containerized ones. A few nurseries grow stocky, robust, real trees. Here are some things to look for in a healthy tree:

✔ **Good roots:** The root system should be proportional to the canopy and well branched and fresh, displaying a lot of young root shoots. Seeing the whole root system is easy with a bare-root tree. Avoid containerized trees with roots coming out the drainage holes in the bottom of the pot, and follow the other tips on picking healthy plants in Chapter 16. The root ball of a B&B tree should be firm and 10 to 12 times the diameter of the trunk measured 6 inches above the soil. (A tree with a 2-inch trunk should have a root ball 24 inches in diameter, for example.)

Grab the trunk and push it back and forth. A well-rooted tree is immovable; a poorly rooted one wiggles around in the soil. Examine the trunk where it enters the soil, looking for *girdling roots* that circle one another — a sure sign of problems.

✔ **Trunk flare:** The trunk of a healthy tree widens as it enters the ground. If you see a trunk that plunges straight into the soil like a telephone pole, that tree has been planted too deeply to do well.

✔ **Happy branches and good crotches:** The canopy of the tree should be nicely proportioned, with evenly spaced branches. Examine the *crotches,* which are where branches come together; they should be wide and strong. V-shaped crotches indicate weak attachment and the probability of catastrophic failure in some future windstorm. Avoid trees with wounds and clumsy pruning cuts that left stubs. Check for cracks where branches meet the trunk. If the tree is tied to a stake, be sure that the ties aren't girdling the trunk.

Planting a tree properly

To plant a tree properly, read the general planting instructions in Chapter 16 and follow these additional tips for trees:

- Set the tree at the right height and make sure it sits on undisturbed soil.
- Lift by the root ball, not the trunk, to prevent strain on the root system.
- Carefully straighten the tree so the trunk is vertical.
- Make sure that the best side of the tree is visible.
- Staking weakens trees. If the tree is robust and well grown it won't need staking unless there are extreme wind conditions. Remove the nursery stake and see whether the tree remains upright. If you stake it, be sure the ties are loose to allow a little movement (see Figure 17-2). Large trees may need to be supported with guy wires instead of stakes.

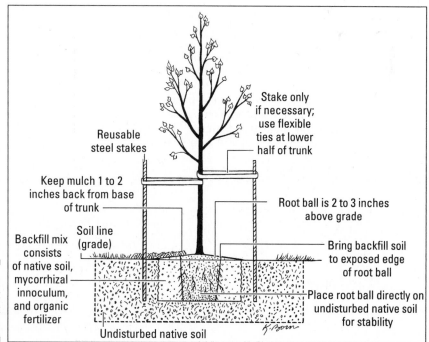

Figure 17-2: The correct way to plant a tree.

Stake only if necessary; use flexible ties at lower half of trunk

Reusable steel stakes

Keep mulch 1 to 2 inches back from base of trunk

Root ball is 2 to 3 inches above grade

Soil line (grade)

Backfill mix consists of native soil, mycorrhizal innoculum, and organic fertilizer

Bring backfill soil to exposed edge of root ball

Place root ball directly on undisturbed native soil for stability

Undisturbed native soil

Tree care during the early years

Care of your newly planted tree is critical to its long-term health. There's not much to do, but it's important to do it right. Read on for details.

- ✔ **Pruning young trees:** The pruning you do on your new trees will set their course for life, determining their shape, strength, and overall health. It's easy to do, but it's critical that you do it right and not do too much. Develop a central trunk with main scaffold branches spaced evenly along and around the trunk. Eliminate any tight crotches as well as any branches that are crossing, rubbing, damaged, weak, oversized, or redundant (see Figure 17-3). See Chapter 20 for more pruning advice.

  Some folks will tell you that a newly planted tree should be heavily cut back. Poppycock. A young tree needs every leaf to develop a healthy root system. Prune with a light hand, following the previous instructions.

- ✔ **Establishment watering:** Two of the biggest reasons trees don't establish properly are underwatering and overwatering. Monitor the soil with a probe or shovel to make sure the root ball doesn't dry out. If your soil drains poorly, be sure you don't drown the tree.

- ✔ **Fertilizing and pest control:** Assuming that you fertilized well at planting time and chose species well adapted to your site, your trees shouldn't require feeding for months or years. If growth slows abnormally, broadcast a balanced organic fertilizer throughout the root zone, and water it into the top 12 to 18 inches of soil. Watch for and promptly treat insect damage and disease.

- ✔ **Protection:** Keep gophers under control. Build sturdy cages around your trees if deer or other browsers are a problem. Shade or whitewash your sun-sensitive trees to protect them against sunscald. Stake securely if strong winds are a consideration.

Shrubs in the Sustainable Landscape

Shrubs are often the easiest group of plants to care for, assuming that you've chosen well. When properly used, shrubs demand little in the way of fertilizer, water, and other resources. In fact, a good shrub is as sustainable as anything you can imagine, getting all it needs from sun, soil, and rain. If I've convinced you that you need to include a few shrubs in your landscape, read on for more information.

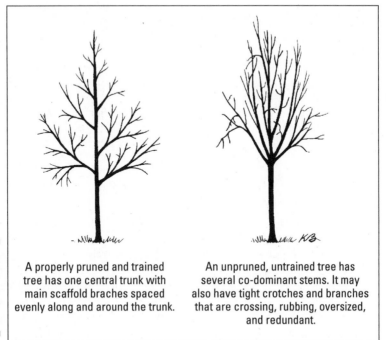

Figure 17-3:
Comparing a
pruned and
unpruned
young tree.

A properly pruned and trained
tree has one central trunk with
main scaffold braches spaced
evenly along and around the trunk.

An unpruned, untrained tree has
several co-dominant stems. It may
also have tight crotches and branches
that are crossing, rubbing, oversized,
and redundant.

Considering types of shrubs

A *shrub* is a woody plant that lives more than one season, is smaller than
a tree, and is larger than a perennial plant. Shrubs can be *arborescent* (tree-
like), upright, mounding, spreading, or prostrate. Shrubs can be *deciduous*
(losing their leaves in winter, such as *Forsythia* and roses), *broadleaf evergreen* (holding on to their leafy growth year-round, like lavender and camellia), or *coniferous evergreen* (with needle- or scalelike foliage, such as yew
and juniper). Shrubs bloom in different seasons, and many offer colorful
fall or winter foliage. Speaking of color, don't overlook shrubs that are
variegated (with multicolor leaves). Thorny or prickly shrubs can be useful
at boundaries as barrier plants.

Knowing what shrubs can do for you

Shrubs are the ultimate sustainable multitaskers. They can screen out undesirable views, create private spaces, exclude unwanted visitors, block wind,
define boundaries, subdivide large spaces, create a stunning accent, soften

the lines of your house, provide a background for smaller plants, act as erosion-controlling ground cover, provide food and concealment for wildlife, and bear fruit and other food for you. Here are tips on a few key uses of shrubs:

- ✔ **Hedges and screens:** Using shrubs as untrimmed screening plants is a lot less work than planting a sheared hedge. Choose evergreen shrubs of the proper size for boundary plantings and let them do their thing without trimming. If space is limited, or if you're looking for a formal effect, a clipped hedge is the way to go. Unfortunately, Mother Nature didn't make many plants that are 2 feet wide and 8 feet tall, so the gardener is forced to train larger plants into that form. If space is really limited, try a fence covered with vines; you'll get the effect of a hedge with much less width and less care.

- ✔ **Specimen shrubs:** A striking plant, when used individually at a focal point in the landscape, is called a *specimen.* Choose something with an *open habit* (with branches showing through the foliage), interesting branch structure, fabulous flowers, or some other attention-getting characteristic. Keep it separate from adjacent shrubs and place compatible perennials at its feet for a lovely scene.

- ✔ **Massing:** To cover large areas with tall, easy-to-grow plants, use masses of shrubs, mixing a few varieties that vary in texture, foliage color, flower color and season, and habit. Consider the year-round appearance, making sure that the shrub displays something for every season, whether it be foliage, flowers, fruit, or attractive bare branches. Avoid random one-of-each plantings; repeat varieties through the area.

- ✔ **Foundation plantings:** Planting shrubs all around the house has been out of fashion for quite a while. But shrubs located strategically to soften or accent the lines of the house are still welcome. Try planting shrubs far enough away from the house that they can be enjoyed from both inside and out.

Buying quality shrubs

Shrubs are long-lived plants and, along with trees, form the backbone of the garden. For that reason, choosing well is important. Buy shrubs in smaller container sizes unless you need mature plants immediately for a party or wedding. A 1-gallon shrub often overtakes a 5-gallon or 15-gallon shrub of the same variety in just one or two growing seasons.

When shopping for shrubs, choose varieties that are well adapted to your climate, that thrive with minimal inputs of water, fertilizer, and the like, and that are the right size for the space you have. See Chapter 16 for more information on selecting healthy, vigorous plants.

Make sure that your shrubs aren't poisonous, especially if little kids or pets are around. Some shrubs — such as yew, rhododendron, and oleander — are highly toxic.

Working with shrubs

The rules that apply to other types of planting also apply to shrubs; see Chapter 16 for the dirty details. Plant clipped hedges 3 to 4 feet apart in most cases, depending on the kind of plant you're using.

Except for hedges, pruning should be done from the inside out, removing conflicting, damaged, weak, or dead branches. Many shrubs can be rejuvenated by cutting them back hard, or even to the ground, every few years as needed. For basic care information, see Chapters 20 and 21.

Chapter 18

Enhancing Your Landscape's Sustainability with Smaller Plants

. . . .

In This Chapter

▶ Laying the groundwork with perennials, annuals, and biennials

▶ Filling in with bulbs, ground covers, grasses, and vines

▶ Considering succulents and cacti

▶ Fitting food into your landscape

▶ Growing plants for special situations and container gardening

. . . .

*W*elcome to the wonderful world of the smaller landscaping plants, the nonwoody things that add so much charm and function to the garden. You could create a lovely planting of just trees, shrubs, and mulch, but small-scale companion plants add a lot to the personality of a garden. Remember, too, that many kinds of nonwoody plants serve practical functions in addition to being ornamental. Perhaps most important of all, diversity increases stability and, therefore, sustainability.

Planting Perennials for Beauty and Habitat

Perennial plants are those that live for more than two years. They're generally nonwoody, and most of them die back in winter in colder areas. Perennials are often grown for their colorful flowers, but many are valuable for other reasons. In the sections that follow, I introduce you to perennials and their functions; I also show you how to select perennials and put them to good use in your garden.

Making pals with perennials

Perennials are perfectly attuned to the low-impact, low-maintenance philoso-phy of sustainable landscaping, making them the perfect companions to your garden. Consider some of the benefits that perennials bring:

- They're among the easiest flowering plants to maintain, requiring only occasional *deadheading* (removing the dead flowers) and an annual hard pruning at the end of the season. (See Chapter 20 for details on caring for perennials.)

- A well-chosen perennial requires little supplemental watering or fertiliza-tion and resists attacks by pests and diseases.

- If given adequate space to grow, perennials don't need to be pruned to control their size.

Perennials also are revered for their colorful flowers, which are attractive to the following groups:

- **Birds:** Many birds depend on perennial plants for food, shelter, and nesting materials. For example, red flowers, especially tubular ones, provide nourishment for hummingbirds.

- **Bees and beneficial insects:** Many flowering plants attract bees, an insect that's having a difficult time these days due to diseases and loss of habitat. Many perennials, such as goldenrod, lamb's ear, and Shasta daisy, provide habitat for beneficial insects that reciprocate by helping to keep your garden free of pests.

- **Animals:** Rabbits, deer, and other mammals feed on perennials. As long as this doesn't result in destruction of your plantings, it can help return wildlife to communities. You can even get your property certified as a wildlife habitat; visit www.nwf.org/backyard for information.

- **Humans:** Culinary herbs, such as thyme, oregano, and mint, are easy to grow and are long-lived. Other perennials offer food — and you have choices beyond the usual asparagus, rhubarb, and artichokes. For example, primroses, daylilies, and hyssop all have edible parts. Perennial plants have medicinal uses, too. Consider the easy-to-grow *Aloe vera,* lemon balm, lavender, and feverfew. Visit www.altnature.com for more on medicinal perennial plants.

Choosing and using perennials

Perennials vary widely in their tolerance for sun or shade, wet or dry condi-tions, cold or mild climate, and type of soil. They come in a wide range of sizes, too. They span the range of flowering periods from spring through fall,

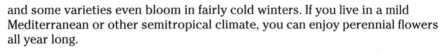

and some varieties even bloom in fairly cold winters. If you live in a mild Mediterranean or other semitropical climate, you can enjoy perennial flowers all year long.

Perennials demand little and live a long time; that's why they're a welcome element in the sustainable landscape.

When selecting perennials, avoid Saturday Morning Syndrome: choosing plants impulsively because they're looking all cute at the nursery. Instead, take the time to make a plan before you head out. Here are some things to keep in mind:

- Decide on a color scheme.
- Research climate-adapted varieties that will work in your location.
- Make a wish list and then choose the most compatible plants from that list, making sure they have the same growing requirements and look good together.
- Repeat varieties throughout your planting so you don't get the one-of-each look. Include six to ten varieties in any given area, using at least three plants of each variety.
- Mix varieties that have compatible foliage colors and textures.
- Consider the overall form of the plants: mounding, spiky, and so on, and combine forms that look good together.
- Mix plants that have different seasons of bloom.
- Vary the height and width of the plants you choose.

Look in a gardening encyclopedia for lists of perennials that are suited to your region. Such lists show plants by color, season of bloom, soil or light requirements, and other characteristics. Comb the lists for things that appeal to you, cross-checking to be sure that your candidate plants meet all your requirements. Then take your list to a local nursery to check availability, discuss possible combinations with nursery staff, and see the plants. Observe mature specimens in actual gardens if possible.

Mail-order nurseries offer unusual perennials. The plants often cost more than what you'd find locally, but it may be the only way to obtain hard-to-find species that you'll never run across at the local chain store.

After you've picked out your plants and made a plan, you're ready to put 'em in place. Keep in mind that most perennials are best planted in the fall. This matches their natural growth cycle, reduces the amount of water needed to get them established, and improves their chances for survival. Follow the standard planting instructions in Chapter 16.

Adding Annuals and Biennials for Color and Wildlife

Annuals live a year, set seed for the next generation, and croak. "Live fast, die young" is their philosophy. Examples of annual plants are petunias, cosmos, and pansies. *Biennials* take a slightly different track, hanging around for a year as somewhat unimpressive green blobs and then doing the flower-and-kick-the-bucket thing the second year. Examples are sweet William and foxglove.

Gardeners choose annuals and biennials for three reasons: color, color, and color. But they can also provide nectar for insects, pollen for bees, seed for birds, and browse for animals.

Considering the sustainability of annuals and biennials

When you think about those massive beds of marigolds and petunias that some gardeners laboriously renew every spring, you may conclude that annuals and biennials are about as far from sustainable landscaping elements as nuclear-powered riding mowers. But some of them are most welcome in the sustainable landscape.

For example, native wildflowers thrive on natural rainfall and reseed themselves to come back year after year. They're just what native insects and animals need for habitat. You can't get more sustainable than that, and they're beautiful to boot. Even nonnatives offer pollen for the bees.

Selecting and using appropriate annuals and biennials

When you choose annuals and biennials, select varieties that fit with your overall planting scheme and that can take care of themselves. Check the *hardiness* (in gardening parlance that's how cold-tolerant a plant is, not how tough it is) and earliest-planting-date information on the seed packet if you're planting from seed (the most sustainable way to go). Hardy plants can overwinter as seeds in the ground; tender ones that can't take freezing winters should be planted in spring, whether from seed or plants. You can also find half-hardy annuals and biennials that put up with yucky cold weather but not frost. Let natives go to seed instead of cutting them back before their natural life cycle is completed.

Making wildflower meadow magic: Not so easy

The fact is that a wildflower meadow (which is different from the types of meadows I suggest as lawn substitutes in Chapter 19) is one of the most daunting challenges in the gardening world. Yes, making a native meadow is righteously sustainable, and you can try to your heart's content. But if you don't eliminate the weed seeds first, and if you don't follow up with diligent weeding and protection from browsing animals and other pests as the young meadow develops, you'll end up with something fit only for a pass with the rototiller. Further, most of the so-called wildflower mixes available for sale aren't true to the mix of species in any real meadow and almost certainly aren't tuned to your particular location. Nevertheless, you can succeed with a small wildflower meadow if you follow these tips:

✔ Choose a custom mix of truly local wildflowers; see a reputable local seed dealer for advice.

✔ Spend several months sheet-mulching (see Chapter 16) before you sow your seeds.

✔ Plant the wildflower meadow at the right time of year for your location. Check with your seed dealer for advice, or read the label on your seed packet.

✔ Plan to spend time hand-pulling tiny weeds out of wildflower seedlings.

If you're successful, you'll have a great display of color in the spring, and some plants may come back the following spring. Try sowing smaller quantities of wildflowers in perennial borders and turf-type meadows. Remove little patches of mulch to expose bare ground, loosen it a bit with a cultivating fork, sow a few seeds (just a few!), and top-dress with a ¼-inch thick layer of fine compost or similar organic matter. Nature will do the rest.

Consider growing all your annuals from seed; it's the most resource-efficient (and sustainable) way to obtain them. Start seeds in flats or small pots and move them into the garden later, or sow the seeds directly into ground that has been weeded and lightly raked to loosen the soil. Save and trade seeds with other gardeners, too. If you buy annuals in pots or packs, avoid overgrown plants that are already in bloom.

Brushing Up on Bulbs and Bulblike Plants

Bulbs (and their close kin rhizomes, corms, and tubers) are among the loveliest and easiest garden plants. Examples of bulbs include tulips, hyacinth, crocuses, and daffodils. A bulb's vertical, strap-shaped foliage and stunning flowers add a lively bit of punctuation (think exclamation point) to perennial beds and meadows. Bulbs live for many years. Most of them die back after they flower, spending the winter underground to emerge and bloom again in spring.

Bulbs are considered sustainable because they require little or no care once established. Plus, native bulbs in your garden help preserve wild species and provide sustenance for native creatures. However, never dig bulbs from the wild or purchase dug bulbs from unscrupulous dealers. There's no need to destroy nature to get plants.

Here are some tips for using bulbs successfully and easily:

- ✔ Use bulbs in drifts and masses, or salt them among other small plants. Bulbs belong in meadows, where they add diversity.

- ✔ Many bulbs are among the first plants to bloom in spring. They can be planted in mixed borders for an early show.

- ✔ Many bulbs naturalize, increasing their numbers annually to form sizable, dense populations that need little care.

- ✔ You don't need to dig bulbs up and put them in storage every year. If a bulb needs that kind of treatment, it isn't adapted to your climate.

- ✔ Follow the package instructions on planting depth, which can be critical to their success.

- ✔ Plant bulbs in chicken-wire baskets and cover the soil with wire to protect them from squirrels, gophers, and birds.

- ✔ Allow the foliage of most bulbs to die down naturally to feed the bulb for the following year's performance.

Walking on Living Carpet: Perennial Ground Covers

In some ways, *ground cover* is a dubious term. As the term is commonly used, it means a low-growing nonwoody perennial plant that sprawls across a wide area. Meadows are a special type of ground cover; see Chapter 19 for more on them. The idea of ground covers seems to be twofold:

- ✔ To play the role of lawn, visually and sometimes functionally.

- ✔ To outcompete weeds for a carefree sward of greenery and flowers.

These ideas are lovely, and in some situations they actually work. At other times, the solution becomes the problem because of poor plant selection. Tread carefully in the world of ground covers, and find out what really succeeds before committing to a plan of action.

The main pitfalls of the ground-cover approach have to do with the nature of the chosen plants. Following the "right plant, right place" dictum can result in a successful, more-or-less-bulletproof planting. But a careless choice can create a disaster. Here are the major ills of common approaches:

✔ **Weeds:** Weeds show up through underground or aboveground runners and by way of seeds. If the ground-cover planting is too low to the ground or contains bare spots, weeds and germinating weed seeds can get right to the sunlight and take control quickly. At that point, you face laborious hand-weeding or the use of herbicides.

The sustainable approach is to choose plants that are at least 1 foot tall so they shade the soil and keep weeds down. Use a drip system to irrigate instead of keeping the soil surface constantly moist with an overhead sprinkler system, which creates a perfect environment for seed germination. Choose drought-tolerant plants and water little or not at all; seeds germinate only during the wet season.

✔ **Invasiveness:** Many ground covers are viney and try to grow out of bounds. Some, like ivy, are so aggressive that you'd swear they're going to grow into the next zip code. With plants like this, there's nothing you can do except keep cutting them back.

Pick plants that have a *determinate growth habit,* meaning that they grow to a certain relatively predictable size and stay there. Plant them far enough from edges to eliminate the need for trimming. In other words, keep a plant that grows to 4 feet in diameter at least 2 feet from the edge of the bed it's in.

✔ **High water use:** Many drought-tolerant ground covers are available; pick one of those instead of a thirsty variety.

✔ **Bees:** Bees pollinate crops, make honey, and are smart, cute, and utterly essential to life on Earth. But stepping on bees isn't good for neither man nor bees, especially if you're allergic to them. Avoid bee-attracting varieties like clover or Lippia for walk-on ground covers.

Getting Ornamental with Grasses

There was a time when grasses in the yard were either lawn or weeds. Then some folks in Europe began growing grasses for their beauty — not perpetually crew cut and indistinguishable from one another, as in a lawn, but placed as individual plants in flower beds and allowed to grow to their full glory. It took gardeners a while to get used to seeing fully grown grass plants without yanking them out by the roots. But the charms of grass prevailed, and many gardeners came to love ornamentals. In the sections that follow, I describe the benefits and pitfalls of growing ornamental grasses, and I explain how to sustainably use and maintain them.

Understanding ornamental grass basics

Ornamental grasses range in size from 6-inch-tall *Fescue* to clumps of *Miscanthus* that grow 8 feet tall or higher. Even bamboo is technically a grass. Grasses can be sustainable elements in the landscape as long as they're climate adapted, noninvasive, and the right size.

Read up on the grasses in a good plant encyclopedia or one of the many books that specialize in ornamental grasses. Ask other gardeners or local nursery people about what works best in your area.

Here are some of the basic benefits of using grasses:

- ✔ Many species tolerate or prefer poor soil and require little or no fertilizer.
- ✔ Unlike lawn grasses, they don't need much in the way of water.
- ✔ They're generally pest free.
- ✔ They sequester a lot of carbon, which helps mitigate global warming.
- ✔ They grow quickly and live a long time in most cases.
- ✔ They resist browsing by deer and other animals.

On the other hand, grasses do have some problems:

- ✔ **Weeds:** The most vexing problem is weeds. If you've ever tried to pull two grassy plants apart, you know that it's like trying to break up a dogfight. Multiply this situation by a yard full of grasses and you've got yourself a hobby. The answer is to choose drought-tolerant varieties and be sure to pull weeds when they're young.
- ✔ **Invasiveness:** Avoid using invasive varieties, such as fountain grass, pampas grass, big and little bluestem, *Miscanthus,* and *Nassella tenuissima*; they become weeds, and some can even harm wild ecosystems. They can be nearly impossible to get rid of. What's harmless in one area can be pernicious in another, so check ornamental grass books for bad guys and talk to your local cooperative extension office for locally troublesome species.
- ✔ **Fiery dispositions:** Some grasses are highly flammable. In fact, most wildfires start in dry grasses. Irrigate enough to keep them green, and periodically remove dead foliage by hand or cut the plants back hard in early spring.

Integrating grasses sustainably into the landscape

Ornamental grasses make great specimen plants, ground covers, and mass plantings. They even grow in containers. Mixing grasses with perennials and shrubs gives your landscaping a natural feel. Here are some basic considerations for working grasses into your plantings:

✔ **Cool and uncool grasses:** Grasses fall into two categories: *cool season* (which are most active at . . . guess what time of year?) and *warm season* (which do better in that other time of year). Mix cool- and warm-season grasses for year-round interest. Winter brings a fourth season of beauty to many grasses if you wait until spring to cut them back.

✔ **Runners and clumpers:** *Running grasses* spread, often vigorously, by underground shoots; they can be handy for erosion control, but many of them can get out of hand quickly and become nuisances. *Clumping grasses* hang out in one place and don't get in anybody's face; they're easier to live with.

✔ **Light:** With a few exceptions, grasses like full sun, so plan to use them in open areas where they'll get at least half a day of the stuff. In shadier areas, try grass-like rushes and sedges.

✔ **Special effects:** Exploit the unique charms of grasses: their fountain-like growth habit, the graceful way they move and rustle in the wind, the way morning and afternoon light settles in the foliage. Plant grasses to the west of a bench or patio for a wonderful backlit sunset show. Use the showy blooms in flower arrangements. Plant a tall specimen grass where you want an eye-catching vertical element.

✔ **Soil stabilization:** Take advantage of the extensive root system of grasses to knit unstable soil together. However, see Chapter 14 for an important caveat about preventing landslides.

Keeping your garden from becoming a pain in the grass

Assuming you've chosen your grasses well, you shouldn't have much trouble with them. Here's a rundown of tasks that you may or may not need to do:

✔ **Water:** Many grasses are happy with rainfall alone, but some need supplemental irrigation. Many drought-tolerant grasses can tolerate wet soils, but they may grow too lush and floppy in wet soil, and they may end up being short lived, too.

Drip, overhead, and hand watering are all okay. Wet the soil 12 to 18 inches deep. Water as seldom as you can get away with.

✔ **Fertilize:** Most grasses don't need fertilizer; in fact, overly fertile conditions encourage weak growth. Especially avoid excess nitrogen, which produces lush foliage to the point where it can be a problem.

✔ **Avoid pests and diseases:** Overwatering and overcrowding can encourage diseases. Gophers will eat grasses from underground, so plant them in protective wire baskets (see Chapter 16 for details). Other critters will browse on your grasses from time to time; remember that grasses are here for just that purpose and can't be hurt by a little grazing.

- ✔ **Get control of weeds:** Carefully remove young weeds, roots and all. Wetting things down first helps a lot. Don't let the weeds get too big, or you'll end up lifting and dividing the grass (or removing it altogether) just to get the weeds out.

- ✔ **Cut back:** Some grasses can go along for years with no pruning, but most look better (and are safer in a fire) if you cut them back hard annually in early spring. You may also want to try combing dead foliage out with your hands (wear gloves). Meadows can be mowed — or grazed, if you happen to have a few head of cattle around.

Walking a Vine Line

Vines have a special place in the landscape. They can be useful for small or narrow spaces, but they can also be problematic, growing into trees and invading spaces not meant for them. Using vines well can result in a richer garden environment; misusing them can cause grief.

Understanding nature's di-vine strategy

Vines developed as a way to exploit limited sunlight in forests where the light is taken by the trees, leaving little for smaller plants. Vines tolerate shade when they're young and scramble to the tops of the trees to get to the sun, spreading out as soon as they reach the canopy. All vines compete with their host trees, and some — like the strangler fig of tropical rain forests — ultimately kill the tree and become trees themselves by developing huge trunks and branches. Some introduced vines such as the infamous kudzu in the Southern U.S. have become a severe problem with no solution in sight. If all this sounds kind of violent or at least rude, it is. *Natural* doesn't always play gentle.

When properly chosen and planted in a suitable location, the right vine can be just the ticket for special garden needs. Vines need more trimming than other plants, but sometimes that's a small price to pay to get a lot of function.

Here are some general things to consider to make vines work for you:

- ✔ **Using vines:** Make use of vines to cover fences where you have no space for a hedge. Plant them on walls to help insulate the house and conceal bad architecture. Send them over the hill to control erosion.

- ✔ **Choosing a climbing style:** Some vines twine around their support; others wrap small tendrils around the stems of other plants; still others stick by means of little *holdfasts,* which look like teeny lizard feet. Some vines just sprawl. Choose a vine type that grows on the support you plan to offer it. (Holdfasts, by the way, are well named; they can be nearly impossible to get off if you want to paint.)

✔ **Deciding between evergreen or deciduous vines:** Evergreen vines hold their leaves all year; deciduous ones lose them in winter. Choose evergreens for screening purposes.

✔ **Attracting wildlife:** Many vines attract and nurture butterflies, birds, and bees. Vines can also attract rats, which is not so good unless you happen to love rats.

✔ **Building a support system:** Make your support strong, because mature vines can be surprisingly heavy. A building will do as long as you're willing to keep the vine trimmed away from eaves and openings. Install horizontal stainless steel wires on fences, and hand-train the vines onto them. Make trellises out of natural materials such as the whiplike branches pruned from deciduous fruit trees.

You may be tempted to grow big vines on overhead pergolas. What usually happens is that all the leaves and flowers grow on top, where all the light is, and you end up sitting underneath looking at dead stuff and wondering when the rats are going to start jumping on your head. And when the time comes to paint, you'll wish you'd never heard the word *vine*. If your pergola is ugly, tear it down; don't make things worse by trying to hide it with a vine. Also, go ahead and let a vine climb up to the second story if you like spending your weekends teetering high on a ladder with electric hedge clippers in your face.

Avoid growing vines on power poles. They draw attention to the pole and make the utility companies unhappy, because they have to keep cutting back the vines. Keep them out of trees, too.

✔ **Planting different combinations:** Try planting two vines that bloom in different seasons for a longer display of color.

Letting vines feed you, too

Everyone knows about the grapevine, but many other vines also produce edible fruits, including passion fruit; kiwi; and cold-hardy arctic kiwi, berries, hops, and chayote. Don't forget annual vines such as peas, beans, squash, and melons. Food-bearing vines can grow in places where fruit trees and vegetable beds would never fit, and they often put the fruit at a nice pickable level to eliminate stooping and climbing.

If you're in the market for a couple of food-bearing vines, first pick things you actually like to eat so the food doesn't go to waste. Choose varieties that work well in your region. Check for resistance to local diseases and pests too. Be sure your soil is suited to the vine you're choosing, and find a sunny spot where it will perform well. Finally, make sure you provide sturdy support as well as a way to conveniently get to it in order to pick the fruit and prune.

Seeking the Super-Sustainable Succulents and Cacti

You either love or hate succulents and cacti. If you hate them, you don't have to read this section; you'll still be welcome in the sustainable-landscaping club. If you love them, you'll discover an amazing array of shapes and forms. Succulents and cacti can't be touched when it comes to sustainability. In the following sections, I describe how succulents and cacti function, and I also explain how you can choose them and use them.

Getting the scoop on succulents and cacti

Generally, succulents and cacti like sun, but some varieties tolerate shade. They prefer warmer climates (USDA Zones 8 to10; see Chapter 4 for details on hardiness zones), but some grow as far north as parts of Canada. Because they hold water in their tissues, they're very drought tolerant, though many can accept limited regular watering under otherwise good growing conditions. They use one third to one half the water of turf. Pests and diseases are rare; and there are few, if any, invasive varieties. Succulents and cacti are among the easiest, most bulletproof plants for the sustainable landscape.

Knowing what to consider for the succulent garden

Consider these factors before you start buying every cactus in sight:

- **Placement:** Locate succulents on the sunny south side of a house or building, where reflected heat and the warmth retained in the walls will help them endure cold nights. Choose a location with good air circulation as well. Place thorny plants away from paths and other traffic patterns.

- **Arrangement:** Succulents and cacti rarely grow only with others of their kind in nature. It's okay to have an all-succulent/cactus garden, but it's okay to mix them with other kinds of plants. Just be sure to group them with plants that have similar water needs. Use the bold forms as specimen or accent plants. Silhouette them against walls. Play with the many foliage colors.

- **Drainage:** Succulent plants grew up in places with gravelly soil and fast internal soil drainage. Give it to them. Give them drought. Give them sun. Leave them the heck alone. They'll love you for it. If you're one of those people who waters every day, stay away from succulents, because they hate that kind of attention.

✔ **Feeding and watering:** Go easy on the fertilizer, and apply it only during the active growing season (and only in small doses). However, don't use it unless you see actual nutrient deficiencies. Withhold fertilizer and water during fall and winter.

Handling thorny plants is tricky. Succulents are much heavier than other plants because of the water in their tissue, so they can be top-heavy. And a top-heavy succulent can lead to accidents that cause you painful injury. Many succulents are also brittle and need to be handled with care. This is extreme gardening, so wear thick leather gloves, a heavy, long-sleeved shirt or jacket, heavy boots, and eye protection, and wrap the plants in newspaper or a piece of old carpeting. If you get pricked, clean the wound promptly and thoroughly to avoid infection.

The Best Use of Land: Growing Food

People went kind of crazy after World War II. Huge cars with tailfins, Twinkies, and big front lawns consumed the affections of "modern" Americans. One of the casualties was homegrown food, a common part of life before then. Times have changed again, and it's time to get back to growing our own groceries. Feeding your family is the very best use of your land — and not as difficult as you may think.

When it comes to sustainability, you not only make good use of your land by growing food to feed your family, but you also reduce farm-to-plate transport from miles to feet and eliminate fossil-fuel use. Perhaps the best benefit is the fact that homegrown food is utterly fresh, delicious, free of pesticides, and fun to grow. You can enjoy varieties that are vastly more flavorful than anything you'll buy at the supermarket. If you have kids, introduce them to the art of food growing; they may need this knowledge more than we do.

The following sections introduce the benefits of growing your own food and provide pointers on growing the best garden full of a variety of foods.

Picking through food-plant principles

Food doesn't need to be relegated to a sad corner of the backyard as though it were some kind of blight. True, tomatoes and a few other crops are a bit homely as the season winds to an end, but most food plants are every bit as lovely to look at as so-called ornamentals, which of course leads to the idea of mixing food and ornamental plants. To me, nothing is lovelier than a garden filled with fruit trees; grapevines; perennial crops like asparagus and rhubarb; and annual crops such as lettuce, peppers, and eggplants mixed in with flowers and shrubs. The abundant food forest, overflowing with yummy edibles, has become a staple of the sustainable garden.

Growing food doesn't have to be labor intensive. The truly lazy gardener can concentrate on permanent crops, such as fruit trees and perennial veggies, but even annual crops can be easy if you observe a few principles:

- ✔ Prepare your soil well, but only one time. (You'll find out why in a minute.) Choose a level, sunny spot for your annual crops. Make sure that the native soil is good, or build raised beds and import decent soil. Add compost and fertilizer, and water it in well.

- ✔ Select crops that you actually like to eat. Kohlrabi looks cool, but if you detest its flavor, it's going to go to waste.

- ✔ Grow plants from seed (indoors to get an early start), or make things really easy and buy starts in six-packs. Choose organically raised varieties, if they're available.

- ✔ Add balanced organic fertilizer and a little compost at planting time, and water your new plants as soon as they're in the ground.

- ✔ Cover the entire area with organic mulch — prunings, purchased mulch, or tree chips. When spread out 3 to 4 inches thick, mulch will keep water in and weeds down. Mulch is the key to success without a lot of work. Replenish the mulch as it decomposes.

- ✔ When you want to add plants, instead of tilling or digging the whole area, just move bits of mulch out of the way and plant into the soil, replacing the mulch when you're done. Ba-da-bing: an ecosystem!

Check out the Path to Freedom Web site (www.pathtofreedom.com) to find out what one family has done to maximize productivity on its small suburban lot. It's truly astonishing how much you can harvest from the most ordinary property by devoting as much space as possible to food production and using intensive gardening practices. See the appendix for more information on developing a food forest.

Bringing in perennial food plants

In between annual veggies and fruit trees are the perennial crops, ones that live for many years without replanting. Some of them are quite familiar; asparagus, artichokes, and rhubarb come to mind. They go in the ground one time and then provide you great groceries for many years with little effort other than harvesting.

Perennials help build good soil; use few resources; extend the harvest season beyond what annuals can deliver; and can be part of a *perennial polyculture,* a diverse ecosystem of productive plants of all types. Perennial food crops don't replace annual crops; they add another dimension to your food system.

Perennials are easy, but they aren't perfect. Some are slow to begin producing, and a few can become weedy. Still, perennial food plants are worth exploring even if you just stick to rhubarb.

Sharing the wealth: The foodshed idea

Once you get hooked on growing your own food, you can take it to the next level by sharing the food surplus with your neighbors. Nearly every food gardener has a surplus now and then, and it often goes to waste because the family just can't eat that much broccoli at one sitting. The answer is to organize a *neighborhood foodshed,* which is like a watershed except that it's apples and peaches and onions that flow to a central point in the neighborhood where folks gather to trade food, swap growing tips, watch the kids play, and make friends.

Because the food is both grown and transported without the use of fossil fuels, it's the most efficient way imaginable to feed people. You can even go a step further and tune the neighborhood for a balanced diet by adding crops as needed and optimizing the use of the land.

Foodsheds are about much more than just food; they're also about building community and having fun. Visit my Web site www.owendell.com for a complete how-to on starting and managing your own foodshed.

You may be surprised by how many foods come from perennial plants other than the Big Three (asparagus, artichokes, and rhubarb). Depending on your climate, you may want to try some of these crops. Unless otherwise noted, these will grow in most climates and soil types (and all these are attractive plants that you don't need to hide behind the garage):

✔ Jerusalem artichokes (not artichokes and not from Jerusalem; how this species got its name is a mystery)

✔ Chayotes (mild to moderate climates)

✔ Scarlet runner beans

✔ Bananas (for the very mildest climates only)

✔ Sweet potatoes (not for very cold climates)

✔ Ultra-drought-tolerant prickly pear cactus, which makes nutritious fruit; the young leaves, called *pads,* can be cooked as vegetables (not for extremely cold climates)

✔ Daylily flowers, which some folks eat

✔ Taro (if you live in a mild climate), from which you can make poi

✔ Bamboo shoots from specific varieties of bamboo

For more information, check out these Web sites: Edible Forest Gardens (www.edibleforestgardens.com) and Plants for a Future (www.pfaf.org).

Discovering the secrets of savvy farmers

Farmers work with soil and plants every day. The best of them can teach the home food grower a thing or two about keeping the harvest coming and the land healthy, not to mention how to do it without wrecking yourself in the process. Here's some of the collective wisdom of sustainable agriculture:

- ✔ **The farm, large or small, is an ecosystem.** The interactions of plants, animals, insects, bacteria, fungi, soils, air, water, and minerals are complex, and it's essential to understand all elements of the system, not just plants. In fact, by mimicking the processes of natural ecosystems, you'll get better results with less work.

- ✔ **Keep your eyes open.** Watchfulness, keen observation, and thinking for yourself can make all the difference between success and failure. Small things, if unobserved, can cause problems.

- ✔ **Feed the soil, and the soil will feed us.** Keeping the soil in good health is the heart of good food-growing practices. Because food production involves extracting elements from the system (the food we eat), nutrients have to be brought back in the form of compost, compost tea, humanure (yes, that), or organic fertilizers. Even more important, beneficial soil microorganisms, such as soil bacteria, mycorrhizal fungi, and earthworms, need to be kept in good health, because they're the basis for the health of the plants. Organic farmers say, "Healthy soil equals healthy food equals healthy people."

- ✔ **Don't cultivate.** Turning soil usually does more harm than good. No-till farming practices, combined with regular use of mulches on the surface, protect and improve soil structure and improve yields. When you have decent soil in place for your mini-farm, leave it alone.

- ✔ **Encourage diversity.** Plant many varieties, and rotate your crops so they don't deplete the soil. Include legumes, such as fava beans, that absorb nitrogen from the atmosphere and deliver it to the soil. Also include plants such as yarrow, dill, cilantro, clover, and tansy to attract beneficial insects that will stick around and control pests.

Growing Specialty Plants for Sustainable Uses

If you want to turn your property into a bastion of sustainability, make it work harder. Go back to our roots, to the time when people used their land to meet their needs, raising plants and animals that were useful to them — a time that included most of human history until very recently. No laws (except the foolish ones that force people to grow front lawns) prevent you from raising plants that do something besides look pretty. Consider some of the things you can do with common garden plants:

- **Garden goodies:** Garlic, coriander, and many other plants make effective natural insecticides. Garlic is also a fungicide, as are impatiens. The juice of walnut leaves kills some weeds.

- **Household helpers:** Shampoo your hair with rose of Sharon extract, wash your clothes with soapwort (used since the Middle Ages), and repel moths with lemon rind. In the kitchen, clean the pots and pans with scouring rush, store things in bottle-gourd containers, and hasten the ripening of fruit with dandelion roots (when put in a closed space with the fruit, dandelion roots give off ethylene gas which initiates ripening).

- **Building materials:** If you're really ambitious, you can grow your own lumber or make things from bamboo, but those options are only the beginning. How about building a room addition using home-grown cattails for insulation, Western red cedar bark for roofing, walnut-shell extract for wood finishing, horsetail for sandpaper, and glue made from garlic juice? There's even a rust preventive made from hemlock trees!

For much more information on plant uses, from handy to bizarre, check out the Other Uses page at the Web site of Plants for a Future (www.pfaf.org).

Making Use of Potted Plants

Nothing is quite as endearing as a cluster of terra cotta containers spilling over with a froth of colorful flowers and fascinating plant forms. Nearly every gardener succumbs to this temptation at some point. Many gardeners fail and never try again. That's a shame, because growing potted plants doesn't have to be difficult. But pots are a tough growing environment, and you have to know what you're doing. This section gives you the lowdown.

Knowing when to pot and when to not

Unless you live where no open ground is available, don't depend on potted plants to form the backbone of your landscape. No plants are native to pots, and most plants wouldn't be caught dead in a pot. Well, actually, they're caught dead in pots all the time; that's the problem. A plant in a pot is slowly being tortured to death, because there's just not enough root run for any but the smallest or most highly specialized plants.

Still, there's a time and place for potted plants. If your garden consists of a balcony or patio, pots are the only way to go. Very urban properties often have little soil, and the gardener turns to containers to satisfy the urge to grow things. Every landscape will benefit from the judicious placement of a few good potted plants, though, because they add a lot of charm to paved areas, entries, and other hardscaped places where growing plants in the ground is impossible. Potted plants also make the garden look finished because the pots themselves become an art feature. Go easy on pots, but indulge yourself in a few here and there.

Determining the best plants for pots

You can plant nearly anything in a pot as long as you understand the implications. Consider the facts about each of the following categories:

- **Annuals and perennials:** Annuals and perennials offer seasonal color.

- **Bulbs:** Bulbs can come and go without much care.

- **Shrubs, fruit trees, and even vegetables:** These plants all work in containers. They require more attention to watering and fertilizing when they're potted than they would if they were in the ground, and they may never do quite as well as they would in the ground. If you want to keep them from year to year, count on repotting them every year or two.

- **Succulents and cacti:** Succulents and cacti are the most bulletproof plants for containers because they store water in their tissue, tolerate drought very well, seem to be okay with confinement, and won't wilt or die if you neglect them now and then. Any plant with succulent tissue has evolved in a dry environment, where the camel-like strategy of holding on to water is a key to survival. They bring that strategy to your veranda and make life easy for you.

  Besides, succulents and cacti are amazingly diverse and strikingly (sometimes weirdly) beautiful. You can keep them in the same pot for years without any apparent harm, and if the kid you're paying to water them while you're on vacation forgets, the plants will be fine when you get home.

- **Monocots:** Plants in the grass, lily, iris, orchid, sedge, palm, and agave families (among others) are members of the class of plants called *monocots.* The name comes from the fact that germinating seeds of these plants have one seed leaf, the first juvenile leaf that emerges from the seed, called a *cotyledon.* For some reason, monocots are much more tolerant of the crowded conditions of a container than their counterparts the *dicots* (plants with two seed leaves like most shrubs, perennials, and annuals). This means that you can enjoy monocots in containers for a long time before you have to repot them. Many varieties thrive for years in very crowded, rootbound conditions.

Avoid planting vines in pots and then training them on a wall or arbor. This arrangement will work for a while, but eventually you end up with a sorry-looking mess because the vine will outgrow the pot and die on you in a highly visible way. Vines belong in the ground.

Caring for potted plants

As with all things sustainable, setting things up right makes living with container plantings much easier. And knowing what to do over the long haul can make a believer out of you, even if you've failed with pots before. Follow these considerations:

- ✔ **Containers:** If you're buying a new container, sustainable choices include terra cotta (glazed or unglazed), wood, recycled plastic, or even the new ultra-sustainable pots made from the hulls of grain. Repurposed containers can be anything that strikes your fancy. I've seen plants in coffee cans, old shoes, brake drums, hollowed-out stones or tree stumps, clay sewer pipes, and wheelbarrows.

  Make sure that your container has a drainage hole in the bottom; if it doesn't, carefully drill one with a masonry bit. The pot should be sturdy and weather-resistant. Very porous containers need watering much more often; sealing the inside with roof sealant helps retain water. Avoid moss-lined baskets, because they don't thrive unless they're watered nearly every day in summer. Putting plants in a plastic pot and then inside a more attractive outer pot makes care a lot easier and helps soft, low-fired pots last longer.

- ✔ **Soil:** Commercial potting soils have improved a lot over the past few years. Many good organic products are available. Soil for pots is lighter than what's in the ground and in most cases doesn't even contain any actual soil. Lightness offers fast drainage and makes it easy to move plants around, but it also means that the soil will dry out fast and won't hold nutrients as well as heavier soils.

  You can add manures, compost, or real soil to commercial potting mix, or you can make your own from scratch. Incorporate some mycorrhizal fungi at planting time to bring life to the soil; this addition can make a huge difference. Polymers (special additives that hold water) are controversial; I don't recommend them.

- ✔ **Planting:** Be sure that your plants are healthy and well-watered. Knock plants out of their pots by turning them upside down while holding the soil in place with your hand and then giving the top edge of the container a gentle tap on the edge of the pot you'll be putting them into. The plants should slide right out. Check for a well-developed root system, discard any plants with circling roots, and give the roots a little back-scratch to loosen them up before sinking them into their new home.

As with any planting, don't plant too deeply, and water thoroughly as soon as you're done. Adding mulch on top of the soil helps save water and keeps the roots insulated.

✔ **Fertilizing:** Use an organic complete fertilizer. Potting soil contains few natural nutrients, so you have to supply everything. Quality fertilizer makes all the difference. Fertilize every month or so during the growing season (except for succulents and cacti, which need much less), or try a slow-release fertilizer made for pots.

✔ **Watering:** Plants in pots need watering much more often than if they were in the ground, and missing a watering can be the beginning of the end for delicate species. If you water by hand, fill the pot at least twice to make sure the water goes all the way to the bottom of the root ball and to flush out any salts that may have accumulated. Apply enough water so that some of it leaks out the drainage hole. If you can place pots in the rain now and then, they'll really appreciate the purer water.

If your pots are on an automatic irrigation system, put them on their own valve, and program the controller to water them at least every two to three days in summer (depending on the weather) unless they're succulents or other very drought-tolerant varieties. Consider running water into a big stew pot while you're waiting for the hot water to arrive at the kitchen tap and using the saved-up water for your potted plants. Finally, self-watering planters with a reservoir and a wicking system make watering a simple matter of refilling the reservoir now and then.

Remember that cacti and succulents need a resting period in fall and winter. Bring them into a brightly lit room if you live in a cold climate, and protect them from rain during the cool season.

Chapter 19

Exploring Lower Impact Lawns and Sustainable Lawn Alternatives

In This Chapter

▶ Critiquing the conventional lawn

▶ Making lawns less bad

▶ Relying on lawn alternatives

*I*t's time to have a look at that lawn of yours. Eighty percent of U.S. homes have lawns, so odds are that you're the owner of one. You're either stuck with or in love with one, wondering how you can reconcile lawn ownership with sustainability. No lawn will ever be 100 percent sustainable, but you can do plenty of things to mitigate their negative effects. Lawns even have a few good points.

Lawns are usually the most consumptive element in a typical landscape. But here's the good news: Lawns are the low-hanging fruit on the sustainable tree. Getting your lawn working better goes a long way toward improving the sustainability of your property. I go into ecological lawn care in Chapter 22. For now, in this chapter, I provide you with some info on making your lawn more sustainable, or at least less bad.

Getting the Dirt on Lawns

If you have a lawn, you're not alone. NASA took some photos from space and concluded that the United States alone has 31,630,000 acres of lawn. (NASA also wanted me to tell you that it's time to clean out your gutters.) That's nearly twice the size of the 100 largest U.S. cities put together. If only turf were a truly beneficial element of gardening, we could be proud of our accomplishment. (How did we get to this point, anyway? See the nearby sidebar "The lawns that ate America" for some background.)

The lawns that ate America

Lawns got off to a poor start. They became popular in the 1600s, when British landowners began to compete to see who could take the most arable land out of production and plant it with the brazenly useless crop of turf. The English climate is ideal for such a silly pursuit, of course, with its constant supply of moisture, agreeable native grasses, and plenty of sheep to keep the results cropped into respectability.

For a long time, lawns were exclusively for the privileged. But two mid-19th-century inventions, one coming closely on the heels of the other, are responsible for the stunning explosion of turf, especially in the New World. First, vulcanization of rubber permitted the development of reliable garden hoses, which were essential for watering, especially in the drier climate of North America. Next, the invention of the mechanical lawn mower enabled the average sheepless homeowner to keep turf under control. The lawn soon became a symbol of democracy and prosperity, enabling the humblest suburbanite to enjoy the fantasy of being the lord of the manor.

Over time, lawns turned into an industry, and today $30 billion a year is spent in the U.S. just on professional lawn care, not to mention the efforts of homeowners themselves and the vast array of technologies that are thrown at modern lawns. This situation wouldn't be so bad if it weren't for the negative impacts of turf: global warming, noise from powered equipment, probable to definite risks of cancer and other diseases from turf chemicals (see the study by Cornell University at `envirocancer.cornell.edu/turf/index.cfm` or visit `www.chem-tox.com/pesticides`), water and air pollution, fossil-fuel use, habitat destruction, soil degradation, excess water consumption, mountains of clippings, and golf. Oh. Sorry, golfers. But really, couldn't you play on mulch?

Lawns have become a symbol of consumerism gone mad, and they pretty much deserve their bad reputation. Check out Figure 19-1 for an idea of how lawns adversely affect the environment.

Despite what the lawn industry — which is made up of sod and seed producers, fertilizer manufacturers, irrigation system companies, lawn care businesses, and others — says, lawns aren't all they're cracked up to be. Look at some of the negative effects of lawns that you'll never see in an ad for lawn care products:

- ✔ **Air pollution:** Because mowers, edgers, trimmers, and so on operate without smog devices, they're responsible for at least 5 percent of U.S. air pollution. Each mower emits 80 pounds of carbon dioxide per year, generously contributing to global warming.

- ✔ **Wasted water:** Lawns suck water like crazy. Between 30 and 60 percent of urban fresh water in the U.S. is used to keep lawns alive. Lawn water use amounts to 270 billion gallons per week, which is three times what's put on irrigated corn. It's enough to grow 81 million acres of organic food. So is it better to have 31 million acres of lawn or 81 million acres of pure, fresh food?

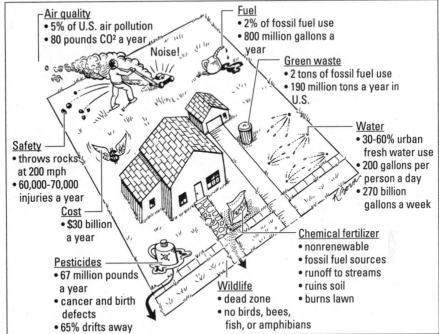

Figure 19-1:
The effects
of lawns.

Air quality
• 5% of U.S. air pollution
• 80 pounds CO_2 a year

Noise!

Fuel
• 2% of fossil fuel use
• 800 million gallons a year

Green waste
• 2 tons of fossil fuel use
• 190 million tons a year in U.S.

Water
• 30-60% urban fresh water use
• 200 gallons per person a day
• 270 billion gallons a week

Safety
• throws rocks at 200 mph
• 60,000-70,000 injuries a year

Cost
• $30 billion a year

Pesticides
• 67 million pounds a year
• cancer and birth defects
• 65% drifts away

Wildlife
• dead zone
• no birds, bees, fish, or amphibians

Chemical fertilizer
• nonrenewable
• fossil fuel sources
• runoff to streams
• ruins soil
• burns lawn

✔ **Overuse of fossil fuels:** Each year, $5.25 billion is spent on fossil fuel–based lawn fertilizers. The Environmental Protection Agency (EPA) says that Americans burn 800 million gallons of gas in their mowers each year. Lawn care equipment (mowers, edgers, trimmers, and so on) accounts for 2 percent of American fossil fuel use.

✔ **Excessive use of dangerous pesticides:** Sixty-seven million pounds of synthetic pesticides go on American lawns each year. Only 35 percent of those pesticides actually reach the plants; the rest drifts off to do harm. This leads to water and air pollution, global warming, loss of wildlife and beneficial insects, and numerous diseases (cancer, birth defects, and heart disease, for example).

✔ **Damaging fertilizers:** Chemically based fertilizers are made from nonrenewable fossil fuels and other nasty stuff. They leach into the water supply and kill lakes by nourishing algae blooms that suck all the oxygen out of the water. Unlike gentle natural fertilizers made from organic sources, chemical fertilizers are salts that have a terrible effect on soil well-being; they kill the beneficial soil microorganisms on which the grass depends for its health. They also disappear suddenly, leaving your lawn without adequate nutrients.

✔ **Harm to wildlife:** Lawns are dead zones for wildlife. Compared to a mixed planting of trees, shrubs, perennials, and annuals, a lawn contains almost no biodiversity and offers little or no habitat value. Plus many common lawn chemicals are toxic to bees, fish, and birds. Even the family dog isn't safe; there's twice the incidence of lymphoma and bladder cancer in dogs that live around pesticide-treated lawns.

✔ **Creation of green waste:** A typical $\frac{1}{3}$ acre lawn generates almost 2 tons of clippings a year. That's slightly shy of 190 million tons in the U.S. alone. Most of that is taken away in a fossil-fuel consuming truck and put in a landfill where it will never again be part of a living system.

✔ **Safety concerns:** There are around 70,000 severe lawnmower accidents per year in the U.S. alone. Don't believe me? Think of it this way: A rotary mower can fire rocks at 200 miles per hour. Also consider what happens when you try cleaning out the chute while the mower is still running.

✔ **An abundance of noise.** Stop with the racket already! Imagine your neighborhood on a Saturday morning without all the lawnmowers and blowers going at once. How peaceful that would be. Peace and quiet isn't an impossible dream.

✔ **High costs:** Suppose you pay a gardener $50 a visit to mow your lawn. And suppose you live in a mild climate like mine where mowing is a year-round job. If you do that for 20 years, not accounting for inflation or raises for the poor sucker, you'll spend more than $50,000. This number doesn't even count the water, fertilizer, sprinkler repairs, replacement, weed control, and all the rest.

Having said all that, however, there are *a few* advantages to having a lawn:

✔ A recent independent study found that if lawn clippings are left on the lawn after mowing, lawns can sequester significant quantities of carbon, which helps mitigate global warming — a big plus. (See the later section "Grasscycling" for more info.)

✔ Grassed areas (as long as they aren't compacted or growing on heavy soil) absorb water readily, so they can soak up a lot of stormwater, preventing urban flooding and allowing groundwater recharge.

✔ They produce oxygen, cool the air, and trap dust and crud.

✔ Lawns don't burn, so they're handy if you live in a high fire hazard area.

✔ They're soft and safe to play on.

✔ They reduce glare.

✔ And hey, they're pretty.

Are these benefits justified in light of the problems that lawns create? Differing schools of thought exist, and no solid data takes into account the mitigating effects of organic lawn care.

Whatever the bottom line, lawns probably aren't going away any time soon, if ever. It's better not to have a lawn, but if you have one or want one, you can minimize its destructive effects by using one or more of the alternatives I present in this chapter.

Minimizing the Impact of the Lawn

You do have options. You can change your lawn and the way you manage it with significant positive results. Most of the changes aren't difficult or expensive. Some of them are even free and result in immediate savings in water and labor. None of it is rocket science. In the following sections are some initial thoughts; visit Chapter 22 for a detailed rundown on lawn care the sustainable way.

Reducing its size

Consider how much turf you require. Unless you have an actual need for a big lawn, such as hosting regulation tackle football games, there's no reason to support the typical suburban ⅓ acre of turf. Grow lawn where it will really be used, and use the rest of the space for perennial beds, an orchard, vegetable gardens, or native plantings. Your costs will go down and benefits will go up, and the environment will love you. Never use a lawn for ornamental purposes.

Create a long, narrow lawn that allows for most normal uses and cuts the unnecessary girth. A gardener I once met called this design a *lap lawn*.

Changing to low-maintenance grasses

You can choose from many kinds of lawn grasses, some less troublesome than others. As with any plant, different varieties of lawn grass vary in their susceptibility to pests and diseases, their need for water, their resistance to weeds, and their need for mowing and other care. If you'll be installing a new lawn or replacing an old one, pick a low-care variety that

- ✔ Is suited to your region
- ✔ Is resistant to pests and diseases
- ✔ Uses the least amount of water possible

Beating the lawn police

Of all crazy things, many communities and homeowner associations actually demand that residents own and maintain conventional lawns. They fine or even arrest violators, criminalizing those who prefer wildflowers, vegetables, or perennial borders over turf (as well as those who don't mow often enough). Some homeowner associations can even lay claim on your property for your defiance of their regulations.

If you live under such oppressive conditions, lobby for change. Organize like-minded neighbors to educate the community about the negative effects of turf and the benefits of sustainable landscaping, and offer good examples of beautiful, sustainable lawn alternatives. If you're up for it, defy the law and make an example of your yard. You're sure to make people think, and perhaps you'll be able to make a real difference in your community.

Hybrid tall fescues are the current candidates in many areas, but the best choice varies from place to place. Talk to experienced lawn professionals who are familiar with local conditions.

Improving water management

Most people are overwatering their landscaping, and lawns are getting most of this largesse. Good water management involves a bit of education and some careful attention to changing conditions, not simply watering on a fixed schedule that ignores actual water need. Water management doesn't cost a penny, and you'll start seeing lower water bills right away. Visit Chapter 9 for complete information on ways to manage your water properly.

You have a huge opportunity to save water (and money) just by tuning up your lawn sprinkler system. A permanent, well-designed irrigation system is the most sustainable way of watering a lawn, but it has to be kept in good condition with regular maintenance. Simple adjustments, such as re-aiming heads, cleaning plugged nozzles, and moving heads to improve coverage and eliminate overspray onto pavement, can make a big difference. See Chapter 10 for details.

Exploring Lawn Alternatives

Suppose that you're ready to scrap your lawn and do something more sensible. Bravo! That's a smart move, especially considering the wide of variety of low-maintenance alternatives that use much fewer resources after they're established.

Playing with the meadow idea

Everywhere you look, people are taking out their lawns and replacing them with meadows. The transformation has been described as a "revolution," and it's surely one of the bright spots in modern horticulture. Instead of fertilizing and watering to make grass grow and then ruthlessly decapitating it every week with snarling fossil-powered lawn mowers, the meadow owner enjoys a more tousled, natural-looking turf made up of native or climate-compatible nonnative grasses, grass-like sedges, or herbaceous plants such as yarrow. Check out the fine-looking meadow in Figure 19-2.

Meadows have many advantages over grass lawns. Consider the following:

- ✔ **Meadows need mowing rarely (or never).** A sedge meadow, for example, can be mowed a couple of times a year to freshen it up, or it can be left to its own devices. If you want a clipped look, many meadow plants can take regular mowing.

- ✔ **Meadows require much less water and fertilizer than lawns do.** Properly chosen plants that are put in favorable locations have little if any trouble with pests and diseases.

- ✔ **Meadows can be more diverse than lawns.** Meadows provide a tough, playable, beautiful surface as well as habitat for beneficial and native insects such as butterflies.

Figure 19-2:
A typical meadow.

Courtesy of Owen E. Dell

Meadow plants

Meadow plants fall into three basic categories:

- **Grasses:** These are chosen for their attractive unmowed appearance and overall low maintenance. These plants can be native or otherwise as long as they're easy to live with.

- **Sedges:** Sedges look like grasses but are in a different family of plants. They're fresh looking, tolerant of a wide range of conditions, and easy to live with. A few species can be moderately invasive and should be surrounded by an underground plastic root barrier.

- **Perennials:** These flowering plants, such as yarrow, develop a tight turf.

You can (and really should) mix several kinds of plants in your meadow. Diversity makes any meadow a richer habitat that's more adaptable to varying conditions and much more interesting to look at.

How to make a meadow

Creating a meadow isn't much different from putting in a lawn. Soil preparation is the same. Here are the basics:

1. **Kill weeds using the sheet-mulching technique described in Chapter 16.**

2. **Rototill the soil (one of the few times this is a good thing to do for your soil), incorporating an inch-thick layer of good quality compost.**

3. **Level the area and compact it gently with a lawn roller.**

4. **Install your sprinkler system.**

   Sprinklers are the best way to water a meadow wherever there are long periods of drought during the growing season. Even though watering will be less than with a lawn, it won't be zero.

5. **Put in the plants.**

   Depending on the species you choose, the plants can be planted from seed or small pots. In some regions, certain meadow mixes are available as sod.

Lawn Care For Dummies, by Lance Walheim and the National Gardening Association (Wiley), has all the information you need on putting in a new lawn.

Establishment of some meadow species can involve more work than a lawn because the plants are slower to mature, meaning that you'll have to pull weeds for a while longer than usual. But that's a small price to pay for years of easy care and low impact.

Meadow management

Living with a meadow is pretty easy, given that the plants in a meadow don't care whether you pay much attention to them. Mowing can be challenging if the plants are very overgrown; a weed whacker or hand shears can work better than a mower in some cases.

As for watering meadows, try letting it go until you see signs of stress (slowing of growth, change in color, droopiness). I'll bet the intervals between waterings will be longer than you think.

Fertilize once or twice a year, but only if growth is slow. That's really about it. A meadow is supposed to be easy to maintain — and it is.

Choosing walk-on ground covers

You can use various kinds of ground covers in place of a lawn. The main difference between a ground cover and a meadow is the degree of traffic that the plants can tolerate. Meadows are fine with normal lawn use, whereas ground covers are better off with only occasional foot traffic, because they're more easily injured or recover more slowly. Ground covers provide the look of a lawn where you want a broad swath of something low to set off other, taller plantings and where you can tolerate limited access and use.

Most ground covers offer fewer benefits and require more care than meadows do, but your actual experience will depend on the plants you choose. Look into varieties that are suited to your region and then choose plants that thrive in your particular conditions. Planting and establishing a ground cover is similar to what's needed for a meadow. See Chapter 18 for more on ground covers.

Covering an area with mulch

There's a time and place to lay off the green stuff and simply cover the earth with a layer of organic mulch. Mulch is a low-care surface that's well suited to paths and open areas where a living element isn't needed. Sometimes, mulch is a temporary solution while you're killing weeds or waiting to decide how to develop a space. At other times, it's a great permanent element in the landscape, offering weed control, water conservation, soil improvement, erosion protection, and a nice natural appearance. It's cheap, too. Check out Chapter 16 for the lowdown on mulch.

Thumbs down: Avoiding phony grass

As with so many things these days, some of what passes for green materials is anything but. For instance, phony plastic lawns are all the rage in some circles. Some communities even give rebates to homeowners who replace their living lawns with artificial ones. Manufacturers point out that a fake lawn uses no water and needs no mowing, fertilizer, or pesticides.

Nonliving turf worsens the urban heat island effect, uses materials that are made from fossil fuels (and may contain toxic elements), eliminates even the paltry life-giving benefits of real grass, and creates a potential waste-stream nightmare at the end of its service. Throw in the fact that synthetic turf does require some water to keep it clean, contributes to stormwater pollution because it offers no biofiltration, and gets dangerously hot in summer, and you can see that plastic lawns are a very bad idea.

Living lawns are a huge part of the negative environmental impact of land-scaping, but substituting a sea of plastic is going in the wrong direction. A far better alternative is to install a meadow of native grasses or other perennials. Better yet, put in a diverse garden of useful plants that wildlife will appreciate and that you'll enjoy for food.

Chapter 20

Examining the Essentials of Sustainable Garden Care

....

....

*I*n my many decades of creating and maintaining landscaping, no client has ever asked me for a high-maintenance garden. Never. It's safe to assume that few people see weeding, mowing, pest control, and pruning as "fun" lifestyle elements, yet people accept these chores as though they had no choice. Even avid gardeners grow weary of some of the maintenance tasks their gardens require.

Most everyone accepts the myth that a proper garden needs a lot of care and nurturing, but such high maintenance is unnecessary. Instead of playing God with your landscape — pruning things into submission, deciding what lives and what dies, and arranging your little world just the way you want — sustainable gardening recognizes that your garden is part of a larger, natural system.

In this chapter, you discover sustainable maintenance techniques that affect the environment and your pocketbook less, yet still deliver the beautiful landscape you're longing for.

Understanding the Importance of Sustainable Maintenance

Nonsustainable maintenance affects the environment, your pocketbook, and you personally in several ways:

- ✔ The annual 60 trillion British thermal units (Btu) of energy used to mow lawns in America is equivalent to 200 billion hours of human work.

- ✔ Eighty percent or more of the total cost of a conventional landscape goes to maintaining it over a 20-year lifespan. That's tens of thousands of dollars or more that you don't really need to spend.

- ✔ Fertilizer-laden water seeps into groundwater and runs off to pollute streams and destroy lakes.

- ✔ Pesticides blow away during application to affect what the chemical industry politely calls *nontargeted recipients,* such as kids in their classrooms, beneficial insects, and wildlife.

- ✔ Pesticides also *volatilize* (a fancy way of saying that they evaporate), causing air pollution.

- ✔ Howling motors annoy whole neighborhoods.

A sustainable landscape, by contrast, exists in a peaceful state within its boundaries and causes no harm to others. The strongest smell escaping from it is the fragrance of the freesias; the loudest noise comes from the songbirds.

Minimizing Maintenance with Sustainable Design

Natural ecosystems don't need maintenance. You don't see anybody out in the wilds pruning, fertilizing, or weeding nature; it takes care of itself! Nature's got that homeostatic edge — the natural balance of forces that keeps things from falling apart.

Compare that with what would happen if you left your landscaping unattended for a while. Suppose you were to put a chain link fence around your property, turn off the utilities, walk out, and lock the gate. What do you think the place would look like if you came back after one year without any care whatsoever: no watering, no fertilizing, no mowing, and no pruning? If you answered, "It would look like crap," you'd likely be right. Most landscapes need constant attention to prevent the forces of entropy from tearing them apart. Think about it. Without watering, plants would die. Without pruning, some plants would grow completely out of bounds and smother smaller ones. Without pest and disease control, weak plants would soon succumb.

What's different about landscaping that it needs so much attention? The answer is that most landscaping hasn't been set up according to the rules of nature. It's created without much thought for what's required to keep it in one piece. Flimsy structures, inefficient irrigation systems, plants that are too big for the spaces they're in or that are prone to diseases — all these factors add up to a battleground, with the hapless homeowner in the middle. More important, the system as a whole is dysfunctional because the inter-relationships of elements aren't present or aren't working.

The poor, nonsustainable design of most landscapes increases the need for maintenance. That's a shame, because the following simple rules of sustain-able design make life easier for the gardener as well as for the garden:

- ✔ Plants are selected for their overall reliability and for their compatibility with local conditions: soil, climate, microclimate, and watering regimen.
- ✔ Plants are given room to grow so that they don't need to be pruned to control size.
- ✔ Plants are drought tolerant and pest resistant.
- ✔ Plants are long-lived to minimize the need for periodic replacements.
- ✔ Plants have been inoculated at planting time with mycorrhizal fungi to help them work more efficiently.
- ✔ The irrigation system is built to match the soil and plants.
- ✔ Watering is facilitated by a smart controller or by a good management plan for a conventional controller or manual system.
- ✔ Mulch covers the earth to help keep the water in, keep weeds down, and preserve the soil's well-being.
- ✔ Hardscape elements, such as patios, walls, and other structures, are designed for minimal care with no need for special cleaning or refinishing.
- ✔ Hardscape elements are built to last for decades (or longer).

In a properly designed garden, maintenance is a steady series of small tweaks, not violent blitzes of hyperactivity. To tune up your maintenance routine, make a list with two columns. Put the gardening work you love in one column and the gardening work you hate in the other. Use the rules of sustainable landscaping to eliminate as many of the items in the second list as possible. Set up a smoothly functioning landscape system — an ecosystem. Then put the fate of the garden in the hands of nature, relegating yourself to the role of gentle nurturer — an assistant, not the boss. Your services will still be needed, but in smaller quantities. You can enjoy the garden instead of struggling with it. You'll save money, too! See Part II of this book to learn more about how to design a sustainable landscape that really works over the long haul.

Purging Your Power Equipment to Please the Planet

When I show people what I use to maintain my garden, they stare in disbelief. I love tools, and over the years I've owned nearly everything made for gardening and landscaping work. But can you guess what I use in my own garden? A pair of hand pruning shears, a small trowel, and sometimes a weeding tool known as an *asparagus knife*. Oh, I have other tools. I use a shovel to plant big things, and a hose to water. I have lots of stuff out in the garage, and once in a while I actually use something for a special task. But mostly, the pruning shears and the trowel are it. Together, they cost around $80. I have to laugh when I look at these gardening catalogs full of gadgets that I have no use for.

Then there's power equipment. Do you need to eliminate it from your tool kit if you want to garden sustainably? The best answer is that by creating a sustainable garden, you've eliminated so much of the usual work that tools — both manual and powered — are much less necessary.

When you face a laborious task, ask yourself whether hand tools will get it done without much fuss. If you truly need the help of modern technology, choose a newer model that complies with current efficiency and pollution standards, and rent or share tools with neighbors if you can.

To help you power down, in the following sections I discuss the impacts that power equipment has on the environment and your pocketbook. I also give you some good alternatives to power tools.

Understanding the effects of power tools

Some of the most pernicious elements of the maintenance picture are power lawn and garden tools: mowers, blowers, chain saws, string trimmers, and the like. Add up the effects of fossil fuel use, air pollution, noise, health problems, injuries (to you and your plants), and the infrastructure that supports mechanized garden care, and you have a real mess.

It's true that power equipment saves a lot of hand labor, but when you take the work of manufacturing, maintaining, and paying for it, much of its alleged efficiency disappears in a cloud of exhaust smoke. It's also true that the gas engines that power this equipment have become cleaner and quieter, but that's only because the U.S. Environmental Protection Agency ordered manufacturers to improve the dismal record of their products. And there's still a long way to go.

Adjusting to alternatives for power garden equipment

I don't have a lawn — just a tiny meadow that I never mow. I have a vine on the house that I shear back (with electric hedge trimmers) once or twice a year. If I got rid of that vine, I wouldn't need the hedge trimmers. Believe me, it's tempting. I practice chop and drop, and I mulch, so there's no need for a string trimmer. I never turn over the soil, even in my vegetable garden, so I don't need a rototiller. I get more food than I could ever eat without lifting a finger except to plant the little fellers and pick the produce. Perhaps you have more work to do in your garden than I do. That's cool. I understand. But I bet that in most cases, you'll still do fine without power tools.

The Cheat Sheet lists some simple sustainable choices to replace power equipment. Some of these options take more effort to use but have a much lower impact when you look at the big picture.

Going with green cleanup gear

One piece of power equipment — the leaf blower — is particularly galling to many people. Here's a little advice that will make your life easier and keep you out of trouble with the neighbors and wild-eyed enviros like me: No blowers. Let me say that again. No bloody blowers, okay? There may be a legitimate use for these growling, pollution-flatulating, dinosaur-juice-sucking, dust-cloud-making, disease-spreading little contraptions, but I'll be darned if I know what it is.

Ordinary housekeeping tasks, such as cleaning pavement, can be done with time-honored gear: a rake, a broom, or even a palm frond. The only energy they use is yours, and unless you sing while you work, they're pretty quiet. If hardscape surfaces drain into planter beds that could use the water, feel free to hose them off, especially if you use a low-volume nozzle. If the water would go into the street or a drain and be wasted, use a broom.

Pruning Established Plants

I love to prune. It's a way of making a plant look more graceful without imposing much on its basic character. When you get hooked on real pruning, you'll never butcher another innocent plant.

Unless you're doing topiary or clipping a formal hedge, pruning is not about sculpting plants into shapes: It's about developing a sturdy, healthy, graceful branching structure and allowing the natural form of the plant to express itself with just a little help from you.

You can't achieve this goal by standing outside the plant with a clattering hedge trimmer in your hands; you have to stick your head, or your whole self, *inside* the plant and prune from there, using pruning shears to remove offending growth one branch at a time. Very few people, professional garden-ers included, have any idea how to do this. So you're about to become one of the in crowd (or perhaps it's the in-the-shrubbery crowd). The following sections describe the proper way to prune.

First, make sure that your tools are sharp and well adjusted. Do most of your pruning in winter or spring, depending on the type of plant, but remove damaged or dangerous branches at any time. Look up specific information on the species you're working on, because pruning techniques vary from one plant to another. When trees grow too big for you to prune safely, put them in the hands of a certified arborist (see the "When it's grown: Involving an arborist" section later in this chapter).

Examine the subject

First, take a long look at the plant, inside and out. Identify branches that are damaged, weak, crossing, or growing out of bounds (refer to Figure 17-3 in Chapter 17 to see how unhealthy tree branches look; this applies equally to smaller plants). Decide whether you'll be making major changes such as removing large limbs, or simply opening the interior and improving the structure.

In most cases, the less pruning you do, the better. You're gently nudging the plant toward its own perfection, not brutalizing it into a form of your choosing. Pruning is collaboration, not war.

Do the big stuff first

Take out any major branches that are problematic because of size, condition, or shape. Be sure that you want them out, because they're not easy to put back on. Figure 20-1 shows you how to cut large branches safely without harming yourself or the plant.

Big limbs are a lot heavier than you might think, and there's a danger of injury, so let a pro do the pruning work if you aren't certain whether you can handle it. If you do make a big cut, don't seal it with anything; sealing is ineffective and can even seal in problems.

If you have shrubs that send many canelike branches up from ground level, you can refresh them by cutting up to $1/3$ of the branches to the ground. This will bring new vigor to a weakly-growing shrub.

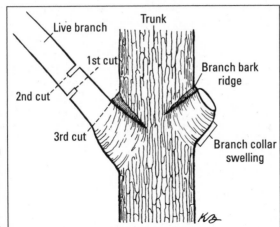

Figure 20-1:
Pruning
large
branches.

Pay attention to details

Your goal is to open the center of the plant and create a graceful branch structure. Do this by thinning out the inner structure of the plant, removing smaller branches and twigs that are dead, weak, or growing toward the center of the plant. Remove as little living foliage as possible — never more than f$1/3$ of the total and ideally much less. A before-and-after example is shown in Figure 20-2. Don't cut too close to a bud; leave a short bit of stem just above it (see Figure 20-3).

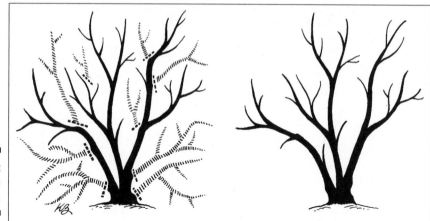

Figure 20-2:
How to thin
a shrub.

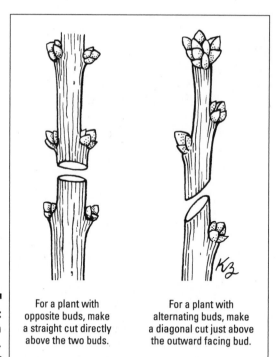

Figure 20-3:
Cut above a
bud.

For a plant with
opposite buds, make
a straight cut directly
above the two buds.

For a plant with
alternating buds, make
a diagonal cut just above
the outward facing bud.

Prune to increase density

Some plants respond well when you cut just the tip growth back to a bud,
as shown in Figure 20-4. This technique, which makes the plant fuller and
more compact, is known as *heading back*. But do this only if you really

want a tighter plant; in most cases, this practice ruins the natural form, and it may disrupt flowering on plants that bloom at the ends of their branches.

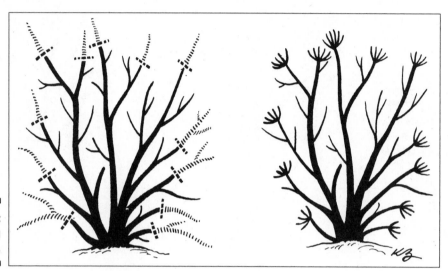

Figure 20-4:
Heading
back.

Treat fruit trees differently

Each type of fruit-bearing tree has its own pruning requirements, and it's important to prune these trees properly so you get a good crop of fruit. This subject is beyond the scope of this book; visit www.ces.ncsu.edu/depts/hort/hil/ag29.html for a good fruit tree pruning primer.

Shear your hedge with the proper tools

The formal sheared hedge has its place in the sustainable landscape. True sustainable hedge care requires holding a small goat up to the hedge while it gnaws the hedge into the proper form. If you don't have a goat, try hand hedge clippers. Electric hedge trimmers are okay, especially if your house is equipped with solar power. Gas-powered hedge trimmers aren't okay, but you already knew that.

Shear hedges so the sides are slanted inward, with the top narrower than the bottom (see Figure 20-5). That way, the surface receives more sunlight, and the hedge plants do better.

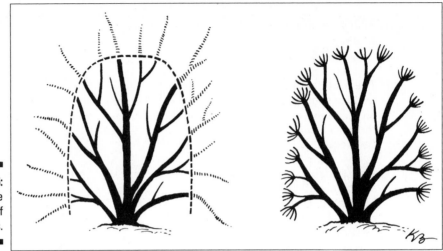

Figure 20-5:
Taper the
sides of
hedges.

When it's grown: Involving an arborist

Trees quickly grow beyond the ability of a home gardener to care for them safely and effectively. It's best to hire a professional to perform an annual tree health and safety inspection, checking for signs of damage, disease, dangerous limbs, and poor growing conditions. If work is needed, instead of trying to save a little money by doing it yourself, let a pro handle it.

Anyone with a chainsaw can claim to be a tree expert, but real professionals are certified by the International Society of Arboriculture (ISA), the Tree Care Industry Association (TCIA), or the American Society of Consulting Arborists (ASCA). Don't jeopardize your trees by putting them in the hands of a self-appointed expert. Real arborists have to pass rigorous exams for their certification. Ask to see their credentials, get a certificate of insurance so that you're protected if an accident occurs, and of course get a written estimate. To find out more, visit: ISA (www.isa-arbor.com); TCIA (www.natlarb.com); ASCA (www.asca-consultants.org).

If a tree "expert" advises you to top a tree, send him packing. *Topping* is the practice of whacking the upper portion of limbs off to make the tree smaller. This practice is discredited, and no qualified professional proposes it. Topping trees ruins their structure and creates the danger of falling limbs. A tree that has grown too big can be controlled by *crown reduction,* which is a non-harmful pruning technique for making a tree smaller.

Forgoing Fertilizer: The Fine Art of Chop and Drop

The traditional cycle of "fertilize, grow, prune, dispose of the prunings, and fertilize some more" is wasteful, expensive, and damaging to the environment. Americans put more fertilizer on their landscaping than is used in all the world's underdeveloped countries to grow food. It's shameful, especially considering how unnecessary it is.

A sustainable garden doesn't get pushed hard to grow only so you can cut it all down and throw it away. Plants can live quite well on their own droppings. This is nature's way: stuff falls off the plant and returns to the system. Hauling it away and then importing synthetic fertilizers is cuckoo. True, there are times when you should fertilize (to give your plants a boost or to stimulate growth of young plants). But if you help the plant recycle its own waste, it will reward you with steady, healthy growth.

One of the key elements in sustainable maintenance is not allowing anything to escape from the system. Rather than bag up your prunings, keep them on site to cycle the valuable nutrients they contain back into the soil. The laborious way to recycle pruning debris is to compost it, but even that's working too hard. The easy way is to cut the leftovers into little pieces as you prune and allow them to fall directly at the feet of the plant that produced them. I call this practice *chop and drop*. It's a silly way of reminding myself that stuff that grew in Spot A should remain in Spot A. Chop and drop keeps the nutrient loop very tight and minimizes effort on your part.

Chop and drop saves labor in addition to saving money. Yes, you do have to cut things up, but because you're helping to form a mulch layer, you'll weed and water much less. And you won't have to dispose of the stuff or spread fertilizers (or work to pay for them).

I should acknowledge that hacked-up plant parts can look less than properly suburban. If you can't stand the appearance, cover the choppings with nicer-looking mulch, such as bark or chips. Or stuff your choppings beneath the skirts of the plants where they can do their thing unseen.

If you do fertilize, use organic fertilizers that come from natural, renewable sources and that are gentler on the plants and soil microorganisms. Visit Chapter 16 for more on this.

Weeds Be Gone: Managing Weeds without Hurting the Environment

The conventional gardener turns to chemical herbicides and violent practices to eliminate weeds. Because growing conditions in a conventional garden are often hospitable to weeds, all the weeding in the world won't keep them from coming back. The sustainable way is to change the conditions, which allows you to enjoy a weed-free ecosystem with little or no effort.

Getting to know weeds

Weeds are plants that people moved from one place to another on the backs of domestic animals, in soil used as ballast on ships, or as imported garden or farm plants that didn't know where the property lines were. Some weeds are native, but most are imported. Knowing all this doesn't change the fact that weeds will enter your life even if you have the most sustainable landscape on the planet.

Weeds are ultra-successful plants. They grow fast, out-compete more delicate plants, suck all the water, and make lots and lots of babies. Some weeds even poison the soil around themselves so that nothing else will grow. Weeds kick butt.

Creating an unfriendly environment for weeds

We have weeds because we create situations in which they feel at home. In these situations weeds encounter the thing they love most: open ground. Weeds see open ground and they just giggle with delight, and then they get to work procreating.

Weeds do the job of pioneering in open space, to be succeeded by later, larger plants that form a more stable long-term plant community. In this fact lies the answer to the problem of weeds: Create the stable plant community, and the weeds won't show up because their niche is already filled. If you don't believe it, just look at where the weeds grow. You won't find many in unfavorable locations with dense permanent growth.

Trying out types of weed controls

Here are some great strategies that really work. Use them, and your weed problem will gradually decline to nearly nothing. Really.

- ✔ **Physical controls:** Use plants that are at least knee-high for most of your landscaping. Maintain a 3- to 4-inch-deep layer of organic mulch in all beds and open areas. To get rid of a strong stand of established weeds, sheet mulch the area. (Visit Chapter 16 for details on sheet mulching.) Use a drip system (see Chapter 8) to keep as much of the soil surface dry as possible. Pull weeds when they're young and before they set seed.

- ✔ **Biological controls:** Goats, geese, ducks, chickens, and other browsing animals eat weeds (as well as desirable plants). So do certain insects for a limited range of weed species. You can even find *mycoherbicides* — fungi that destroy weeds.

- ✔ **Chemical controls:** You probably know the name of a certain herbicide that seems to work very well. (I would never mention it in a family book like this one.) People love it. It's a lot more hazardous than you've been told, however. What's more, after 30 years of using it in massive quantities worldwide, we seem to have as many weeds as ever. Does it sound like something's wrong? There is.

    You don't need that harsh chemical stuff. Sheet mulching works better. If you want to kill existing weeds, spray them with horticultural vinegar (this is a strong acid so be careful when you apply it), or use corn gluten meal to suppress the development of weed seedlings, including crabgrass. (See Chapter 22 for the full scoop.)

Bundle Up: Winterizing Your Plants

The best strategy for helping your plants to get through the winter in good health is to make sure they're hardy enough to tolerate local worst case conditions. But sometimes even sustainable plantings need help with this.

For example, young plants need special protection for the first few winters. Provide burlap screens for wind and frost protection (see Figure 20-6), and maintain winter mulch around young plants. Wrapping the trunks and main branches of young trees and shrubs to protect against sunscald can create more problems than it solves; use wrapping judiciously, and remove it as soon as conditions permit. Make a tent of boards to prevent snow loads from damaging delicate plants.

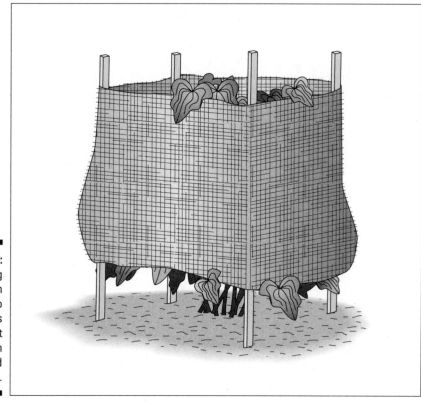

Figure 20-6:
Wrap young
plants in
burlap
screens
to protect
them from
wind and
frost.

Some plants that keep their leaves all year can dry out in winter. Protect them with a cover of evergreen boughs or an antidesiccant spray.

If extreme conditions are coming, treat even established plants as you would young ones. To prevent breakage, knock snow off limbs before it freezes. Low spots and open ground are colder than south-facing walls and the spaces under eaves. Cold air flows to low places just the same as water, so you can predict where the coldest places will be by looking at your land. Exploit warmer microclimates by planting less hardy varieties there. Prepare your plants for frost by not fertilizing from late summer onward and by keeping soil moist as frost approaches.

Chapter 21

Pest and Disease Control the Sustainable Way

A sustainable garden starts with good design, including plants that are well adapted to your conditions and inherently resistant to pests and diseases. A sustainable garden also includes healthy soil teeming with good microorganisms that help fight bad things. But plants do get stuff, and when they get stuff, you have to deal with it. Pests and diseases don't run rampant through a healthy ecosystem; they're signs of out-of-balance conditions. Correct those conditions and the problems probably will go away.

Animals, however, will run rampant through most any ecosystem. They can be infuriating to deal with, yet some animals are welcome in the sustainable garden. In fact, most animals are a mix of good and bad. For instance, moles eat troublesome soil-dwelling pests but also damage lawns with their mounds. And of course native animals have a right to coexist with us. There are ways to live with the animals rather than exterminate them. This chapter tells you how to manage pests, diseases, and animals the sustainable way.

Integrated Pest Management: The Smart Way to Deal with Problems

Integrated pest management (IPM) is a strategy for dealing with pest and disease problems in an intelligent, nontoxic way. It consists of regular, careful monitoring of the garden ecosystem to identify unhealthy conditions, coupled with a stepped approach that starts with the least-toxic method and moves up the scale only if necessary. You need to know a great deal about the problem to control it effectively with IPM — you can't just spritz toxic pesticides all over the yard. IPM consists of these steps:

1. Improve growing conditions and eliminate whatever caused the problem. By cutting back on fertilizer use, for example, you reduce soft-tissue growth and make plants less susceptible to aphids and sucking insects.

2. Try simple mechanical actions like washing pests off with a jet of water or using sticky barriers to keep pests out of trees.

3. If the pests crawl back, more draconian methods come into play. Release beneficial insects or apply microbial controls.

4. Only if the first three steps fail, consider using least-toxic sprays.

5. If all else fails, replace sickly plants with something sturdier.

Controlling Creepy-Crawlies

Instead of using hazardous pesticides in your garden, opt for insect management that involves the three Ps:

- **Predators:** Beneficial insects that eat pests
- **Parasites:** Beneficial insects that lay eggs on pests (the eggs hatch and destroy the pests)
- **Pathogens:** Diseases that kill the pests but not your plants

The strategy you choose depends on the particulars of the situation. Work with local IPM practitioners until you get a feel for how the system works. Look for a pest control company that uses the terms "IPM" or "organic" in their advertising, and insist on nontoxic approaches.

Understanding problems with conventional pest control

The more pesticides you use, the more pests you have. Insects breed so rapidly that new generations are quickly born with natural resistance to the pesticides. The chemical industry constantly battles to come up with new formulations that will outevolve the pests — and it isn't winning. Add to this the toxic legacy of so many often-unregulated and untested chemicals, and you have cause for concern about conventional approaches to keeping pests at bay.

Because of the inherent dangers involved, the use of pesticides by licensed professionals and farmers is highly regulated. Yet many of the same chemicals that require application permits and recordkeeping when used by pros can be applied by untrained homeowners with no oversight. Keep in mind that just because you can buy something at the nursery doesn't necessarily mean that it's safe. For detailed info, including an extensive database of toxicity information on pesticides, visit the Pesticide Action Network North America Web site at www.panna.org.

Beneficials are your buddies: Getting to know the good insects

Beneficial insects feed on or parasitize harmful insects. Most everyone knows that ladybugs eat aphids, but ladybugs are only the beginning. One of the most voracious predators is the green lacewing, which is omnivorous and easy to establish in your garden. Other good beneficials include parasitic wasps, which feed on aphids, whiteflies, caterpillars, and other insects; beneficial beetles, which eat mealybugs and scale; and mites that eat thrips.

As long as you don't spray pesticides in your yard, some beneficial insects are already present. If the native populations aren't sufficient to take care of problems, you can buy beneficials from nurseries or insectaries.

Before introducing anything to your garden, find out exactly what insects you have by taking samples to your local cooperative extension office for identification. Then work with a supplier to choose an appropriate beneficial. Beneficials have to be released properly to survive and do their jobs. Get specific release information when you purchase your beneficials.

You can also plant to attract beneficial insects. Common edibles such as dill, caraway, cilantro, and fennel feed the good bugs as well as you. Ornamentals work too; cosmos, yarrow, tansy, alyssum, evening primrose, and others attract lacewings, ladybugs, parasitic wasps, and other beneficials.

Using beneficials takes a little thought, but discovering this hidden aspect of life on your property is fascinating, and this technique really works. For interesting reading on beneficial insects, visit a pioneering insectary's Web site: Rincon-Vitova Insectaries at www.rinconvitova.com.

Making use of microbial controls

Microbial insecticides are diseases (aka pathogens) that kill pests. A common example is *Bacillus thuringiensis* (Bt), which kills various species of caterpillars. Bt is easy to apply, harmless (unless you're a caterpillar), and very effective.

Each microbial is specific to particular pests. So, as with beneficial insects, you need to carefully match one to the other. Find out if microbial controls are effective against your particular pest by asking your local nursery what it recommends.

Using least-toxic pesticides carefully

Insecticidal soaps, oil sprays, and botanical pesticides (made from plants) are examples of pesticides that have low toxicity to *nontarget organisms,* such as you and your family, birds, and other wildlife. They're handy for spot treatments of serious outbreaks where resident beneficials aren't up to the job.

Use least-toxic chemicals carefully, because they can kill beneficials too. Also, regular dependence on these pesticides — even relatively safe ones — can cause pest populations to develop resistance to the pesticides. Also, be sure to always follow label instructions when you use any pesticide.

Dealing with common pests: An insect-by-insect guide

There are many pests, of course, but there are also many sustainable strategies for dealing with them. Here are some of the main pests of home gardens and some tips for dealing with them:

- **Ants:** Ants prefer to nest in dry-baked soil, so mulching can be an excellent strategy. Try insect growth regulators or nontoxic baits containing boric acid or *diatomaceous earth* (an abrasive material).

- **Aphids:** These insects are prolific yet relatively easy to control with natural enemies, such as ladybugs, lacewings, and syrphid flies. Avoid overfertilization, prune away highly infested plant parts, and control ants (which farm aphids, increasing their populations).

- **Cutworms and grubs:** Birds and predatory insects feed on these bugs. If that tactic fails, use Bt insecticide, neem oil, or beneficial nematodes.

- **Japanese beetles:** Treat with milky spore disease or parasitic nematodes.

- **Mealybugs:** Control ants, avoid harming natural predators, introduce predatory insects, and spot-treat with insecticidal soap or oil.

- **Scales:** Encourage natural enemies by avoiding pesticides and planting flowering plants for habitat. Oil sprays can be effective, but timing is critical; check with your nursery for details.

- **Snails and slugs:** Use a nontoxic bait that breaks down into fertilizer. Or try putting some beer in a pie pan or special bait station. The snails and slugs get smashed, party down, and die.

- **Thrips:** Introduce natural enemies, such as predatory mites, and avoid shearing or overfertilization, which produces soft, vulnerable growth.

- **Whiteflies:** These insects can be difficult to control, but parasitic wasps can keep populations down. Insecticidal soaps and oils also help.

Critters! Sensible Vertebrate Control

Think of nuisance animals as big bugs with backbones. What insects do on a small scale, animals do in broad sweeps. Nothing tests the gentle gardening spirit like a raccoon attack on the pond or a visit by hungry gophers. Integrated pest management (which I introduce earlier in the chapter) applies to big pests too.

Gophers, moles, and voles

Gophers till the soil and aren't all bad, but they can be among the most destructive and irritating garden pests. It's no fun to watch your prize kohlrabi get sucked underground in front of your eyes. Enclose plants in chicken wire cylinders with openings no smaller than 1 inch (use bottomless cylinders for woody plants so their roots will escape and not be choked by the wire). Surround beds with an underground fence of *hardware cloth,* which is a welded wire mesh. Pit gopher snakes or cats against gophers; plant daffodils or oleanders around your property; or if all else fails, trap the beasts.

Daffodils and oleanders are poisonous to people and pets too, however, so use them with care.

Moles are actually beneficial, eating grubs and other soil insects. Leave them alone unless they're really damaging your lawn by making raised mounds. Sadly, there's no proven nonviolent way to control moles. They scoff at noisemakers, stinky repellents, and other kindly approaches. They can only be deterred by trapping. If you feel that murder and sustainability are compatible, set out two or more mole traps along an active run. Or let natural predators, such as owls or neighborhood cats, do your dirty work.

Voles are more aggressive and can harm plants. Repel them with commercial repellents or predator urine, exclude them with wire barriers, or trap them in a humane trap and release them in a faraway field.

Rats! (and mice)

I wish I had better news, but there's no nice way to deal with rats and mice. You have only a few nonlethal options:

- ✔ **Good housekeeping:** Keeping your property clean helps minimize the problem. Eliminate piles of junk and thick vines where rodents like to hang out, and don't leave pet food outdoors.
- ✔ **Barriers:** Use wire screens to close off openings to the house.
- ✔ **Security:** Close the pet door at night.

But when it comes to *really* getting rid of these critters, it's no more Mr./Ms. Warm-'n-Fuzzy Ecoperson. You have to kill them. With traps. Don't use bait unless you want to poison your pets and wildlife. As for repellents, what in creation would ever repel a rat?

Putting up an *owl box* — a manmade nest for one of the greatest killers of all time — helps to a point. To find out how to build an owl box, visit www.owlpages.com.

Raccoons and other medium-size critters

Vertebrate pests, as the pros call the medium-size critters, can be exasperating. Some can be adorable too: fuzzy little bunnies that eat your plants and bushy-tailed ground squirrels that undermine your patio. They were here first, and we have no right to exclude native animals from our environment. Some species, such as raccoons, opossums, and skunks, seem to be making a comeback in many neighborhoods as they adapt to a changed environment. I believe that they have rights and that their contributions to the suppression of still smaller pests need to be taken into account. Still, we gardeners need to set some boundaries. Consider the following options for nontoxic control:

- ✔ Remove attractions such as pet food from outdoor areas.
- ✔ Eliminate den sites near the house by cleaning up brush and wood piles.
- ✔ Place fencing around vulnerable plantings, such as veggie beds.
- ✔ Chase them off with special motion-sensing sprinkler heads.
- ✔ Spray repellents or predator pee around the yard.
- ✔ Trap them or call your community's animal control department for help.
- ✔ Get a dog (or, I'm told, a llama) to keep animals at bay.

Deer and other macrovertebrates

Macrovertebrates, such as deer, moose, and elk, can make a real mess of a garden, especially when drought or fire deprives them of their customary wild food sources. A determined animal can be difficult to stop, but some strategies work against them:

- ✓ **Unpopular plants:** Choose plants they don't like; you can find lists of these plants in gardening books and on Web sites.

- ✓ **Barriers:** Protect browsable plants by placing sturdy wire cages or netting around the plants, or string fishing line across the animals' paths to trip them up and spook them. Two 4- to 5-foot tall fences running parallel to each other and spaced 3 to 5 feet apart can keep deer out of an area pretty reliably.

- ✓ **Smelly substances:** Try repellents containing chili peppers, rotten eggs, and other nasty substances. Other things that sometimes work are bars of Irish Spring soap (its unique fragrance is not well loved by deer), baby powder, fabric-softener sheets, and predator urine. Most of these items are easy to use, but if you're planning to get your own urine sample from the neighborhood mountain lion, you may want to think twice. Believe it or not, wild-animal pee is for sale at progressive nurseries and online. Choose urine that matches that of local predators the deer know and fear.

You're dealing with smart animals here. They'll quickly get wise to your tricks, so plan on changing tactics regularly. For more on deer management, visit `attra.ncat.org/attra-pub/deercontrol.html#exclu`.

Putting Yourself on Disease Control

Diseases can be tricky to control. Sometimes a plant collapses suddenly and you can't determine the cause. Disease organisms are present everywhere all the time; only when conditions become favorable for them do they go into action. Many soil pathogens, for example, wait for soil that's warm and wet at the same time; they're harmless unless both conditions are present.

The best way to prevent disease outbreaks is to choose resistant plants and then eliminate any conditions that are conducive to problems. These include over- or underwatering; poor soil conditions, such as heavy or badly-draining soil; bad air circulation; and too much shade for sun-loving plants (and vice versa). Diseases will attack stressed plants first.

Fungi good and bad

If you've read Chapter 16, you know how important fungi are, especially mycorrhizal fungi that team up with your plants to improve their uptake of water and nutrients. Most fungi are essential. Without them, the planet would have long ago been buried in undecomposed waste. Still some fungi, such as Phytophthora root rot and oak root fungus, attack living plants, causing decline and even death. Some fungi are really nasty and can be very difficult or (I hate to have to tell you) impossible to control.

Most fungus attacks result from poor growing conditions. Change the growing conditions, and in many cases you might eliminate the problem. For example, overwatering gives a big thumbs-up to wicked little fungi, such as phytophthora root rot, oak root fungus, pythium, and others. The fungi are always present in the soil, waiting for conditions favorable to their development. Change your habits, give the plants what they need, and the fungi will disappear like the Wicked Witch of the West.

One promising new approach for controlling soil-borne fungal diseases involves applying bacterial inoculants to the soil. These inoculants take up space that otherwise would be occupied by fungi. A healthy soil food web is no place that harmful fungi want to hang out.

Fungi are proving to be among the most useful living things. For a fascinating look, check out *Mycelium Running: How Mushrooms Can Help Save the World* (Ten Speed Press) by visionary mycologist Paul Stamets.

Viruses

Plant viruses are incurable; often, the best strategy is to remove the afflicted plant. On the other hand, viruses rarely kill woody plants, being content with merely distorting the foliage. Viruses can lay dormant for decades, waiting for the right plant to show up. Genetic susceptibility is the critical element; even ideal growing conditions won't prevent an infestation.

You can work around viruses by keeping plants vigorous so they're better able to resist the effects of an infestation. Sanitation can also help. Remove infected plants from the property immediately (don't compost them).

Chapter 22

Opting for Organic Lawn Care

. . . .

In This Chapter

▶ Creating conditions for lawns to thrive

▶ Feeding your lawn

▶ Mowing and watering tips and tricks

▶ Controlling pests, diseases, and weeds the sustainable way

▶ Getting rid of your funky old lawn

. . . .

*T*he most sustainable lawn is no lawn at all. The second best approach is to have a meadow instead of a lawn (see Chapter 19 for details). Meadows do most of the things that lawns do, including tolerate moderate traffic and play. But when you need a conventional lawn (for lawn games or other legitimate uses, or to comply with neighborhood regulations), try to keep it as small as you can and care for it in such a way that you create the least impact possible.

The shift to organic lawn care has been huge. People are fed up with spreading poisons all over their yards. According to *Popular Mechanics* magazine, the number of U.S. households purchasing natural fertilizers increased from 2.5 million to 11.7 million between 1998 and 2003. During the same period, the number of households practicing natural pest control went up from 1.8 million to 10.9 million. That's a revolution!

People wouldn't be using organic methods if they didn't get results. Organic lawn care isn't just for hard-core enviros; it's also a well-developed system with a lot of great science behind it. Suppose you hate the environment. Fine. Organic lawn care will still save you time and money, and at the same time it'll deliver a great-looking, robust lawn. In this chapter, I show you how to make it happen.

You can find a lot more great information on lawn care in *Lawn Care For Dummies,* by Lance Walheim and the National Gardening Association (Wiley). Consider it a companion volume to this chapter.

Putting Healthy Conditions First

Set up a healthy environment, and you'll have much less trouble with your lawn. Proper lawn-growing conditions include the following:

- **Good soil:** Lawn grasses need soil that's loamy, fertile, and fairly high in organic matter. Too much clay inhibits root development; the roots can easily be overwatered or compacted. Too much sand creates a soil that dries out too fast and doesn't hold nutrients well. Get a soil test to see whether your soil will have to be modified or replaced (see Chapter 16 for details). If the soil is poor, you're better off fixing that first.

- **Enough sun:** The best place for a lawn is in full sun.

- **Proper varieties of lawn grasses:** Choose a seed mix that's adapted to your particular climate. Include several varieties of grass that adapt to slightly different growing conditions. If you have shady areas, include some shade-tolerant varieties.

- **Minimum competition from neighboring trees:** Tree roots are shallow and extensive (See Chapter 9). They find lawns quickly and suck the life out of them. The lawn is small and weak compared to the trees, so it loses the battle. Place your lawn as far away from trees as you can.

- **Adequate water:** Be sure you have enough pressure and volume to operate a sprinkler system (see Chapters 7 and 8 for details), and take community watering restrictions into account. If you're on a well or other private water supply, find out whether there's a consistently adequate supply of water.

Fertilizing the Sustainable Way

The major nutrient that lawn grasses require is nitrogen, followed by phosphorous, potassium, and sometimes trace elements such as iron. Nitrogen is volatile and needs to be applied regularly. However, many people overapply lawn fertilizers thinking that more is always better. Instead, test your soil to find out exactly what the lawn needs (see Chapter 16).

If you have to fertilize your lawn, follow these simple guidelines:

- **Go organic.** Organic fertilizers nurture soil life; harsh chemical ones harm it. Organics last longer, won't burn the lawn if they're overapplied, are made from sustainable natural sources rather than fossil fuels, are less likely to leach into groundwater or streams, and are less expensive in the long run.

✔ **Know how much fertilizer to apply.** Lawns need 1 pound of *actual nitrogen* per 1,000 square feet at each application, with an annual total of 1 to 5 pounds, depending on soil type, grass variety, and growing conditions. The percentages of the Big Three (nitrogen, phosphorous, and potassium) in a fertilizer are listed on the bag — shown as 10-5-5, for example, indicating 10 percent nitrogen and 5 percent each of phosphorous and potassium.

To avoid damage to waterways and groundwater through leaching of nutrients, replace only what's been used instead of dumping on a set amount of fertilizer each time.

✔ **Know when to fertilize.** Two feedings a year are usually enough to encourage good root development and prepare the grass for strong growth in spring. Make fall your primary feeding time. Avoid fertilizing too early in spring, because it encourages the development of diseases. Warm-season grasses should be fed in summer only; cool-season grasses shouldn't be fed in the heat of summer.

Organic fertilizers are dependent on soil microbes to convert their nutrients to a form that's available to the grass. The microbes are on duty when soil temperatures are on the warm side, so organic fertilizers won't do much good in cold weather.

There's more to good fertilizing than just nitrogen. Keep these tips in mind to keep your lawn looking lush:

✔ A monthly application of seaweed extract (kelp) provides valuable *trace elements* (nutrients needed in smaller quantities). This seaweed application is a natural way to boost the performance of your lawn.

✔ Good organic fertilizers contain humic acids, which increase the availability of nutrients, improve soil structure, enhance photosynthesis and protein synthesis, and improve root function. These fertilizers enable you to use less nitrogen, which means less waste and pollution.

✔ The *pH* (a measure of whether the soil is acidic or alkaline) of your lawn should be between 6.3 and 6.8. Adding lime to your soil (the mineral, not the fruit) can reduce acidity; adding sulfur can reduce alkalinity. Maintaining optimum pH helps keep weeds and diseases from becoming a problem, reducing or eliminating your need to use chemicals.

✔ Adding compost or *compost tea* (a specially prepared living solution of compost that's available at some nurseries) once or twice a year can revitalize the soil food web and contribute nutrients. (See Chapter 16 for details.)

Aerating and Renovating Your Lawn

Aeration is the practice of removing cores from the root zone of turf to reduce how compact the roots are and to allow water and fertilizers to penetrate. Clay soils are especially susceptible to compaction.

Aerate in spring or fall, when temperatures are low. Use a gas-powered or small foot-powered aerator that removes small cores of soil (see Figure 22-1). Don't use a spading fork or spikes that don't take cores, because they compact the sides of the holes they make. Remove nine to ten cores per square foot of lawn. Follow up by raking compost into the holes.

Renovation, also called *dethatching,* is a method of combing *thatch* (built-up dead grass) from the turf. Thatch inhibits the penetration of water, fertilizer, and air, and it can encourage certain diseases and pest problems. Thatch is most prevalent in lawns that are overfertilized, especially Kentucky bluegrass.

If the soil food web is in good shape, the beneficial bacteria, insects, and earthworms will consume thatch and keep the soil open. But conditions are sometimes less than ideal due to inherent soil conditions, such as heavy clay, compaction due to heavy use, or regrettable lapses of good practice. That's when it's prudent to step in and fix the situation.

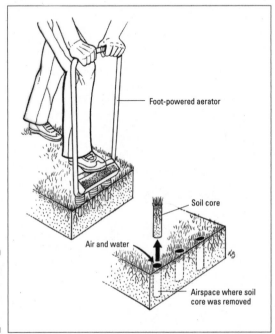

Figure 22-1:
Using a foot-powered aerator.

Foot-powered aerator

Soil core

Air and water

Airspace where soil core was removed

Working with an organic lawn care company

Caring for one's own lawn is a basic duty of modern homeownership. But there are certainly reasons to hire someone to mow, fertilize, weed, renovate, and otherwise nurture your lawn for you. Take laziness, for example; it's one of my favorite motives for paying people. Or busyness, distaste for the activities of lawn care, physical inability to do the work, or excessive income. For whatever reason, hiring a lawn service can be a load off your shoulders.

Be sure you choose a lawn care company that has a genuine commitment to the sustainable way. Some services sneak the chemicals in when you're not looking or use the same equipment for chemical and organic lawn care, resulting in contamination. Others don't really understand the principles behind organic lawn management and don't deliver good results. The sustainable approach has been around long enough, and enough training is available, so there's no excuse for poor performance.

Ask questions about the approach the lawn care company is proposing, and use the information in this chapter to see whether its program conforms to accepted sustainable practices. Get specifics about the materials the service will be using and the strategies it recommends for your particular situation. Get a detailed written management plan and a fixed price as well as the usual references and written contract.

No gardening service, organic or otherwise, can keep things perfect all the time; nature just has too many variables. But be sure to maintain open communication with the workers to be sure that you understand what they're up to and that you'll be aware of any problems that come up.

Renovate in late summer, and do so only if thatch is at least $1/2$ inch thick. Here's how.

1. **Remove the thatch.**

   Use a power lawn rake (a machine that combs thatch out of the lawn) or a special hand renovating rake if you're doing a small area.

2. **Overseed (apply lawn seed onto the prepared surface of the lawn).**

3. **Top-dress (cover the seed) with a $1/4$-inch layer of compost.**

   Use about 20 cubic feet of mulch per 1,000 square feet of lawn area.

4. **Water to bring the seed to life.**

It may be cheaper to hire a lawn company to aerate and renovate for you. (Check out the nearby sidebar, "Working with an organic lawn care company," to be sure you're working with a reputable and sustainable company.)

Giving Your Lawn Just Enough Water

Water properly and you'll have few problems; screw it up, and nothing else will go right. Nearly everybody waters too much. A few people water too little. Very few people water just the right amount. If your lawn is constantly soggy and squishy, you're overwatering. If you step on the lawn and it doesn't spring back, or if your lawn is crunchy and dying out in places, chances are you're not watering enough. See Figure 22-2 for what happens to grasses and their root systems with varying amounts of water.

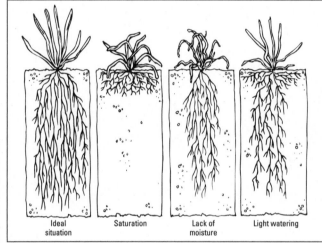

Figure 22-2:
The effects
of different
approaches
to watering.

| Ideal situation | Saturation | Lack of moisture | Light watering |

Visit Chapter 9 for details on proper watering. For now, remember the following key points:

✔ **Most lawns need 1 or 2 inches of water per week, including rainfall.** That inch of water will penetrate 6 to 12 inches into the soil, depending on your soil type (deeper in sandy soils than in clay soils).

✔ **Water more often in sandy soils, less often in clay soils, but never water more than three times a week.** Once a week is usually fine, but the frequency depends on weather conditions. The hotter, drier, and windier the weather, the more often you have to water.

✔ **Water to replace what's been used and no more.** Use a soil probe to examine soil moisture. If the soil is damp in the root zone, you don't need to water. If you step on the grass and it doesn't spring back when you remove your foot, it's time to water.

✔ **Water early in the morning.** Never water at night or in the heat of day unless your lawn is in urgent need of water.

> ✔ **Pay attention to drought tolerance.** Among cool-season grasses, fescues are the most drought tolerant; bluegrass and rye are the least. Warm-season grasses tolerate more drought than cool-season ones. There's no such thing as a drought-tolerant lawn, so keep it small. (Find out more in Chapter 19.)

Smart Mowing Means Good Growing

Mowing with a power mower causes noise and pollution, and it uses fossil fuels. Mowing is dangerous. Mowing is bad. Flip to Chapter 19 to read more about the effects of mowing. In the meantime, this section provides some tips for mowing as smart and sustainably as possible.

Besides watering, mowing is the other most-important lawn care practice. You should mow your lawn high (and no, I don't mean under the influence). Maintaining grass at the proper height preserves plenty of leaf surface so that photosynthesis is maximized and plenty of sugars go into the roots to strengthen them (plants are sugar junkies). Mowing high encourages deep rooting and soil building. It also helps shade out weeds, encourages grass to spread by sending out underground runners, discourages pests (what's better than a discouraged pest?), and keeps diseases at bay.

Mow cool-season grasses, such as fescues, bluegrass, and rye 2 to 3 inches high. Mow warm-season grasses, such as Bermuda grass, no more than 1 inch tall.

Here are a few other mowing mantras to keep in mind:

> ✔ Mow when the grass needs it, not just because it's Saturday morning.

> ✔ Use a mulch mower or mulching blade to return the clippings to the lawn by practicing *grasscycling* (see the upcoming "Grasscycling" section). Grasscycling can account for up to 30 percent of the total nitrogen requirements of the average lawn, and it eliminates the need to dispose of the clippings.

> ✔ You can mow right over fallen leaves, and they, too, can return to the soil. Contrary to popular belief, this practice doesn't cause thatch buildup.

Mowtown: Alternatives to fossil-powered mowing

People mow because the grasses they use in lawns are bred to be mowed. They mow because society says mowing is the right way to keep a lawn. They mow because a cropped turf is a playable, attractive surface. They mow, and mow, and mow, burning up dinosaur juice and making noise and pollution in the process. Yet you can mow in less damaging ways.

Muscle-powered push mowers (also called *reel mowers*) work very well. They use no fuel unless you count what you had for breakfast. They're quiet. They always start. They let you mow the lawn *and* get your exercise at the same time, which is perfect for busy people. They work well as long as you don't let the lawn grow too long before mowing. Because a reel mower shears the grass off like a pair of scissors would, it makes a cleaner cut than the typical rotary mower. One of these mowers is a feasible option if your lawn is smaller than 3,000 square feet, made up of a fine-bladed and not-too-wiry grass variety, and is on relatively level ground.

If you have a bigger lawn or tough grass, use an electric mower, which requires about half the energy of a gas mower and can be less polluting, depending on the source of the electricity (solar panels on your roof would be ideal). Modern electric mowers are cordless, quiet, and efficient, and they always start.

Or try the classic solution: sheep. The town of Curitiba, Brazil, uses a flock of municipal sheep to mow the parks. Grass co-evolved with browsing animals, so this method isn't such a big leap. The sheep fertilize, too. If you happen to have one or more domestic ruminants, turn them out on the lawn.

Taking good care of your mower can make a difference. Reel mowers need sharpening and adjusting now and then to keep the cut clean and minimize the effort it takes to push them. Electric mowers need little care other than keeping the blade sharp. If you have a gas mower, keep it tuned up so it pollutes as little as possible, and sharpen the blade so it doesn't have to work so hard.

Grasscycling

Bagging grass clippings is unnecessary and wasteful. After all, it removes valuable nutrients and organic matter from the system for no reason. A better alternative is *grasscycling* (also known as *mulch mowing*) — the practice of leaving clippings on the lawn so they return to the soil through the process of decomposition. Grasscycling can reduce the need for nitrogen (the key element in lawn fertilizer) by 30 to 50 percent.

The idea that leaving the clippings on the lawn causes thatch is a myth. If you have a mulching mower, it will automatically cut the grass into very fine bits that will decompose quickly and then blow them down into the lawn, where they'll get right to work recycling nutrients. Many regular mowers can be equipped with a grasscycling kit. You can use a regular mower as-is as long as you cut the grass often enough that you aren't removing more than an inch of the blades at any one time. Be sure to mow when the grass is dry so the clippings are distributed more evenly.

Fighting Lawn Pests and Diseases without Chemicals

Like giving yourself a healthy diet, exercise, and good living conditions, taking care of your lawn's soil makes all the difference. An overfertilized and overwatered lawn is the perfect place for pest and disease problems to develop. So is one that isn't mowed at the right height or isn't mowed often enough. The traditional approach is to attack the problem with chemicals, but that doesn't work if the cause of the problem isn't resolved.

Pests and diseases are present in every lawn, but they lay dormant until conditions are right for their development. Any problem depends on the presence of three elements: a disease or pest, a host (your lawn), and conditions favorable to the problem. Eliminate the conditions, and the problem will go away without the need for toxic pesticides or other chemicals.

The following sections introduce you to pest and disease control the sustainable way.

Controlling lawn pests: Grubs, bugs, and other subsurface lurkers

Sometimes good conditions aren't enough to stop a problem; and other times it isn't possible to optimize conditions for one reason or another. That's when you step in with some natural controls, which are available from nurseries and insectaries. The following are tips on dealing with some of the most common lawn insect pests (see Figure 22-3):

✔ **Grubs, armyworms, and cutworms:** These soil-dwelling larvae cause patches of lawn to die off and also attract varmints that dig up the lawn looking for them. Grubs are susceptible to many natural controls, so you may not need to take any action. You can inoculate the soil with beneficial nematodes (roundworms); introduce parasitic wasps; or treat with *Bacillus thuringiensis* (Bt), a disease of caterpillars that's harmless to anything else. Japanese beetle grubs are treatable with milky spore disease; one fall application lasts for decades.

✔ **Sod webworm:** These larvae make small patches of dead grass in summer. You'll see moths flying around the lawn and can find green pellets of *frass* (a nice word for poop) in the grass. Keep grass mowed high, aerated, and well watered to minimize the problem. If those techniques fail, control with Bt or parasitic nematodes. Some varieties of rye and fescue lawn grasses contain *endophytes* (beneficial fungi that attack webworms and other pests).

✔ **Chinch bugs:** These winged insects are easily controlled by regular watering, which encourages the development of fungi that attack the bugs. Keep thatch removed, too. As with webworms, grass varieties containing endophytes also help.

✔ **Billbugs:** These tiny beetles can be controlled with endophytic grasses or parasitic nematodes.

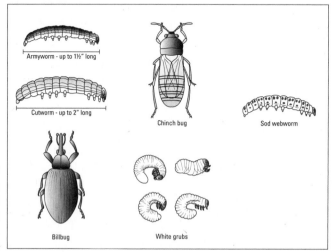

Figure 22-3: Common lawn insect pests.

Treating lawn diseases

Many species of fungi and other diseases attack lawns that aren't in good condition. Lawn diseases usually announce their presence with patches of dead grass. The way the patches spread and the shape and color they take on can indicate (to a trained eye) the type of problem that's lurking beneath the surface. See *Lawn Care For Dummies* for details on identifying diseases.

Lawn diseases are nearly impossible to control with chemicals, but good lawn care usually keeps the diseases at bay. The best strategy is to avoid overfertilizing, which produces susceptible growth. No organic fungicides are available, but seaweed has been effective in some cases.

If diseases are persistent, renovate the lawn and seed with a mixture of disease-resistant grass varieties. See the earlier section "Aerating and Renovating Your Lawn" for further details.

Whacking Weeds the Natural Way

Make your lawn dense and vigorous so it outcompetes the weeds: Plant the proper varieties, nurture the soil, mow high and often to prevent seed-set on annual weeds, water deeply and infrequently, and reseed bare spots quickly. Any vacancies will likely fill up with weeds, not desirable grasses. Monitor weed development, and eradicate newcomers early.

Even with the best of care, you still get some weeds. This ain't the Garden of Eden. Outsmart them. Try these tips:

- ✔ **Fix the pH.** Dandelions, for example, like a soil pH of around 7.5 (slightly alkaline); adjust the pH so it's between 6.3 and 6.8, and the dandelions will diminish.

- ✔ **Fertilize when necessary.** The medic plant and clover are indicators of low nitrogen, so fertilizing a little more often will put them at a disadvantage.

  By the way, clover absorbs nitrogen from the air and puts it into the soil, where grasses can use it. Clover was a common feature of lawns until chemical-company propaganda convinced people that it was a weed. It also attracts bees, however, so it's hazardous to those with bee allergies.

- ✔ **Yank them out by hand.** Hand-pulling weeds can be laborious, but it works fine if you stay on top of it. Many non-backbreaking weeding tools are available.

- ✔ **Be uncultivated.** Don't cultivate the soil if you have perennial weeds; it can disperse rather than discourage them.

- ✔ **Dress with vinegar.** Using horticultural vinegar to spot-treat weeds works really well. (For details, visit www.usda.gov and search for "vinegar weeds.")

  Only low-test food-grade vinegar is legal to use in the garden; stronger 20-percent concentrations work great but aren't yet approved by the EPA.

- ✔ **Apply corn gluten meal.** This type of meal kills crabgrass. Apply 20 pounds per 1,000 square feet in early spring or late summer. You should get 50 to 60 percent crabgrass control in the first year and 90 percent by the third year.

  Corn gluten meal works against many other weeds and also acts as a gentle organic fertilizer. Don't seed after applying it, though, because it inhibits germination. Spread the meal with a fertilizer spreader, water afterward, and then let the lawn dry out for two to three days.

Replacing an Old Lawn

At some point, a lawn gets old. The exact longevity of a lawn depends on many factors: local growing conditions, type of lawn, level of care, degree of use, and the presence of pests, diseases, and weeds. Unfortunately, there comes a time when it's necessary to turn the old clunker in for a new model.

In some cases, renovating and overseeding your washed-up lawn with fresh grass is sufficient (see the earlier section "Aerating and Renovating Your Lawn" for details). But when you're faced with a lawn that's mostly weeds, full of holes, and generally pathetic, it's time to roll up your sleeves and start over. Some work is involved, but replacing a lawn isn't that difficult for the average gardener. Here's how to do it:

1. **Strip the old sod off.**

   Using a hand sod cutter or a (I'll look the other way) pollution-spitting gas-powered sod cutter, which you can rent. Compost the sod. (See Chapter 16 for details on composting.)

2. **Rototill the soil, incorporating a 1-inch-thick layer of good organic compost into the top 5 or 6 inches of native soil.**

   This method brings life to the soil and gives you an organic-matter content that's ideal for turf grasses.

3. **Finish-grade the area, being sure to direct water away from the house.**

   If your soil is sandy or loamy and drains well, consider making the lawn concave so that it soaks up rainwater, which will reduce dependence on irrigation. However, this technique isn't a good idea for heavy or easily compacted soils, where heavy use may be a problem if the soil is frequently wet — especially if you live on a geologically unstable site.

4. **Install a sprinkler system if you'll be using one.**

   You have a few system options to choose from; see Chapters 7 and 8 for the scoop.

5. **Use sheet mulching to kill the weeds.**

   If you have persistent perennial weeds that come back from the roots, visit Chapter 16 for info on sheet mulching.

6. **When you're sure that the weeds are gone, remove the mulch and cardboard, and seed or sod the new lawn.**

For specific information on installing a conventional lawn, refer to *Lawn Care For Dummies.*

If you want to go one better than lawn, put in a meadow. Meadows require much less watering, fertilizing, and mowing than lawns do; they're also diverse and beautiful, and you'll be the envy of all your neighbors. Visit Chapter 19 for details on low-impact lawns and lawn alternatives.

Part VI
The Part of Tens

The 5th Wave   By Rich Tennant

"I used an all natural method of pest control,
but we're still getting an occasional
vacuum cleaner salesman in the garden."

In this part . . .

*I*n this part, check out the ten quick projects that will make your yard more sustainable right away. They don't cost much or require heroic efforts, and they can make a big difference. I'm talking about simple things like making your lawn smaller, using mulch to keep weeds out and conserve water, and growing food. You can do these things.

And be sure to study the ten mistakes to avoid. A little knowledge will keep you out of trouble. These mistakes are "I can't believe I did this" bonehead things like poisoning the neighborhood with wicked pesticides or not giving plants enough room to grow (so you end up cutting them back all the time). They're easy situations to avoid, and you'll appreciate knowing about them.

Chapter 23

Ten Projects That Pay You and the Environment Back Big Time

In This Chapter

▶ Completing projects that help you save money

▶ Benefiting the environment with a few simple fixes

*I*n this chapter, I introduce some projects you can tackle right away (for relatively little or no money!) that make a big difference to you and the environment. They're all easy, and most of them don't require the use of heavy equipment, chiropractors, or bad language. Enjoy.

Make Your Lawn Smaller

Most lawns have parts that are never used for anything other than giving the lawn mower its weekly workout. Do what savvy sustainable landscapers everywhere are doing: Cut that lawn down to size! (Refer to Chapter 19 for the scoop on lawns and lawn alternatives.) Make a *lap lawn* — a phrase coined by a gardener I once met. Long and narrow, this type of lawn is still perfectly suited to hosting a friendly game of catch or a chase with the family pooch. After its midriff bulge has been whacked away, your svelte new lawn is ready for sustainable action. Consider a maximum size of 20 by 40 feet — a total of 800 square feet. If you can do with less, great.

In making the lawn smaller, you create new borders. Plant these borders with useful, beautiful, climate-appropriate plants that need less care, water, and fertilizer than the original lawn did. Drip-irrigate and mulch the borders to save water. Don't forget to move your sprinkler heads to the new edges of the lawn to save more water (and money).

Tune Up Your Sprinkler System

Out-of-whack sprinklers result in water waste and poor lawn performance, so you need to give the system a tune-up every so often. Turn the system on one valve at a time so you can test it and get everything working right. (See Chapter 10 to find out how to maintain your irrigation system.)

Reprogram Your Irrigation Controller

Conventional irrigation controllers have no idea how much water your plants need. They're just timers, faithfully carrying out whatever instructions you gave them the last time you programmed them. Umm, you *did* adjust your controller at some point, right?

If you haven't, now is the time. Get out the instruction book for your controller so you can make sense of the simple-yet-often-obscure ways of programming these pesky beasts. Then read Chapter 9 of this book to discover how to make seasonal adjustments to your controller. Reprogramming your irrigation controller isn't terribly difficult, and it saves you a bunch of money. Your plants will thank you, too.

Install a Smart Irrigation Controller

If you don't want to reprogram the controller you already have (see the preceding section), yank that old clunker off the wall and put in a smart controller. A smart irrigation controller receives signals from — get this — outer space. These signals reset the controller's program continuously, based on current meteorological data taken from local weather stations.

To install and program a smart controller, you just have to answer simple questions about your soil, plants, and so on. You tweak it a bit over the first few weeks, and when you're done, you probably never have to touch it again.

These units have generated water savings of 25 to 50 percent, which means that your water bill will go down. Even better, you can gloat when the neighbors come over. Sustainability is just the coolest thing. See Chapter 9 for more on smart water management.

Many water districts offer rebates for installing smart controllers.

Axe Your Overgrown Plants

Take note of how many hours per month you spend keeping plants from growing too big for the space they're in. You could've spent that time enjoying a nice, sustainable activity, such as loafing.

Plants don't ask you how big you want them to be. If they're programmed to get 100 feet tall, they always try to do so. So if you want an 8-foot-tall plant, you need to choose one that grows to 8 feet at maturity. Then you'll never have to trim it. Plus, it looks better and is healthier when left alone. (And you'll look so relaxed in that hammock.)

Pull Up Sissy Plants

Go around your yard with a shovel and perhaps a digging bar, swiftly and mercifully eliminating namby-pamby plants of whatever kind. Or at least move them where they'll perform better, if location is the problem. Probably 80 percent of gardening problems are caused by 20 percent of plants. You know which ones they are. Go get 'em.

My favorite sissy plant to weed out is the rose. I know the term may offend some people, but hybrid tea roses aren't so great at taking care of themselves. It hurts me to ponder the rust, the leaf spot, the bugs, and all the other ills and ailments that plague these pitiable creatures. I consider it a public service to replace them with something a little more durable.

Dump Your Chemical Arsenal

Exactly what excuse does anyone have for holding onto that noxious-smelling collection of insecticide, weed killer, and fert-'n'-hurt? C'mon — you know you'll never use that stuff again. You're a sustainable gardener now! Put your old chemicals in a sealed container and then take them to your local hazardous-waste collection center for safe disposal. Then go home, perform a cleansing ritual or two in your garage, and get on with your life. Feel good knowing that you'll probably never have to make the trek to the toxic dump again.

Some of this stuff is truly treacherous to your health, so be sure to wear protective gear and be very careful not to spill anything.

Trade Your Power Tools for Hand Tools

Shop around for some truly good, lifetime-quality hand tools, and leave the power ones out at the curb for some other fool to struggle with. You'll be glad you did.

Power tools actually don't save much effort. First, you have to work pretty hard to earn the money to buy them. Then you have to store them somewhere, do tune-ups and repairs, fuel and oil them, wipe them down and sharpen the blades, and adjust the dang carburetor over and over because nobody but the high priests of internal combustion can get it right the first time. Besides all that, think about the number of times you've pulled the starter cord with no result. Must be in the thousands, right? You could've had the lawn mowed with a simple push mower by the time you regained your composure and got that wheezy old mower running.

Mulch Your Beds

Naked beds don't work. The soil dries out too quickly, root systems suffer heat and cold, weeds come up everywhere, rain washes earth away, beneficial soil microorganisms suffer, drip tubing shows, mud sticks to your boots . . . I could go on and on. In nature, organic material rains down from plants constantly, creating mulch and returning valuable nutrients to the soil. The sustainable landscaper mimics this elegant system by practicing chop and drop pruning (refer to Chapter 20) and by spreading some form of organic mulch on the surface of the soil. For more on mulching, see Chapter 16.

Grow Food

What better use can you have for your land than growing your own food? The list of advantages is a mile long (but I won't bore you with the details). Plant a few crops that are easy to grow in your area and then devote a little time, money, and effort to reap the rewards. Flip to Chapter 18 for more information about sustainable veggie gardening.

Chapter 24

Ten Totally Nonsustainable Landscaping Mistakes and How to Avoid Them

In This Chapter

▶ Knowing the nonsustainable landscaping pitfalls

▶ Avoiding resource- and money-sucking mistakes

Considering all the nonsense that's out there about landscaping and gardening practices, I don't think you need to feel bad about committing some of the gaffes listed in this chapter. After all, it's human nature to think that if everyone's doing something, it must be right.

Yet many common gardening practices are foolish, and imitating them doesn't help anyone. If you're wasting time and money or creating a big environmental impact, now is the time to change your ways. A little knowledge and willingness to change behavior can solve the majority of gardening problems in a big hurry, with no downside and often little or no cost.

Making Hasty Decisions

The first rule is to slow down. Very few landscaping emergencies exist at any time — and none at all exist during the early stages of your project. The best gardens have been developed over years, decades, and even centuries. Take your time.

There's a phenomenon that I call *Saturday Morning Syndrome*. Here's how it works: You get up on Saturday morning and say, "Hey, today is the day I landscape my yard! All right!" You drive down to the nursery, where you pick out a bunch of plants you've never even heard of before and a bag of soil amendment; maybe you throw in a fountain that caught your eye and a couple of plaster gnomes. You come home with your stuff and spend the rest of the day trying to figure out what to do with it. Because you don't have a clue what the plants want or how big they get, they eventually kick the bucket; lift your house off its foundation; or grow into the next block, strangling small children along the way. The fountain doesn't go with the house. And the gnomes? Well, I won't even go there.

You're going to live with your new landscaping for a very long time. Why not do yourself a favor and give the design phase all the attention it needs? You'll be happy you did. The chapters in Part II can help.

Not Giving Plants Room to Grow

Each plant has a genetic destiny. Its ultimate size is built into its DNA, and you can't do a thing to change it. Based on a rigorous scientific survey — one that involved walking around my neighborhood looking at all the plants that want to be much bigger than the spaces they're in — I estimate that 40 percent of all gardening work consists of cutting things back. This is madness. And of course, it's also nonsustainable, because it requires fossil fuels to run the hedge trimmers and truck the decapitated plant parts to the landfill. Fortunately, you can employ a simple solution.

Check the mature height and width of the plant in any good gardening book or on a good gardening Web site. Or see what the tag that comes with the plant says. And believe it. Make sure to place each and every plant so that it has room to grow — make sure it's far enough from other plants, paved surfaces, and structures. (Check out Chapter 16 for more information on giving plants the room they need.) That way, you'll never have to prune your plants.

Ignoring Growing Conditions When Planting

Plants are living things, and they need what they need. Planting a shade-loving plant in the hot sun or a drought-loving plant in a wet spot is a recipe for failure. So is putting a delicate plant where it'll be pummeled by wind. Once again, the simple solution is to match your plants carefully to the conditions you have. Flip to Chapter 16 for some pointers.

Note: At times, it makes sense to change *conditions* to accommodate plants that normally wouldn't be happy in that particular spot, but it's far wiser, easier, and more sustainable to choose plants that will be happy with things as they are.

Overwatering

There's something satisfying about watering — so satisfying that overwatering is among the most widely practiced of gardening mistakes. Not only does overwatering waste water that could be used for better things, but it also kills plants or makes them grow too fast so that they become soft and vulnerable to problems. Overwatering costs you a lot of money, too!

If you have a manual watering system (or if you water by standing at the business end of a hose), be sure to use a soil probe or put a shovel into the soil to check moisture levels before you water. Don't depend on the surface appearance of the soil; conditions may be quite different down where the roots live. If the soil is dry 6 to 12 inches below ground, consider watering — depending, of course, on the root depth of the plants in the area.

If you have an automatic controller (see Chapter 7 for details), be sure to reprogram it periodically to account for seasonal changes in water use. The heat of the summer increases water demand, but then many people forget to turn the controller back down in the fall. Refer to the water management information in Chapter 9 or talk to your local water purveyor for specific programming suggestions. Better yet, invest in one of the new smart controllers; these devices automatically adjust to ever-changing conditions.

Using Chemical Fertilizers

Many chemical fertilizers are made from natural gas and other nonsustainable resources. They also often have a *high salt index,* which means that they salt the soil, making conditions tough for the many beneficial microorganisms on which your plants depend for true well-being. Also, many chemical fertilizers act very quickly, which means that they can burn plants by overloading them with excessive nutrients — and then go away, leaving the plants stranded. Using chemical fertilizers on plants is like expecting your body to live on coffee and chocolate bars. It's tempting but not so healthy.

Sustainable gardeners depend on organic fertilizers that provide nourishment for the entire soil food web, not just the plants (see Chapter 16 for details). Organic fertilizers are made from renewable natural sources rather than petroleum. They're much less likely to cause pollution from runoff and to leach into groundwater. And they don't burn plants. They apply nutrients gradually — as plants prefer — and stick around for the long haul.

The truly sustainable landscape doesn't depend on fertilizers, because nutrients never leave the site. Everything that's pruned from a plant is returned to the soil in the form of compost or sheet mulch (find out more in Chapter 20). It's fine to use fertilizers for the occasional special treat or when nutrient levels need to be high for spring growth or other situations, but your plants should be able to coast along on their own waste most of the time.

Being Hooked On Pesticides

Tell me that you don't use harsh chemical pesticides. Please. They're so unnecessary! Plants get pests for any number of reasons, generally because something is wrong with the growing conditions: too much or too little water, sickly soil, oddball weather conditions, and so on. The pests know a stressed plant from a happy one, and they make their move when a plant's defenses are down. Pests also attack soft growth, which can be a result of overwatering.

A well-planned landscape has little need for conventional pesticides, which cause pollution and health risks. Still, even in the most sustainable gardens, a plant may suffer an attack of some kind. Your first line of defense should be to evaluate growing conditions and make any necessary improvements. Then sit back and watch for positive change. More often than not, the newly healthy plant will defend itself without any further help from you.

The other cool thing that happens is that beneficial insects often move in to mop up the pests for you. If not, organic remedies are available for most pest and disease problems; you should have no trouble finding a treatment that's consistent with sustainable practices. If all else fails, take the plant out and replace it with something tougher. Visit Chapter 21 for more information on combating pests and plant diseases.

Applying Harsh Chemical Herbicides

You end up with weeds because nature fills voids — and not usually with azaleas. Weeds are aggressive, opportunistic plants that are poised to exploit any gap in vegetation. When conditions are right, weeds happen.

Weed growth and the use of herbicides are the result of design failure. Correcting the problem with proper planting and mulch is easy. For instance, if you make sure that every square inch of your garden is filled with robust plants or covered with weed-discouraging mulch, you greatly reduce the problem; as a result, you don't need to use herbicides. Then you can deal with the few remaining weeds (yes, you'll still have some) by hand-weeding or using some horticultural vinegar spray when they're young. (See Chapter 22 for what you need to know to get started.)

Choosing Power Tools When Hand Tools Would Do

Power tools seem to make your gardening life easier, but when you factor in all the variables — working to buy and maintain them, keeping them adjusted and running properly, storing them, using gas and oil to keep them going, and dealing with the impact of eventual disposal — they really aren't that great a deal. Add in the terrible noise and air pollution, and what you get is a high-tech train wreck.

Sure, sometimes power equipment is the best way to go if you want to get the job done in a reasonable period of time, but remember that humans built the Giza pyramids and Stonehenge and a whole lot of other stuff by hand. Why have we gone soft on our ancestors?

If you have a lawn, consider using a push mower (see Chapter 22) or try converting the lawn to a natural meadow that requires little or no mowing. Drag out those rusty old hedge shears and give them a whirl on the hedges; your pecs will perk up marvelously. Just remember that the key is to design (or redesign) your property so that power tools just aren't necessary. You want to design so that everything is in a state of balance that makes all that hard work a thing of the past.

Tilling the Soil

Everyone has been taught that fluffy, thoroughly cultivated soil is the very best stuff for your plants. As it turns out, that's not true. Instead, cultivating soil destroys its texture, along with the elegant network of mycorrhizal fungi and other beneficial organisms that are essential to the well-being of your plants. Tilled soil can become clumpy or powdery, and the effects are worse if the soil is wet when tilled. Tilling also turns up weed seeds and can undo years of patient weeding in a single, pollution-spewing pass.

Yes, tillers suck up dinosaur juice (also known as fossil fuels) and spit out smog and noise just like all other power equipment. Tsk, tsk. Not sustainable. Not sustainable at all.

Tilling the soil to grow plants is like tearing the roof off your house to let a little fresh air in. The sustainable way is to practice *no-till* or *low-till* growing. For the home gardener, this ancient practice involves covering your vegetable garden with an organic mulch, which keeps weeds down, reduces water use, and returns nutrients to the soil. Place plants in small, hand-dug holes within the mulch, never again turning the soil over. Mulch may not be as sexy as a big plot of fragrant, fluffy black earth, but it's a whole lot better for the environment, your plants, and you. (Find out much about mulch in Chapter 16.)

At times, you have to do grading during the course of constructing your new landscape, and you may be tempted to soften the soil with a rototiller. Resist — the same soil damage will occur. Instead, water if necessary to bring soil to proper physical condition; then grade by hand (or with minimal use of heavy equipment in large areas).

Unimproving the Soil

One of the biggest myths in landscaping is that you have to "improve" the soil to get the best performance from plants. The truth is that you really can't fix soil. Some pioneering research in the 1970s proved that in most cases, amending soil is detrimental both to the soil and to the plants. Here are several reasons:

✔ Incorporating amendments into the soil displaces nutrients and reduces its water-holding capacity in many cases (depending on your soil type).

✔ Fluffy, highly porous planting pits invite rainwater in, drowning the plants if internal soil drainage is poor.

✔ Conversely (and perversely), those fluffy pits dry out much faster than the surrounding native soil during dry periods, so plants suffer.

✔ Roots circle around in soft, amended soil and never venture out into the native soil where they belong, especially in clay soils.

Spend your time and money improving the soil food web by inoculating it with mycorrhizal fungi, beneficial bacteria, and other living goodies — not by working on the texture.

Chapter 16 gives you the scoop on soil improvement. In the long run, of course, it's far better to match plants to the soil you have.

Appendix

Planning for Special Situations

*T*his appendix provides example landscape plans for special situations that may apply to you. Remember that landscaping isn't just about making your yard pretty. Landscaping also does stuff; it improves the environment in many ways. If you find yourself with a particular challenge, such as having a property in a high fire hazard area or in a hot climate, look through this chapter for examples of how to work with these issues. Or you may have specific sustainability goals, such as attracting wildlife, improving the watershed, or amping up your food-growing chops; all this is covered too.

The Housewarming (And Cooling) Landscape

By placing trees at strategic locations around your yard, you can make your house more comfortable all year long. *Deciduous* trees (ones that lose their leaves in winter) provide shade in summer, keeping your house cool, and let in the sun during the winter, making your house warmer and sunnier. On the windward side, evergreen trees get in the way of the wind, creating a calm zone on your property. Shoot, you can even use trees and shrubs to funnel cooling winds onto your property. Hardscape can help too: Fences and walls direct air movement, and overhead structures shade hot spots. Look at Figure A-1 to see cool ideas for keeping your home comfy.

Visit `www.greenbuilder.com/sourcebook/LandscapingEnergy.html` for a rundown of strategies for modifying microclimates and saving energy with landscaping.

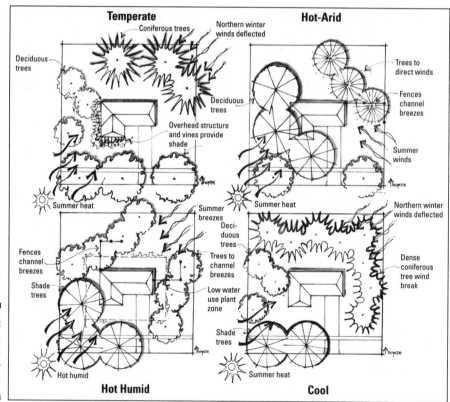

Figure A-1: Modifying the climate on your property.

The Fire-Wise Landscape

If you live in an area with a history of catastrophic wildfires, you're at risk of losing your home. Create defensible space around your home by thinning overgrown vegetation, replacing highly flammable plants with low-growing and succulent varieties, removing lower limbs from trees, eliminating or modifying wooden structures, keeping your property tidy, and keeping plants well watered. Also consider building masonry patios (made of stone, concrete, or other nonflammable material) instead of wooden decks and using steel fencing or masonry walls instead of wooden fences. Make your house less flammable by enclosing eaves and installing a "Class A" fireproof roof and fireproof siding.

No landscape is ever completely fire-safe, because anything will burn in a violent wildfire. But the strategies in this section improve your chances. Get the lowdown at the Firewise Communities Web site (`www.firewise.org`). See Figure A-2 for a diagram of a typical fire-wise landscape.

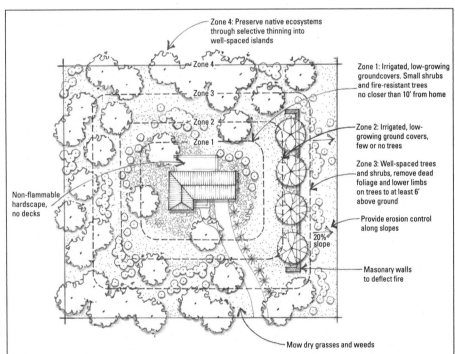

Zone 4: Preserve native ecosystems through selective thinning into well-spaced islands

Zone 4

Zone 3

Zone 2

Zone 1

Zone 1: Irrigated, low-growing groundcovers. Small shrubs and fire-resistant trees no closer than 10' from home

Zone 2: Irrigated, low-growing ground covers, few or no trees

Zone 3: Well-spaced trees and shrubs, remove dead foliage and lower limbs on trees to at least 6' above ground

Provide erosion control along slopes

Non-flammable hardscape, no decks

20% slope

Masonary walls to deflect fire

Mow dry grasses and weeds

Figure A-2:
The fire-wise landscape.

The Watershed-Friendly Landscape

We all live on a watershed. The rainfall that hits your roof and land runs into the street, where it contributes to urban flooding and pollution of streams, lakes, and oceans. If you make your landscaping absorbent, the ground soaks up that good water instead of wasting it. Provide plenty of planted areas instead of just pavement, make pavement permeable (see Chapter 12), create low spots in the terrain that will soak up water (see Chapter 8), build *rain gardens* (any planting that's irrigated by channeling rainwater from adjacent roofs and surrounding areas into the planted area), and swear off chemicals that could leach into the environment. You could even plant the roof of your house! (Chapter 12 discusses the ecoroof.) Refer to Figure A-3 to see how to make a watershed-friendly landscape.

By creating a watershed-friendly landscape, you'll save money on water, your plants will be happier with pure rainwater, and the environment will be eternally grateful to you. For further details, check out the watershed page of my Web site at www.owendell.com/watershed.html.

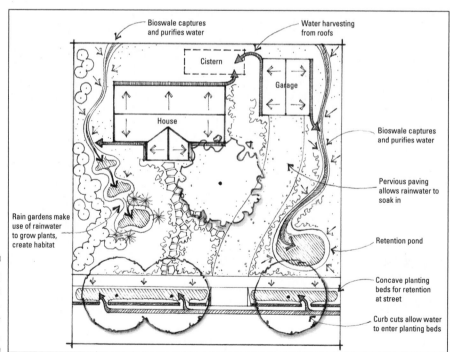

Figure A-3: The watershed-friendly landscape.

The Wildlife Landscape

Critters. Some people love 'em; some people hate 'em. The truth is that you probably don't want to attract bears, wolves, or rattlesnakes to your backyard; they're better off in the wilds. But lots of other animals, birds, and insects are an important part of a sustainable landscape.

Maintaining a wildlife-friendly landscape isn't just about attracting beneficial insects like honeybees, which pollinate your food crops. Foraging animals, such as skunks and opossums, can help keep the pest population down. Provide food, shelter, and water for native critters, and the whole system benefits. For an example, see the Missouri Department of Conservation's "Landscaping for Backyard Wildlife" page at mdc.mo.gov/nathis/ backyard/backwild. Check out Figure A-4 to discover ways to attract wildlife to your yard.

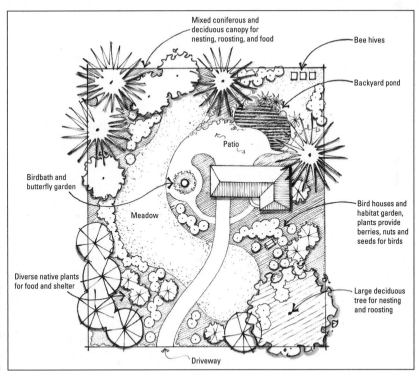

Figure A-4:
The critter-
friendly
landscape.

The Food Forest

You eat, right? Well, why not eat from your own land? Growing food is easy, especially if you develop a stable food forest that uses the laws of nature to support a permanent edible ecosystem made up primarily of fruit trees and perennial plants that are durable, easy to care for, and well adapted to your climate and soil. A food forest also includes compatible animals, pollinators, water-harvesting systems, and annual food plants, such as broccoli and tomatoes. It's a complex ecosystem that looks great, feeds your family, and is good for the environment. That homegrown food sure is tasty, too! Check out the food-forest info at the Permaculture Institute's Web site (www.permaculture.org/nm/index.php/site/Permaculture-Food-Forest). Refer to Figure A-5 to see what a food-oriented landscape looks like.

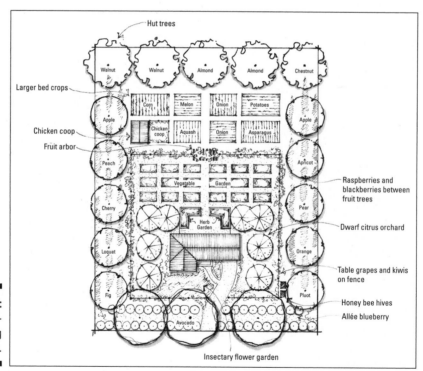

Figure A-5: The food-bearing landscape.

Index